FUNDAMENTALS OF INTERNATIONAL ECONOMICS

CONSULTING EDITOR

WILLIAM LETWIN

LONDON SCHOOL OF ECONOMICS

Fundamentals of
INTERNATIONAL
Economics

Imanuel Wexler

UNIVERSITY OF CONNECTICUT

Random House / New York

For
My parents,
my teachers,
and my students

Preface

"A good textbook," one of my colleagues once observed, "should be capable of teaching itself." In writing this book, I have tried to keep this advice in mind. I have resisted the temptation to write either an encyclopedic volume which would leave the teacher little to add in class, or one which would oblige him to spend most of his time explaining the material itself. Hopefully, the result is a balanced text that enables the teacher to build an international economics course around it and permits the undergraduate student—economics major or visitor from another academic discipline—to acquire an understanding of the subject without difficulty.

Underlying the book is the proposition that a close interrelationship exists between international trade and economic growth. In fact, I begin and end by calling attention to the role of international trade in promoting growth and economic well being. Also, throughout the book frequent references are made to the impact of trade on growth and of growth itself on trade. A corollary theme is that changing economic conditions, whether they lead to, or are caused by, changes in trade patterns, are bound to give rise to problems which concern both the individual trading nations and the world at large. Therefore, solutions to many of these problems must be sought in international cooperation rather than in national isolationism. Finally, the book devotes considerable attention to what has become, in recent years, one of the major and most dynamic developments on the international scene—the emergence of regional economics blocs.

The book is divided into six major parts and may be used in either a one- or a two-semester course (with additional outside readings). I am convinced that in order to appreciate the significance of international trade, the student must first view the phenomenon of international trade within the context of a nation's total economic activities. Accordingly, Part I examines in some detail the relation between foreign trade and the problems of economic growth and stability. Part II consists essentially of the theoretical explanation of how trade patterns are established and how international prices are determined under free-trade conditions, while Parts III and IV address themselves to the various obstacles that in reality may obstruct or distort the free flow of international trade. Part V is largely a historical account of the major developments in international economic relations during the last one hundred fifty years; and Part VI examines the recent trend toward regional economic integration among both developed and underdeveloped nations.

For assistance and advice during the course of writing I am especially grateful to Professor William Letwin and Professor William R. Allen, both of whom read the entire manuscript and made many valuable comments and useful suggestions. I am also indebted to my colleague at the University of Connecticut, Professor Galvin G. Gall, whose critical observations helped improve several chapters. Three of my former students, Mrs. Roberta Carey, Mrs. Holley Ulbrich, and Mr. Thomas Standish, deserve special mention for their advice and encouragement. I alone, of course, bear full responsibility for the final product.

STORRS, CONNECTICUT

I. W.

Contents

ix

Part III: B A R R I E R S   T O   F R E E   T R A D E :
*International Monetary Problems
and Solutions*

———

Part IV: B A R R I E R S T O F R E E T R A D E :
Private and Public Policies

Part V: FREE TRADE VERSUS PROTECTION
IN A CHANGING WORLD

Part VI: THE REGIONAL APPROACH TO FREE TRADE

PART I

GROWTH, INCOME, AND TRADE

1

Specialization, Trade, and Economic Growth

Ask yourself the following question: What is perhaps the most often-declared economic objective of present-day societies? The answer can be summed up in two words: Economic growth. Technically defined, this means an increase in *per capita* real income (i.e., total national income divided by the number of people within the nation). An increase in real national income means an increase in the total output of goods and services, and for *per capita* real income to increase, the rise in total output during a particular period must be larger than the rise in population. Hence, in a narrow sense, economic growth can be thought of as a process by which more goods and services become available to satisfy the needs and desires of society.

Yet broadly speaking, economic growth can be conceived of as a process leading to an improvement in living standards, the latter being measured not only by the *quantity* but also the *quality* of available goods, as well as by the amount of effort spent in obtaining them. Indeed, in its broad sense, economic growth implies that the members of society have at their disposal greater amounts and a wider variety of goods than they had before, and, at the same time, can enjoy more leisure time.

A great variety of causes may play a role in inducing economic growth and promoting higher living standards. In this book we shall be concerned with one of the most important of these causes: international trade. The connection between international trade and growth is often obscured by the general tendency to regard foreign trade as inherently different from domestic trade. There are, to be sure, some major differences between them, which will become apparent as we go along. But in essence, the two are the same—both are motivated by the same considerations and both exert a favorable influence on economic growth. Indeed, to understand the role of international trade, one must first consider the causes and consequences of domestic trade.

Specialization and Trade

Economic growth depends not so much on the quantities of the resources available to society as on the ways in which these resources are organized in the course of production. The more efficient the methods of production, the larger the output that can be obtained from a given amount of labor and capital, that is, the higher the level of productivity.

It was precisely this idea which Adam Smith expressed by suggesting that ''The greatest improvement in the productive powers of labour . . . seem[s] to have been the effects of the division of labour.''[1] On this score, as on others, he has since been proven right. The division of labor, or *specialization,* means the splitting up of a productive process—for example, automobile production—into smaller and simpler processes, to be handled by different people and machines. And the direct results of such an organization are two: Not only does each worker become more adept at his specific task, but the time that would have been lost by shifting from one operation to another can now be saved. The result is a far larger output of automobiles than would have been possible if each worker were to build a car from start to finish all by himself.

Nor is this all. The concept of specialization extends beyond the internal organization of single firms or industries. It underlies the economic organization of society as a whole. Not only differences in individual skills, but also differences between geographical regions offer a

[1] Adam Smith, *The Wealth of Nations* (New York: Modern Library, 1937), p. 3.

compelling argument in favor of specialization. For example, due to climatic differences, oranges are grown in Florida, corn and wheat in the Midwest, and cotton and sugar in the South. Similarly, steel production was developed in regions lying close to sources of coal and iron ore; and the textile industry settled originally in New England, where streams and rivers provided water power for the mills. These examples of regional specialization point up a fundamental idea: Since society's resources are limited, they must be utilized in the most efficient (lowest cost) manner.

Specialization not only increases the efficiency of existing resources, it also facilitates the accumulation and use of additional ones, particularly capital. As productive processes become more specialized, they provide the incentive for greater use of specialized machinery and equipment, and the use of such tools tends to increase efficiency still further. This effects savings in costs that enable society to accumulate more capital and to devote more effort to technological research and development. Thus, specialization, technology, and capital grow together and exert a favorable influence on productivity and growth.

What determines the extent of specialization? Another of Adam Smith's famous statements provides a clue to the answer. The division of labor, he argued, depends on the extent of the market.[2] To this should be added that the extent of the market is itself affected by the degree of specialization. In general, the larger the market, the greater the opportunities for specialization; and the more extensive the specialization, the larger becomes the market (i.e., its ability, or capacity, to absorb a large output of goods and services). In the final analysis it is not the size of an area or the number of people that determines the ability to absorb output. Rather it is the total income, or purchasing power, that the people have. Chicago, for example, has fewer people and spreads over a smaller area than, say, Peru; but the former, by virtue of its higher total income, constitutes a larger market than the latter.

The functional relationship between market size and the scope for specialization is not difficult to perceive. A market capable of absorbing only a small volume of output does not justify the use of highly specialized methods of production. A large market, on the other hand, encourages both specialization and technological advances, and thereby helps economic growth. If proof of this is required, one need not search very

2 *Ibid.,* p. 17.

far for it. It is generally agreed that the size of the American market has been the most important underlying cause of the great economic strides made by the United States. And the continuous growth of this market has in turn been influenced by extensive specialization and expanding trade.

It is important, however, not to lose sight of the basic connection between trade, specialization, and economic growth. By extending the market, trade, in effect, influences the methods and organization of production; for it permits and encourages specialization, and thereby promotes productive efficiency. It is primarily in this sense that trade can be regarded as a generative power for growth. In the words of a distinguished economic historian: "The ultimate explanation of the progressive economic history of Europe compared with other continents is that the simple facts of geography . . . were exceptionally favorable to trade and the progressive extension of the market."[3]

International Trade and Economic Growth

The wider the market, the greater the possibilities for specialization. And what better way to enlarge the market than to extend it beyond the confines of national boundaries? International trade is simply an extension of domestic trade; the result is a market comprising many countries rather than a single one. Indeed, the expansion of the international economy during the past century and a half continuously opened up new opportunities for specialization throughout the world. And in many cases, foreign trade was the driving force which stimulated a domestic economy and launched it on an accelerated path of economic growth.

The most direct benefit of international trade is also the most obvious. Just as individuals differ in skills and aptitudes, so nations differ in natural and man-made resources. And it is foreign trade that makes it possible to exploit such differences. To put it another way, foreign trade provides the opportunity for an *international division of labor* that leads to a better allocation of resources and greater productive efficiency in every country. Yet substantial as the gains from specialization may be, they constitute only one aspect of the contribution of

[3] H. J. Habakkuk, "The Historical Experience on the Basic Conditions of Economic Progress," in Barry Supple (ed.), *The Experience of Economic Growth* (New York: Random House, 1963), p. 113.

international trade to growth. The experience of the nineteenth century indicates that trade does much more than provide a large market. During that period trade served as an "engine of growth"[4]—a means by which rapid economic growth in one country was transmitted to other less developed areas. The center of economic progress was Great Britain, and the recipients of its benefits were the so-called "regions of recent settlement": Canada; Australia; New Zealand; some countries in South America and Africa; and to a certain extent, the United States.

Underlying this process was a unique combination of forces. Economic growth was transmitted to the newly developing areas through a fast growing demand for their exports (raw materials and foodstuffs) which was accompanied by tremendous amounts of investment directed to them from England. This, it has been argued, was perhaps the most spectacular feature of nineteenth century international trade, the volume of which increased by 270 per cent between 1850 and 1880, and by 170 per cent between 1880 and 1913.[5] Most of the foreign investment was induced by the prospects of a continuously rising demand for primary products, and was specifically designed to develop additional sources of supply. Yet the periods during which this demand was at its peak did not always correspond to the periods of great capital exports. In any event, part of this investment was used to finance other projects for example, railroad construction—in the newly developing regions.

It would be difficult to measure exactly how much of the rapid growth during the nineteenth century was accounted for by the trade-investment combination and how much was due to other factors. Yet there can be no question that international trade ranks very high among the contributors to this phenomenon—so high, in fact, that the great English economist Alfred Marshall said: "The causes which determine the economic progress of nations *belong to the study of international trade*."[6]

In contrast it is often argued that as an "engine of growth," inter-

[4] This expression was coined by D. H. Robertson in "The Future of International Trade," reprinted in *Readings in the Theory of International Trade* (Philadelphia: American Economic Association, 1949), p. 501; reprinted from *Economic Journal* (March, 1938), pp. 1–14.

[5] R. Nurkse, *Patterns of Trade and Development* (New York: Oxford University Press, 1961), p. 19.

[6] Alfred Marshall, *Principles of Economics,* 8th ed. (New York: Macmillan, 1952), p. 270. (Italics added.)

national trade has not performed as well in the twentieth century as it did during the nineteenth. Specifically, this argument refers to and draws upon the experience of today's underdeveloped countries. These nations —comprising two-thirds of the world's population and much of its geographical area—have a major feature in common: extremely poor living conditions and a strong desire to remedy this situation. Having, in many cases, won political independence only recently, these countries have mounted an all-out assault on their economic ills, an assault designed to start them on a course of rapid economic growth. Yet while the growth of the advanced countries has continued at a fairly high rate, the progress of the underdeveloped nations has been generally very slow; hence the charge that the gap between the rich and the poor countries has actually been widening and that this trend is in part augmented by the nature of the trading relations between the two groups.[7]

Does this mean that international trade should be written off as a growth-inducing factor insofar as the underdeveloped countries are concerned? Definitely not. It is true that the conditions which facilitated the international transmission of growth during the nineteenth century are almost completely absent now. The demand for primary products, which are the major exports of underdeveloped countries, has been growing slowly in recent years (an important exception is the demand for oil). At the same time, private foreign investors shy away from these countries and for obvious reasons: lack of profitable investment opportunities, political instability, etc. It seems almost as though present conditions have conspired to prevent the underdeveloped countries from enjoying the fruits of progress made elsewhere.

Yet these circumstances do not alter the case for international specialization; it is still as valid as ever. More important, the indirect benefits that international trade can bestow upon today's developing nations exceed, both in magnitude and variety, those which could have been expected a century ago.

In the nineteenth century it was primarily one country, Great Britain, that provided financial and technical resources for economic development in the "regions of recent settlement." Today the underdeveloped coun-

---

[7] This view has been expressed most vigorously by the Swedish economist Gunnar Myrdal. See his *An International Economy* (New York: Harper & Row, 1956).

tries can borrow such resources from a number of highly industrialized countries. And although *private* foreign investment does not play as large a role as it once played, long-term development loans from governments and international institutions, as well as outright financial grants and free technical advice have taken its place. Moreover, present technology is far more advanced and diversified than it was a hundred or even fifty years ago. And through trade, the benefits of modern technology are increasingly being shared by the underdeveloped countries.

Nor are the underdeveloped countries the only ones that presently stand to benefit from trade. The advanced nations are no less dependent on trade today than they were during the nineteenth and early twentieth centuries. If anything, their dependence has increased with time; for having geared their economies to highly specialized patterns of production and trade they should be all the more anxious to maintain them. Moreover, continuous growth, along with the burden of aiding the less developed nations, requires the most efficient use of available resources. No country, however advanced it may be, can ignore the contributions which international trade can make toward that end.

Conclusions

All in all, international trade still remains one of the basic factors promoting economic growth and higher standards of living. As times change, the patterns and composition of trade also change. But while some countries may be favored by particular changes, others may be adversely affected. Because of this, foreign trade is often made a scapegoat; it is blamed and punished for all sorts of economic ills, and at times the punishment has been greater than the alleged crime.

This is not to suggest that trade cannot have unfavorable effects. Fundamental changes in trade patterns require adjustments; yet the process of adjustment may be a painful one. There are, as will be seen later, instances when one can indeed point an accusing finger at some byproducts of international trade. What is important, however, is not the accusation *per se* but the national policies to which it may give rise. It may be necessary at times to adopt measures that would restrict foreign trade temporarily. But a country that pursues restrictive trade policies as a matter of course must in the long run pay a heavy price : It is denied opportunities for greater economic efficiency and for a rapid rate of growth.

2

Trade and Economic Stability

BY THEIR OWN ADMISSION
most governments nowadays are committed not to one but to three basic
economic goals. In addition to their concern with growth, they strive
to maintain stability and to assure an equitable distribution of the
national wealth. That this trio—growth, stability, and equity—has come
to share a place of honor on the official list of economic objectives is
not surprising. For although they may at times give rise to conflicts in
policy, these objectives are basically complementary. The achievement
of one is often a prerequisite to the achievement of the other.

We are not so much concerned, however, with the economic role of
modern governments as we are with the impact of international trade on
various aspects of economic life. Yet inasmuch as these have come to be
identified with specific policy objectives, we can organize our inquiry
along corresponding lines and consider, in turn, the effects of trade on
growth, on stability, and on equity. Following this order, we began by
examining the relation between trade and growth and, in the process,
established certain basic propositions. In later chapters we shall subject
these findings to a more rigorous analysis and see how they stand under
fire. But for the moment we can proceed to the next item on our list and

ask: Does international trade exert a stabilizing or a destabilizing influence on the level of a country's economic activities? Or, to pose the question in more general terms, what are the effects of trade on the level of, and changes in, national income?[1]

We may begin by considering the forces that determine the level of national income in the absence of foreign trade. The next two sections will deal with what is commonly referred to as a "closed economy," and will seek answers to two basic questions: (1) Under what conditions would national income tend to remain at a particular level? and (2) What would cause it to fluctuate (to move to a higher or lower level)?

Income and Income Changes in a Closed Economy

The student undoubtedly recalls that a country's national income, commonly referred to as Gross National Product, is defined as the total market value of all goods and services produced during the year, as measured by total expenditures in that year. Total expenditures, however, do more than just measure the value of national output; they do, in fact, represent aggregate demand in the economy. Aggregate demand may in turn be broken down into several components, each identified by a particular type of expenditure.

For analytical purposes it is convenient to distinguish between three major categories of expenditures that together constitute total demand. By far the largest component consists of expenditures for consumer goods—or, more precisely, "private consumption expenditures." Another component consists of "private investment expenditures," representing the demand of business firms for capital goods. To these we add "government expenditures," consisting of public outlays for both consumption and investment goods. Thus, total expenditures for goods and services (GNP) originate from three sources of demand: consumer demand, business demand, and government demand. If we denote these components by $C, I,$ and G respectively, we write,

$$GNP = C + I + G$$

Yet if Gross National Product represents total realized expenditures—that is, expenditures that were actually made—it must also repre-

---

[1] The effects of trade on the distribution of national income, i.e., on equity, will be treated in subsequent chapters.

sent total realized incomes. The logic here rests on the simple fact that expenditures made by buyers are, in effect, the incomes received by sellers; the aggregate amount spent on the national output must be the amount received by its producers. Incomes thus received are used in three ways: A portion is earmarked for tax payment; a major part is spent on current consumption; and some is saved. If we denote aggregate income by Y, consumption expenditures by C (corresponding to the C in the previous equation), savings by S, and tax payments by T. We can then write,

$$Y = C + S + T$$

The two equations just developed can now be placed side by side:

$$GNP \text{ (aggregate expenditures)} = C + I + G$$
$$Y \text{ (aggregate income)} \quad = C + S + T$$

Hasty conclusions, however, should not be drawn about the relationship between income and expenditures by reading into the two equations more than is warranted. We have here merely two identities, each describing an *ex post* phenomenon—that is, something that has already taken place. Indeed, only when viewed through *ex post* glasses can aggregate income be definitely said to equal aggregate expenditures, and the two equations written as

$$C + S + T = C + I + G$$
$$Y = GNP$$

or

Now, according to Keynes, national income will reach an equilibrium level when aggregate intended expenditures are exactly equal to aggregate income. Put differently, national income would tend neither to rise nor to fall if the aggregate income, earned in the process of producing the national output, were to be intentionally spent in its entirety. This is understandable. For if the current level of national output is to be justified, its total cost—as measured by the incomes earned by factors of production—must be at least covered by an equal amount of sales proceeds—as measured by total expenditures. Indeed, if total *intended* expenditures are less than total *expected* income, producers would be inclined to cut production back, causing national output to fall. Conversely, if intended expenditures exceed expected income, production would tend to increase, thereby raising national income to a higher level.

Yet whether or not intended aggregate expenditures will, in the end, be equal to aggregate income can hardly be known in advance. Since decisions to consume are made independently of decisions to produce, it is only by chance that total demand might equal total supply. Hence, if an equilibrium *is* reached, it is more by accident than by design. Nevertheless, it is possible to specify the conditions that must be met if an equality between intended aggregate expenditures and aggregate income—that is, equilibrium—is to be achieved.

For simplicity's sake, let the financial activities of the public sector (i.e., tax receipts and government outlays) be excluded.[2] We then have

$$GNP = C + I$$
$$Y = C + S$$

Equality between total income and total expenditures demands that

$$C + S = C + I$$

But since the C's on both sides are by definition the same, the equality between each side of the equation depends on the equality between intended S and I. Only when intended savings (S) are equal to intended investment expenditures can aggregate income and aggregate expenditures have the same value. Thus, only when

$$S = I$$
$$C + S = C + I$$

To push the discussion a step further, if investment expenditures are greater than savings (i.e., $I > S$), aggregate demand ($C + I$) is greater than the value of current output, as represented by income ($C + S$). In this case there will be a tendency for production and, with it, national income to increase. If, on the other hand, savings are greater than investment (i.e., $S > I$), total demand is smaller than the current supply, causing production and income to fall.

To sum up: National income is in equilibrium—tends to stay at a particular level—only when aggregate expenditures (GNP) are equal to aggregate income (Y). For this to occur, savings must be equal to in-

---

[2] This can easily be done by assuming that the government budget is in balance, i.e., tax receipts are exactly equal to government expenditures. In that case, G and T simply cancel each other out.

vestment expenditures. An excess of savings over investment would cause national income to fall whereas an excess of investment over savings would cause it to rise.

One question still remains: Should national income be forced out of equilibrium, what would be the magnitudes of its changes? For an answer, we turn to the next section and enlist the aid of a well-known concept—the national income multiplier.

The National Income Multiplier

In equilibrium

$$C + S = C + I$$

or

$$S = I$$

Theoretically, this equality—and hence an equilibrium level of national income—can be disturbed by a change in any one of the three variables C, S, or I. Yet experience indicates that current expenditures for consumption, as well as current savings, are closely related to the current level of income. A change in C (or in S) is more often caused by, rather than the cause of, a change in income. Indeed, the causative relationship between a change in income and the resulting change in consumption expenditures has been dignified by the term *marginal propensity to consume*. The marginal propensity to consume is defined as the amount allocated to consumption out of each additional dollar of income, and can be expressed as $\triangle C / \triangle Y$.[3] A similar relationship has been established between income and savings and is called the *marginal propensity to save*. Defined as the amount allocated to savings out of each additional dollar of income, this can be written as $\triangle S / \triangle Y$. Thus, a change in income (either positive or negative) will normally induce a change in consumption and a change in savings, the sum of which will be equal to the change in income itself (i.e., $\triangle Y = \triangle C + \triangle S$).[4]

While both consumption and savings are generally determined by

[3] This relationship also applies to a decrease in income. Thus, the marginal propensity to consume also indicates the amount by which consumption is curtailed when income is reduced by one dollar.

[4] Since tax payments are not assumed, any income earned is either spent entirely on consumption or is partly spent and partly saved.

income, the same cannot be said for investment. Decisions to increase or decrease investment expenditures are apt to be made with an eye to the future rather than to the present. Current income is much less of a factor in business demand for investment goods than expectations as to the future level of income. Even though investment decisions may be affected by the current level of economic activities, they are much more influenced by other considerations. Hence it is in changes of investment ($\triangle I$) that we are most likely to find the cause of an initial change in national income in a closed economy. But since a change in investment will probably lead to reinforcing of changes in other sectors of the economy, the consequent change in national income may be several times greater than the original change in investment itself.

Here is where we call forth the multiplier principle. This concept can help explain the process whereby an initial change in investment may induce a larger total change in national income.[5] And at the same time, the multiplier can suggest the possible magnitude of such changes in income. To observe the multiplier process at work, consider the following example.

Assume that out of each additional dollar's worth of income, 80¢ is spent on consumption and 20¢ is saved. This can be expressed by saying that the marginal propensity to consume (MPC) is .80, or ⅘, and the marginal propensity to save (MPS) is .20, or ⅕.

Suppose that when the economy is in equilibrium (i.e., $C + S = C + I$), there occurs a net increase in investment of $100. This adds $100 to the income of those engaged in the production, or sale, of capital goods. They will spend a portion of this new income ($80) on consumption, thus adding to the incomes of the suppliers of consumption goods. The latter will in turn spend ⅘ ($64) of *their* newly acquired income, causing a still further rise in the demand for goods and services. And so on. Increased demand will stimulate increased production and, with it, a rise in employment and income throughout the economy. If this process is traced, step by step, to its conclusion, it will show the total rise in national income initiated by the original rise in investment expenditures. Part of this process is shown in Table 2.1.

---

[5] When income is at a given level, however, a change in *any* type of expenditure can constitute the initial cause of changes in income. Although we will use changes in investment to illustrate the multiplier process, the same principle applies to autonomous changes in government spending, consumption expenditures, and so on.

TABLE *2.1* Increments to National Income Resulting from a Single Investment Expenditure

$$(MPC = 4/5; MPS = 1/5)$$

Income expend. period	*Original change in I*	*Increments to national income in the form of additional expenditures for consumption* $(\triangle C)$		
1	100			
2		80		
3			64	
4				51 20
5				40.96
6				32.77

Table 2.1 takes us only through the first several rounds of income and expenditure increases, but it serves to illustrate the basic principle of the multiplier process. One characteristic of this process is apparent at once: The stream of *additional* consumption expenditures flows in a diminishing order of magnitude. This, however, is not surprising. At each stage, a portion of the income received leaks out into savings, thus reducing the income received at the next stage. Indeed, it is this leakage (the size of which is determined by the marginal propensity to save) that eventually brings the process to a stop.[6] For as the amounts spent on consumption become smaller and smaller so do the increments to national income, until finally they are negligible.

Adding the figures in the table, we find that the total rise in national income is

$$100 + 80 + 64 + 51.20 + 40.96 + 32.77 = \$368.93$$

Since at each stage consumption expenditures are $4/5$ of income, we get the same result by writing

$$100 \ (1 + 4/5 + 4/5^2 + 4/5^3 + 4/5^4 + 4/5^5) = \$368.93$$

Thus, if we denote the marginal propensity to consume by *c*, we can generalize our example by writing

$$\triangle Y = \triangle I \ (1 + c + c^2 + c^3 + c^4 + c^5 + \ldots c^n)$$

[6] The expansionary process will end when the additional income created generates an amount of additional savings that equals the initial change in investment; i.e., when $\triangle S = \triangle I$. However, the multiplier effect will itself come to an end unless, of course, additional investment is continuously injected into the economy.

where

$$\triangle Y = \text{total change in national income}$$
$$\triangle I = \text{the initial change in investment}$$
$$n = \text{the number of income-expenditure stages}$$

Mathematically, the expression within the parentheses can be written as $1/1 - c$, and the formula becomes

$$\triangle Y = \triangle I \cdot \frac{1}{1 - c}$$

But since the sum of the MPC and the MPS must be equal to one, it follows that $1 - MPC = MPS$. Using s to denote the MPS, we arrive at

$$\triangle Y = \triangle I \cdot \frac{1}{s}$$

In a word, the total change in national income is given by the initial change in investment multiplied by the reciprocal of the marginal propensity to save. This reciprocal is called the *multiplier;* its value determines by how much we can expect income to rise (or fall) as a result of an initial rise (or fall) in investment expenditures.

Applied to our specific data, the formula yields the following result:

$$\triangle Y = \triangle I \cdot \frac{1}{s} = 100 \cdot \frac{1}{\frac{1}{5}} = 100 \cdot \frac{5}{1} = 100 \times 5 = 500$$

The *multiplier* in this case is 5; but it could easily have been either larger or smaller, depending on the value of the MPS. For example, when the MPC is $\frac{2}{3}$, the MPS must be $\frac{1}{3}$, and the value of the *multiplier* is only 3. In that case, an initial $100 rise in investment would produce only a $300 total rise in national income. Thus, the higher the value of the *multiplier,* the greater the impact of a change in investment on subsequent changes in income, and vice versa. But the value of the *multiplier* itself depends on the value of the MPC. The higher the MPC, the smaller must be the MPS, and therefore the larger its reciprocal. Put differently, the greater the proportion of additional income spent on consumption, the smaller the leakage into savings, and hence the larger the total increase in national income.

Foreign Trade and Income Changes: The Foreign-Trade Multiplier

Still excluding the public sector, we may now drop the assumption of a closed economy and bring foreign trade into the picture. To do so we must take cognizance of two variables—exports (X) and imports (M)—which were previously omitted from our national income equation. Specifically, we must bear in mind that in an open economy, consumption expenditures (C) represent expenditures on *all* goods and services consumed, regardless of whether they were produced at home or were imported. But although they are included in consumption (C), expenditures on imports cannot of course be considered as expenditures on *domestically* produced output. Hence, they must be subtracted from the aggregate expenditure equation (GNP). On the other hand, exports, which represent expenditures on domestically produced goods sold to foreign countries, must be added to the GNP equation. Thus, in an open economy we have

$$GNP \text{ (aggregate expenditures)} = C + I + X - M$$
$$Y \text{ (aggregate income)} = C + S$$

Yet whether the economy is closed or open, equilibrium still requires an equality between aggregate income and intended aggregate expenditures. Consequently, equilibrium in an open economy can be achieved only when

$$C + I + X - M = C + S$$
or
$$I + X - M = S$$

Our concern, however, is still with the causes and consequences of changes in national income. And although in this section we address ourselves mainly to the influence of foreign trade on national income, we can employ some of the basic propositions and analytical concepts which were developed in the last two sections. The key to the analysis that follows is the notion that an autonomous increase (or decrease) in expenditures will jolt national income from equilibrium, and as it spreads through the economy will cause it to rise (or fall) by a larger amount. The total size of the change depends, as we have seen, on the value of the *multiplier,* the latter being the reciprocal of the marginal propensity to save. Bearing all this in mind, consider the effects of autonomous changes in exports, assuming there are no autonomous changes in any other variables.

Since exports represent expenditures on goods sold to foreign buyers, they must at the same time represent income received by exporters. A sudden increase in exports means that exporters are receiving a larger income than before. Like all good citizens, they will spend a portion of this additional income on consumption goods, thereby initiating the familiar income-expenditure flow throughout the economy. In this fashion a rise in exports can trigger a larger increase in national income, similar to one initiated by a rise in investment expenditures. Yet in this case, the multiplier process is subject to an additional constraint that is absent in a closed economy and whose influence we must now take into account.

The constraint referred to above, is none other than the tendency of consumers to spend part of their income on imported goods and services. Because payments for imports are made to foreign rather than domestic suppliers, they cannot be considered a part of the domestic income-expenditure stream. Such payments, in fact, constitute a leakage out of the stream and serve to reduce its size in the same manner as do leakages into savings. Thus, although foreign trade can—through a rise in exports—stimulate an expansion of the national economy, it contains a built-in feature that limits the size of this expansion. It is called the *marginal propensity to import* (MPM), defined as the portion of an increase in income that is spent on imports $(\triangle M/\triangle Y)$. To appreciate its effects, consider this example.

Assume, as before, that out of each additional dollar of income 80¢ is allocated to consumption and 20¢ to savings. But now suppose that of the 80¢ spent on consumption 20¢ is spent on imported goods, leaving only 60¢ for domestic expenditures. In terms of propensities, this may be expressed as follows:

$$MPC = \tfrac{4}{5}$$
$$MPM = \tfrac{1}{5}$$
$$MPS = \tfrac{1}{5}$$
$$MPC - MPM = \tfrac{4}{5} - \tfrac{1}{5} = \tfrac{3}{5}$$

With this information, let us trace an autonomous rise in exports of $100 through the economy, in the same manner as before. The first recipients (exporters) of the additional income will save $20, spend $20 on imports, and purchase $60 worth of domestic goods. Recipients of these $60 will in turn allocate $36 of their increased income to domestic consumption, $12 to the purchase of imports, and $12 to savings. And so on down the line.

What will be the total increase of national income when the expansionary process finally ends? Recalling the expression for the multiplier, and adding into it the marginal propensity to import (m), we can write:

$$\triangle Y = \triangle X \cdot \frac{1}{1 - (c - m)}$$

where

$\triangle Y$ = total change in national income
$\triangle X$ = the initial change in export
$c - m$ = the difference between the MPC and the MPM

We can rewrite the above as follows

$$\triangle Y = \triangle X \cdot \frac{1}{1 - c + m}$$

but since $1 - c = s$, we finally arrive at

$$\triangle Y = \triangle X \cdot \frac{1}{s + m}$$

The expression $1/s + m$ is called the *foreign-trade multiplier;* when it is multiplied by the initial rise in exports ($\triangle X$), it indicates the total subsequent increase in national income ($\triangle Y$). In practice, however, the foreign-trade multiplier can be used in conjunction with any autonomous rise (or fall) in expenditures. For in an open economy, changes in income may owe their origin to either external or internal forces, or both. Indeed, it would be more accurate to include investment as well as exports in our formula, and express changes in income as

$$\triangle Y = (\triangle I + \triangle X) \cdot \frac{1}{s + m}$$

where

$$\triangle Y = \text{total change in national income}$$
$$\triangle I = \text{autonomous change in investment}$$
$$\triangle X = \text{autonomous change in export}$$
$$\frac{1}{s + m} = \text{the foreign-trade multiplier}$$

Yet since in our present case, any changes in investment have been ruled out, the multiplier yields the following result:

$$\triangle Y = (0 + 100) \cdot \frac{1}{\frac{1}{5} + \frac{1}{5}} = 100 \cdot \frac{1}{\frac{2}{5}} = 100 \cdot \frac{5}{2} = 100 \times 2.5 = 250$$

Compare this result with the one obtained earlier, under the assumption of a closed economy. Although in both instances $100 of autonomous expenditures was injected into the economy, the total rise in income now is half as large as it was before (250 as compared with 500). How so? The explanation lies, of course, in the different values of the respective multipliers. In the closed economy the multiplier was $\frac{1}{\frac{1}{5}}$, or 5, while in the open economy it was found to be half as large (i.e., $\frac{1}{\frac{2}{5}}$, or 2.5). This is hardly surprising, for we already know that the value of the *multiplier* varies inversely with the proportion of any additional income that leaks out of the expenditure stream: the larger the leakage, the smaller the value of the multiplier. And while in a closed economy we have to contend with only one such leakage (i.e., the MPS), the existence of foreign trade adds another, the MPM. Together, the MPS and the MPM constitute a larger total leakage than the MPS alone. Consequently, the value of the multiplier in an open economy must be smaller than it is in a closed economy.[7]

Stripped of its mechanical formalities, the foregoing analysis suggests that an autonomous rise in expenditures in an open economy would result in a smaller total increase of national income than would an equal rise in a closed economy. But inasmuch as the multiplier process can work in reverse—that is, induce a multiple contraction of income—the fact that the foreign-trade multiplier is small may actually prove a blessing in

---

[7] Unless, of course, the marginal propensity to import is assumed to be zero—an unrealistic assumption at best.

disguise. For when an autonomous *fall* in expenditures sets off a chain of falling incomes and expenditures, the foreign-trade multiplier will serve to dampen the downward movement of national income, thereby lessening its total contraction. By the same token, should inflationary pressures gather momentum—as when a rise in expenditures occurs at a full employment level of national income—foreign trade would provide an outlet for some of the excess expenditures and arrest the inflationary spiral.[8] Thus the presence of foreign trade—represented by the foreign trade multiplier—constitutes an element of stability that does not exist in a closed economy.[9] And although, as we will soon see, foreign trade has its destabilizing aspects, these do not stem from the size of the *foreign-trade multiplier* itself.

Interaction Between External and Internal Forces

To simplify matters, we have thus far treated separately those forces that originate *within* an economy and those that are thrust upon it by foreign trade. Moreover, we have focused attention only on the direct consequences of autonomous changes in expenditures, ignoring any secondary repercussions to which they may give rise. This exercise led us to two major conclusions. First, national income can be jolted from a particular level by either internal or external forces; secondly, income changes will be smaller in an open economy than in a closed one.

Although correct as far as they go, these conclusions must be modified if they are to offer greater insight into the working of an open economy. For in the real world the level and course of economic activities are influenced not only by direct actions of different variables but also by their *inter*actions. Nor are the effects of such actions and interactions confined within political boundaries. More often than not, economic changes in one country spread willy-nilly to other countries. And although the oft-heard claim that "whenever the United States

[8] The outlet through which expenditures are siphoned off is none other than the marginal propensity to import. Moreover, imports, by increasing the total supply of goods, relieve the pressure on domestic supply and check the upward movement of prices.

[9] For a fuller discussion of this point, see C. P. Kindleberger, *Foreign Trade and the National Economy* (New Haven: Yale University Press, 1962), Chap. 13.

sneezes the rest of the world catches cold'' is a bit of an exaggeration, it nevertheless contains a germ of truth. Foreign trade *is* a means by which economic fluctuations can be transmitted—for better or for worse—from one country to another. Just how extensively it influences domestic stability (or instability) can be easily appreciated if we throw our previous assumptions to the winds and consider the following examples:

Suppose that a sudden rise in investment stimulates, via the multiplier process, a subsequent rise in income in the United States. As income rises, so will imports. And since one country's imports are another country's exports, other nations will now experience an increase in *their* exports and incomes. Rising incomes in countries abroad will also stimulate their imports. Some of these will be purchased from the United States, thus causing an increase in American exports and a further rise in American income. Moreover, a rising demand for exports may induce additional investment expenditures that, in their own right, will reinforce the upward movement in national income. As a result, a further increase in imports may be expected that would further augment the rise of incomes abroad. And so on.

It is easy to visualize the extent to which this process can be carried, especially if many countries are simultaneously involved. Whether such a process will be sustained for a long time or end abruptly depends on a great many variables and hence cannot be fully foreseen. But this much is fairly certain: The interaction between domestic and external variables can produce a far greater increase in income than is possible in a closed economy.

The same process, however, may work in reverse. A fall in one country's income, due to a fall in investment or in its exports, may result in curtailment of its imports, which would depress other countries' incomes, causing them to import less. As a result, exports and incomes throughout the trading world would be reduced still further. In short, foreign trade may combine with domestic forces to produce a worldwide contraction of economic activities, worsening the internal decline experienced by any one country. Moreover, the internal decline itself may have been initially caused by external forces, thus adding insult to injury.

Yet foreign trade may still prove to be a source of stability, especially to countries whose exports enjoy a high (or rising) demand abroad.

In such cases, a decline in, say, domestic investment, which would normally lead to a fall in income, may be offset by an equal or greater rise in exports. The rise in exports would either prevent income from falling or actually cause it to rise. Moreover, such a rise may provide a stimulus to investment, which was lacking before, and thus start the economy on an upward path.

Conclusion: Growth versus Stability

In one way or another, foreign trade exerts a constant influence on the level of a nation's economic activities. It can stimulate a lagging economy and launch it on a rapid advance, or it can reverse an upward trend and precipitate a severe economic decline. The experience of the nineteenth century, discussed in Chapter 1, attests to the favorable contribution of trade to growth. But at the same time it suggests that the extent of such a contribution depends on the existence of particular circumstances. This chapter lends support to this contention. Given the "right" circumstances, foreign trade can render great service in expanding output, employment, and income. At other times, however, the "trade" winds may blow in an opposite direction.

All of this, of course, bears directly on our immediate concern with the question of stability. Since growth and stability are closely related objectives, the effects of trade on one of them are likely to influence the pursuit of the other. Yet the effects of trade on growth may at times run counter to what is deemed desirable from the viewpoint of stability, and vice versa. Thus, depending on which of these objectives is emphasized at a particular moment, trade may be regarded either as a welcome guest or as an intruder.[10] Or one might say that the presence of foreign trade may be taken either as an aid to policy or as a constraint upon it. Yet in either case, its influence could not be ignored.

[10] More will be said in Part III about possible conflicts between domestic objectives and the influence of foreign trade.

3

A Portrait of Trade and Growth:
The Balance of Payments

Changes in a country's foreign trade affect, and are affected by, changes in its national income. Response to such changes depends not only on their magnitude but also on their character. To put it differently and more comprehensively, the interrelationship between trade, growth, and stability involves both the type and the size of changes in a country's domestic and international economic activities.

In the preceding chapter we distinguished between two types of foreign-trade transactions—exports and imports—and considered their influence on variations in income. This enabled us to simplify our analysis and to spotlight the basic relation between income and trade. But in order to appreciate more fully the role of international trade we must examine its composition in greater detail by referring to an important economic document: the balance of international payments.

Meaning and Nature of the Balance of Payments

A country's balance of international payments, or simply the balance of payments, is a record of all the economic transactions between that country[1] and the rest of the world during a given period of time, usually one year. As with most national income statistics, the balance of payments indicates the money value of the country's foreign-trade transactions, and these values are usually expressed in terms of the country's own currency. For example, England's balance of payments is given in pounds (£), Germany's in marks (DM), and that of the United States in dollars. Finally, the balance-of-payments statement presents the aggregate values of the major items entering foreign trade rather than a detailed breakdown of all individual transactions.

It is possible, of course, to draw up a balance-of-payments statement that would describe separately the trade of the reporting country and one or a few of its trading partners. In fact, some countries provide balance-of-payments information concerning their trade with geographical areas—for example, the trade of the United States with Latin America, with Western Europe, and so on. By the same token (though for different reasons) some countries, including the United States, compile and present balance-of-payments data on a quarterly as well as on an annual basis. For our purposes, however, the balance of payments can be taken to represent the total value of a country's trade with the rest of the world, summarized over a period of one year.

Before examining the actual make-up of a balance of payments, let us discuss a few balance-of-payments principles. Theoretically the balance of payments can be conceived of as a sort of double-entry-bookkeeping device, in which each transaction is given equal credit and debit entries. Those familiar with accounting principles should disregard the conventional method of distinguishing between credits and debits. For when these terms are used in connection with the balance of payments, they acquire a special meaning and are not handled in the same manner as they would be in ordinary bookkeeping practices.

The balance-of-payments statistician considers and records a given transaction as a debit (minus) if it gives rise to payment by the home country to foreign countries. Conversely, any transaction that gives rise to payment by foreign countries to the home country is entered as a credit (plus). Debit transactions are often referred to as "payments"

---

[1] Residents, business firms, and institutions of the country engage in such transactions. But for convenience we lump all these together under the term "country."

(money outflows) while credits are commonly expressed as "receipts" (money inflows). But this apparently simple distinction is misleading. For balance-of-payments transactions are classified, not according to actual payments and receipts, but according to the direction of payment they would normally involve. For example, exports of goods and services are recorded as credits (+) not because exports in themselves are receipts, but because they entail payments by foreign countries. Similarly, commodity imports are entered as debits (−) because the importing country must sooner or later pay for them.

To put it more succinctly, all transactions that give rise to money claims on the reporting country by foreign countries are regarded as debits, while all transactions that give rise to money claims on foreign countries are considered credits. How these claims are actually settled— that is, how payments are actually made—is a different question and will be discussed shortly. But this much can be noted now : When all credit transactions and all debit transactions are added, their respective totals must equal each other; a country's balance of payments must always balance.

The fact that total credits and total debits are equal is often explained by accounting logic or, more specifically, by the double-entry-bookkeeping nature of the balance of payments. Thus, one may argue that since each transaction results in equal debit and credit entries, total debits should equal total credits. But in reality it is well-nigh impossible to match the credit and debit side of each and every transaction. For in drawing up a balance of payments the statistician is plagued by various discrepancies between debits and credits. These discrepancies—which among other things arise from inaccurate estimates, insufficient data, and different methods of valuation[2]—militate against an overall arithmetic equality between credit and debit items. More often than not, the statistician is obliged to add a balancing item—Errors and Omissions— in order to achieve an accounting balance between the two sides (or columns) of the balance of payments.

---

[2] For statistical purposes, internationally traded goods can be valued either on an f.o.b. (free on board) or c.i.f. (cost, insurance, and freight) basis. The former indicates the value of goods at the point of exportation; the latter, at the point of importation. This means, however, that a country that values its exports on an f.o.b. basis and its imports on a c.i.f. basis is bound to run into statistical discrepancies in recording its foreign-trade transactions.

Nevertheless, total credits and total debits do tend to be equal during any given period. But this equality results not so much from accounting magic as from the basic economic principle that, in order to buy goods and services from others, a country—like an individual—must be able to pay for them. And though the "ability to pay" does not necessarily mean the possession of ready cash, it does mean that a country cannot currently spend abroad a greater amount than it currently earns, unless it somehow manages to obtain the means of payment that can make up the difference. Conversely, a nation's current sales to foreign countries can exceed its current purchases from them only if that nation is willing to supply its foreign customers with the means of financing their excess purchases.

We can further appreciate the significance of this principle and its relevance to the balance of payments if we note that exporters in each country must ultimately be paid in their own currency. An American exporter, shipping automobiles to England, usually insists that final payment be made in dollars, not in British pounds. Similarly, a German exporter of beer ultimately demands payment in marks, for he must use marks to pay his employees or to buy groceries. Consequently, in order to finance its purchases (debit transactions) from other countries, a country must lay claim to a sufficient amount of their currencies. It can do this in a number of ways; for example, it can sell goods and services to them, borrow abroad, and receive grants or donations from other countries—all of which constitute credit items in its balance of payments.

To sum up, the balance of payments tends to balance because, broadly speaking, it is a record describing the ways and means that a country uses to finance its purchases from other countries during a given period of time. And since the debits incurred through purchasing must be matched by credits, which are the means of payment, it follows that total credits and total debits must be equal.

Structure of the Balance of Payments

While it identifies a country's international transactions according to the *direction* of payments (incoming and outgoing) that they involve, the balance of payments also classifies them along functional lines. Transactions fall into four major categories: the current account, unilateral transfers, the capital account, and the gold account. This breakdown is commonly referred to as the "horizontal" division of the balance of payments, as distinguished from its "vertical" division into credits and debits. But terminology aside, the important point is that each balance-of-payments transaction is classified in two ways: It is entered either as a credit or a debit item, and it is also recorded in the major category that best describes its nature or function.

The functional classification gives details about the composition of a country's foreign trade. Just how revealing is the information contained in the balance of payments? This will become apparent as we examine each of its major components. When carefully analyzed, such information can be of great value in suggesting the nature of a country's economic position.

THE CURRENT ACCOUNT

It is often suggested that in order to appreciate the effects of a country's foreign trade on its current level of income, one need only look at the current account of the balance of payments. This suggestion is not without merit. For in the current account are recorded those transactions that represent the current flows of goods and services between the reporting country and the rest of the world. And since flows of goods must entail flows of payments, in one direction or another, the current account may be likened to an income-expenditure statement, reflecting sales to, and purchases from, foreign countries. Thus, expenditures that foreign countries make for domestically produced goods constitute income for the reporting country, and can be added to its national income. On the other hand, purchases of goods and services *from* foreign countries constitute expenditures and must be subtracted from the national income of the reporting country.

Indeed, if we think of a country's national income as the sum total of expenditures made for currently produced domestic output (i.e., GNP), we can include the current account in it by writing the basic GNP equation, which was developed in Chapter 2, as follows:

$$GNP \text{ (aggregate expenditures)} = C + I + G + X - M$$

where

X = current exports (i.e., the value of goods and services sold
to foreign countries)

and

M = current imports (i.e., the value of goods and services bought
from foreign countries)

If current exports and current imports happen to be of the same
value, they merely cancel each other in the above equation, and the
expression $Y - M$, sometimes called "net foreign investment," is equal
to zero. In this case, the total value of GNP remains unaffected by the
country's transactions on current account. But if, as is usually the case,
the current account shows either an excess of exports over imports or an
excess of imports over exports, the difference between the two must be
considered in computing the GNP. Accordingly, whenever exports exceed
imports, the value of $X - M$ is added to the GNP; but should imports
exceed exports, the difference is subtracted from the GNP. Thus, depending on the actual balance between the values of exports and imports, the
current account may contribute either to an increase or a decrease in the
current level of national income.

TABLE *3.1*   Model of a Current Account (in dollars)

Item	Credit (+)	Debit (−)
Merchandise:		
Commodity exports	10,000	
Commodity imports		6,000
Services:		
Transportation	1,000	2,000
Travel	2,000	1,000
Interest and dividends	1,500	400
Banking and insurance	300	100
Miscellaneous	200	
Total, goods and services	15,000	9,500
Balance on current account	+5,500	

What sort of transactions enter into the current account? As we see
in Table 3.1 the current account consists of two major subdivisions:

merchandise and services. Of the two, the former is nearly always the more significant.[3] It includes commodity exports, which, because they give rise to claims on foreign countries, are recorded in the credit ($+$) column; and commodity imports, which appear in the debit ($-$) column.

Under services, often referred to as "invisibles," one finds a variety of items. Most of these—for example, transportation services, travel and tourism, banking and insurance services—are self-explanatory. One need only ask whether the service in question has been rendered to or by foreign countries in order to record it in the appropriate column.

But one item—interest and dividends—requires a few words of explanation. This item represents payments (or receipts) arising out of present and past investment activities; the "service" in this case consists of providing capital (e.g., loans). And although transactions representing foreign investment activities are recorded in the capital account of the balance of payments, income from such investments is included in the current account. Thus, dividends received by an American who owns shares in a British corporation, or interest received by an American holder of a British government bond, are entered as credits in the current account of the United States balance of payments. Conversely, dividends paid by an American corporation to its foreign stockholders, or interest due foreign holders of United States government securities, represent debit items in the current account of the United States balance of payments.

The difference between total credits and total debits in the current account is called the "balance on current account." In Table 3.1 this difference is positive, reflecting an excess of receipts over payments, or a surplus on current account. Had payments exceeded receipts, the net figure would have been entered with a minus sign, and the balance of trade would be said to reflect a deficit. Yet the balance on current account is not the final measure of a country's foreign-trade position. Nor is a surplus or a deficit on current account synonymous with the often-heard terms "balance-of-payments surplus" and "balance-of-payments deficit." Indeed, all we can conclude from a country's "balance on current account" is that it currently spends either more or less for foreign goods and services than it currently earns by providing goods

---

[3] There are, of course, exceptions to this rule; but merchandise exports and imports generally comprise the major items of current-account transactions.

and services to other countries. To find out how such discrepancies between current receipts and expenditures can be offset, we must examine the rest of the country's balance-of-payments statement.

UNILATERAL TRANSFERS

This category of the balance of payments consists of what may properly be termed "one-way" transactions; or, to be more precise, transactions that involve flows of payments in one direction without corresponding flows of goods and services in the other (or flows of goods in one direction without corresponding flows of payments in the other). Such transactions include personal and institutional remittances and gifts, and public grants and donations. At times they may also take the form of reparations or indemnity payments by one government either to another country or to private citizens of that country.

TABLE *3.2* Model of a Unilateral Transfers Account (in dollars)

Item	Credit (+)	Debit (−)
Private:		
Personal remittances	50	200
Institutional remittances		300
Governmental:		
Grants and donations		1,000
Indemnities and reparations	150	
Total	200	1,500
Balance on Unilateral Transfers		−1,300

Unilateral transfers are entered in the balance of payments either as credits or debits, depending on the direction of their flow. From the viewpoint of, say, the United States, any remittances made by its government or citizens to foreign countries are considered debit items. Conversely, remittances received by United States citizens and institutions from abroad are entered as credits. A simple illustration can explain the justification for this procedure. Suppose you donate $100 to a French orphanage by mailing a check in this amount, drawn on your local bank, to Paris. This constitutes a unilateral transfer of funds from the United States to France. As a result, the recipient of your check has a claim of $100 on the United States (or, more specifically, on your bank). According to our definition, any transaction that gives rise to a claim on the reporting country is registered as a debit in its balance of payments. On the other hand, if a Frenchman sends a gift of money to a relative in the United States, the transaction would be entered as a credit in the United States balance of payments, since in this instance the American recipient of the gift would possess a claim for payment on France.

Over a given period of time a country is both a recipient and a dispenser of unilateral transfers. Hence, the statistician who draws up the balance of payments is normally concerned only with the overall balance in this category. He will often distinguish between private and public transfers of funds, but he will record their totals, as well as the total for the entire category, either as a *net* credit or a *net* debit balance.

THE CAPITAL ACCOUNT

If the current account of the balance of payments describes a country's foreign trade in goods and services, the capital account records those transactions involving exchanges of money for evidence of credit or debt. Purchases and sales of stocks and bonds, lending and borrowing, increases and decreases in bank balances—these are the types of transactions that make up the capital account. Hence a country's capital account is a record of changes in its foreign assets and liabilities vis-à-vis the rest of the world.

To avoid a misunderstanding about the nature of the capital account, it is important to emphasize that, in recording capital-account transactions, the statistician assigns a debit sign to capital outflows and a credit sign to capital inflows. Thus, when one purchases securities from a foreign company or government, this involves an outflow of capital. Also regarded as capital outflows are loans to foreign countries or the repayment by domestic residents of loans obtained from foreign sources. Consequently, all these transactions are entered as debit items in the capital account. On the other hand, the sale of securities by domestic corporations or the government to foreign residents, the borrowing of funds from abroad, or the receipt of payment on loans to foreign countries—all of these constitute capital inflow at the time they take place and hence are recorded as credit items.

One can easily appreciate the reasoning behind this by applying the basic distinction between credits and debits to the transactions that comprise the capital account. For example, the purchase of foreign securities is considered a debit because this gives rise to a foreigner's claim for payment. Similarly, a loan to a foreign country provides that country with a claim on the lender, and the transaction must therefore be regarded as a debit in the lender's balance of payments. When the loan, all or part, is repaid, the position is reversed. The claim now is on the foreign country, and the transaction calls for a credit entry in the balance of payments of the country being repaid.

The same reasoning lies behind the treatment accorded to changes in bank balances. Thus, an increase in foreign-owned accounts in American banks is recorded as a credit because it involves a capital inflow into the United States. A reduction in such accounts is entered as a debit, since it represents an outflow of capital from this country. The reverse is true for changes in American-owned accounts, held in foreign banks. An increase in such accounts constitutes an outflow of capital from the United States and is entered as a debit, while a decrease is regarded as a capital inflow and is recorded as a credit.

The following rule may be helpful. From the standpoint of balance-of-payments accounting, exports (or outflows) of capital entail the same direction of payment as do imports of goods and services. Both give rise to claims for payment on the reporting country; hence both are debits. Conversely, imports (or inflows) of capital can be likened to exports of goods and services; they involve claims on foreign countries and are therefore entered as credits in the balance of payments of the reporting country.

Table 3.3 shows that capital flows are classified either as short-term or long-term, depending on the maturity characteristics of the credit instrument involved in any given transaction. Transactions that involve claims payable on demand, or due for payment within one year, are classified as short-term. In addition to bank balances and currency holdings, short-term transactions include treasury bills, call loans, drafts, acceptances, and so on. Under long-term transactions are recorded sales and purchases of stocks and bonds, long-term loans, and direct investments.

Capital transactions may also be classified according to type of creditor and debtor. Thus, the capital account usually distinguishes between

TABLE *3.3*   Model of a Capital Account (in dollars)

Item	Credit (+)	Debit (−)
Long term:		
Direct investment		3,700
Purchases and sales of securities	150	400
Long-term loans	50	
Short term:		
Changes in holdings of currencies		20
Changes in bank balances		80
Purchases and sales of short-term government securities	120	300
Misc. short-term capital	80	100
Total	400	4,600
Balance on Capital Account		−4,200

transactions by the government and other official institutions, and those that are carried out privately. This distinction is useful in ascertaining the extent of governmental participation in international financial activities at various times. But the reasons for such participation may not always be apparent from the balance-of-payments data alone. In any event, it hardly matters at this stage of our discussion whether it is public or private capital flows that predominate in the capital account.

What does matter, however, is that the capital account, like the two previously discussed categories, contains both credit and debit transactions, and that when these are added, the net balance may turn out to be either negative (−) or positive (+). The meaning of each of these possible outcomes should now be fairly clear. In a word, a net balance with a minus sign reflects an excess of capital outflow over inflow, or a net export of capital; a positive balance indicates the opposite—an excess of capital inflow over outflow, or a net import of capital.

THE MONETARY GOLD ACCOUNT

A gold-producing country, such as South Africa, might well regard its sale of gold to other countries exactly as it does the sale of diamonds or any other commodity. From South Africa's viewpoint, gold exports constitute just another credit item, to be included in the current account. From the viewpoint of most countries, however, the export and import of gold represent special transactions and are recorded in a separate balance-of-payments category—the gold account. It should be noted here that it is movements of *monetary* gold—that is, gold held by governments and/or central banks as official monetary reserves—which are recorded in the gold account.[4] Thus, unlike all other balance-of-payments categories, the gold account consists exclusively of official transactions: transactions that are undertaken either by the government or by the country's central bank.

The reasons for, and the implications of, such transactions will be discussed in detail in Part III. At the moment we may simply observe that gold exports (sale of gold to foreign countries) are recorded as credits, while gold imports (purchase of gold from foreign countries) are entered as debits. The same procedure is followed even when the gold that is sold or bought is not actually shipped from one country to another, but is merely earmarked for the account of the purchaser. For example, an increase in the amount of gold earmarked by foreign central banks for the account of the American government is considered a gold import into the United States; it is thus entered as a debit item in the United States balance of payments. Conversely, an increase in the amount of gold earmarked by the Federal Reserve authorities for the account of, say, France, is regarded as a gold export from the United States, and hence a credit item in its balance of payments. The actual shipment of earmarked gold does not constitute a new transaction and is not recorded as such.

THE BALANCE OF PAYMENTS:
AN OVERALL VIEW

Having examined the major balance-of-payments components separately, we may now pull them together and view the balance of payments as a whole. Table 3.4 presents figures for the United States balance of payments for 1966.

---

[4] More recently, however, it has become customary to record gold movements with other transactions involving changes in monetary reserves (i.e., official holdings of foreign currencies). See Table 3.4.

The table is mostly self-explanatory. Thus, with respect to the current account, the figures reflect a sizable excess of current earnings over current expenditures, yielding a surplus on current account of about $5.1 billion. Yet this surplus was more than offset by the net debit balances on the unilateral transfers and capital accounts. These two categories constitute a total outflow of over $6 billion. Moreover, the balance of payments in 1966 featured some $383 million of unrecorded debit transactions, represented by the item errors and omissions. When these are added to the other debit balances, the sum total of debit items becomes $6,526 million. In short, in 1966 the total outflow of payments from the United States exceeded its surplus on current account by $1,424 million (subtract $5,102 million from $6,526 million). And it was this figure that in 1966 represented our so-called balance-of-payments deficit, the implications of which will be discussed in subsequent chapters.

Deficits, however, cannot be left hanging in midair; they must be offset if for no reason other than to assure equality in total debits and credits. Accordingly, in looking over Table 3.4, we observe two items that together account for a credit balance of $1,424 million. These are: (1) changes in U.S. gold and foreign currency holdings, and (2) changes in United States liquid liabilities to foreign accounts. Changes in United States liquid liabilities include essentially transactions of the capital-account type—in other words, increases in foreign-owned bank balances (in dollars) and sales to foreigners of United States government securities. But because these transactions are conducted under special circumstances, they are not recorded in the capital account itself, and instead are presented separately.

Viewed in its entirety, the United States balance of payments for 1966 represents transactions totaling some $44.5 billion, of which about $43 billion, or over 90 per cent, are exports of goods and services. These figures reveal that the United States is the world's largest exporting, as well as importing, nation. Indeed, during the past twenty years or so, no other country has been able to make such a claim. It may therefore come as a surprise to discover that the foreign trade of the United States constitutes only a small portion of its national income. In 1966, for example, the GNP of the United States stood at $739.6 billion; out of this total, exports came to about 7.5 per cent and imports to a little over 5 per cent. Although these proportions have varied from year to year, they

TABLE *3.4*   United States Balance of Payments, 1966
(in millions of dollars)

	Credit (+)	Debit (−)
Current Account		
Merchandise	29,168	25,510
U.S. military sales and purchases	847	3,694
Transportation	2,589	2,914
Travel	1,573	2,657
Investment income	7,245	2,074
Miscellaneous	1,572	1,088
Total, goods and service	43,039	37,937
Balance on Current Account	5,102	
Unilateral Transfers		
Private remittances (net)		647
Government grants, excluding military (net)		2,278
Balance on Unilateral Transfers		2,925
Capital Account		
U.S. private capital flow (net)		
Direct investment		3,462
Other long term and short term		670
U.S. gov't, excluding official reserve transactions (net)		
Long term		1,266
Short term		265
Foreign capital flow (net)		
Direct and other long-term investment	2,176	
Short term	269	
Total, capital flows	2,445	5,663
Balance on Capital Account		3,218
Errors and Omissions (net)		383
Settlement of Deficit		
Changes in U.S. official holdings of gold and convertible currencies (net)	568	
Changes in U.S. liquid liabilities to foreign accounts (net)	856	
Balance on Settlement Account	1,424	
Total, all transactions	44,463	44,463

Source: *Survey of Current Business*, U.S. Department of Commerce (Washington, D.C.: Government Printing Office, June, 1967), p. 23.

have in general remained relatively small compared with those of most countries. In fact, the United States may be singled out in this respect as a unique case. For while its volume of foreign trade is larger than that of any other country, it seems less dependent upon it than the great majority of countries.

Whatever one may choose to make of this paradox, this much is certain. Any conclusions about the relation of a country's foreign trade to its national income must rest on detailed statistical information concerning the magnitude and types of its international economic transactions. The balance of payments is the major source of such information.

The Balance of Payments as an Analytical Tool

Apart from its virtues as a comprehensive statistical record, the balance of payments is a useful analytical tool. In an immediate sense, balance-of-payments information serves as an important guide to the formulation of commercial and trade policies. Yet even the choice of *domestic* economic policies is often based on balance-of-payments data. Indeed, some of the fiscal and monetary measures instituted in recent years by the U.S. Treasury and the Federal Reserve have been influenced by our balance-of-payments position, and particularly by our concern over the persistent outflow of gold.[5] Nor is the United States the only country in which balance-of-payments considerations influence or dictate economic policies. Most countries, in fact, look to their balance of payments when contemplating important policy measures.

In later chapters we shall discuss in some detail the role played by the balance of payments in determining foreign and domestic economic policies. At the moment, however, we are mainly concerned with the ways in which balance-of-payments data can help us understand the relation between growth, stability, and trade. Will a careful reading of a country's balance of payments enable us to draw meaningful conclusions about its economic posture and/or problems? Will we learn something about its experience with economic growth by tracing its balance of

[5] Among these measures are the restriction on the value of tariff-free goods that American tourists may bring back from abroad, and the recent imposition of the "interest-equalization" tax on interest and dividends received by American holders of foreign securities.

payments through successive years? The answer to both questions is "yes."

Indeed, in drawing up the balance of payments we have already noted that the current account can provide clues to the relationship between the values of a country's exports and imports, and the current level of its national income. We may now add that *changes* in a current-account surplus or deficit are equally significant when it comes to an analysis of changes in national income. After all, changes in exports and/or imports may initiate an increase or decrease in income; and, as we saw earlier, the amount of the initial change—as well as the value of the foreign-trade multiplier—will determine the amount of such increases or decreases.

In terms of the analysis developed in Chapter 2, we may say that changes in the current-account balance correspond to the familiar "autonomous changes in exports" ($\triangle X$). Thus, an autonomous rise in exports (a positive $\triangle X$) may be regarded as an increase in the size of a current-account surplus or a decrease in the size of a current-account deficit. Conversely, an autonomous decline in exports (a negative $\triangle X$) can mean either a decrease in the size of a surplus or an increase in the size of a deficit. In other words, *net changes* (increases or decreases) *in the size of the surplus or deficit on current account,* when multiplied by the foreign-trade multiplier, indicate the extent to which national income may rise or fall as a result of autonomous changes in foreign trade. Accordingly, a net increase in a surplus or a net decrease in a deficit would tend to increase national income, whereas a net decrease in a surplus or a net increase in a deficit would tend to decrease it. Of course, in order to obtain information about such changes, we must consult the balance of payments.

The usefulness of the balance of payments in an analysis of a country's economic conditions or problems does not end here. In addition to indicating the amount and direction of net changes in the balance on current account, the balance of payments reveals some of the immediate causes of these changes. There may be a number of such causes, each with its own implications. For example, one may ask whether an increase in a current-account surplus (or a decrease in a deficit) was caused by an increase in exports or a decrease in imports. Similarly, one may ask whether a decrease in exports or an increase in imports was responsible for a decrease in an existing surplus (or an increase in an existing deficit). Such questions must be answered before we can attempt a meaningful evaluation of a country's economic condition. And once again the balance of payments may provide the information leading to some of the answers.

To illustrate, consider a case close to home. From 1947 to 1966, the United States consistently enjoyed a surplus balance on its current account. Yet the size of this surplus (Table 3.5) has changed from year to year. Moreover, a comparison of 1947 and 1966 yields a seemingly curious phenomenon: In 1947, the current account registered a surplus of about $11.5 billion, whereas in 1966 the surplus amounted to only $5.1

TABLE *3.5* Summary of Current Account in United States Balance of Payments 1947–1966
(in millions of dollars)

Year	Exports of goods and services* (+)	Imports of goods and services (−)	Surplus on Current Account
1947	19,737	8,208	11,529
1948	16,789	10,349	6,440
1949	15,770	9,621	6,149
1950	13,807	12,028	1,799
1951	18,744	15,073	3,671
1952	17,992	15,766	2,226
1953	16,947	16,561	386
1954	17,759	15,931	1,828
1955	19,804	17,795	2,009
1956	23,595	19,628	3,967
1957	26,481	20,752	5,729
1958	23,067	20,861	2,206
1959	23,476	23,342	134
1960	26,974	23,206	3,769
1961	28,311	22,867	5,444
1962	29,790	24,964	4,826
1963	32,353	26,436	5,917
1964	37,017	28,457	8,560
1965	39,147	32,203	6,944
1966	43,039	37,937	5,102

* Excludes transfers under military grants.

Source: *Survey of Current Business*, U.S. Department of Commerce (Washington, D.C.: Government Printing Office, 1948–1967).

billion. Does this mean that American exports of goods and services declined from 1947 to 1966? Or, to put it differently, was the total value of United States exports of goods and services smaller in 1966 than in 1947? Definitely not. A quick glance at the export column in Table 3.5 confirms the fact that United States exports amounted to some $23 billion more in 1966 than in 1947. The same column also reveals that since 1958 the value of United States exports has increased every year. How then are we to explain the variations in the surplus on current account?

A closer look at Table 3.5 answers the question. From 1947 to 1966, despite declines in some years, the overall trend was upward for both exports and imports. But the rate at which imports and exports rose was not the same during this period. For example, from 1958 to 1959, exports increased by $409 million, while imports rose by $2,481 million. In other words, between 1958 and 1959 imports increased much faster than exports, thereby reducing the surplus from $2,206 million in 1958 to $134 million in 1959. On the other hand, between 1963 and 1964 exports rose by $4,664 million, while imports increased by only $2,021 million; as a result, the surplus increased from $5,917 million in 1963 to $8,560 in 1964. Between 1964 and 1966, however, imports again rose faster than exports, thus causing a decline in the surplus.

The above example clearly demonstrates that changes in a surplus (or a deficit) on current account are due to the direction and size of the changes in exports and imports. And although the balance of payments does not itself explain *why* exports rose or fell faster than imports (or vice versa) over a given period of time, it may suggest where the answer might ultimately be found. At the same time, it may enable us to make an intelligent guess as to the possible effects of a particular change in the current account upon the level of economic activities at home and abroad.

Yet while the data in the current account can be related to the current level of, and changes in, a country's national income, it sheds little light, strictly speaking, on its basic economic character: We cannot generally tell, by looking at the current account and knowing nothing else about the country, whether its economy is highly advanced or underdeveloped. Nor can we tell what kinds of goods—for example, raw materials or manufactured goods—the country exports and imports, since the current account does not give a detailed commodity breakdown.

Without such information we can only guess at the country's stage of economic maturity as compared with that of countries with which it trades. In short, we find no reflection in the current account of the country's growth-through-trade experience, or its level of economic maturity. We must turn for these to another major component of the balance of payments : the capital account.

In this connection it may be convenient to think of the capital account as a record of a country's international lending and borrowing activities. And although the mechanical details of such activities—that is the credit instruments involved in the various transactions—need not concern us here, we must raise the following two questions : (1) Is the country a *net borrower* (a net importer of capital) or a *net lender* (a net exporter of capital) ? and (2) Does its capital account consist mostly of long-term or short-term capital movements? Answers to these questions can easily be determined from data in the capital account, and lie at the heart of our inquiry. For it is largely by the type of capital that it lends or borrows that we can judge a country's stage of economic development.

Consider first the question of foreign lending and borrowing. The very fact that one country is able to export sizable amounts of capital, while another must import capital, is highly significant. Indeed, the ability to spare capital for foreign lending, without neglecting the investment needs of domestic industries, indicates a relative abundance of capital. Conversely, the need to borrow from abroad usually reflects a domestic scarcity of capital. And since capital accumulation is both a requisite for, and a consequence of, economic growth, we may assume that countries that can supply capital to others have already achieved a fairly high level of economic maturity, whereas those that depend on external sources for it are still in early or intermediate stages of economic development. Translated into balance-of-payments terms, this means that a country whose capital account shows a *persistent* debit balance can generally be regarded as an economically advanced nation. On the other hand, a *persistent* credit balance on capital account suggests that the country is probably a developing nation.

The word "persistent" has been emphasized because without it our interpretation of the capital account loses some of its validity. For it is quite possible that during a given year, or over a period of several years, a fairly well-developed economy may have net *inflows* of capital; and it is also possible that the balance of payments of an economically *under-developed* nation may reveal that in a given year the country *exported* more capital than it imported.[6] Hence, only by observing the behavior of the capital account over a considerable number of years can we draw any conclusions about the relation between a country's capital flows and its level of economic maturity. Bearing this in mind, we may tentatively conclude that a country whose balance of payments shows persistent net outflows of capital is more likely to be economically mature than a country with persistent net inflows of capital.

But we must observe not only the direction of capital flows, but also the types of capital that a country borrows or lends. Although we must postpone to a later chapter a more detailed examination of international capital movements, we may distinguish now between short-term and long-term capital flows. In general, movements of short-term capital reflect short-run changes in market conditions rather than basic structural conditions of the economies involved. Put differently, short-term capital flows are said to be activated by temporary market phenomena—for example, changes in interest-rate differentials between domestic and foreign money markets, or a need for short-term credit to offset a temporary deficit. Hence, the fact that a country is experiencing net inflows of short-term capital cannot be taken as proof that it is economically underdeveloped. By the same token, net outflows of short-term capital cannot be interpreted to mean that it has a highly mature economy.

In assessing the basic economic position of a country in relation to other countries, we must be guided by its experience with long-term capital movements. In particular, we must look to long-term capital flows that are autonomous in nature—motivated primarily by profit considerations rather than by a desire to offset deficits or surpluses in other categories of the balance of payments. Such profit-motivated capital flows usually take the form of direct investment, purchase (or sale) of long-term securities, and long-term loans. And although governments, as well as private citizens, may engage in profit-motivated, capital-account

---

[6] Also relevant is the fact that wealthy people in an underdeveloped country may, from time to time, choose to invest their wealth abroad rather than at home. Such capital outflows may in some years be equal to, or greater than, the capital inflows into the country.

transactions, we think of autonomous long-term capital flows as being typically private undertakings.

To sum up, the direction taken by private long-term capital flows gives us the answer to our basic question : Is the country whose balance of payments we examine a developed or a developing nation? Accordingly, we can now amend our previous conclusion as follows: A country with persistent net *outflows* of private long-term capital is more likely to be economically mature than a country whose balance of payments shows persistent net *inflows* of private long-term capital. In countries whose governments actively participate in international economic transactions, however, the direction of a *combination* of private and public long-term capital flows reflects the countries' basic economic positions.

The Balance of International Indebtedness

Unlike the balance of payments, which summarizes a country's foreign-trade transactions over a given *period* of time, the balance of international indebtedness states a country's total claims on other countries, and vice versa, at a given *moment* in time. In other words, the balance of international indebtedness indicates the international capital position of a country, as reflected by the total value of its outstanding investments abroad, and by the total value of outstanding investments made in it by foreigners.

In a country's balance of international indebtedness, investments made by its residents and institutions in foreign countries represent assets, or claims on foreigners, and investments made in the country by foreigners represent liabilities. When total claims and total liabilities are balanced against each other, the country emerges either as a *net creditor* or a *net debtor* vis-à-vis the rest of the world. Table 3.6, which presents the United States balance of international indebtedness for selected years, bears this out. Thus, during World War I, this country changed from a net-debtor to a net-creditor position, and maintained this position during the 1920's and 1930's. In 1940 and 1945, it had a small net indebtedness on its international capital account. But since 1946, the United States has maintained a net-creditor position, a position which it is unlikely to lose in the foreseeable future.

TABLE *3.6*   United States Balance of International Indebtedness
Selected Years, 1908–1965
(in billions of dollars)

Year	United States investment abroad	Foreign invest- ment in the United States	United States net position ([−] debtor)
1908	2.5	6.4	− 3.9
1914	3.5	7.2	− 3.7
1919	7.0	3.3	3.7
1924	10.9	3.0	7.0
1930	17.0	8.4	8.8
1935	13.5	6.4	7.1
1940	12.3	13.5	− 1.2
1945	16.8	17.6	− .8
1946	18.7	15.9	2.8
1950	32.8	19.5	13.3
1955	44.9	29.6	15.3
1961	75.0	46.9	28.1
1963	88.1	51.5	36.6
1964	98.7	56.5	42.2
1965	106.1	58.9	47.2

Source: *Historical Statistics of the United States,* U.S. Department of Commerce (Washington, D.C.: Government Printing Office, 1960); and *Survey of Current Business,* U.S. Department of Commerce (Washington, D.C.: Government Printing Office, August, 1962, and September, 1966).

The terms "net debtor" and "net creditor" are not particularly meaningful, however, without additional information about the types of claims and liabilities that each involves. And although Table 3.6 indicates only the total foreign assets and liabilities of the United States, a balance of international indebtedness is usually divided along the same lines as is the capital account in the balance of payments. Thus, one finds in the balance of international indebtedness both the short-term and long-term claims and liabilities of the country, and these are further classified as "private" and "governmental" sectors.

This kind of information can be misleading, however. For example, one ought not hastily conclude that a country that is a net creditor on its international capital account is necessarily better off than one that is a net debtor. Nor should one assume that net-credit and net-debit positions on the balance of international indebtedness correspond respectively to net-credit or net-debit balances on the capital account of the balance of payments. And most important, one should not associate a balance-of-payments surplus or deficit in a given year with a net-credit or a net-debit position in the balance of international indebtedness. Indeed, only three generalizations can safely be made about the relation between the balance of payments and the balance of international indebtedness. First, a country's balance of international indebtedness is a reflection of past transactions in the capital account of the balance of payments. Second, the assets and liabilities in the balance of international indebtedness give rise to current receipts and/or payments of interest and dividends; and these, as we have seen, are recorded in the current account of the balance of payments. Finally, the information contained in the balance of international indebtedness may give some indication of the ability or inability of the country to liquidate its foreign assets quickly, in the event that balance-of-payments difficulties make this necessary.

Nevertheless, the balance of international indebtedness has its virtues. As a statistical record, it contains information that cannot be found in the balance of payments; and although such information by itself is rather limited in scope, it can be of great value when used in conjunction with balance-of-payments data. Indeed, the balance of payments and the balance of international indebtedness complement one another; between them they cover, in a statistical sense, all of the important aspects of a country's foreign-trade relations and thereby describe the country's international economic position. In turn, they can be used to analyze the interrelationships between the country's foreign trade, and its past and present experience with economic growth and stability.

PART II

PATTERNS OF
FREE TRADE

4

<hr>

Foundations of International Trade Theory: The Classical Approach

<hr>

DESPITE OCCASIONAL ALLEGA-
tions to the contrary, the classical economists left us a rich and useful
legacy. Their preoccupation with the economic problems of their day
produced many analytical tools and concepts that serve as the foundation of modern economic analysis. This is especially true of trade theory.
Here, more than in any other field of economics, the classical writers
provided the mold that shaped most subsequent explanations and anal-
yses of foreign trade.

Basic Questions and Assumptions

Three broad questions define the framework within which the classical economists explored the implications of foreign trade.

1. What is the basis for trade, and what goods does a country
   export and import?
2. On what terms are the traded goods exchanged?
3. Should disturbances occur in the trade pattern, what forces
   will bring about an adjustment, and how will they do so?

The answers to these questions evolved over a period of years and incorporate the intellectual efforts of such men as David Hume, Adam Smith, David Ricardo, John Stuart Mill—and others of lesser fame. The cohesive body of thought thus formed has come to be known as the classical theory of trade. Nowadays, however, it is customary to treat the various aspects of international trade separately and to draw a distinction between the pure theory and the monetary (or balance-of-payments) theory. The latter, to be discussed in Part III, deals with typical problems of adjustment referred to in the third question above. The pure theory, on the other hand, deals with the more fundamental questions that concern the basis for, and the gains from, trade. Here the classical economists made their most lasting contributions.

Theory, however, was not the major objective of the classical economists. Their analysis was designed primarily to influence policy matters: to discredit protectionism and to promote the free-trade idea. More specifically, they sought to demonstrate that, in the absence of restrictions or obstacles, certain beneficial trade patterns would tend to become established. Yet in order to simplify the analysis and to focus attention on this major contention, they made use of an impressive array of assumptions.

Only a few of these assumptions were stated explicitly; most were implied either in the analysis itself or in the conclusions drawn from it. By far the most important assumptions were: that productive factors can move freely within a country; that they are completely immobile between countries; and that the money supply of a country consists of gold and/or gold substitutes. These, as we will see, were absolutely indispensable to the central argument.[1] Surrounding them, and varying in importance, were other assumptions: that the cost of production is measured by the cost of labor; that price relationships within a country are based on the cost of labor embodied in a unit of each commodity; that resources in all countries are fully employed; that production takes place under conditions of constant cost; that trade is carried on between two countries, each of which produces only two commodities; that technology does not change; that there are no transportation costs; that pure competition prevails; and that the value of goods exported by a nation equals the value of the goods it imports.

[1] The third assumption belongs to the monetary theory of trade and will be referred to in Part III.

Thus fortified, the classical economists were prepared to do battle with protectionism.

Absolute Cost Advantage

One of the first salvos in that battle was fired by Adam Smith whose argument rested on the familiar virtues of specialization. "It is the maxim of every prudent master of a family," wrote the venerable Scotsman almost two hundred years ago, "never to attempt to make at home what it will cost him more to make than to buy."[2] By the same token, "If a foreign country can supply us with a commodity cheaper than we ourselves can make it, better buy it of them with some part of the produce of our industry, employed in a way in which we have some advantage."[3]

The advantage to which Smith refers is termed *absolute cost advantage,* and may be illustrated—along with its reverse, absolute cost disadvantage—as done in Table 4. 1.

TABLE *4.1*   Cost of Producing a Given Output

Country	Cost (*man-hours*)	
	Textile (1,000 yds.)	*Steel (1 ton)*
United States	20	5
England	10	15

Compare the costs of steel and textile production in the United States and England. In terms of labor units, England can produce 1,000 yards of textile cheaper than they can be produced in the United States. On the other hand, the United States can produce one ton of steel cheaper than can England. Thus, England is said to have an absolute cost advantage over the United States with respect to textile, while the United States possesses an absolute cost advantage over England with respect to steel. England should, therefore, specialize in the production of textile, and exchange some textile for steel imported from the United States; the

[2] Adam Smith, *The Wealth of Nations* (New York: Modern Library, 1937), p. 424.

[3] *Ibid.*

latter should concentrate on the production of steel, and exchange some of it for textile imported from England.

The early case for free trade rested essentially on this kind of reasoning. It was argued that trade enables countries to import, in exchange for their own products, those commodities which can be produced at home only at a greater absolute cost than that prevailing abroad. As a consequence, all products would tend to be produced in those countries where the costs of producing them would be lowest.

All well and good. But suppose a country does not have an absolute advantage in *any* line of production, while another is so well endowed that it has an absolute advantage with respect to *every* commodity it produces. Take England and the United States, for example. Let us assume that the United States can produce both steel and textile more cheaply than England can. Under these circumstances, is there scope for specialization and trade between the two countries? If so, what should England sell to the United States and the United States to England?

David Ricardo answered these questions by showing that trade can be carried on profitably between two countries even if one can produce both commodities more efficiently than the other.[4] His analysis also indicated what commodities should be exchanged.

The Principle of Comparative Costs

According to Ricardo, *relative* rather than absolute cost differences determine trade patterns. A country need not necessarily specialize in commodities it can produce at lower cost than other countries, and import those that cost less abroad. What matters is the extent to which costs in one country are higher (or lower) than in another. Thus, even if it possesses an absolute cost advantage in all the goods it produces, a country can still benefit from trade—provided that its advantage is greater in some products than in others. And a nation with

[4] Ricardo's contribution is contained in Chapter VII of his *Principles of Political Economy*, first published in 1817. It has been claimed that Ricardo's theorem had already been formulated by Robert Torrens two years earlier. The latter, however, was unaware of the implications of his idea. See G. Haberler, *A Survey of International Trade Theory*, Special Papers in International Economics, no. 1 (Princeton University, International Finance Section, July, 1961) p. 7.

absolute cost disadvantage in all of its lines of production can nevertheless take its place in international trade, if its disadvantage is less in some products than in others. For under trade, each country would tend to specialize in, and export, those goods that it can produce *comparatively cheaper*, and import those which are comparatively expensive to produce at home.

To illustrate this principle of comparative costs, consider Ricardo's own famous example involving England and Portugal, each producing wine and cloth.

TABLE 4.2 Cost of Producing a Given Output

Country	Cost (*man-hours*)	
	Wine (100 gals.)	*Cloth (100 yds.)*
Portugal	80	90
England	120	100

Costs of producing both wine and cloth are lower in Portugal than in England. But a comparison of the figures reveals that Portugal's cost advantage over England is greater in wine than in cloth production. And although England suffers from absolute cost disadvantage in both goods, its disadvantage is less in cloth production. Portugal should therefore specialize in wine and exchange some of it for English cloth; and England should specialize in cloth and exchange it for Portuguese wine. Each country would then be able to import the commodity it wants at a lower real cost than it could be produced at home.

The skeptic can verify the above claim by assuming, as did Ricardo, that 100 gallons of wine are exchanged for exactly 100 yards of cloth. Portugal could then obtain, for the cost of 80 man-hours, what would cost 90 man-hours to produce domestically; and for 100 man-hours England could obtain what, in the absence of trade, would cost her 120 man-hours to produce. To put it another way, Portugal could obtain more cloth per unit of wine exported than she could by diverting domestic production from wine to cloth; and England could obtain more wine per unit of cloth exported than by diverting production from cloth to wine at home.

At this point, let us pose an obvious question: If wine and cloth can be produced more cheaply in Portugal than in England, would it not make sense for labor and capital to move from England to Portugal and for both commodities to be produced in their entirety there? It might! Here, however, the assumptions concerning factor mobility and immobility come into play. Regional cost differences within a country can effect movement of productive factors; industries try to locate in areas of low production costs. Labor and capital, however, are not free to move from one country to another in order to exploit favorable production possibilities. The benefits of higher productivity (and hence low cost) in one country can be transmitted to another only through trade. Thus, movements of goods provide a substitute for movements of factors between countries. And each can employ its own resources where they are relatively most efficient or relatively least inefficient.

Ricardo's emphasis on *comparative* costs reflects a more refined, though perhaps less obvious, concept of specialization. And his contribution is regarded as the cornerstone of the pure theory of international trade. Yet while he showed what goods would be exported and imported, he failed to answer—and, for that matter, to ask—another important question: On what terms will the goods be traded? His failure to do so left the theory incomplete. For, as we will soon see, the *terms of trade* reflect the relation between the prices a country receives for its exports and the prices it must pay for its imports; or, more simply, this is the ratio of international prices. As such, the terms of trade provide at least some measure of the gains from trade, and indicate how these gains might be distributed among the trading partners. Whatever his reason, Ricardo did not consider this question. John Stuart Mill, writing some years later,[5] answered it while developing what has come to be known as the theory of international values.

The Terms of Trade

Although Mill is generally credited with explaining how the terms of trade are determined, part of the explanation can be inferred from

[5] Mill set forth his ideas in essays written in 1829 and 1830. These essays were published in 1844, in a book entitled *Essays on Some Unsettled Questions of Political Economy.* See J. B. Condliffe, *The Commerce of Nations* (New York: W. W. Norton, 1950), p. 199.

Ricardo's theorem. The connection between the principle of comparative costs and the terms of trade can be illustrated more clearly, however, with the aid of a version that differs slightly from the one used by Ricardo. Such a version was, in fact, employed by Mill who expressed the principle, not in terms of cost differences in the production of a given output, but in terms of different outputs produced at a given cost (or labor input):

T A B L E *4.3*   Outputs of a Given Labor Input

| Country | *Output of* | |
	Steel	Textile
United States	10	5
England	2	3

In the United States, a given amount of labor (e.g., X man-hours) can produce either 10 units of steel or 5 units of textile. In England the same amount of labor can produce only 2 units of steel or 3 units of textile. Clearly, the United States possesses an absolute advantage over England in the production of both steel and textile; yet its comparative advantage is in steel. England's comparative disadvantage lies in textile. Accordingly, the United States will export steel to England and the latter will export textile to the former. But at what rate would textile and steel be exchanged?

In the absence of trade, each country can increase the production of one commodity only by switching some labor from the production of the other commodity.[6] Hence the cost of textile is, in effect, the amount of steel which can be produced by the labor necessary to produce an additional unit of textile; the same applies to the cost of steel. In the United States the same amount of labor can produce twice as many units of steel as units of textile—or, twice as much labor is needed to produce a unit of textile as a unit of steel. By giving up 1 unit of steel, the United States can gain only ½ unit of textile. Therefore, unless it can get *more* than ½ unit of textile in exchange for 1 unit of steel, the United States will not find it advantageous to trade. In England, an increase of 1 unit in steel production involves a loss of 1½ units of textile. Consequently,

[6] On the assumption that in each country labor is fully employed.

England will enter trade only if she can obtain the additional unit of steel by exporting *less* than $1\frac{1}{2}$ units of textile.

The domestic cost ratios[7] in the countries involved will set the *limits* on the range of possible terms of trade. Only those terms which fall within this range could be acceptable to both countries. In our example the range is

	Steel	*Textile*
	1	more than $\frac{1}{2}$
or		less than $1\frac{1}{2}$
	Textile	*Steel*
	1	more than $\frac{2}{3}$
		less than 2

An exchange of 1 unit of steel for 1 unit of textile would be acceptable—and beneficial—to each country. But so would any other ratio that falls within the range. A moment's reflection will reveal, however, that the benefits from trade to a given country may be larger or smaller, depending on the actual terms of trade. For example, an exchange of 1 steel for $\frac{5}{8}$ textile would favor England, whereas 1 steel for $1\frac{1}{4}$ textile would favor the United States. What, then, determines exactly the terms of trade?

Given the limits set by the domestic cost ratios, the terms of trade will depend, according to Mill, on *reciprocal demand*—that is, each country's demand for the other's product, expressed in units of its own exports. Thus, England's reciprocal demand indicates the amounts of steel it wants, and the amounts of textile it will offer in exchange, at various price ratios (of steel and textile). The reciprocal demand of the United States is its demand for textile in terms of the amounts of steel it offers in exchange. The stronger the demand for an imported product, the more exports are offered for it, and hence the more favorable the exchange ratio to the exporting country. Thus, if England's demand for steel is sufficiently strong, given the United States' demand for textile, the terms of trade would probably settle nearer to the British domestic cost ratio. Conversely, the stronger the demand of the United States for textile, given England's demand for steel, the closer will the terms of trade approach its own domestic cost ratio.

---

[7] These cost ratios are also the domestic price ratios—i.e., the ratio at which steel and textile exchange for each other in the market.

But for trade to balance, the value of each country's exports must equal the value of its imports. Mill argued that this condition (equilibrium) would be fulfilled only if one price (or exchange) ratio prevails: the ratio which simultaneously equates the quantities demanded (and supplied) by one country to the quantities supplied (and demanded) by the other. His explanation of how the terms of trade are determined is the equation of reciprocal demand.[8]

This rule—often called the *law of reciprocal demand*—says that the terms of trade in our example will be established by the price ratio at which the quantities of steel demanded (and textile offered) by England match the quantities of steel offered (and textile demanded) by the United States. To illustrate, suppose that at a given price ratio England offers 50 units of textile in exchange for 40 units of steel. If, at the same price ratio, the United States happens to demand 50 units of textile and offers 40 units of steel in return, the equilibrium condition is met. What are the terms of trade in this case? They are 5 textile: 4 steel—in other words the international price ratio is 1 steel: 1¼ textile, or 1 textile: ⅘ steel. It is easy to see that the terms of trade are actually the reciprocal of the international price ratio. Thus

	International price ratio	*Terms of trade*
	1 steel: 1¼ textile	5 textile for 4 steel
or		
	1 textile: ⅘ steel	4 steel for 5 textile

A change in either the price of steel or the price of textile will alter the international price ratio, and with it the terms of trade. The various causes and effects of such changes will be discussed in Chapters 6 and 7. For the moment we might note that the *law of reciprocal demand* is, as Mill himself stated, "but an extension of the more general law of value, which we called the equation of supply and demand."[9] Essentially, then, this "law" is an expression of a familiar economic principle, that equilibrium is established when the quantity supplied is equal to the quantity demanded. Yet Mill's use of this principle marked a great

---

[8] Mill did not himself use the term "reciprocal demand." He spoke of the "equation of international demand" or the "law of international values." See J. Viner, *Studies in the Theory of International Trade* (London: George Allen & Unwin, 1955), p. 536.

[9] John Stuart Mill, *Principles of Political Economy* (London: Longmans, Green & Co., 1909), p. 592.

advance in the development of international trade theory. For by considering demand as well as supply, Mill provided a more complete explanation of trade than any previous economist. And although his was not the last word on the subject, there can be no question that he contributed greatly to the classical doctrine.

Mill, in effect, served as a bridge between the classical and modern analysis of international trade. His chief contribution—the "law of reciprocal demand"—stemmed from and supplemented Ricardo's principle of comparative costs. These two theorems contain most of the classical explanation of trade; they tell which goods will be exported and imported by each country, and on what terms these goods will be traded. Neither principle by itself could provide the answers to both questions. But together they enabled the classical economists to throw light on the possible contributions of trade to a country's well-being and growth.

Indeed, the classical economists could take credit for being the first to show how trade can enable each country to utilize its resources efficiently and thus increase its real income. And although some of their assumptions are today regarded as weak and unrealistic, their analysis established a firm basis for subsequent theoretical developments. Not surprisingly, these later efforts were largely spent in attempts, more or less successful, to overcome some of the earlier analytical weaknesses. And in the process, a modern theory of trade has been developed.

5

Modern Trade Theory: Supply

EVEN SOME OF THE CLASSICAL economists recognized that some of their assumptions served to load the dice in favor of free trade. For example, Mill, as well as Ricardo before him, admitted that the assumption about the international immobility of labor and capital was unrealistic. But since this assumption was indispensable to the classicals' case, Mill hit upon a compromise. For purposes of analysis, he defined international trade as the exchange of goods by areas among which productive resources *cannot* be moved easily.[1] This definition still underlies the modern theory of trade.

A much more serious defect in the classical analysis is found in two other assumptions: (1) that labor is the sole factor of production, and (2) that the value of goods is derived from their labor content. These assumptions were an integral part of the labor theory of value which, as we have seen, played an important role in classical economics. It was used to show that by transferring labor from one line of production to another, goods could be substituted for each other in proportion to their cost. The amount of labor required to produce different goods determined the rate of exchange—or simply the price ratio—between them. And it

[1] J. B. Condliffe, *The Commerce of Nations* (New York: W. W. Norton, 1950), pp. 174–175.

was, after all, these price ratios that indicated whether or not comparative advantages existed.

That these assumptions drew heavy criticism and were rejected as invalid is easy to understand. First, labor is not homogeneous and hence not perfectly transferable from one occupation to another. Second, labor is only one of several resources used in the production of goods. Consequently, the values (or prices) of different goods cannot be compared merely in terms of their labor content. And since classical analysis was based on precisely such comparisons, is it any wonder that its critics questioned its conclusions?

While reliance on the labor theory of value proved a major weakness of classical analysis, however, it destroyed neither its logic nor its conclusions. In fact, later developments in the theory of international trade have made it possible to express the classicals' reasoning in more realistic terms and thus strengthen their major contention.

We turn now to one of the most significant contributions of the modern theory.

Opportunity Cost and Production Possibilities

The assumptions of the labor theory of value can easily be replaced with a more valid one: that, assuming the availability of all its resources, a country can shift some of them from one line of production to another. If this assumption is accepted, then the price ratio (or rate of exchange) between commodities can be obtained from their *opportunity costs*. The opportunity cost, say, of steel is the amount of textile that must be given up to get an additional amount of steel—regardless of whether it was labor, capital, or some other factor that was shifted from textile to steel production. The same goes for textile: Its opportunity cost is the amount of steel that must be sacrificed for an additional quantity of textile.

Application of the opportunity-cost concept to international trade theory, by Professor G. Haberler,[2] provided a more realistic way of explaining comparative-cost differences and the benefits from trade. To observe the concept at work, consider the following example in Table 5.1.

[2] G. Haberler, *The Theory of International Trade: With Its Application to Commercial Policy* (London: Hodge, 1950).

TABLE 5.1 Production Possibilities in the United States and England

	Full Employment Output	
Country	Steel (no textile)	Textile (no steel)
United States	50	100
England	20	80

Assume that when all its resources are fully employed, the United States can produce either 50 units of steel and no textile, or 100 units of textile and no steel, or some combination of the two (e.g., 10 steel and 80 textile; 20 steel and 60 textile; and so on). England, also utilizing all its resources, can produce either 20 units of steel, or 80 units of textile, or some combination of the two. The various production possibilities in England and the United States can be described graphically by means of *production-possibilities* or *transformation* curves.

CONSTANT COSTS

Each point on a production-possibilities curve represents a certain combination of steel and textile that can be produced when the country's resources are fully employed. More important, the slope of the curve indicates the opportunity-cost ratio between these goods: the amount of one that must be given up to produce an additional unit of the other. And because the production-possibilities curves in Figure 5.1 are straight lines, they reflect a *constant-cost* condition of production—that is, the rate at which steel and textile can be transformed into one another remains the same at all levels of output. In this case the slopes of the curves indicate not only the cost ratios, but also the domestic price ratios in our two countries. Thus, in the United States, steel and textile always exchange for each other at a rate of 1 steel for 2 textile (or 1 textile for ½ steel), while in England the rate is 1 steel for 4 textile (or 1 textile for ¼ steel).

Lest it be overlooked, our curves also reveal that while the United States is superior to England in the production of both steel and textile, its comparative advantage lies in steel. One can easily verify this by

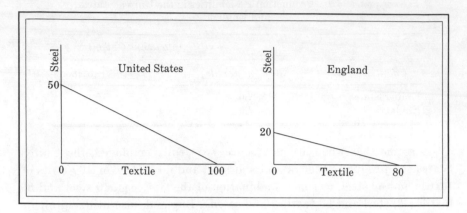

FIGURE *5.1* Production-Possibilities Curves (Constant Cost)

comparing the maximum outputs of steel and textile in the two countries: The United States can produce more than twice as much steel as
England (50 as compared with 20), but its production of textile sur-
passes that of England by only 25 per cent (100 as compared with 80).
England's comparative disadvantage is therefore in textile. Under these
circumstances, and given the differences in their domestic price ratios,
trade can be established to the mutual benefit of both countries.

For a case in point, consider Figure 5.2, as viewed through British
eyes. Given her supply of resources and moving along her own production-possibilities curve, England can transform textile into steel at a rate
of 4 to 1. Thus, if she happens to produce and consume at point *A* (i.e.,
20 units of textile and 15 units of steel), she must give up 4 units of
textile in order to obtain an additional unit of steel. England would be
better off, however, if (with the same supply of resources) she could exchange textile for steel at the rate prevailing in the United States (2:1),
as reflected by that country's production-possibilities curve. For in this
case, steel could be obtained at half the price it commands at home; or, to
put it differently, each unit of textile would exchange for twice as many
units of steel as it does now. Failing to reach such a favorable position,
however, England might still improve her lot if, by trading with the
United States, she could exchange textile for steel at less than a 4 to 1
ratio.

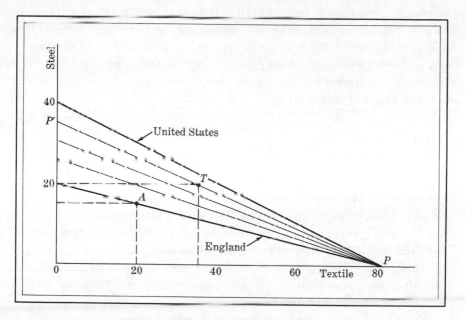

FIGURE *5.2*   Possible Gains from Trade (England)

Thus, from England's viewpoint, any one of the lines drawn from point *P* to the steel axis, and falling between the two production-possibilities curves, represents a rate of exchange that is more favorable than her own domestic price ratio. What the actual international price ratio (the terms of trade) would be is impossible to say; this depends on demand as well as on cost conditions. But as long as England can import steel in exchange for textile at a lower price than the domestic one, she benefits from specializing in textile and exporting some of it in exchange for steel. For example, if the international price ratio were to settle at *P–P'*, England may find herself at point *T,* consuming more steel (20 units) *and* textile (35 units) than at point *A*. She would be able to do so by devoting all her resources to textile, producing 80 units, 45 of which are exported in exchange for 20 units of imported steel.

As for the United States, it can obtain textile from England on better terms than at home. For by trading steel for textile at the international price ratio, the United States can obtain more than 2 units of textile for each unit of exported steel (or, 2 units of textile can be obtained for less than 1 unit of steel). Hence, it would pay the United States to devote its resources to steel production, and exchange some of it for imported textile.[3] We might add that under the condition of constant costs both countries would tend toward complete specialization—that is, after trade has opened up, the United States would tend to produce only steel, and England only textile.

INCREASING COSTS

The condition of constant costs is the exception rather than the rule in real life. As more and more resources are shifted from textile to steel production (or vice versa), some are likely to be less productive in their new occupation than in their old one. After a while, larger and larger amounts of one commodity must be sacrificed in order to obtain additional amounts of the other. To put it differently, after a point each additional unit of steel (or textile) will cost more in terms of textile (or steel) than the previous unit. Here lies the essence of *increasing costs* which can be described graphically as follows.

Figure 5.3 shows that an increasing-cost production-possibilities curve is concave with respect to the points of origin. As in previous figures, each point on the curve represents a certain combination of steel and textile obtainable at full employment of resources. But the rate at which these goods exchange for each other keeps changing. This becomes clearer if we trace changes in physical quantities along the steel and textile axes. Thus, starting from point *T* and moving to the left, we observe that successive reductions (of equal size) in textile output yield smaller and smaller additions to steel output. Sliding down from point *S*, we note that larger and larger amounts of steel must be given up in exchange for equal increases in textile output. An increasing-cost production-possibilities curve adds some analytical complications. For although the slope of the curve indicates the cost ratio between steel and textile, it does not—in contrast to the *constant-cost* curve—indicate their domestic price ratio. Still, it is an effective tool; it reveals that trade can exist where there are comparative-cost differences.

[3] This can be shown graphically by redrawing the curves in Figure 5.2 so as to equate them at a point on the steel axis. Try your hand at it and see what happens.

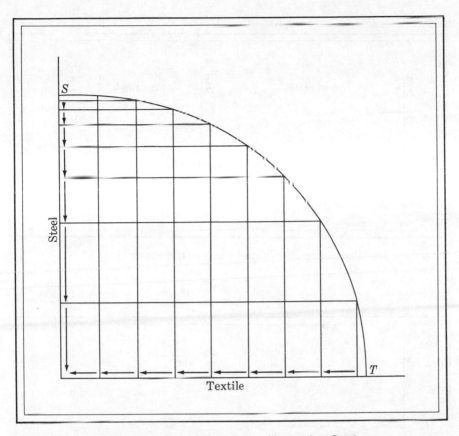

FIGURE 5.3   Production-Possibilities Curve (Increasing Cost)

In Figure 5.4 it is unmistakably clear where each country stands: The United States has a comparative advantage in steel, while England has a comparative disadvantage in textile. As we will soon see, the difference between this case and that of constant costs lies in the absence of complete specialization: Neither country will devote all its resources to the production of only one commodity even after trade is under way. Yet both countries can benefit from trade, as long as the international price ratio is more favorable than their domestic price ratios.

Figure 5.5 shows England's position before and after trade. Let line *XY* represent the domestic price ratio of steel and textile. Then, in the

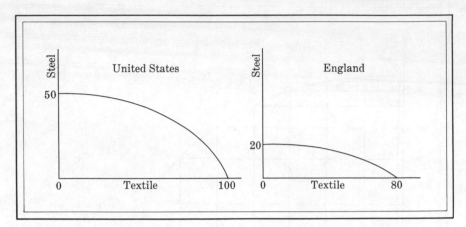

FIGURE *5.4* Production-Possibilities Curves (Increasing Cost)

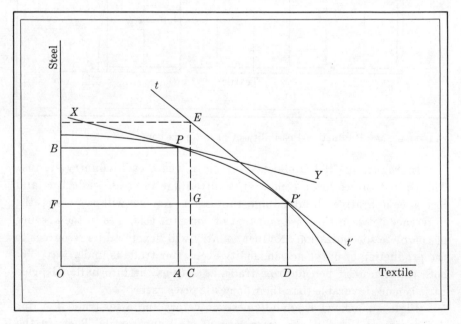

FIGURE *5.5* Possible Gains from Trade (England)

absence of trade, the combination of steel and textile produced and consumed in England will correspond to point P. For at that point the relative marginal costs of production are equal to the relative prices of the commodities in question—in other words, this is an equilibrium position. Accordingly, England will produce and consume OA of textile and OB of steel. Now suppose that by trading with the United States, England is faced with a price ratio represented by the line t–t'; this line is tangent to the transformation curve at point P'. (This means that at point P', the international price ratio is equal to the domestic cost ratio of steel and textile) England will now devote more resources to textile (producing OD of textile), and less resources to steel (producing only OF of steel). But by exchanging some textile for steel from the United States, England would actually have more of both commodities: It will export CD of textile and import GE of steel, thus ending up with OC of textile (which is greater than OA), and CE of steel (which is greater than OB). These results are summarized in Table 5.2.

TABLE 5.2 Effects of Trade on Production and Consumption
(in England)

	Before Trade		Under Trade	
Commodity	Production	Consumption	Production	Consumption
Textile	OA	OA	OD ($> OA$)	OC ($> OA$)
Steel	OB	OB	OF ($< OB$)	CE ($> OB$)

Similar results can be shown for the United States. By concentrating more heavily on steel production and exchanging some of it for textile from England, the United States would end up with more of both commodities. In short, trade enables the two countries to employ their limited resources more efficiently. As a result, both can enjoy an increase in the amount of goods available for consumption.

No explanation of trade would be complete, however, if it did not settle another important question: What causes the differences in comparative costs among nations?

Underlying Causes of Trade: Factor Endowments and Factor Proportions

Aided by the labor theory of value, the classical economists attributed comparative differences in costs—leading to absolute differences in prices—to differences in labor productivity. To them, one country's ability to produce a certain good more cheaply than another country indicated a more highly productive labor force. Yet this identification of low cost with high labor productivity does not in itself explain *why* labor is more productive in one country than in another. Nor can it account for the differences in cost and price even between countries whose labor forces are considered equally well-trained and skilled.[4] In any event, rejection of the labor theory of value as unrealistic renders meaningless any explanation of trade couched solely in terms of labor costs and/or labor productivity.

A more convincing explanation of the causes underlying trade has been formulated, in recent times, by the Swedish economist, Bertil Ohlin.[5] His explanation rests on two well-established propositions: that countries are differently endowed with productive resources (e.g., land, labor, capital, and so on), and that resources are used in different combinations in the production of different goods.

Since neither natural nor man-made resources are distributed evenly throughout the world, each country finds itself with an abundant supply of some resources but with a small supply of others. While this bit of common knowledge hardly requires elaboration, we might note that the relative supplies of various productive factors generally determine the relative prices of these factors. Where land is plentiful in relation to the size of the labor force, rents tend to be low and wages high. Similarly, where the amount of capital is small relative to labor—as it is in most underdeveloped countries—interest rates tend to be high and wages low.

Observe that relative rather than absolute differences in factor

---

[4] Today one cannot really explain differences in productivity, costs, and prices between, say, the United States and most Western European countries by saying that labor in the United States is so much more superior to labor in Europe. The evidence simply does not support such a contention.

[5] B. Ohlin, *Interregional and International Trade* (Cambridge: Harvard University Press, 1933).

endowments explain why labor and/or land are cheaper than capital in some countries while in others the reverse is true. No one doubts, for example, that the United States is blessed with more labor and capital than, say, England. Yet in relation to the huge capital stock at its disposal, labor in the United States is the scarce factor, and hence its price is relatively high. In England, where the per capita supply of capital is smaller than in the United States, labor emerges as the relatively abundant factor, and its price accordingly is low. Similarly, because capital is relatively abundant in the United States but relatively scarce in England, its price is low in the former and high in the latter.

Bearing all this in mind, consider now the second proposition of Ohlin's thesis. Technologically speaking, it requires more labor than capital or land to produce some commodities, and more land or capital than labor to produce others. And although it is possible sometimes to vary the proportions of different factors in the production of a particular good, limits exist beyond which one factor cannot be substituted for another in any given line of production. Thus, commodities can be generally classified according to the factor proportions, or *intensities*, involved in their production.[6] Steel, for example, is a capital-intensive good; so are automobiles, farm machinery, airplanes, and others. Wheat and cotton, on the other hand, are land-intensive commodities, while textile, woven baskets, polished glassware, and others may be regarded as labor-intensive.

One may rightly conclude that where labor is relatively abundant, labor-intensive goods can be produced more cheaply in relation to capital-intensive goods. On the other hand, where land and/or capital are relatively abundant, capital-intensive and/or land-intensive goods are relatively less expensive to produce. Here we find the answer to the riddle: It is international differences in relative scarcity or abundance of factors, coupled with different technological requirements, that give rise to differences in comparative costs and provide the basis for trade. Thus, a country will have a comparative cost advantage in those goods (and hence will export them) that require large proportions of its relatively abundant—and therefore inexpensive—factor. Conversely, a country will

---

[6] Such classification assumes, of course, a given state of technology. Factor intensities may—and do—change as a result of technological innovations. Thus, labor-intensive commodities may become capital-intensive, and so on.

import those goods that require large proportions of its relatively scarce —and therefore expensive—factor.

To be sure, the broad classification of factors into land, labor, and capital is as much—if not more—of a simplification as the classical notion of a homogeneous labor force. Land is not the same everywhere; nor is one country's capital stock of the same quality or type as that of another. Cost (and price) differences between countries are, therefore, often the result of *absolute* differences in factor endowments—that is, possession by some countries of one or several resources that other countries lack.[7] Still, Ohlin's thesis provides a logical explanation of trade patterns that are based on comparative cost differences.

Putting the explanation to an empirical test, however, may at times prove embarrassing. Thus, because the United States is clearly a capital-rich country, compared with the rest of the world, one would expect it to export capital-intensive, and to import labor-intensive, goods. Yet a recent statistical study puzzled not only its readers but also its author, Professor Wassily W. Leontief, by yielding exactly the opposite result: that America's exports are labor-intensive while its imports are capital-intensive.[8] Despite the flurry of debates that these findings stirred up, the so-called "Leontief Paradox" remains unsolved.[9] As such, it serves as a reminder that no theoretical principle, however sound, should be made the basis for sweeping generalizations concerning the patterns or composition of international trade.

Some Effects of Trade: Equalization of Factor Prices

Although trade is initiated basically by commodity price differences, one of its major effects is to equalize the prices of traded goods. In fact, were it not for transportation costs and/or market "imperfections," each

[7] Climatic conditions, soil characteristics, and mineral deposits are all cases in point. A country either has them or does not.

[8] See Wassily W. Leontief, "Domestic Production and Foreign Trade: The American Capital Position Re-examined," *Proceedings of the American Philosophical Society*, Vol. XCVII (September, 1953).

[9] For one of the more recent attempts to explain the "Leontief Paradox," see William Travis, *The Theory of Trade and Protection* (Cambridge: Harvard University Press, 1964).

internationally traded good would sell everywhere for the same price.[10] In addition, international trade tends to equalize the prices of productive factors, especially those that are used to produce the traded goods. Complete equalization of factor prices is no more likely—in fact, much less likely—than complete equalization of commodity prices.[11] Yet the mere tendency toward it gives rise to important policy questions in each nation. These will be discussed in a later chapter; at the moment we will illustrate the process itself.

Consider again our two countries, England and the United States, and assume that the former is relatively rich in labor, and the latter relatively rich in capital. Since the opening of trade will alter the production patterns in each country, it is bound to have an effect on the demand for the productive factors involved. More specifically, trade will cause an increase in the demand for the relatively abundant factor (capital in the United States, labor in England), thereby making it less abundant and more expensive. At the same time, demand for the relatively scarce factor (labor in the United States, capital in England) will decrease, reducing its scarcity and therefore its price. (See Table 5.3.)

TABLE *5.3*   Effects of Trade on Relative Factor Supplies

	United States		England	
Factor	*Before Trade*	*Under Trade*	*Before Trade*	*Under Trade*
Labor	Scarce	Less scarce	Abundant	Less abundant
Capital	Abundant	Less abundant	Scarce	Less scarce

Specialization and increased exports increase the use of the relatively abundant factor. Conversely, imports reduce the pressure on the supply of the relatively scarce factor. Thus, although absolute supplies of both factors may remain the same, changes in demand for them cause

[10] Market ''imperfections'' will be dealt with in Part IV. Transportation costs are the subject of the next section of this chapter.

[11] Only under very restrictive (hence unrealistic) assumptions will complete equalization of factor prices occur. For the theoretical formulation of this proposition, see Paul A. Samuelson, ''International Trade and the Equalization of Factor Prices,'' *Economic Journal* (June, 1948); and ''International Factor-Price Equalization Once Again,'' *Economic Journal* (June, 1949).

changes in their relative prices. And the changes in demand for factors are, after all, the result of changes in production patterns, brought about by trade.

Exceptions to this process occur where differences in comparative costs stem, not from different factor endowments as such, but from the economies of scale that are associated with mass production. Certain manufacturing processes are subject to the principle of increasing returns (or decreasing costs) : Up to a point, as output expands, productive efficiency rises and unit-costs fall. Yet savings in cost due to large-scale operation can be realized only if the market can absorb a large output of the product(s) in question; for where the market is small, large-scale production cannot be justified on economic grounds. It therefore comes as no surprise that, compared to countries whose domestic markets are small, large countries can better enjoy the cost advantage—and tend to specialize—in the production of goods that are best produced on a large scale. The fact that a domestic market is small, however, does not necessarily preclude specialization based on increasing returns. For the mere opening or expansion of international trade widens the market, and thus permits the introduction of mass production methods. Indeed, much of the trade between industrial countries—be they large or small—can be explained by historical patterns of specialization arising out of large-scale economies.

Sources as well as implications of economies of scale will be discussed further in Chapter 20. For the moment, let us note that where differences in comparative costs are fundamentally the result of increasing returns, there need not be a tendency for equalization of factor prices once trade opens up. In fact, there is little reason to expect such equalization if the trading partners have similar factor endowments to begin with, or if specialization had taken place in each country long before trade ever started.

Transportation Costs, Trade, and Location

Transportation costs, briefly alluded to in the preceding section, will now be considered in some detail. These costs—for example, freight, insurance, loading, unloading—strongly influence the volume of trade as well as its geographical patterns. We have thus far ignored these costs because we have been mainly concerned with the causes and benefits of trade in general, and not with specific trade flows. Yet in order to explain why trade flourishes between some regions and is merely a trickle between others, transportation costs must also be considered.

The most obvious result of these costs is to raise the price of imported goods, thereby reducing the demand for them. Less obvious, perhaps, is the fact that no trade in a particular good can take place if the cost of transporting it from one country to another exceeds the difference in production cost between these countries. For example, if it costs $50 to produce a ton of steel in country A and $60 in B, a transportation charge of $10 or more per ton will eliminate the cost advantage of A over B, and with it the basis for trade in steel between them. Similar examples may explain why some commodities do not enter international trade at all, and why others are traded only in small quantities.

More often, however, transportation costs influence the *patterns* of specialization and trade rather than the total volume of internationally traded goods. Other things being equal, the greater the distance between two regions, the higher the cost of transporting goods from one to the other. But since "other things" are seldom equal, geographic distance does not always impede trade between two areas. Also important are the actual routes taken and the type of transportation used. Thus, it usually costs more to ship goods over land than by sea (or rivers); and where goods must travel on land for a long distance, it costs less to ship them by rail than by truck. Also relevant are such factors as weight, bulk, and/or perishability; these affect the cost of packaging and handling goods, as well as the method of transporting them. All in all, transportation costs are not always proportionate to distance; they are determined by a combination of different factors, and vary greatly from commodity to commodity.

Variations also exist between costs of transporting finished goods, and transporting the raw materials from which they are made. On the basis of such variations and the reasons behind them, patterns of specialization and trade can often be explained. Since the location of industries is partly governed by the need to minimize transportation costs, commodities can be classified according to the site of their production : They can be *market-oriented, supply-oriented,* or *neutral.*

Goods that gain weight or bulk during the manufacturing process are generally more costly to ship than the raw or semiprocessed materials used in their production. Hence, industries producing such goods (e.g., automobiles, bottled soft drinks, ink) tend to locate near the market where the finished product is sold. Also market-oriented, but obviously for different reasons, are highly perishable goods (e.g., fresh milk, bread and bakery products) and service industries (e.g., laundries, restaurants).

On the other hand, where the cost of transporting the raw materials to the market exceeds the cost of transporting the finished article, industries are attracted to the source of raw-materials supply. Prominent examples of *supply-oriented* industries include steel, lumber, sugar refining, vegetable canning. In all these cases, large quantities of raw materials are used up during the manufacturing process, and the finished product is less heavy and/or bulky, and hence more easily transportable, than the raw materials (or fuels) used in its manufacture. Thus, steel is generally produced near coal deposits, because large quantities of coal in relation to iron are required. Other examples: lumber, which is processed at the site of timber resources and shipped to the market in finished form; sugar, which is extracted from cane or beets and is refined nearby; and aluminum, which is refined near the source of fuel (electric power) rather than at the source of raw material (bauxite).

Finally, where transportation costs are insignificant in relation to the cost of production, or where the manufacturing process causes little changes in weight or bulk, the industries concerned have no strong reason to be attracted to either the market or the source of raw materials. Consequently, the location of these so-called *neutral* industries will be determined less by transportation costs than by other forces. Such an industry, in fact, may owe its present site to some historical accident which at the time had little to do either with local availability of resources or with considerations of transportation costs. Once established, however, the industry may have been able to develop the necessary resources on the spot or to obtain them from other places. Or, it may have moved on and sought its fortunes elsewhere.

Many examples can be given to illustrate the various impacts of transportation costs on industry location. But this subject belongs more properly to another branch of economics that is growing rapidly: the *theory of location*. Analytically, the theory of location makes no distinction between regional and international patterns of specialization; it seeks to provide a *general* explanation of industrial location, based on considerations of space and transportation costs. For this very reason, however, its methods can be usefully applied to both domestic and international problems. Indeed a day may come when the theory of international trade will be reduced to the position of a special case within a general framework of location theory.

Summary

Of the three questions raised by the classical economists, only the first has been dealt with in this chapter: Why do nations trade and what goods are exchanged between them? The answer, although couched in the language of modern economics, remains essentially the same: International trade is based on differences in comparative costs, and the latter also determine what goods will be exported and imported by different countries.

The major cause of comparative-cost differences lies in unequal factor endowments among countries, coupled with the fact that different commodities are produced with different factor proportions. But differences in comparative costs may also be due to economies of large-scale production, in which case trade will flourish even between countries with similar factor endowments.

Sharing in the determination of trade patterns are transportation costs. In raising the prices of imported goods, transportation costs act either as a complete or a partial barrier to trade between some regions. More often, however, they are influential in determining the geographic location of manufacturing activities and, as a result, the patterns of specialization.

All of the above—factor endowments, economies of scale, transportation costs—have one thing in common: They affect trade through their influence on the costs of the goods involved. In short, they are forces which underlie the *supply* side of the international market. But supply conditions, as represented by comparative costs, can tell only part of the story—what goods are likely to be exported and imported, and by whom. In order to determine at what prices, and in what quantities, goods will be traded, we must switch to the demand side and consider its role in international trade.

6

Modern Trade Theory: Demand and the Terms of Trade

FOLLOWING IN THE FOOTSTEPS of John Stuart Mill, a number of writers continued to explore the forces which determine the gains from trade and their distribution. Outstanding among them was Alfred Marshall (1842–1924), who both clarified and further developed Mill's theory of international values. Although the details of Marshall's theoretical explorations need not detain us here, the analytical tools which he developed are of immediate interest. For with these tools we can tackle the second major question that was raised in Chapter 4: On what terms will goods be traded internationally?

Reciprocal Demand, Offer Curves, and the Terms of Trade

It will be recalled that Mill suggested that, within the limits set by domestic cost ratios, the terms of trade will be established through the equation of reciprocal demand. But it was Marshall who introduced the *reciprocal-demand curve*—also known as the *offer curve*—thereby making it possible to follow Mill's reasoning more precisely. Generally defined, the reciprocal-demand curve of country A is simultaneously A's

79

demand curve for country B's products and A's supply curve of its own exports. Thus, A's offer curve indicates how much it would demand from, and offer to, B at different prevailing prices. And depending on its desire for the imported products, as well as on its domestic production possibilities, A would offer more (or less) of its own exportable products for a given quantity of imports from B.

In reality, a country's demand for imports and its supply of exports are composites of many goods and services, involving trade with many countries. Indeed, Marshall's reciprocal demand was conceived in terms of bales (or bundles) of exportable goods exchanged for bales of importables.[1] Yet in order to illustrate the principle of reciprocal demand, we may refer to our simple analytical world—consisting of two countries and two commodities—and recall the situation depicted in Figure 5.2 and reproduced below.

The slopes of these *constant-cost* production-possibilities curves indicate, for each country, not only the domestic cost ratio between steel

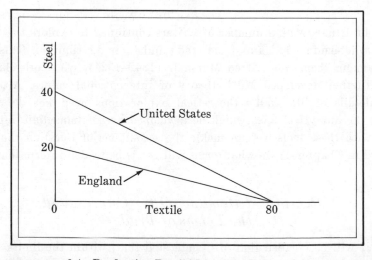

FIGURE *6.1* Production Possibilities (England and
the United States)

[1] See G. Haberler, *The Theory of International Trade: With Its Application to Commercial Policy* (London: Hodge, 1950), p. 150.

and textile, but also their price ratio. And since we are concerned at present with price ratios rather than cost ratios, we may draw the curves showing them as positively sloped *price lines*. Of course, the slope of each of these price lines is identical with the slope of the production-possibilities curve to which it corresponds.

In Figure 6.2 the price lines indicate that no international exchange is likely to take place outside the limits set by the domestic price ratios (i.e., 1 steel for 2 textile in the United States and 1 steel for 4 textile in England). To put it another way, the lines set the limits within which the international price ratio (terms of trade) must fall.[2] Each country,

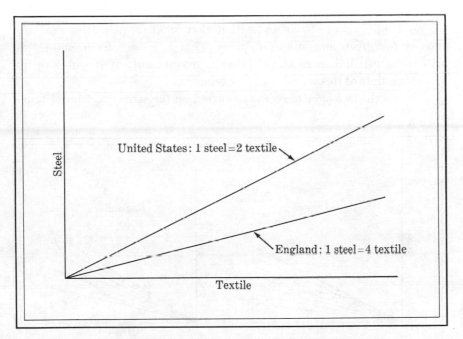

FIGURE *6.2*   Relative Prices of Steel and Textile (England and the United States)

[2] This must be qualified. For although the terms of trade are unlikely to fall *outside* the limits set by the domestic price ratios, they may settle at one limit or the other—especially if the trading countries are of unequal size. In this case, the terms of trade may be set by the domestic price ratio of the large country, thereby enabling the small country to reap large benefits from trade.

however, would behave according to its own self-interests, and this behavior would be reflected in its offer curve, as shown in Figure 6.3.

At any given price ratio (indicated by the slopes of the price lines), each country would offer to, and demand from the other, certain quantities of steel and/or textile. Thus, starting from its domestic price line, the United States offer curve consists of a series of points,[3] showing the amounts of steel offered at various prices for given amounts of textile. Likewise, the British offer curve shows the various amounts of textile England is willing to offer in exchange for given amounts of steel. A similar pattern can be detected along each offer curve. Initially, each country is willing to part with increasing quantities of its product in return for additional imports. Beyond a certain point, however, the offer curves bend backward—an indication that smaller quantities are now offered for given amounts of imports. That is to say, each country is willing to demand more of the other's product only if it can give up lesser amounts of its own product in exchange.

When the two offer curves are charted on the same diagram (Figure

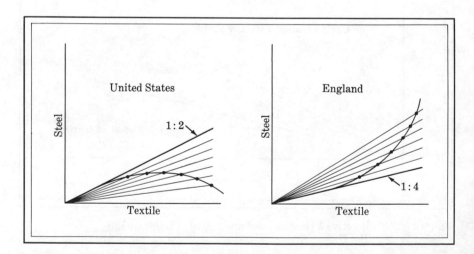

FIGURE *6.3*   Offer Curves of the United States and England

[3] The considerations that govern the exact location of these points wiH be discussed in the next section.

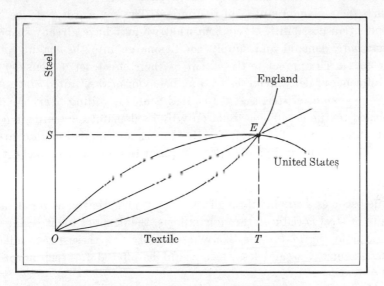

FIGURE *6.4*   Determination of the Terms of Trade

6.4), they almost invariably intersect. At the point of intersection (E), the amounts of steel offered, and textile demanded, by the United States just equal the amounts of textile offered, and steel demanded, by England. At that point the reciprocal demands of the two countries are equal, and equilibrium in their trade is established. The slope of the line OE indicates the one, and only one, price ratio that brought about the equation of reciprocal demand. This price ratio is none other than the terms of trade.

The Ingredients of Reciprocal Demand

Now that the terms of trade have been established, we may ask: What lies behind the offer curve? Or more specifically, what forces determine the actual quantities offered and demanded by each country at different prices?

We have a clue to the answer in the suggestion made earlier that, depending on its desire for the imported product and the production possibilities at home, a country would offer more (or less) of its own exports for a given quantity of the import. The key words, "desire" and "production possibilities," confirm what we may have already suspected —that *both* demand and supply conditions go into the making of the offer curve. To appreciate the extent of their effect, let us consider first the influence of demand on the trading behavior of the United States.

The amount of steel that the United States is willing to exchange for imported textile is influenced not only by its demand for textile, but also by its desire, or need, for steel itself. If steel commands a high degree of preference domestically, only small quantities of it are likely to be offered *at any price ratio,* and vice versa. But even if textile is strongly preferred initially, the demand for it may weaken as more and more textile becomes available through imports. Concurrently, as the domestic supply of steel is reduced through exports, the demand for it (relative to the demand for textile) is likely to increase. As these two tendencies grow stronger, less and less steel would be offered for each additional unit of textile.

Meanwhile, on the supply side, another combination of forces is at work. Involved are the production costs of both steel and textile, whose ratio, as we saw earlier, is indicated by the slope of the production-possibilities curve. Here we must distinguish between two cases : (1) constant costs, and (2) increasing costs. Under the former, the domestic cost ratio will always remain the same, specialization will be complete, and the amounts of steel offered for given quantities of textile will be solely influenced by demand considerations.

With increasing costs, however, specialization will be less than complete, and the quantities of steel and textile exchanged will be partly determined by cost conditions. Thus, so long as textile can be obtained from abroad at a lower cost (in terms of steel) than it can be produced domestically, larger quantities of steel will be produced and offered in exchange for it. (Observe the first portion of the offer curve.) But as domestic production of steel increases, the cost of steel, relative to textile, rises; and after a while it may no longer pay to shift resources from textile to steel production and offer the additional steel for imported textile. In fact, when the cost (or price) of importing textile—as measured by the amount of steel given up in exchange—equals the cost of producing it at home, specialization stops : No additional resources will be shifted from textile to steel. Beyond this point, lesser amounts of steel would be offered for a given quantity of imported textile, as reflected by the backward-bending section of the United States offer curve.

Similar considerations underlie the British offer curve. Although in this case textile is being offered and steel demanded, the forces of supply and demand are just as influential in determining the actual quantities traded. Reciprocal demand, then, simply *combines* the two major elements that govern the behavior of any free market. Thus, in the international market, supply and demand dictate what goods will be exported and imported by each country and—through the equation of reciprocal demand—on what terms these goods will be exchanged.

Changes in the Terms of Trade: Gains or Losses?

Supply and demand conditions do not stay the same for long. Constant changes in tastes and preferences, as well as changing levels of incomes, affect the demand, while new discoveries and technological innovations influence the conditions of supply. And a change in either supply or demand is inevitably reflected by a change in a country's offer curve.

Whatever the exact cause, a change in the offer curve of either trading partner will alter the international price ratio and with it the terms of trade. This can be easily verified by Figure 6.5. Originally, the terms of trade were established by the line *OA*. If the United States curve shifts to the right and England's curve remains the same, the new terms of trade are indicated by *OB*. Should the British curve shift to the left and that of the United States remain the same, the terms of trade will move to *OC*. Finally, should both curves change at the same time, the new terms of trade will be *OD*. We might note that a shift of the United States curve to the left, or of the British curve to the right, would produce different results from those shown here. In fact, the student might assume such shifts and draw the resultant terms of trade.[4]

At stake, however, is an important issue: What are the implications of changes in the terms of trade for each trading partner? In Figure 6.5, is the United States better off at *OB* than *OA?* If so, is England worse off? And what about the situation at *OD?* Are both countries better off,

---

[4] Keep in mind that the new terms of trade will be affected by the magnitude as well as the direction of the shifts.

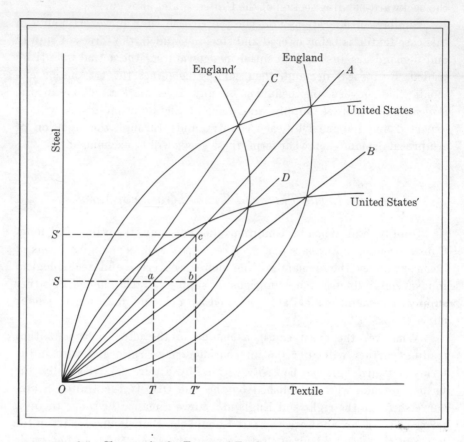

FIGURE 6.5   Changes in the Terms of Trade

or worse off, than they were at *OA?* More important still, what is the significance of being "better off" or "worse off"?

A moment's reflection, and a closer look at Figure 6.5, sheds some light on the matter. Compare, for example, point *a* (lying on *OA*) and point *b* (lying on *OB*), and consider what the difference between them is. At point *a*, the United States was willing to offer *OS* of steel in exchange for *OT* of textile, while at point *b*, *OS* of steel is exchanged for *OT'* of textile. In other words, the change in the terms of trade, from *OA* to *OB*, has enabled the United States to acquire, for the same quantity of exports, a larger quantity of imports.

Switching to England, let us compare points *c* and *b*. At point *c*, England exchanged *OT'* of textile for *OS'* of steel, whereas at *b*, she offers the same amount of textile for *OS* of steel. That is to say, a given quantity of British exports now commands a smaller quantity of imports from the United States. We may therefore conclude that the terms of trade have changed in favor of the United States. This change reflects either a rise in the price of steel (in terms of textile) or a fall in the price of textile (in terms of steel).

The shoe might be on the other foot, however, if the price of textile rises or the price of steel falls. In this case, the terms of trade would move from *OA* to *OC*, and England would find herself in a more favorable position. If both curves shift simultaneously, either outcome may result, depending on the magnitude of the individual shifts. While in our example the Yankees seem to have benefited from such a shift (compare *OD* with *OA*), this need not always be the case.

But to speak of the terms of trade as favoring one country or another is in itself misleading. For although the above analysis is correct as far as it goes, it emphasizes only one criterion by which gains or losses from trade are assessed: the relation between export and import prices. Thus, the fact that the terms of trade may have moved against England and in favor of the United States simply means that the prices of British exports to the United States have declined in relation to the prices of American exports to England.[5] More information as to the cause of the price change is needed before any meaningful assessment of England's new trade position can be made. And even with such information, it is not always possible to reach a definite conclusion one way or another.

Nevertheless, the terms of trade have been widely accepted as an index by which to measure *trends* of gains from trade and several concepts of terms of trade have been developed. Let us examine them and briefly evaluate their usefulness.

Terms of Trade Concepts

Net-barter terms of trade. All our previous references were made to the so-called "commodity" terms of trade, also known as the "net-barter" terms of trade. Since they are the easiest to measure statistically,

---

[5] Or, British imports are now relatively more expensive (in terms of its exports).

they are the ones most frequently used. What they measure, of course, are changes in the ratio of export prices to import prices; and these changes are reflected in the movements of the terms of trade themselves (i.e., the ratio at which the traded goods are exchanged). If we let Px and Pm stand for the average prices of exports and imports respectively, then the net-barter terms of trade are represented by Px/Pm.

To measure changes in this ratio, we divide the change in export price by the change in import price between two periods of time. Thus

$$\text{change in } Tn.b. = \frac{Px_1}{Pm_1} \bigg/ \frac{Px_0}{Pm_0} = \frac{Px_1}{Px_0} \bigg/ \frac{Pm_1}{Pm_0}$$

where the subscripts $_0$ and $_1$ stand for the base period and a subsequent one. If, between the two periods, export prices have trebled and import prices have only doubled, the terms of trade will register an improvement of 50 per cent, computed as follows

$$\frac{300}{100} \bigg/ \frac{200}{100} = 150$$

Should import prices rise more than export prices, the terms of trade are said to have deteriorated. For example

$$\frac{150}{100} \bigg/ \frac{200}{100} = 75$$

As stated previously, movements in the net-barter terms of trade merely record changes in the relative prices of exports and imports. Neither the reasons behind such changes nor any other facts are revealed by the statistical results. One cannot tell, for example, whether a country whose terms of trade have improved (or deteriorated) is actually importing (or exporting) more than before; or whether the quality of its imports and exports has changed. Nor does a movement—for better or for worse—in the net-barter terms of trade indicate the state of a country's balance of payments. In short, the ease with which these terms of trade can be calculated does not mean that they are a reliable indicator of a country's gains or losses from trade. Although useful, they must be used with care.

Gross-barter terms of trade. Devised by the late Frank Taussig of Harvard, this concept purports to overcome at least one weakness of the commodity terms of trade. It focuses, not on changes in export and import prices, but rather on changes in their physical quantities. "Cross-barter" terms of trade are represented by the ratio Qx/Qm, where Qx and Qm are the quantities of exports and imports respectively. Changes in this ratio are calculated as follows

$$Tg.b. = \frac{Qxl}{Qml} \Big/ \frac{Qxo}{Qmo}$$

A rise in the numerical value of these terms of trade means either that the volume of exports has risen relative to the volume of imports, or that the volume of imports has fallen relative to the volume of exports. A fall in the value of the index signifies the reverse: Either the quantity of exports has fallen relative to imports, or the quantity of imports has risen relative to the volume of exports. Beyond that, the gross-barter terms of trade tell us nothing. Consequently, an improvement or deterioration in this index is of little help in judging whether a country's gains from trade have increased or decreased.

One might, of course, interpret a fall in the gross-barter terms of trade as favorable, for it means either that a smaller quantity of exports is given up for the same quantity of imports, or that a larger volume of imports is now being obtained for the same quantity of exports. But when it comes to a rise in the value of the index, no welfare judgment can be made without knowing *why* exports have risen or imports fallen.

Income terms of trade. This third concept gives us something that makes more sense, for it attempts to provide a measure of a country's capacity to import, given its income from exports. "Income" terms of trade are arrived at by multiplying the price of exports (Px) by the quantity of exports (Qx), and dividing by the price of imports (Pm).

$$Tinc. = \frac{Px \cdot Qx}{Pm}$$

An improvement in a country's income terms of trade implies that the country can—if it wishes—buy more imports than it could have before. This improvement can come about either because export prices have risen, or import prices have fallen, or because the physical volume of exports has increased. Conversely, a deterioration in the index may be due to a fall in export prices, a rise in import prices, or a decrease in the volume of exports. But while the statistical results reveal nothing new about the underlying cause, many economists regard this concept as a more valid measure of gains than either of the preceding two. And with good reason. For as a country's capacity to import increases, the country can better avail itself of the basic benefit of trade : It can buy more goods from countries where they are produced efficiently, while devoting more of its own resources to lines of production in which those resources are efficient.

Factoral terms of trade. Although they are the least amenable to statistical measurement, "factoral" terms of trade are an important concept for analytical purposes. Their major purpose is to adjust changes in the net-barter terms of trade for changes in productivity occurring between two periods of time. And since changes in productivity alter the factor content of traded goods, the factoral terms of trade in effect represent an attempt to measure changes in the ratio at which factors of production exchange for each other through trade. Developed by Professor Jacob Viner, these terms of trade are of two kinds: "single-factoral" terms of trade, which correct a country's commodity terms of trade for changes in productivity in its own export sector; and "double-factoral" terms of trade, which also take into account changes in productivity in foreign industries that supply the country with its imports.

Single-factoral terms of trade are obtained by multiplying a country's net-barter terms of trade (Px/Pm) by the productivity index (Kx) in its export sector. Thus

$$Ts.f. = \frac{Px}{Pm}.Kx$$

To illustrate, suppose that, between the two periods of time under consideration, productivity has increased by 5 per cent and the commodity terms of trade have registered a 10 per cent improvement. The single-factoral terms of trade will be $1.10 \times 1.05 = 1.15$. This means that a unit of a productive factor, employed in the production of exports, can now buy 15 per cent more imports than before—a clear gain in real terms.

To obtain the double-factoral terms of trade, we divide the above expression by the foreign-productivity index (Km), thus

$$Td.f. = \frac{Px}{Pm} \cdot \frac{Kx}{Km}$$

An improvement of, say, 10 per cent in the double-factoral terms of trade implies that one unit of a productive factor can buy 10 per cent more units of foreign factors of production than before. In practice, however, neither the double- nor the single-factoral terms of trade can be calculated or even clearly defined. They are mainly useful in suggesting that changes in a country's commodity terms of trade may be accompanied by increases in its productive efficiency. And such increases may either augment an improvement or offset a deterioration in the country's commodity terms of trade.

Current account terms of trade. Now we introduce a new and final concept. This focuses on the relation between export receipts and import expenditures, and is intended to shed light on a country's balance-of-payments position. "Current-account" terms of trade are computed by multiplying net-barter by gross-barter terms of trade. Thus

$$Tc.a. = \frac{Px \cdot Qx}{Pm \cdot Qm}$$

Although this measure suffers from the same basic weakness as most of the other concepts (it does not reveal the reasons for a particular change), it has at least two virtues. First, it can indicate whether a country currently has a surplus ($Tc.a.>1$) or a deficit ($Tc.a.<1$) in its trade balance. Second, changes in this ratio over a period of time suggest the nature of the country's position: Is it blessed with a continuous surplus or afflicted with a continuous deficit?

Information of this kind has great significance. For, as we will see later, a persistent surplus in the current accounts usually implies an accumulation of gold and/or foreign exchange which can be used in time to finance a larger volume of imports. On the other hand, a deficit that persists may lead to gold and foreign-exchange losses. Even if currently covered by capital imports, such a deficit points to the possibility of a day of reckoning in the future, when foreign loans will have to be repaid out of export earnings. But more about this later.

So much for the current-account terms of trade. In summing up this section, we must concede that none of the terms of trade is a foolproof index of gains or losses from trade. For while each of the concepts provides a specific measure of trends, none of the measures is sufficiently comprehensive to serve as a general indicator of a country's well-being. Consequently, an improvement or a deterioration in any of the terms of trade cannot in itself justify the conclusion that a country is either better off or worse off. This is not to suggest that the terms of trade are analytically, or even statistically, useless. Rather it is a reminder that, like most other tools of economic measurement, they must be used very carefully and with constant awareness of their limitations.

A Summing Up

Having journeyed through the "pure" theory of international trade, it will be helpful to recall some of the important milestones along the way.

Starting with the absolute-cost-differences explanation of trade, à la Adam Smith, we moved on to Ricardo's more sophisticated principle of comparative costs. And, accepting comparative-cost differences as the basis for mutually beneficial trade, we then inquired into their underlying causes. We found these to be differing factor endowments among nations, and also economies of large-scale production.

Yet comparative-cost data merely provide an account of supply conditions. As such, they may indicate a likelihood of trade, but cannot describe what will actually happen once trade opens up. To find out the terms under which goods will exchange in the international market, conditions of supply must be considered along with the forces of demand. This, as we have seen, is the essence—and purpose—of reciprocal-demand analysis.

Introduced by John Stuart Mill and further refined by Alfred Marshall, the concept of reciprocal demand enables us to follow simultaneously the trading behavior of two countries—as governed by their respective supply and demand conditions—and thus determine what the terms of trade are likely to be. This concept takes the graphic form of reciprocal-demand curves, in which the point of intersection is really an expression of Mill's "law of reciprocal demand."

This point marks the end of our journey through the pure theory of international trade. Here come to rest, at least temporarily, all the variables whose interactions dictate what, and how much, will be produced, consumed, and traded by our trading partners—and at what prices. This is where equilibrium is established.

7

Changes in Consumption, Production, and Trade

Gaining equilibrium is one thing, retaining that position is quite another matter; equilibrium can be maintained only as long as the basic underlying conditions do not change. In terms of our own endeavor this means that patterns of international trade, which were established by a particular set of supply and demand conditions, would persist only as long as no changes occur on either the supply or the demand side. And although in the model that we used to explain trade (and in the process arrive at equilibrium) any such changes were disregarded, their presence in the real world calls for second thoughts.

In our analytical world we viewed consumption habits as given and fixed. In other words, we assumed that the patterns of demand were governed by an unchanging set of tastes and preferences. As for the underlying conditions of supply, we assumed a constant state of technology throughout the world and fixed, though different, amounts of productive resources in each country.[1] Armed with these ''static'' as-

---

[1] Another important and closely related assumption was that factors of production cannot move *between* countries but are perfectly mobile *within* each country.

sumptions—fixed tastes, fixed technology, and fixed factor supplies—we argued that comparative cost differences provide the basis for, and determine the patterns of, international specialization and trade. Moreover, by combining comparative-cost data with the forces of demand, we were able to show not only what goods would be exported and imported by each country, but also on what terms.

History, however, provides ample proof that trade patterns change as time goes by. In order to explain the nature of such changes, as well as their underlying causes, we must set aside our previous assumptions and accept the fact that in the world as it exists neither demand nor supply conditions remain constant. Indeed, once we admit the possibility that demand and supply are *not* fixed, but may change, our analysis acquires wider and more meaningful dimensions. No longer are we restricted, in explaining trade, to a particular set of economic conditions. Instead, we can relate changes in trade patterns to changes in the economic structures of the countries involved, and thereby explain their origin. In doing so, however, we must distinguish between the various kinds of economic changes that may occur, grouping them under two major headings: changes in consumption (demand), and changes in production (supply). We begin our discussion with the former.

Changes in Consumption

In order to draw attention to the direct benefits of international trade, we have thus far couched our analysis in quantitative rather than qualitative terms. That is to say, we have argued that the opening up of trade would enable each country to increase its consumption of the same goods it had consumed previously. We must recognize, however, that as a result of exposure through trade to new products, consumers in different countries may develop new tastes and discard old consumption habits. Indeed, one of the most frequent by-products of international trade has been the introduction of new commodities into areas where they had not been known before. And having created new tastes, international trade has at the same time provided the means to satisfy them.

So widely accepted are the taste-creating and taste-changing qualities of international trade that they have been designated by the use of a special term—the "demonstration effect."[2] Although this term has been used primarily in reference to a behavior pattern of underdeveloped countries, its significance extends to trade in general. As applied to the underdeveloped areas, it describes their attempts to emulate overnight the living standards of advanced countries; they do so by importing from the latter goods for which they have only recently acquired a taste. Thus, having been exposed to such articles as cars, refrigerators, radios, TV sets, watches, pens, and so on, the underdeveloped countries feel they must have them, too. Unfortunately, this desire often exceeds their ability to pay. The consequences of this will be discussed in Chapter 19.

In its broad meaning, however, the demonstration effect can be observed almost everywhere in the world. The American tourist may discover in London, Paris, Rome, or even Tel Aviv the very brand-name products that he has been accustomed to buy at the corner drugstore back home. Or an Englishman, on a visit to the United States, may soon find that Americans, too, like to drink scotch, drive MG cars, wear Harris Tweed jackets, and, alas, hum along with the Beatles! Just as these and other "foreign" products have found their way into the American home, so nylon stockings, cola drinks, Western movies, chewing gum, and other products are enjoyed by consumers the world over. Such similarities in tastes among nations that are linked through trade are largely due to the workings of the demonstration effect.

Changing tastes and preferences may also be due to changes in income. At low income levels, consumption patterns are characterized by the predominance of so-called "inferior goods"—for example, bread, potatoes, rice, cheap cotton textiles, and so on. But as their incomes rise, consumers try to improve and diversify the contents of their shopping bags. They may reduce or abandon their purchase of some goods and replace them with others. And as their incomes continue to rise, still newer consumption patterns emerge: Smaller proportions of income are spent on essentials and larger proportions on luxury goods.

One should not confuse consumer response to income changes with behavior that is due to the demonstration effect. Although both result in pretty much the same thing—that is, changing consumption patterns— they are separate phenomena. At times, however, they may be linked by a common denominator: international trade. For not only does trade

[2] The term was originally coined by Professor J. Duesenberry; the first to apply it to discussions of international trade was Professor R. Nurkse.

expose consumers to new and different products, but it also raises their incomes. Thus, the opening up of trade may activate simultaneously both the income effect and the demonstration effect, both of which influence consumption behavior.

How do changes in consumption affect the patterns of, and gains from, international trade? Unfortunately, this question is more easily asked than answered. One can describe, of course, specific changes in trade between countries and relate them to underlying changes in their demand conditions. Moreover, one can perhaps imagine the likely consequences for a country whose exports are presently in greater, or lesser, demand than they were before (more about this in Part III). But one is less certain when it comes to judging the welfare implications of qualitative changes. How is one to decide, for example, whether a country as a whole is better off if it imports more steel and less textile than it did before? Similarly, is a country better or worse off with more imported whiskey and fewer imported cars than with less whiskey and more cars?

To be sure, one of the virtues of international trade is the wider choice it offers consumers in each country. What goods they actually choose to consume depends, of course, on their individual tastes and preferences. But whether a particular change in tastes is "good" or "bad" cannot be easily determined; even the consumer himself may not always be sure. In short, changes in consumption help explain *why* certain patterns of trade may have changed in a particular way. But any additional information they reveal should be used with caution and restraint.

Changes in Production

Here we must distinguish between three basic changes that may alter a country's production possibilities and hence its comparative advantage vis-à-vis other countries. These are changes in technology, changes in the amounts of existing resources, and changes in the type of available resources. Taking each[3] of these in turn, we might explore their effects on supply conditions and, through them, on the patterns of trade.

[3] For the sake of convenience, however, we shall discuss the last two kinds of changes under one heading.

CHANGES IN TECHNOLOGY

In a world devoid of technological changes, comparative-cost differences, and hence trade, spring from relative differences in factor endowments. For with a given and unchanging state of technology—a technology freely available to all countries—each country would possess a comparative advantage in those commodities that can be best produced with large proportions of its relatively abundant factor (or factors). It would export these commodities in exchange for goods whose production requires large proportions of its relatively scarce factor. Yet to assume that technical capabilities are the same everywhere and that technology remains constant is to misrepresent reality. Indeed, the introduction of new products, the development of new productive techniques, the improvements in productive organization, and so forth, suggest that technical changes have been the rule rather than the exception during the past century or so.

That technology is *not* the same everywhere is attested to by the fact that, despite similarities in factor endowments in two given countries, one may be able to produce certain commodities more efficiently—and hence more cheaply—than the other. And even where differences in factor endowments do exist, the actual patterns of trade are often determined by differences in existing levels of technology. In fact, technological differences, rather than different factor endowments, account for a considerable volume of international trade. While this is especially true today, it has always been true to some extent. Thus, during much of the nineteenth century, England built up a large export trade on the basis of her technical superiority in the production of many manufactured goods. But as other countries caught up with her, some items of British exports—most notably textiles—diminished in importance and were replaced by goods in whose production England could still maintain a technological lead. For more recent examples of trade patterns based on technical differences, one has only to look at the type of goods exchanged between the United States and Western European countries, and those exchanged among European countries themselves (e.g., electrical equipment, chemicals, aircraft, automobiles).

Even more striking in this connection are some of the trade flows between the developed and underdeveloped countries. To be sure, many of the products that the latter export to the former—especially raw materials—are the result of differences in factor endowments. But consider the fact that a country such as the United States actually exports agricultural products to countries where land and labor are relatively (and in some instances, absolutely) more abundant. Such peculiarities can be explained if we realize that advanced technology can enable a country to alter basic processes of production. Thus, technical know-how has often enabled the United States to transform land intensive or labor intensive processes into capital-intensive processes. As a result, the United States has gained a cost advantage over other countries, even in the production of goods requiring large proportions of these countries' abundant factors.

Yet technology does not stand still. The introduction of new commodities is often accompanied by innovations in production techniques. Thus, capital-intensive industries may become, by comparison with newer lines of production, labor-intensive. Such industries may now provide the less developed countries with the chance to start their own manufacturing activities. For as technical knowledge spreads from the advanced to the developing areas of the world, the latter may be able to use *their* abundant resources to produce commodities that they previously had to import from the former.[4] However, the spread of technical know-how is not restricted to one channel, leading from the developed to the under-developed countries, but occurs among the industrial countries themselves. For while the introduction of a new product or a new technique may bestow upon the innovating country an advantage over others, its lead may gradually diminish or disappear as the innovation passes into the hands of competitors who successfully imitated it.

It is now fairly obvious that changes in technology—whether they occur one at a time or in several countries simultaneously—are likely to affect existing trade patterns. But the nature of a particular change in trade will depend to a large extent upon the kind of technological change behind it. Generally speaking, changes in technology are mostly of two

[4] Examples include such items as textiles, shoes, processed food, cosmetics, household goods.

kinds: They consist in the introduction of new products, or in the improvement of efficiency in production (leading to a rise in productivity) in existing industries.[5] Moreover, technological changes may be concentrated either in industries whose products are already traded internationally (i.e., exported or imported by a particular country) or in industries that cater solely to the domestic market (e.g., laundries and restaurants). Industries serving the domestic market do not concern us here, for any technological advances they make will have little effect on trade patterns. Hence, we look to technological changes in industries serving international markets for a clue to specific changes in international trade.

When a change in technology results in an increase in productivity, it is likely to lead to cost reduction. If such reductions occur in export industries, they may well result in an expansion of trade. For as the prices of a country's exports decline, more of its products may be demanded abroad. On the other hand, if a rise in productivity—and the subsequent reduction in cost—comes about in industries whose products are already competing with imports, the result may be a contraction in the volume of trade. It is possible, moreover, that increases in productivity in import-competing industries will reverse the *direction* of trade : For example, two countries may export to each other goods that they previously imported from each other. Yet although history abounds with examples illustrating the impact of changes in productivity on international trade, this does not justify any generalizations as to their ultimate effects. While certain changes may prove beneficial to all countries concerned, others may be harmful.[6] In any event, one can never be absolutely sure that it was indeed a particular change in productivity that caused a particular change in trade patterns.

Similar ambiguities beset any inquiry into the effects of technological changes involved in the introduction of new products. One may reasonably surmise that changes of this kind would generally stimulate

[5] The invention of the steam engine and the introduction of the assembly-line technique are cases in point.

[6] One might note in this connection J. R. Hicks' famous argument that the import-biased changes in American productivity have worked to the benefit of the United States but to the detriment of Western Europe. See his ''The Long Run Dollar Problem. An Inaugural Lecture,'' *Oxford Economic Papers*, New Series 5 (1953).

trade. For if the demonstration effect is in operation, the appearance of a
new product in one country would be followed by a demand for it by
other countries, thus increasing exports of the country that originated it.
And since a rise in exports usually leads to an increase in incomes, it
might be expected to stimulate imports as well.

Yet such favorable results cannot be taken for granted. For one
thing, consumers abroad may greet a new product with much less
enthusiasm than do consumers at home; in this case the hoped-for
increase in exports may not materialize. Second, if the product has
been developed by an import-competing industry, its appearance may
actually result in a reduction in imports. And although reductions in
imports resulting from new-product development may be somewhat offset
by increasing exports of other goods, the net effect of such changes on
trade cannot be easily calculated. More will be said in a later section
about the relation between technological changes and changes in trade.
For the moment, let us turn to the other supply-changing force—changes
in factor endowments.

CHANGING FACTOR ENDOWMENTS

Neither the amounts nor the kinds of a country's productive resources are fixed and unalterable. Its labor force can be increased or
decreased by population changes and its stock of capital can grow
through increased savings; these are familiar and indisputable facts. But
even the supplies of natural resources can change over time. Thus, land
reclamation, continued explorations, and discoveries of mineral deposits
add to existing quantities and types of a country's natural wealth, while
reckless use of natural resources depletes the supply. Finally, if we
reject, as we must, the notion that factors of production are immobile
internationally,[7] we remove another barrier to the possibility of changing factor endowments. Indeed, such changes may owe their origin to
external as well as to internal causes.

Historical evidence lends support to this claim. One need only call to

---

[7] Actually, this notion came under heavy attack, over thirty years ago, by
Professor J. H. Williams. See his "The Theory of International Trade Reconsid-
ered," *Economic Journal*, Vol. XXXIX (June, 1929). It might also be recalled that
Mill had felt uneasy about the same notion even earlier.

mind the Irish immigration or the importation of Chinese labor to the United States during the latter part of the nineteenth century, to see that changes in a country's human resources may originate either at home or abroad. Similarly, international flows of investment, both past and present, indicate that the accumulation of capital is often the result of two forces: domestic savings *and* capital imports. Moreover, international factor movements affect not only the amounts of resources in various countries, but also their quality. Thus, with immigration come new skills, especially when the movement of people is from advanced to underdeveloped countries. And capital imports usually bring with them technical knowledge and entrepreneurship, thereby enabling the receiving country to make better use of its resources or to develop new ones.

But the main issue is not that factor endowments may be changed by external as well as internal forces. What does matter is the possibility that such changes will alter the relative supplies of factors in different countries. And since comparative-cost differences rest on relative differences of factor endowments, a change in the latter is likely to be followed by changes in the former. Thus, as shown in Figure 7.1, country A starts out with a comparative advantage in, say, land-intensive goods, because

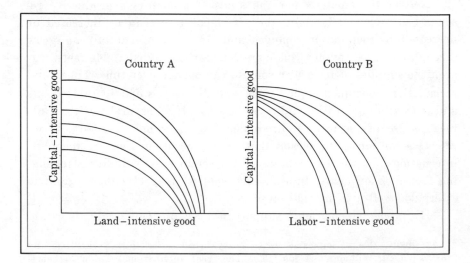

FIGURE *7.1*   Changes in Comparative Advantage Due to
Changing Factor Endowments

land is its relatively abundant factor. But through the continued accumulation of capital and/or the depletion of land, it may come to possess a comparative advantage in capital-intensive products. On the other hand, country B, which was initially well endowed with capital as compared with other countries, may find its comparative advantage shifting from capital-intensive to, say, labor-intensive commodities.

That these are not merely theoretical possibilities is forcefully illustrated by historical experience. During most of the nineteenth century, Great Britain could rightfully boast of relative abundance of capital compared to the rest of the world. Yet during the same period many forces of change were at work, making this claim less and less valid as time went on. The United States, for example, was being transformed from a land-rich to a capital-rich nation, while in some Western European countries labor was being steadily replaced by capital as the relatively abundant factor. Nor were other regions of the world spared the winds of change. Immigration and capital imports on the one hand, and internal developments on the other, combined to alter relative factor supplies in several South American countries, and in Australia, New Zealand, Canada, and other nations. By the time the twentieth century rolled into its second decade, these changes in factor endowments had already made their mark on the patterns of international specialization and trade.

This should not come as a complete surprise. After all, if changes in relative factor endowments alter a country's comparative-advantage position, they are bound to affect its trade relations with other countries. And since the particular set of comparative-advantage positions that had existed at the beginning of the nineteenth century no longer held true one hundred or so years later, is it any wonder that the network of world trade has changed[8] accordingly? Here, indeed, lies the major significance of changing factor endowments: Because such changes alter comparative-cost relations, they help to explain changes in trade patterns among different nations.

An important point, however, is that international trade may often

---

[8] The most striking changes, of course, were the weakening of Britain's position as the world's leading exporter of manufactured goods and the rise in other countries' share of total world trade. For a more detailed historical account of trade changes during that period, see S. B. Clough and C. W. Cole, *Economic History of Europe* (Boston: D. C. Heath, 1941).

be the very instrument that causes factor supplies to change. Or, if trade does not actually initiate such changes, it may accelerate their pace. For example, the flows of investment in the nineteenth century from England to the "regions of new settlements" were essentially the result of trade patterns. The demand for raw materials and foodstuffs on the one hand, and the desire to develop export markets on the other, played a crucial role in bringing about such flows of funds. But in the process the receiving countries were able to accumulate productive resources (capital, skilled labor, and so on) for their own use. More recently, the overseas activities of industries such as petroleum, copper, tin, and aluminum have produced similar, if not as spectacular, results in some of today's developing countries. On the other hand, international trade may accelerate the depletion of some resources, especially those that are used for export purposes; and in so doing it may actually transform a country from an exporter to an importer of certain products.

To sum up: Because changes in factor endowments in different countries bring about changes in their production possibilities, these changes provide the basis for, and an explanation of, the continuing changes in the patterns of international specialization and trade. Yet since production possibilities are influenced by changes in technology, as well as by changes in factor endowments, the impact of the latter cannot always be separated from that of the former—especially when the two kinds of changes occur simultaneously. At the same time, we must note that technological advances may offset the impact of changing factor supplies, thus leaving the actual patterns of trade, if not their magnitude, unaltered. For example, the depletion of arable land in a country specializing in agricultural exports may be accompanied by an increase in land productivity; or, invention of a synthetic substitute may more than compensate for the dwindling supplies of a particular mineral. Under such circumstances, the comparative advantage may not necessarily change; it might, in fact, be reinforced. But regardless of the actual changes in production capabilities in one country or another, chances are that *both* technology and factor endowments had a hand in bringing them about.

Changing Patterns of Trade and Economic Growth

Having described the forces which underlie changes in trade patterns, let us consider how they affect the role of international trade in promoting growth and economic well-being. More specifically, let us ask whether the basic idea about the benefits of international specialization and exchange holds true in a world characterized by constantly changing conditions of supply and demand.

This is not a new question. It reflects a deep concern over a view expressed by many observers during the past thirty years: that rapid technological changes, as well as changing factor endowments, serve to narrow comparative-cost differences and thereby reduce the scope for, and gains from, international specialization. To this, these observers usually add another piece of incriminating evidence: that changes in demand may inflict serious damage on countries whose exports consist of only one or a few products. For such countries, they argue, the risks inherent in specialization far outweigh any of its advantages. Finally, these critics say, the importance of, and dependence on, foreign trade diminishes as countries reach higher and higher stages of economic development. As proof, they point to the fact that for most countries the ratio of foreign trade to total production (GNP) has been declining since the late nineteenth century.[9]

Notwithstanding some elements of truth in these charges, the case for international specialization and trade is not lost. In fact, upon closer examination it becomes apparent that the critics rest *their* case on inconclusive evidence and thereby miss—or choose to ignore—a number of important considerations. In particular, they fail to take into account the *favorable* aspects of the very forces they regard as undermining the foundation of trade. In any case, they ignore the fact that some of the phenomena they decry have often been the consequence, not of free economic forces but of national policies, deliberately designed to subvert the working of international trade.[10]

---

[9] This is true. But since total production has increased rapidly during the same period, the decline in the ratio of foreign trade to GNP does not necessarily mean that trade became *absolutely* less important.

[10] More about this in Part IV.

One cannot deny, of course, that the spread of technology may enable more and more countries to produce a wider range of commodities, thereby reducing their dependence on imports. Similarly, by off-setting either scarcities or the complete absence of certain natural resources, technological advances may permit some countries to maintain a higher living standard than they previously could without the help of foreign trade. Yet nothing in either of these half-truths suggests that living standards cannot be raised to still higher levels if the countries concerned avail themselves of the opportunities offered by international specialization. Nor is it at all certain that the spread of technology would equalize production capabilities to such an extent that the same commodities could be produced everywhere at exactly the same cost. And even if this were the case, there are still bound to remain quantitative differences in productive capacities. That is to say, at a given price some countries would be able *and* willing to supply larger amounts of certain commodities than other countries could offer. Surely, such differences alone point to the virtues of international trade in a world of rapidly growing populations and rising demand for goods and services.

Critics of international trade must also explain their failure to recognize explicitly the great many varieties of commodities that actually enter trade; instead they lump them under two general headings : Agriculture and Manufacture. Such a broad dichotomy does not, as the late Professor Dennis H. Robertson once said,[11] exhaust the truth; for it ignores the tremendous number of variations in each of these groups. Yet when such variations are taken into account, it becomes clear that despite narrowing differences in technology, there is still room for specialization among primary producing and manufacturing countries, as well as among the manufacturing countries themselves.[12] Nor is it fair to imply that most technological changes are biased against imports. For while in many instances this is undoubtedly true, one can point to as many, if not more, cases where technical progress has made trade more profitable and

11 D. H. Robertson, ''The Future of International Trade,'' reprinted in *Readings in the Theory of International Trade* (Philadelphia: American Economic Association, 1949), p. 511.

12 This is borne out by the fact that since 1913 the proportion of world trade that consists of the exchange of manufactures for manufactures has shown no tendency to decline. See Albert O. Hirschman, *National Power and the Structure of Foreign Trade* (Berkeley: University of California Press, 1945), p. 126.

thus contributed to its expansion.[13] And even in instances where technological innovations hurt some imports, they do not rule out the possibility that larger quantities of other goods will be imported.

As for changes in demand, there is no good reason why they should always be presumed to affect trade adversely. To be sure, there are changes and there are changes; but more often than not the demand for imported goods and services has tended to rise rather than to decline with trade. And where a shift in demand is from an imported to a domestic product, it may well be accompanied by an increase in demand for other imported goods. This is not to deny that changes in demand increase the risks inherent in specialization, or that a country whose exports suddenly fall out of favor in world markets may run into serious economic hardships.[14] But risks are part and parcel of any kind of specialization, whether it is among or within nations. Hence, the fact that risks exist should not be taken as proof that an international division of labor is less desirable or beneficial than one that takes place within national boundaries.

In summing up our argument, let us return to the question with which we started: Does international trade serve a useful purpose in a world of changing tastes, changing technology, and changing factor supplies? By now the answer is fairly clear: As long as differences remain in comparative (let alone absolute) costs between nations, a basis exists for mutually beneficial patterns of international specialization and exchange. And although changes in technology and in factor endowments may narrow some gaps in comparative advantage, they may also widen other gaps. More important, while they narrow, or even close, existing gaps in production capabilities, technological advances constantly create new ones, thereby assuring a continuous basis for fruitful specialization and trade. As for changes in demand, unless it can be proved beyond reasonable doubt that they are always biased against imports, we cannot find them guilty of obstructing trade.

Thus, changing conditions of demand and supply do not justify the conclusion that international trade has no virtues as a growth-promoting

[13] Technical developments in the means and methods of transportation are a case in point.

[14] The nature of such hardships and possible ways of adjusting to them will be discussed in Part III.

force. Quite the reverse. Economic growth is itself a dynamic phenomenon, affecting and being affected by economic changes; and few would seriously suggest that changing economic conditions within a country lessen the basic contributions of specialization to economic efficiency and hence to growth. By the same token, one should not dismiss the contributions of *international* specialization to growth, simply because trade patterns in time undergo changes. In fact, one might welcome such changes, for they reflect a process whereby countries adjust themselves to an ever-changing economic environment, and find new ways to exploit the benefits of international trade.

Conclusions: The Dynamic Basis of Trade

We have come a long way from the two-country, two-product world in which basic economic forces were assumed to stand still. That world, to be sure, had its virtues; for it provided us with a simple and uncomplicated model with which to start our explanation of trade. Then, having drawn from that model certain basic conclusions, we were able to test their validity in the real and more complicated world that we know.

This has been our task thus far. What, in essence, are the results?

We can suggest that neither the principle of comparative advantage nor the law of reciprocal demand has turned out to be less valid in a dynamic world than in a static one. That equilibrium is constantly disturbed by changes in its underlying conditions is readily acknowledged. But if trade is allowed to pursue its course freely, its reaction to such changes would still tend to follow along lines of comparative advantage. In other words, as comparative-cost relations change, new patterns of mutually advantageous trade are established. Indeed, this is what we mean by the *dynamic* basis of trade; it is the impact of changing economic forces on trade, and the response of trade to such changes. As long as we recognize this fact, our explanation of trade can be adjusted accordingly.

One last word. Thus far, our explanation of trade has rested on an important assumption: that no obstacles are placed in the way of trade flows. Only in the absence of any barriers could it be argued that trade patterns would follow the dictates of economic efficiency. Unfortunately, this assumption, too, must fall by the wayside and we must take account of a variety of barriers that, more often than not, divert international trade from its natural course or completely obstruct it. We turn now to a discussion of these barriers and their implications.

PART III

BARRIERS TO FREE TRADE: INTERNATIONAL MONETARY PROBLEMS AND SOLUTIONS

8

Foreign Exchange and International Payments

HOW ARE INTERNATIONAL ECO-
nomic transactions financed? This question, which has been mostly
ignored so far, lies at the heart of the monetary (or balance-of-payments) theory of international trade. As briefly noted in Chapter 4,
this "theory"—or, more precisely, this particular aspect of international trade theory—deals with the causes and correction of disturbances in foreign-trade patterns. And since such disturbances are normally reflected in the balance of payments of the country or countries
involved, the monetary theory of international trade can be regarded
as a body of thought concerning the problems of balance-of-payments
adjustments.

Our earlier discussion of the balance of payments (Chapter 3)
suggests that balance-of-payments disturbances consist essentially of imbalances between international payments and receipts, and that the so-
called adjustment process has the task of minimizing or eliminating such
imbalances. Yet because the nature of, and the reasons behind, balance-of-
payments disturbances may vary from time to time and from country to
country, the remedies must depend on the circumstances in each case.
Moreover, in choosing what it regards as the appropriate measures of

adjustment, a country is usually influenced not only by immediate balance-of-payments considerations, but also by the effect of such measures on domestic economic activities. In the next few chapters we shall examine in some detail both the causes of balance-of-payments disturbances and the methods that have been developed to cope with them. We shall also explore the possible conflicts that may arise between balance-of-payments policies on the one hand and domestic economic measures on the other. We shall consider—and this is most important of all—the effects that measures taken to cure balance-of-payments problems have on the patterns of international specialization and trade; and, in particular, the possibility that such measures may obstruct the free flow of goods and services between nations.

But first we must answer our initial question: How are international transactions financed?

Foreign Exchange: Nature, Markets, Functions

As in the case of trade carried on within national boundaries, foreign trade consists of an exchange of goods and services for money, and vice versa. Yet while domestic transactions involve payments and receipts in a uniform currency, which can circulate freely and which is generally acceptable as a means of payment throughout the country, the same is not true of international economic transactions. Indeed, here lies one of the major differences between domestic and foreign trade. Since the latter involves trade *between* countries, its practitioners (importers, travelers, and so on) must contend with different national currencies. Each of these currencies constitutes legal tender only within the borders of the issuing country, and hence is normally unacceptable as a means of final payment to the people of another country. Consequently, the pursuit of international economic transactions requires some arrangement whereby the monetary claims arising out of these transactions can be easily settled. In response to this need an elaborate apparatus has developed over the years, consisting of a variety of money and credit instruments, known collectively as foreign exchange.

Foreign exchange, then, is the term applied to credit instruments (e.g., drafts) denominated in foreign currencies and to actual foreign currencies in the form of coins or paper bills. Of course, foreign exchange refers to the currency or credit instruments of a foreign country, not one's own country. For example, to an American, Italian lire constitute foreign exchange, but to an Italian, dollars constitute foreign exchange. Thus, a draft that is denominated in dollars and drawn by an American seller on an Italian importer is no different, from the seller's viewpoint, from a draft he may draw on his local customers; in each case the currency involved is dollars. But from the viewpoint of the Italian importer, the dollar draft represents foreign exchange. In order to honor it, he must obtain dollars—a currency that he does not normally possess. Suppose, however, that in order to pay for his purchase from the United States, the Italian importer draws a draft, denominated in lire, on his bank in Rome and mails it to the American exporter. In this case, the draft is viewed as foreign exchange by the American exporter, since it is payable to him in a currency that does not constitute legal tender in the United States. Hence, an American exporter receiving a draft denominated in Italian lire (or, for that matter, in any other foreign currency) would naturally look for someone to whom he could sell the draft against payment in dollars. He would probably find such a buyer in the foreign-exchange market.

To appreciate the concept of the foreign-exchange market it should be noted that at all times in most countries, there are likely to be some individuals (and institutions) who possess foreign currencies that they want to convert into their own domestic currency, and others who possess domestic currency who wish to buy foreign currencies. The foreign-exchange market is essentially nothing more than an organizational framework within which buyers and sellers of foreign currencies can meet and transact business. But unlike most market places, the foreign-exchange market is not confined to any one location. That is to say, purchases and sales of any currency can be transacted in any number of places where there is a demand for, or a supply of, that particular currency. For example, an American importer in need of pounds sterling may buy them either in New York or, if the supply there is exhausted, from a bank in London. By the same token, a French exporter in possession of dollars may sell them, against payment in francs, through a bank in Paris, London, Zurich, or New York.

Over the years, however, foreign-exchange operations have tended to be concentrated in a few financial centers; most of the buying and selling of foreign currencies is done ultimately through these centers. Thus, during most of the nineteenth century and the early decades of the twentieth century, most international payments were cleared through London's banking facilities. At the same time, the London capital market served as a major source of funds (credit) with which to finance international trade transactions. More recently, and especially since the end of World War II, New York has become the world's leading financial center; a substantial portion of world trade is financed with dollars. Nevertheless, London and several other European financial centers still account for a considerable volume of transactions involving the sales and purchases of foreign currencies.

It should also be noted that while the ultimate suppliers and buyers of foreign exchange are primarily those who engage in exporting, importing, and foreign-investment activities, foreign-exchange transactions are conducted mostly through and by banks. In other words, banks (especially a few large banks) in major financial centers buy and sell most foreign exchange, either on behalf of their customers or for their own account. And in looking for buyers or sellers of a particular foreign currency, these banks usually rely on the services of professional foreign-exchange dealers. In the foreign-exchange market these dealers perform a service similar to that performed by stockbrokers; in other words, they act as middlemen, or intermediaries, between those who wish to buy and those who wish to sell foreign exchange. And like stockbrokers, they charge a commission for their services.

In addition to buying and selling foreign exchange through currency brokers, banks also deal directly with one another. For example, a bank in Hartford, Connecticut, may arrange with its correspondent bank in New York to transfer funds, in pounds sterling, to London. The New York bank then calls upon *its* correspondent bank in London and arranges for the funds to be paid or credited to the account of a designated payee. A similar transfer, though this time involving dollars, may be initiated by a small country bank in England, working through its correspondent bank in London.

These examples illustrate the most important function of the foreign-exchange market: the transfer of funds (purchasing power) from one national currency to another; or, to put it more generally, the clearing of international payments. In the absence of such a transfer mechanism, an international exchange of goods and services could not flourish. For although internationally traded goods could conceivably be exchanged on a barter basis, the scope of such trade would be limited. In any event, one can hardly conceive of an international exchange of services or international flows of capital based on a barter system. In this respect foreign trade does not differ from domestic trade. Both depend on the existence of an efficient mechanism by which payments can be transferred from buyers to sellers regardless of the distance between them. And just as the banking system within each country makes possible the transfer of funds domestically, so banks, by virtue of their participation in the foreign-exchange market, facilitate the transfer of funds internationally.

Important as it is, the so-called "transfer" function is only one of three functions that are normally expected of the foreign-exchange market. The others are: (1) providing short-term credit with which to finance exports and imports, and (2) providing facilities for minimizing foreign-exchange risks. The latter, often called the "hedging" function, will be discussed in the last section of this chapter.

As for the "credit" function of the foreign-exchange market, it is evident that the availability of credit and credit facilities is as much a requirement for the conduct of foreign trade as of domestic trade. Consequently, the same institutions—that is, banks—that are usually called upon to facilitate the transfer of funds from one currency to another have also come to be regarded as a major source of short-term credit with which to finance exports and imports. Although the technical details of such operations need not detain us here, we might note that the extension of credit to finance international trade differs in only one respect from credit operations involved in domestic commerce: The credit instruments that are used to finance international transactions may be denominated in foreign currencies. Hence, the act of granting (or receiving) credit may often involve a purchase or sale of foreign exchange as well.

To better appreciate the nature of the "transfer" and "credit" functions of the foreign-exchange market, we will now examine the mechanism of international payments.

The Mechanism of International Payments

The various methods and procedures employed to transfer funds from one currency to another, or to extend credit to finance trade, differ from each other in detail. Two basic elements, however, are common to all: (1) the presence of banking facilities in each of the countries between which the transfer takes place, and (2) the use of a credit instrument (drafts, telegraphic transfers, travelers' checks, and so on) Of course, the particular instrument used, and the manner in which the transfer is effected, will depend on the circumstances in each case—particularly on whether the importer or the exporter requires credit. But in this connection the most widely used instruments are the *telegraphic transfer* and the *bill of exchange* (or draft).

The telegraphic transfer is an order, cabled by a bank in, say, New York to its correspondent bank in London, to pay out a specified amount in pounds (£) to a designated person or account. As such, the telegraphic transfer is merely a device by which funds can be transmitted on short notice and without delay. Indeed, the only difference between a telegraphic transfer and an ordinary bank draft (or a check) is that the latter is usually mailed from one location to another, whereas the former is cabled. In all other respects, the two are essentially the same; both constitute an order that is drawn on a bank, either by another bank or by an individual, to pay a certain sum to a designated payee on demand.

A commercial draft or a bill of exchange, on the other hand, is an order that a seller draws on a buyer, directing him to pay a specified amount—either on sight (i.e., upon presentation of the draft), or within a certain number of days after presentation. As in the case of a telegraphic transfer or a bank draft, the bill of exchange may be denominated either in the currency of the seller (exporter) or the currency of the buyer (importer). But when the transaction has been fully completed, neither the seller nor the buyer may have actually seen the other's currency. This is because the foreign-exchange transfer mechanism enables the seller to receive payment, and the buyer to make payment, each in his own currency.

Figure 8.1 shows the transfer mechanism in action. It describes two independent transactions, each involving an exporter and an

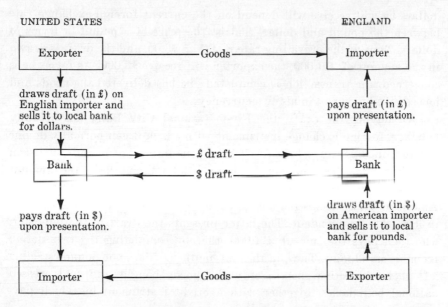

FIGURE *8.1* International Transfer Mechanism

importer. In one case, an American exporter ships (or has already shipped) goods to an English importer, and in the other, a British exporter has sold goods to an importer in the United States. Of course, these two transactions, though unrelated to each other, may occur simultaneously; but this need not be the case. What is important is that in each instance a bank in the United States and a bank in England made possible the transfer of payments from importer to exporter.

Consider first the case of the American exporter and British importer. Each has presumably agreed on the quantity and price of the goods to be shipped, even before the actual shipment takes place. Suppose that under the terms of their agreement payment is to be made in pounds (£) upon arrival of the goods in a British port. Accordingly, once he has shipped the goods, the exporter proceeds to draw a £ draft on the importer, ordering him to pay the agreed amount on sight, either to him personally or to his local bank (let us say that it is the First National City Bank of New York). But since he has little use for pounds, and ultimately wants dollars, the exporter will sell the draft he has drawn to the First National City Bank against payment in dollars. The amount of dollars he will receive will depend on the current foreign-exchange rate between the pound and dollar, that is, the price of a pound in terms of dollars. Thus, if the prevailing rate is £1 = $3.00, and the draft is drawn in the amount of £1,000, the exporter will receive $3,000. As far as he is concerned, the transaction is completed; he has delivered the goods and has received payment in his own currency.

In buying the draft, the First National City Bank has actually bought a foreign-exchange instrument with which it can normally do one of two things. It can sell the draft to anyone in need of pounds, or it can mail it to its correspondent bank in England and have the amount credited to its own account there. In Figure 8.1 it is assumed that the American bank chooses the second course of action; it sends the draft to its British correspondent. The latter presents the draft to the importer, who then pays the sum of £1,000, thereby completing the transaction from his standpoint. Thus, in the end, neither dollars nor pounds sterling left their respective shores; only the goods bought and sold crossed national boundaries, together with a credit instrument by which payment was effected.

There is little difficulty in tracing the other transaction described in Figure 8.1—the one that involves a British exporter and an American importer. Once again, the exporter draws a draft (this time in dollars) on the importer, sells it to his local bank, and receives payment in pounds. The English bank sends the draft to its correspondent bank in New York, which in turn presents it to the American importer. The latter pays in dollars, and these are then credited to the account of the English bank in New York.

Had the importers, in both cases, initiated the payment transaction, the end result would have still been the same. To illustrate, suppose a British importer purchases $3,000 worth of merchandise from an American exporter, agreeing to pay for it upon delivery. When the goods arrive, the importer buys from his local bank a dollar draft, drawn on, say, the First National City Bank of New York, ordering it to pay the exporter $3,000 on demand. The importer pays for the draft in pounds—either in cash or by check—and mails it to the exporter in the United States. Upon receiving the draft, the exporter presents it to the First National City Bank for payment in dollars; and the bank, in turn, debits the account of its British correspondent in that amount.

A slightly different procedure is involved if the importer needs some time in which to sell the goods before he can pay for them. In this case, the exporter might draw a *time* draft, ordering the importer to pay to the bearer the agreed amount within, say, sixty days after delivery of the goods. Having drawn the draft, the exporter might want to hold it until maturity (i.e., for sixty days) before selling it to his local bank. In so doing, the exporter in effect extends credit to the importer, relieving him of the necessity of looking elsewhere for borrowed funds with which to finance his purchase. But if the exporter wants to be paid immediately, he can sell the draft to his local bank at a discount, receiving slightly less than the full amount specified. By buying the draft and holding it until maturity, the bank now exercises the function of extending credit. The remuneration for this function is the difference between the amount it has paid to the exporter and the full amount specified in the draft; it will receive this full amount when it presents the draft to the importer at the end of sixty days.[1]

A more common way of financing imports on credit involves an arrangement initiated by the importer. Take, once again, a British importer who has purchased $3,000 worth of goods from an American exporter but who needs sixty days to pay for them. The importer can arrange through his local bank to draw a time draft, in dollars, on the bank's correspondent in New York, say, the Chase Manhattan Bank, ordering it to pay $3,000 in sixty days to the exporter or to the bearer. This draft is then sent to the exporter who will probably discount it at his local bank, receiving slightly less than $3,000. The exporter's bank, in turn, forwards the draft to the Chase Manhattan Bank for acceptance, and after it has been accepted either sells it in the money market or holds it until maturity. In any event, whoever holds the draft at the end of sixty days would present it to the Chase Manhattan Bank for payment. The bank would pay the full $3,000 specified in the draft and would debit the account of its British correspondent in that amount. As for the importer, he has had two months during which to sell the goods. He now pays his local bank the equivalent sum in pounds (£1,000) plus whatever charges may have been agreed upon in advance.

These examples serve a single purpose: to illustrate how funds can be transferred from one currency to another, and how credit can be extended to finance purchases and sales of internationally traded goods.

---

[1] The bank, however, may choose to sell the draft in the money market before the sixty days are up, in which case it would not receive the full face value.

Although the examples describe different procedures, these can be regarded as variations on a basic theme. For regardless of the particular procedure used at one time or another, the end result is always the same: Importers are able to pay, and exporters are able to be paid, in their own national currencies.

Foreign-Exchange Rates

In describing the international-payments mechanism we have alluded to the fact that prices always exist at which foreign currencies (or, more generally, foreign-exchange instruments) can be bought and sold. These prices, which are listed daily in the financial pages of most metropolitan newspapers, are called foreign-exchange rates. More accurately defined, a foreign-exchange rate is the price of one currency in terms of another. And although it makes little difference in which currency the price is expressed, a foreign-exchange rate may be quoted in one of two ways. Some countries, including the United States, prefer to express the exchange rate as the price, in domestic currency, of a unit of a foreign currency; others quote it as the price, in foreign currency, of a unit of a domestic currency. For example, the foreign-exchange rate between the dollar and the German mark may be quoted either as $1 = DM4 or as DM1 = 25¢. Similarly, the rate between the French franc and the dollar may be expressed either as $1 = F5 or F1 = 20¢.[2]

However it is expressed, the foreign-exchange rate serves an important—in fact, an indispensable—function. For by indicating how many units of one currency must be exchanged for a unit of another, it provides a measure of their relative values for purposes of international trade. As such, it makes it possible to translate domestic costs and prices in different countries into their international price equivalents, and thus to compare the relative prices of different commodities in the international market. To appreciate the significance of this function, try to determine whether it would be cheaper for an American consumer to buy a domestically produced bicycle that costs $50 or a German bicycle that

[2] For a more thorough understanding of exchange-rate quotations, it is a good idea to work through the foreign-exchange listings in the financial pages of a New York or London newspaper. Convert the rates from the domestic to the foreign currency, or vice versa.

costs DM120. You will quickly realize that without the foreign-exchange rate between the dollar and the mark, no meaningful comparisons can be made between the American and German prices. But by knowing that $1 = DM4 (or that DM1 = 25¢), one can easily conclude that German bicycles are cheaper than those produced in the United States; or, to put it the other way around, American bicycles are more expensive than German bicycles. You can easily verify this by multiplying 25¢ by 120, arriving at $30 (less than $50), or by multiplying DM4 by 50, arriving at DM200 (more than DM120). In terms of either currency, German bicycle producers can claim a cost advantage over their American competitors.

If you wish, you may complicate matters a bit by trying to decide whether a Frenchman is likely, under free-market conditions, to buy bicycles from the United States or from Germany. First, compute a *cross rate of exchange* between the mark and the franc, starting with the exchange rate between the dollar and the franc, and that between the dollar and the mark. Thus, if $1 = F5 and $1 = DM4, the cross rate of exchange between the mark and the franc is calculated by dividing 5 by 4, arriving at 1.25. This means that the foreign-exchange rate between the mark and the franc is DM1 = F1.25. Now compare the price, in terms of francs, of German and American bicycles. An American bicycle would cost the Frenchman F250 (= F5 × 50), while a German bicycle would cost him only F150 (= F1.25 × 120). If he wishes to import bicycles from the cheapest source of supply, he should buy them from Germany.

Why is one dollar worth 4 German marks on the one hand and 5 francs on the other? Or, to pose the question in more general terms, what determines the foreign-exchange rates between different currencies? This question is of crucial importance. For since a foreign-exchange rate is essentially a price—the price of one currency in terms of another—it exhibits a characteristic common to all prices: It changes from time to time. In order to assess the effects of changes in foreign-exchange rates, we must first explore the ways in which such rates are determined.

Determination of Foreign-Exchange Rates

Generally speaking, foreign-exchange rates are determined by the forces of supply and demand; the principle involved is the same as that which determines the price of any commodity in a free market. That is to say, the equilibrium price of one currency in terms of another is determined by the interaction between the demand for, and the supply of, that currency. In Figure 8.2, concentrate first on the heavily drawn supply and demand curves. Note that when the exchange rate is £1 = $3, the amount of pounds supplied is equal to the amount of pounds demanded. At any other price, along these two curves, the demand for pounds would either be larger or smaller than their supply. Only £1 = $3 can be considered the equilibrium exchange rate between the pound and the dollar.

But should the demand for pounds increase or the supply of pounds decrease, the price of a pound in terms of dollars would go up. Conversely, should the demand for pounds decrease, or their supply increase, the price of the pound would go down. In either case, however, a new equilibrium exchange rate would be established at the point where supply and demand are equal. Also note that as the dollar price of pounds goes up, the pound price of the dollar necessarily goes down. By the same token, as the dollar price of the pound goes down, the pound price of the dollar goes up. For example, as the price of the pound rises from $3 to $4, the price of the dollar must fall from £1/3 to £1/4. Should the dollar price of the pound fall from $3 to $2, the pound price of the dollar would rise from £1/3 to £1/2.

Figure 8.2 reflects what is commonly termed a system of *freely fluctuating exchange rates*. Under such a system, the forces of supply and demand are the sole determinants of foreign-exchange rates; and as supply and demand change, so do the exchange rates. In actual practice, however, foreign-exchange rates are seldom allowed the kind of fluctuations that might result from the unrestrained operation of free-market forces. For although the system of freely fluctuating exchange rates has its advocates, it is generally recognized that constantly fluctuating rates, especially if the fluctuations are wide, may introduce an element of uncertainty into international trade relations. Consequently, most governments—even those that permit the forces of supply and demand to influence the foreign-exchange market—usually impose limits on the range within which the foreign-exchange rate may fluctuate. Such action is called pegging; the result is a system of *pegged exchange rates*.

Viewed in historical perspective, a pegged exchange-rate system was

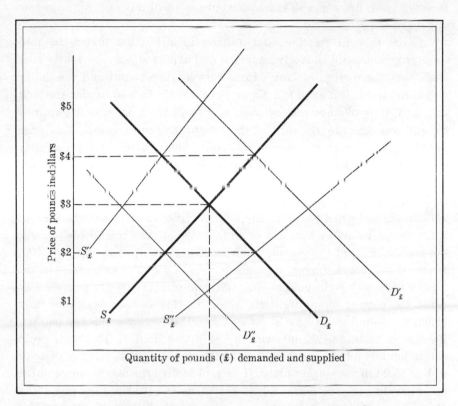

FIGURE 8.2   Exchange-Rate Determination (Freely Fluctuating
Exchange Rates)

maintained automatically by the international gold standard. Under the
gold standard, to which most countries adhered from about 1870 to 1914,
each country defined its national currency unit in terms of a certain
amount of gold (i.e., so many grains of gold per $, £, or other currency
unit). Each government did so by setting an official price per ounce of
gold in terms of its national currency, and standing ready to buy and
sell unlimited amounts of gold at that price. For example, suppose that
under the gold standard the official price of gold is set at $35 per ounce
in the United States and £7 per ounce in England. This means in effect
that the gold content, or mint value, of $1 is equal to 1/35 of an ounce,
while the gold content of £1 is 1/7 of an ounce. Hence, £1 is worth, in

terms of gold, five times as much as $1; or, $5 will buy the same amount of gold as £1.

Given this information, and bearing in mind that under the gold standard, gold could be freely imported and exported, we can rightly conclude that the foreign-exchange rates between the pound and the dollar would be established at £1 = $5, or $1 = £1/5. Indeed, under the gold standard, the exchange rate between any two currencies was determined by, and was equal to, the ratio of their respective mint values. And once established, the foreign-exchange rate could fluctuate only within a fairly narrow range above and below the mint ratio—a range whose limits were set by the cost of shipping gold from one country to another.

To illustrate, suppose that the cost of shipping 1/7 of an ounce of gold from the United States to England, or from the latter to the former, is 2¢. Suppose further that due to an increase in the demand for pounds, the market price of the pound, in terms of dollars, rises to £1 = $5.03. Under these circumstances, it would pay to buy gold with dollars in the United States, ship the gold to England, and sell it there for pounds. For while the cost of obtaining each pound in this fashion would be only $5.02, the pound could be sold for $5.03 on the foreign-exchange market. By the 'same token, no one who, by shipping gold to England, could obtain pounds for the cost of £1 = $5.02, would want to pay the price of £1 = $5.03 in the market place. Hence, in reality the market price of the pound could not even reach £1 = $5.03. Indeed, it would not rise above $5.02. In our example, this rate represents the so-called *gold export point* of the United States—that is, the rate at which gold tends to be shipped from the United States to England and to be exchanged there for pounds. The same rate also represents the *gold import point* of England.

A similar process, working in reverse, is likely to swing into action whenever the market price of the pound falls below the rate of £1 = $5. Thus, should the price decline to £1 = $4.97, it would become profitable to buy gold in England, ship it to the United States, and sell it there for dollars. For since the amount of gold that can be bought for £1 can be sold for $5.00, anyone buying gold in England and selling it in the United States would be able to exchange pounds for dollars at the rate of £1 = $4.98 (i.e., $5 minus 2¢ shipping costs). Given this opportunity, holders of pounds would not offer them for sale at the market price of £1 = $4.97; they would use them instead to buy gold in England and ship it to the United States. As the market supply of pounds decreases and the demand for them increases, their dollar price tends to rise, moving up from £1 = \$4.97 and closer to £1 = \$4.98. Once again, the movement of gold would tend to stop the foreign-exchange rate between the pound and the dollar from deviating by more than 2¢ from the ratio of their mint values. In this case, however, the shipment of gold would set the *lower* limit to the fluctuation in the price of the pound. The rate which reflects this limit (i.e., £1 = \$4.98) is known as the gold export point of England and the gold import point of the United States.

The pegging of foreign-exchange rates under the gold standard was largely the function, or more correctly the result, of private transactions. No governmental interference in the foreign-exchange market was necessary. For, having established an official price at which they stood ready to buy and sell gold, the authorities in each country could rely on private interests to respond to changes in foreign-exchange rates by shipping gold in one direction or another. Indeed, private shipments of gold, initiated whenever the exchange rate moved above or below the ratio of mint values, confined exchange-rate fluctuations to a fairly narrow range. The limits to that range were set, as we have just seen, by the gold export and gold import points, the latter being determined by the cost of shipping gold from country to country.

The disappearance of the international gold standard, a subject to which we shall pay some attention in later chapters, gave rise to new devices for the determination and pegging of exchange rates. One such device, involving direct regulation and control over foreign-exchange transactions, will be discussed in some detail in Chapter 11. At the moment we might observe that under a system of *exchange controls,* free-market forces cannot influence foreign-exchange rates. The authorities set these rates arbitrarily; and because they can rigidly control the supply and demand of foreign currencies, they can maintain the exchange rate at whatever level they consider desirable.

Setting exchange controls aside for the time being, we turn now to what is commonly called a *flexible exchange-rate* system. First appearing during the 1920's, a number of such systems have been in use over the past forty years or so. Although they have varied in detail, they share two basic features: (1) the existence of a free foreign exchange market, in which exchange rates are determined by the forces of supply and demand, and (2) the maintenance of fairly stable exchange rates through official purchases and sales of foreign currencies on the open market. In other words, under a flexible exchange-rate system, foreign-exchange rates, although not rigidly fixed, are not allowed to deviate too far from the rate that the government has officially decided to maintain.

To illustrate : Suppose that, having abandoned the gold standard, the British government decides to maintain the value of the pound, in terms of dollars, at £1 = $4, give or take 2¢. Should market forces push the rate up to £1 = $4.03, the authorities would enter the market, offering to sell pounds for dollars at the rate of £1 = $4.02. Conversely, should the market price of the pound fall to £1 = $3.97, the authorities would offer to buy pounds at the rate of £1 = $3.98. Thus the government actually sets limits—$3.98 and $4.02—on the range of exchange-rate fluctuations that it will permit. For by standing ready to supply an unlimited amount of pounds at the price of $4.02 per pound, and to demand an unlimited amount of pounds at the price of $3.98, the authorities can prevent the pound and the dollar exchange rate from moving above or below these limits. As Figure 8.3 shows, such open-market operations transform the supply and demand curves of the pound into horizontal lines, beginning at the limits established by the authorities.

The operations described above are usually carried out by exchange-stabilization funds. These funds, the best known of which is Britain's Exchange Equalization Account, are endowed by the government with monetary resources with which to finance their open-market activities in different currencies (including the national currency itself). Thus, whenever an exchange-stabilization fund engages in open-market purchases of the national currency, it draws upon its resources of foreign exchange and/or gold. On the other hand, when the fund sells the national currency, it accumulates foreign exchange and gold. The ability of an exchange-stabilization fund to support the exchange rate between the domestic and foreign currencies depends on the adequacy of its resources, especially its foreign-exchange and gold reserves. Should these reserves be exhausted, the fund would be unable to support the value of the national currency on the free market, and the government might be forced to impose direct controls over foreign-exchange transactions. Indeed, the fear of depleting their foreign-exchange reserves, in the face of prolonged market pressure on their national currencies, has often been

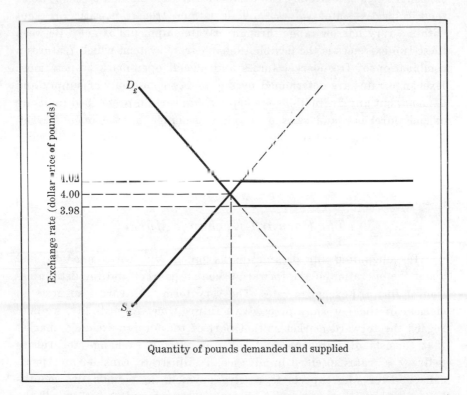

FIGURE *8.3* Exchange-Rate Determination (Flexible Exchange-Rate System)

a major factor in prompting governments to adopt exchange-control systems. For once adopted, exchange controls can effectively prevent market forces from influencing the exchange rate, thus relieving the pressure on officially held foreign-exchange reserves. But more about this later.

Summarizing our findings, we may briefly distinguish between the three basic methods of exchange-rate determination that can operate in the absence of exchange controls. At one extreme is the freely fluctuating exchange-rate system, in which the determination of exchange rates is left entirely to the forces of supply and demand in the foreign-exchange market. At the other extreme is the fixed exchange-rate system, associated historically with the international gold standard. In this system, exchange rates between any two currencies are determined by the ratio of their respective mint values; any deviations from this ratio are kept within a very narrow range through private shipments of gold. Between these two extremes is the flexible exchange-rate system, which features a combination of free-market forces and official open-market operations: Exchange rates are determined by day-to-day conditions of supply and demand, but any fluctuations are kept within certain prescribed limits by official purchases and sales of foreign exchange on the open market. Finally, although no two systems can coexist in one country at the same time, elements of each can be combined in various ways, as will become evident in the course of our discussion in Chapter 12.

The Forward-Exchange Market

In concluding our present discussion, a few words must be said about the operation of the forward-exchange market and the determination of forward-exchange rates. The very term "forward" suggests an element of time, or more precisely, a future time. Accordingly, we may regard the forward market as that part of the foreign-exchange market that consists of purchases and sales of foreign exchange for future delivery, at rates specified in advance. To illustrate, consider an American exporter who expects to receive payment in pounds two months hence, and who, upon receipt of such payment, will want to sell the pounds for dollars. He can enter into an agreement to sell the pounds sixty days from today at a rate decided upon at the time the agreement is made. Or, take an American importer who in sixty days will need a certain amount of pounds with which to honor a sterling draft drawn upon him by a British exporter. The importer can buy these pounds today at a certain price, and expect to receive them around the date on which he must make payment to the exporter.

The rates that govern such transactions are known as *forward-exchange* rates, in order to distinguish them from *spot* rates, which apply to purchases and sales of foreign exchange for immediate delivery. Forward rates are usually quoted for one-month, three-month, and six-month delivery dates, and are listed alongside the spot rates in the financial pages of large-city newspapers. Although the forward rates are quoted (or specified) at the time an agreement is made to buy or sell, payment is not made until the foreign exchange is actually delivered. Thus, a person buying £1,000 for delivery in three months, at the rate of £1 = \$2.76, would pay the \$2,760 that is involved only when the seller delivers the pounds to him. Similarly, anyone selling pounds for future delivery is not obliged to furnish them to the buyer until the date that was agreed upon in the contract.

Why would anyone wish to buy or sell foreign exchange for future delivery? One obvious reason stems from the desire of exporters and importers to protect themselves against possible losses due to exchange-rate fluctuations. Indeed, one of the basic functions of the foreign-exchange market is to enable both exporters and importers to eliminate, or at least minimize, future uncertainties by covering their exchange risks through forward purchases or sales of foreign exchange. To appreciate the significance of this function, consider first the matter of exchange risk from the viewpoint of exporters.

Suppose that an American exporter enters into an agreement to sell \$3 million worth of goods to a British customer, agreeing to receive payment in pounds within three months after delivery of the goods. If at the time the agreement is made, the spot rate between the pound and the dollar is £1 = \$3.00, the exporter calculates that his price is £1 million and would probably quote this amount to his customer. But since his calculation is based on the present rate of exchange, the exporter cannot be certain that the sale of £1 million three months from now would actually fetch \$3 million. If the spot price of the pound at that time is greater than \$3, say \$3.10, the exporter could sell the pounds he has just received for a total of \$3,100,000, thus reaping an unexpected bonus. But if, on the other hand, the spot price of the pound is only \$2.85 when he receives payment, the same £1 million would be worth only \$2,850,000, or \$150,000 less than the value of the goods shipped.

It is against the latter possibility—the possibility of a loss due to a fall in the exchange rate—that our exporter may wish to protect himself. He can do so, thanks to the existence of the forward-exchange market, by entering into an agreement to sell pounds, three months hence, at the same time that he enters into the contract for the sale of goods. The rate governing the forward sale of pounds may be lower than today's spot rate. Indeed, if market dealers expect the dollar price of the pound to fall over the next two or three months, the forward rate may be quoted at, say, £1 = $2.90, and the exporter would receive only $2,900,000 when he delivers the pounds. But by knowing in advance what he will receive in dollars, the exporter is in a better position to quote an appropriate price in pounds to his British client—a price that, when translated into dollars, would cover the costs (including profit) of producing and selling the goods.

While exporters make use of the forward market to protect themselves against the risk of a fall in the price of foreign exchange, importers engage in forward-market activities in order to guard against the opposite risk—the risk that a foreign currency might appreciate between the time they incur the obligation to pay and the time payment must be made in that currency. For example, a rise of a few cents in the dollar price of the pound may mean a considerable loss to an American importer who has to buy pounds at a higher spot price than he had anticipated three months before. Should the importer wish to cover himself against such a loss, he can enter into an agreement to buy pounds for future delivery, at the same time that he incurs the obligation to pay the British supplier. Depending on the market outlook, the forward rate of the pound may be either lower or higher than today's spot rate. But the importer can at least sleep peacefully, knowing that he has protected himself against a possible rise in the price of the pound during the next three months.

In addition to exporters and importers, two other groups may avail themselves of the opportunities offered by the forward-exchange market. One of these consists of investors who wish to take advantage of a differential between interest rates at home and abroad by investing in short-term foreign securities. For example, an American investor who contemplates a short-term British investment can protect its dollar value by selling pounds forward. At the same time that he buys pounds to invest in, say, three-month British government securities, he can contract to sell pounds for dollars three months hence. In this way he can protect himself against a possible fall in the spot price of the pound when the securities mature and he is ready to convert the proceeds into dollars. An Englishman, investing in United States government securities, may follow a reverse course if he expects the price of the dollar, in terms of pounds, to decline between the time he makes his investment and the time the securities mature. He can sell dollars in the forward market at the same time that he buys dollars in the spot market.

International movements of funds for purposes of short-term investment are commonly referred to as *interest arbitrage*. We need not concern ourselves with the mechanics of such movements; it is more important to realize, however, that the prime consideration behind short-term capital flows is their expected rate of return. That is to say, if investors can obtain a higher yield by investing in foreign rather than in domestic securities, they will be inclined to employ their funds abroad. Hence, their forward-market activities are undertaken merely to protect the value of their foreign investment in terms of their domestic currency.

Not so, however, the speculators, who engage in forward-market activities in order to profit from the foreign-exchange transactions themselves. In other words, in entering into a forward sale or purchase contract, the speculator in effect gambles on future movements in the exchange rate, hoping that they will turn in his favor. If he is wrong he may, of course, suffer considerable losses; but if his hunch proves correct, he may reap a handsome profit. Thus, whether the speculator gains or loses depends largely on his ability to guess correctly the future trends of the market—or, more precisely, his ability to *out*guess the market.

Although it is difficult to ascertain the importance of pure speculation in different foreign-exchange markets, there is little doubt that speculative elements exist in almost all transactions involving forward sales and purchases of foreign exchange. Exporters who cover exchange risks by selling foreign exchange forward are actually speculating on the possibility that the spot rate, at the time of delivery, will be lower than the forward rate that governs their forward sale contract. Or, importers cover their risk by buying forward because they suspect that the spot rate, at the time they will need the foreign exchange, will be higher than their forward purchase price. Should their expectations suddenly shift, they will rush to take different forward positions—positions they would consider more advantageous.

Yet neither the activities of speculators nor of exporters and importers determine, under normal market conditions, the forward-exchange rate between a domestic and a foreign currency. That rate, or more correctly, the *relation* between the spot and forward rate is influenced primarily by the difference between short-term interest rates at home and abroad. Put differently, the demand and supply of forward exchange for purposes of covering interest-arbitrage transactions largely determines the relation between the spot and forward-exchange rates of the currency involved. And although the action of pure speculators may at times strongly influence the forward rate, more often the difference between the spot and forward rates tends to equal the difference between the prevailing short-term interest rates in the domestic and foreign money markets.

This is easy to appreciate. As long as the difference between the spot and forward rates is smaller than the interest-rate differential between two money markets, short-term funds would tend to flow toward the market with the higher interest rate. And inasmuch as such flows would presumably be covered against exchange risks, their very existence would increase the demand for spot exchange and the supply of forward exchange (of the currency in which the higher-yielding assets are denominated). Consequently, the spot rate would tend to rise and the forward rate would tend to fall, in relation to each other, until the difference between them would just about equal the interest-rate differential between the two money markets. When this happens—as it would under free-market conditions—the flow of funds would stop.

Thus, international differences in interest rates exert a major influence on the relation between the spot and forward-exchange rates. And since interest-rate differentials between money markets often reflect the monetary policies of the countries concerned, it is not surprising that the direction of international short-term capital flows may be influenced by the kind of monetary policies of different countries. Indeed, domestic monetary measures may at times play an important role in affecting foreign-trade relations—a role whose full implications will become increasingly clear as we examine the causes and consequences of balance-of-payments disturbances.

9

Balance-of-Payments Disequilibrium: Causes

I F NOT FOR THE MECHANISM
that can transfer purchasing power from one currency to another, international economic transactions would be mere barter exchanges; they would be limited in scope and confined to a narrow range of commodities. This mechanism, as we have just seen, consists of foreign-exchange markets in which foreign exchange can be bought and sold. And largely because of the facilities provided by such markets, trade can flourish between countries, each with its own national currency and its own monetary system. But although the international-payments mechanism facilitates and promotes the international exchange of goods and services, it cannot automatically produce the foreign exchange that residents of one country may need in order to finance their purchases from another. Indeed, all the foreign-exchange market can do is to bring together buyers and sellers of foreign exchange. The actual demand for, and supply of, foreign currencies arise out of the demand for, and supply of, internationally traded goods and services.

This is an important link between foreign-exchange activities and the balance of payments. Since the balance of payments is a record of a country's international economic transactions, it necessarily reflects its demand for foreign currencies as well as the demand of other countries for its particular currency. Put differently, a country's international transactions, as indicated by its balance of payments, give rise to its demand for, and supply of, foreign exchange during a given period of time. Thus, the transactions which entail flows of payments into the country (exports of goods and services, imports of capital, and so on) constitute the sources of foreign-exchange supply. On the other hand, transactions that result in *out*flows of payments (imports of goods and services, exports of capital, and so on) indicate the country's demand for foreign exchange. It is ultimately in these terms (i.e., the demand for, and supply of, foreign exchange) that the strengths and weaknesses of a country's balance-of-payments position must be analyzed and judged.

Equilibrium and Disequilibrium in the Balance of Payments

An appreciation of the causes and effects of balance-of-payments disturbances must rest on a clear understanding of what is meant by balance-of-payments "equilibrium." Although the term defies exact definition, its meaning may be conveyed by a comparison with its opposite: balance-of-payments "disequilibrium." Hence, as a first step we must distinguish between balance-of-payments equilibrium and disequilibrium. For not only does such a distinction throw light on the nature of balance-of-payments problems, it also provides a useful background against which to consider the various solutions to these problems.

We established earlier a basic principle, namely, that a balance of payments must always balance. It will be recalled that this principle is a direct reflection of the accounting equality between total credits and total debits in the balance-of-payments statement. Thus, by regarding the transactions which entail receipts from other countries as credits and those that involve payments to other countries as debits, the statistician can safely conclude that total receipts and total expenditures are equal, and that the entire statement is therefore in balance. Yet this accounting equality, or statistical balance, represents nothing more than an ex post relationship. In other words, it merely records the fact that over a given period of time the total value of the transactions defined as credits was equal to the total value of the transactions defined as debits. And precisely because it is essentially a relation based on a definition, this accounting equality cannot be taken as proof that the balance of payments was or was not in a state of equlibrium.

But while the statistical balance does not constitute a test by which to judge a country's balance-of-payments position, the manner in which this balance is attained does constitute such a test. For what matters is not the equality between total credits and total debits, but how this equality is achieved and maintained. More specifically, it is the equality or inequality between certain types of credit and debit transactions that determines whether the balance of payments is in equilibrium. In order to appreciate the significance of such relationships, we must classify balance-of-payments transactions as (1) independently motivated transactions, and (2) compensatory transactions.[1]

Simply defined, independently motivated transactions are those that are considered desirable in themselves and are undertaken for their own sake. Typical of such transactions are exports and imports of goods and services, private long-term capital movements, and private gifts and donations. Private short-term capital flows may at times also be conceived of as independently motivated transactions, especially when they are initiated by a desire to exploit interest-rate differentials between countries. As suggested by these examples, an independently motivated transaction is one that is undertaken without particular regard to balance-of-payments considerations, and is uninfluenced by any balance-of-payments problems. Compensatory transactions, on the other hand, are those that are initiated by the need to correct imbalances in one or several categories of the balance of payments. These transactions, which nowadays are carried out almost exclusively by the government or one of its agencies, include the export and/or import of monetary gold, the receipt or granting of short-term credit, and the accumulation or depletion of officially held foreign-exchange reserves. Whatever form they actually take, however, compensatory transactions are what their desig-

[1] These terms are borrowed from L. Yeager. See his *International Monetary Relations* (New York: Harper & Row, 1966), p. 46. Essentially the same distinction has been made by J. E. Meade, using the terms *autonomous* and *accommodating* transactions. See J. E. Meade, *The Balance of Payments* (London: Oxford University Press, 1951).

nation implies; they are intended to offset, or to compensate for, a possible imbalance between independently motivated credit and debit transactions.

What constitutes an imbalance between independently motivated transactions? Suppose that during the course of a given year, a country imported more goods and services than it exported. Does its current-account deficit represent an imbalance that requires compensatory credit transactions in other balance-of-payments categories? Not necessarily. In fact, the current-account deficit may be matched by independently motivated capital inflows; the result is an overall balance between the independently motivated credit and debit transactions. Or, conversely, a surplus on current account may be offset by independently motivated capital outflows, producing once again a balance between independently motivated credit and debit items. Indeed, either one of these cases can represent a state of equilibrium in the country's balance of payments. As long as its independently motivated debit and credit transactions balance each other, the country is living within its means; it need not borrow, nor must it deplete its gold and foreign-exchange reserves in order to help finance the current level of its foreign expenditures.

Matters are quite different, however, when a current-account deficit is not fully balanced by an independently motivated inflow of funds, or when a current-account surplus is more than offset by outflows of such funds (the latter phenomenon has been typical of the United States balance of payments in recent years). In both cases, the outcome can be described as an excess of independently motivated debit transactions over independently motivated credit transactions. Such an excess of debits over credits is called a balance-of-payments deficit; its size is measured by the value of the compensatory *credit* transactions (e.g., sale of gold, depletion of foreign-exchange reserves, short-term borrowing by the government) that are needed to achieve an overall balance in the balance of payments. But should independently motivated credits exceed independently motivated debits, the balance of payments is said to be in an overall surplus position—a situation that stimulates compensatory *debit* transactions (e.g., accumulation of gold and of foreign exchange, granting of loans) by the country in question.

Both a deficit and a surplus, as defined in the preceding paragraph, denote a state of disequilibrium in the balance of payments. Thus, in distinguishing between equilibrium and disequilibrium, one must regard not only deficits, but surpluses as well, as disequilibrating phenomena. For while it is true that a balance-of-payments deficit poses more serious problems than does a surplus, either constitutes a departure from a state of equilibrium. That state, as we have just seen, requires an equality between the independently motivated credit and debit transactions—or, if you like, an absence of compensatory transactions. Hence, any violation of this requirement, whether an excess of debits over credits or vice versa, constitutes a balance-of-payments disturbance, and suggests the need for adjustment measures

Indeed, the only practical difference between a disequilibrium in the form of a deficit and one in the form of a surplus lies in the degree of urgency with which each must be faced. Thus, a country with a balance-of-payments surplus can conceivably continue to accumulate gold and foreign exchange indefinitely. Such a country might, therefore, be inclined to turn a deaf ear to any suggestions that it quickly adopt measures designed to restore equilibrium in its balance of payments. A deficit, on the other hand, cannot be allowed to go on forever. For since definite limits exist as to the amount of gold and foreign-exchange reserves that any one country possesses at any one time, a deficit country is under much greater pressure to apply corrective measures to its balance of payments. If it fails to do so, it runs the risk of depleting its reserves and/or exhausting outside sources of credit, neither possibility can be looked upon with favor.

To sum up: The distinction between equilibrium and disequilibrium seems to suggest that balance-of-payments disturbances are discrepancies between the amount of foreign exchange demanded by, and supplied to, a country while pursuing its ordinary international economic transactions over a given period of time. Put differently, a disequilibrium indicates either that the country currently demands more foreign exchange than it currently earns through normal transactions, or that it currently earns a greater amount of foreign exchange than it needs to cover its current expenditures abroad. There are reasons for such discrepancies, whether they are temporary or prolonged. These reasons must be correctly analyzed in each case before the proper measures can be taken. In the remainder of this chapter we will examine the reasons that may underlie a state of disequilibrium in a balance of payments.

Short-Term (Cyclical) Disequilibrium

Starting from an equilibrium position, a balance of payments may be jolted into a state of either surplus or deficit by any one of countless different forces, or by several of them. And while it would be a hopeless task to catalogue all the influences that can conceivably affect a country's international economic relations, we can identify certain major groups of forces by the types of disequilibria that they are likely to produce. One identification scheme comes readily to mind; it is based on the duration of the disequilibrium itself. With this particular scheme, we may conveniently distinguish between disequilibria that are temporary, fleeting occurrences, and those that tend to persist over a considerable period of time. However, the distinction between short-term and long-term disequilibria does not exhaust all possible bases of classifications; it merely helps to keep our inquiry within manageable limits. With this in mind, we will begin by considering the nature and causes of the so-called short-term disequilibria.

EXOGENOUS CAUSES

Countries whose exports consist largely of agricultural products are often subject to a temporary balance-of-payments disequilibrium caused by purely natural forces. For example, an unusually good harvest may lead to a balance-of-payments surplus one year while an unexpected crop failure may result in a deficit in another year. Such alternations between surpluses and deficits, especially if they occur regularly and are relatively small, do not pose serious problems. For since a surplus period is characterized by the accumulation of foreign-exchange reserves, the latter can be drawn upon during a period of deficit. A similar pattern may be observed in countries whose exports are subject to seasonal cycles of production. During certain months of the year these countries' exports greatly exceed their imports, thus enabling the accumulation of foreign-exchange reserves for use during subsequent deficit periods.

Industrialized countries may also experience temporary balance-of-payments disturbances that are due mainly to natural phenomena. Thus, a sudden crop failure, by reducing the expected supply of domestically produced agricultural products, may necessitate increased importation of foodstuffs. And unless such an increase in imports is matched by an equal increase in exports, it may well result in a deficit. A temporary deficit in the balance of payments of an industrial country can also arise out of prolonged labor disputes and/or strikes. By leading to work stoppages, such strikes reduce either the production or shipments of exports.[2] Moreover, if a strike results in an overall shortage of goods and materials used domestically, it may stimulate an increase in imports; this, together with a possible reduction in exports, would only aggravate the deficit.

In all of these cases, temporary balance-of-payments disturbances were attributed to so-called *exogenous* forces. Now we turn to examine the influence of *endogenous* variables. Two such forces are: (1) changes in income, and (2) changes in price.

INCOME CHANGES

The interrelationship between national income and foreign trade was explored in some detail in Chapter 2. At this point we are primarily concerned, however, with only one aspect of this interrelationship: the influence of changes in a country's national income on changes in its foreign trade.

It will be recalled that a rise in national income is likely to result in an increase in imports, while a fall in income is likely to produce a decrease. This causal relation between income and imports—a relation formalized by the marginal-propensity-to-import concept—bears directly on our present investigation. For since a rise in income will, in general, result in a rise in imports, it is bound to affect the balance between exports and imports, and thus may cause a deficit in the balance of payments. Conversely, a fall in income will probably cause imports to decline and may therefore bring about a balance-of-payments surplus. Such results may not materialize, however, if, at the same time that imports rise or fall, other independently motivated transactions happen to take place in an opposite direction. But if we assume that other transactions retain

---

[2] For example, the recent seamen's strike in England has been blamed, at least in part, for the curtailment of British exports and the aggravation of Britain's balance-of-payments position during the spring and early summer of 1966.

their existing levels, we cannot escape the conclusion that a balance-of-payments equilibrium may be temporarily disturbed by cyclical fluctuations in national income.

This is an important conclusion. It means, in effect, that a balance-of-payments disequilibrium may be rooted in just about any economic force that causes a rise or a fall in national income. Thus, a sudden spurt of domestic investment activity may translate itself into a balance-of-payments deficit; the same goes for a sudden income-tax reduction. Conversely, a decline in investment activities or a rise in income tax may well turn a balance-of-payments equilibrium into a state of surplus.

Going one step further, we must recognize that a balance-of-payments disequilibrium may be caused not only by income changes at home but also by changes in income abroad. For example, a rise in country A's income, and the subsequent rise in the level of its imports, may produce a surplus in country B's balance of payments—if the latter happens to be the supplier of A's imports. Conversely, a fall in A's income may result in a decline in B's exports, and thus precipitate a deficit in its balance of payments. In short, cyclical fluctuations in income, whether originating at home or abroad, are one of the major causes of short-term balance-of-payments disequilibrium. Depending on the direction of such changes, a country may find itself either in a surplus or in a deficit position vis-à-vis its trading partners.

PRICE CHANGES

Price changes in this context refer to general increases or decreases in price levels rather than to increases or decreases in the prices of specific commodities. In other words, by a "price change" we mean a situation that is commonly described either as inflation or deflation. Such price changes normally originate in a discrepancy between the aggregate supply of, and the aggregate demand for, goods and services. Should aggregate demand exceed aggregate supply at the current price level, prices tend to rise, while an excess of supply over demand tends to push prices down.

It is easy to visualize the impact of changes in general price levels on a country's balance of payments. Consider a case where the general price level in one country rises in relation to price levels in other countries.

Faced with rising prices, consumers may well shift some of their purchases from the relatively more expensive domestic goods to the relatively less expensive substitutes produced abroad. In addition, foreign consumers may now demand less of the country's exports and look elsewhere for cheaper sources of supply. Working simultaneously, these two tendencies are apt to produce a deficit in the balance of payments of the inflation-ridden country. Indeed, inflation has traditionally been regarded—and with good reason—as a major underlying cause of a balance-of-payments deficit.

Deflation, on the other hand, is normally looked upon as a source of surplus in the balance of payments. Since deflation is characterized by a decline in the general price level, it may induce consumers to shift their demand from imports to relatively less expensive domestic substitutes. At the same time, falling prices at home may cause an increase in foreign demand for the country's exports. Hence, by causing imports to decline and exports to rise, deflationary price changes tend to produce a balance-of-payments surplus.

A balance-of-payments disequilibrium resulting from general price variations, such as those just described, is usually called a *monetary disequilibrium*. It indicates that the national price level in one country is presumably out of line with national price levels elsewhere.[3] One should not conclude, however, that monetary disequilibrium is necessarily a short-term phenomenon or that it tends to correct itself automatically. Indeed, historical experience indicates that general price movements may persist in one direction or another for a considerable period of time, and that on occasion they may actually be caused and sustained by official actions. This is particularly true with respect to inflationary trends; a certain degree of domestic inflation may be openly tolerated, and at times deliberately encouraged, if it is considered in the interest of some short-term or long-term national economic objective. Under such circumstances, one surely cannot expect the resulting balance-of-payments deficit to disappear without the aid of corrective measures applied directly to the balance of payments itself.

[3] A variation on this theme is often called an *exchange-rate disequilibrium*. It implies that while a country's general price level may be in line with that of another, its currency is either overvalued or undervalued in relation to foreign currencies. But more of this in subsequent chapters.

Yet whether they alternate rapidly between inflationary and deflationary phases, or persist in one phase for a considerable period of time, general price changes can still be regarded as short-term phenomena. These price changes do not in themselves alter the basic economic structure of a nation any more than do cyclical fluctuations in money national income. Hence, a balance-of-payments disequilibrium that is rooted in one or both of these forces does not in itself imply a fundamental change in the patterns of trade between the country in question and the rest of the world. It is precisely for this reason that we can refer to such a disequilibrium as a short-term phenomenon; this is to be distinguished from a long-term disequilibrium, a discussion of which follows.

Long-Term (Structural) Disequilibrium

Broadly speaking, any balance-of-payments disequilibrium can qualify as "long-term" if it simply lasts long enough. Thus, a country that year after year continues to accumulate gold and foreign-exchange reserves may be said to be in a chronic, or long-term, surplus position. Or, a country which over a long period of time must resort to, or depend on, compensatory credit transactions in its balance of payments, can be said to be in a chronic deficit. Such a broad definition of long-term disequilibrium, however, naturally raises the question: How long is long? How long must a disequilibrium persist before it can be called "long-term" as opposed to "short-term"?

No precise answer can be given to this question. In any event, a definition of balance-of-payments disequilibrium, based solely on the length of time involved, misses the crux of the problem. For we do not distinguish between a long-term and a short-term disequilibrium by the element of time alone, but rather by the basic forces that lie behind each of them. Thus, the nature of its underlying causes provides the crucial test as to the type of disequilibrium a country may experience. And having described (in the preceding paragraphs) the character of the causes that may give rise to short-term disequilibrium, we may now distinguish between some of the more important forces behind long-term balance-of-payments disturbances.

Here it would be helpful to recall the discussion in Chapter 7. That discussion dwelled on the relations between changes in the patterns of production and/or consumption, and subsequent changes in the patterns of international specialization and trade. Precisely such changes (i.e., changes that alter comparative-cost relations or basic patterns of demand) will probably produce long-term disturbances in a country's balance of payments. These so-called *structural* changes may come about suddenly, as when a new product or a new technological process makes its appearance, or they may evolve over a period of time (e.g., gradual changes in factor endowments, rising incomes). But in either case they are bound to affect basic trade relations and hence the balance-of-payments position of the country or countries involved.

To illustrate, let us consider first changes in the patterns of demand. As we saw in Chapter 7, both the demonstration effect and rising levels of income may combine to influence the basic tastes and preferences of consumers in different countries. Such changes in consumption patterns may in turn cause either an increase or a decrease in the demand for a country's exports. Depending on which of these shifts in demand has actually occurred, the country's balance of payments may be favorably or adversely affected. For example, a country whose exports are no longer favored in foreign markets, or whose own residents are beginning to express preference for some foreign-made goods, may experience severe balance-of-payments difficulties. Its exports may decline while its imports rise—and either of these tendencies may produce a balance-of-payments deficit. Conversely, a country whose exports enjoy an increase in foreign demand—or whose domestic consumers shift their preferences to locally produced goods—is more likely to find itself with a balance-of-payments surplus—at least, as long as these tendencies continue.

Yet changes in consumption patterns alone do not give rise to structural changes in the patterns of international trade. Changes in technology and changing factor endowments may be equally responsible for changes in the volume and/or composition of a country's exports and imports. We need not dwell here on all the possible causes that may affect the basic structure of productive activities in different countries. Suffice to say that inasmuch as these structural changes translate themselves into changes in comparative-cost relations, they are bound to disturb existing patterns of international trade and, through them, the balance-of-payments positions of the countries involved. An example or two will illustrate the point.

A technological innovation, resulting in substantial cost savings, may give a country an absolute or comparative-cost advantage in the production of an article it had previously imported from other countries. As a consequence, the country may experience a rise in exports and a decline in imports, which together may produce a balance-of-payments surplus. Or, gradual accumulation of capital may enable a primary-producing country to become an efficient producer of manufactured products, capable of competing with previous suppliers in its own domestic market as well as in third markets. And while the country that emerges as an exporter of manufactured products may now enjoy a surplus in its balance of payments, its competitors may be faced with severe balance-of-payments maladjustments.

A sudden loss of capital, typified by wartime destruction of production facilities, may also be regarded as a possible cause of balance-of-payments difficulties. For with its production facilities impaired, a country would have to rely on increased imports (to relieve local scarcities), while at the same time it might be unable to produce enough exports with which to pay for them. Until it could manage to rebuild its productive strength or to develop new lines of production—neither of which can be accomplished overnight—the country would suffer a prolonged balance-of-payments disequilibrium.

A closely related source of structural disequilibrium consists of changes in international flows of long-term capital, especially those that are independently motivated. For example, a country may be able to run a deficit on current account year after year if at the same time it happens to receive private long-term capital from abroad. What is more important, the country's entire range of economic activities may rest on, or be largely governed by, the expectation that the flow of foreign capital will continue indefinitely.[4] Should these capital flows suddenly stop or be greatly diminished, the receiving country may suffer on two counts. First, its balance of payments would probably register a deficit; second, the country's basic economic structure might have to undergo a painful process of reorganization, a process that might further aggravate the balance-of-payments deficit.

[4] Oil-producing or plantation-economy nations are typical examples.

Somewhat less drastic consequences may befall a capital-exporting country if its independently motivated capital outflows exceed its surplus on current account. Although these outflows may not affect the economic structure of the capital-exporting country, they do imply a deficit in its balance of payments. Such a deficit may persist as long as the current account fails to generate a large enough surplus to offset the net outflows of capital, or until the outflows themselves diminish. In any event, while the deficit lasts, it must be offset by compensatory credit transactions, such as the sale of gold, depletion of foreign-exchange reserves, and so on.

Finally, a structural disequilibrium may be rooted in institutional or political changes that alter previously existing patterns of trade. The imposition of restrictive measures by one country on imports from another; the granting of special trade concessions to a particular nation; the formation of closely integrated trade blocs; the disruption of commercial relations during periods of war or political upheavals—all are examples of institutional changes that may influence basic trade patterns. And any fundamental changes in a country's trade relations must inevitably be reflected, for better or for worse, in its balance of payments.

Conclusions: The Need for Adjustments

Our main task in this chapter has been to sort out the major forces that may give rise to a balance-of-payments disequilibrium, and to classify the resulting disequilibrium accordingly. Having done this, we may draw the general conclusion that, depending on the nature of its underlying causes, a balance-of-payments disequilibrium can be regarded as either a short-term (cyclical) or a long-term (structural) phenomenon. Yet this distinction should not be taken to imply that a short-term disequilibrium necessarily requires less attention than its long-term counterpart. For although short-term disturbances may in some instances tend to correct themselves without the aid of specific action by the authorities, it cannot be certain that such a tendency will occur.

Indeed, the very existence of a disequilibrium must invariably set off some kind of reaction. Depending on the severity and duration of the disequilibrium, the reaction may be either automatic and temporary or one that consists of discretionary policy measures. Yet regardless of the actual form it takes, such a reaction reflects what is known as the balance-of-payments mechanism of adjustment. This is discussed in the next chapter.

10

Balance-of-Payments
Disequilibrium: Adjustments

J UDGED HISTORICALLY, THE
balance-of-payments mechanism of adjustment is a product of changing
circumstances and ideas. One cannot really speak of a single mechanism
of adjustment, but must instead refer to specific methods that may be,
or have been, used by different countries, at different times, to correct
their balance-of-payments maladjustments. Hence, our study of the
balance-of-payments mechanism of adjustment is in effect a study of
the development of ideas for remedying an ailing balance of payments
under many different circumstances. Taking this approach, we can
identify three major balance-of-payments adjustments that have evolved
over the years: (1) adjustment through changes in domestic prices and
income, (2) adjustment through freely fluctuating exchange rates, and
(3) adjustment through official variations of exchange rates.[1]

Although each of these notions has its present as well as past
exponents, each has come to be associated with a particular body of
economic ideas and concepts, characteristic of a particular period in
history. Thus, the idea that balance-of-payments adjustments can best be

[1] To these we may add a fourth: adjustment through direct controls over
foreign-exchange transactions. This will be discussed in the next chapter.

accomplished through domestic price changes predominated during most of the nineteenth century and the early part of the twentieth century; this reflected an adherence to the gold standard and an emphasis on a system of fixed exchange rates. A closely related idea—stressing changes in income—grew out of the Keynesian theory of income determination, and relies on such analytical tools as the marginal propensity to import and the foreign-trade multiplier to explain the working of the adjustment process. But the disappearance of the gold standard on the one hand, and the increasing commitments of governments to internal economic stability and full employment on the other, brought about a fundamental shift in the views concerning balance-of-payments cures. The years since World War I have witnessed a gradual disenchantment with the idea of fixed exchange rates and a growing emphasis on exchange-rate variations to effect balance-of-payments adjustments. And while the emphasis on exchange-rate variations has undergone modifications in the past forty years or so, some of the essential elements still form the basis of the present-day international monetary system.

In this chapter, then, we shall trace the evolutionary process reflected in the three ideas given above. We shall do so by considering each of them in turn, noting its basic features as well as the circumstances surrounding its development.

Adjustment Through Price and Income Changes

As we have already seen, the primary task of any balance-of-payments method of adjustment is to reduce or eliminate the discrepancy between a country's current demand for, and current supply of, foreign exchange. Since the demand and supply of foreign-exchange arise mainly out of the demand for imports and the supply of exports,[2] the adjustment process may be regarded as action that is designed to bring about changes in the value of exports and imports. Thus, an existing deficit may be adjusted either by a relative increase of exports over imports or by a decrease in imports relative to exports. Conversely, the adjustment of a balance-of-payments surplus calls for an increase of imports relative

---

[2] For the sake of simplicity, we shall concentrate for the moment on the current account, and ignore the capital account and unilateral transfers.

to exports or a decrease of exports relative to imports. In either case, changes in the relation between exports and imports would be translated into changes in the demand for, and supply of, foreign exchange, thereby correcting the discrepancy between them.

ADJUSTMENT THROUGH PRICE CHANGES: GOLD-FLOW MECHANISM

To David Hume (1711–1776) goes the credit for formulating one of the earliest versions of the gold flow adjustment process—a process based on the proposition that changes in domestic price levels can change the direction and/or volume of international flows of goods and services. Underlying his formulation were two major assumptions, characteristic of the classical school of economics: (1) that the economy is operating at full employment, and (2) that domestic price levels are determined by the quantity of money in circulation. Taken together, these assumptions form the basis of the so-called quantity theory of money, a concept that suggests a direct causal relation between changes in a nation's money supply and changes in domestic prices. According to the quantity theory, an increase in the quantity of money causes prices to rise, while a decrease results in a general price decline.

To this, the classical economists added one other assumption: that the money supply consists of gold and gold substitutes (i.e., paper currency backed by monetary gold reserves).[3] The significance of this last assumption can be readily appreciated. For if gold constitutes both a circulating medium (gold coins) and a reserve against which paper currency may be issued, then changes in the amount of a nation's gold supply are bound to affect the total quantity of money. Under the circumstances, an outflow of gold would reduce the nation's money supply, while an inflow of gold would tend to expand it.[4] And since changes in the money supply would, in turn, produce changes in price levels, it might be concluded that gold inflows would cause domestic prices to rise, while gold outflows would cause them to fall.

---

[3] This was a perfectly legitimate assumption, since up until the 1930's, the money supplies of most countries consisted partly of gold coins and partly of paper currency convertible into gold.

[4] Provided, of course, that the monetary authorities remain neutral and do not engage in offsetting policies.

The essence of the classical approach to the balance-of-payments adjustment process lies in this causal relationship between international gold flows and changes in domestic price levels. To illustrate, suppose that, due to a sudden increase in imports from England, the United States balance of payments develops a deficit. Suppose further that this deficit is financed by shipment of gold from the United States to England. The inflow of gold would result in an expansion of the money supply—and with it a rise in prices—in England. At the same time, the outflow of gold would tend to contract the money supply, and would cause prices to fall in the United States. Rising prices in England and falling prices in the United States would presumably curtail the American demand for British goods and stimulate British demand for American goods. As a consequence, American imports from England would tend to fall while British imports from the United States would tend to rise ; and either one of these tendencies would reduce the deficit in the United States balance of payments and the surplus in England's balance of payments.

Changes in domestic prices and subsequent changes in imports and exports were not the only agents working to restore balance-of-payments equilibrium under the gold standard. Another important consequence of international gold flows was supposed to take the form of changes in short-term interest rates. Indeed, the "rules of the game" during the reign of the gold standard required that the monetary authorities in a deficit country react to gold outflows by tightening credit, thus causing interest rates to rise. Similarly, gold inflows called for an expansion of credit and a fall in interest rates. The reasoning behind these "rules" derived from the proposition that interest-rate differentials between countries would induce short-term capital movements in search of higher yields. Thus, by causing interest rates to rise, a deficit country could presumably attract privately motivated inflows of short-term capital that would help to finance its deficit. In this manner, a deficit would not result in substantial losses of gold. Conversely, a decline of interest rates in a surplus country would be likely to start an outflow of short-term funds, which would offset the current-account surplus and thus check excessive gold inflows.

However, a balance-of-payments adjustment mechanism that is based on changes in domestic prices and/or interest rates need not necessarily depend on the existence of a gold standard. In fact, as long as the monetary authorities are willing to counter a deficit with deflationary policies and a surplus with inflationary policies, the adjustment process may still accomplish its purpose. Put differently, a rise or a fall in domestic prices and interest rates can be induced by deliberate government action; and to the extent that such changes affect the volume of exports and imports, the adjustment process performs its duty.

By the same token, the monetary authorities can undermine the working of a price-adjustment mechanism, particularly if it is based on international gold movements, by preventing prices from rising or falling in response to gold outflows or inflows. Indeed the experience of the late nineteenth and early twentieth century suggests that central banks did not always follow the "rules" of the gold standard. Thus, instead of allowing credit to contract in the face of a balance-of-payments deficit, monetary authorities often engaged in expansionary credit policies designed to keep prices and interest rates at their existing levels. Similarly, the central bank of a surplus country would frequently offset the expansionary effect of gold inflows by tightening credit, thus preventing the general price level from rising and interest rates from falling.[5] In short, central-bank policy often hindered rather than helped the smooth functioning expected of the price-adjustment mechanism under the gold standard. And although the gold standard itself survived until 1914, and was later reinstated for a brief period (1925–1931), the price-adjustment mechanism associated with it proved far less effective in practice than in theory.

ADJUSTMENT THROUGH INCOME CHANGES

Partly because flows of gold in the nineteenth century were relatively small to begin with, but mainly because they did not produce substantial price and interest-rate changes, attention began to shift to other possible explanations of balance-of-payments adjustments under a system of fixed exchange rates. And with the development of the Keynesian theory of income determination, a new approach to the bal-

---

[5] For an illuminating account of central-bank practices during that period, see A. Bloomfield, *Monetary Policy Under the International Gold Standard, 1880–1914* (New York: Federal Reserve Bank of New York, 1959).

ance-of-payments mechanism of adjustment appeared. According to this approach, changes in income, rather than price changes, play a major role in restoring balance-of-payments equilibrium. And although the corrective effect of price changes is not ruled out, it is considered of only secondary importance.

The nature of the so-called *income effect* on the balance of payments can be easily appreciated if we return to some of the concepts that were developed in Chapter 2—in particular the concept of the multiplier. That concept, you will recall, defines the quantitative relation between autonomous changes in expenditures and the subsequent changes in national income. You will also recall that the multiplier, operating in an open economy, is expressed as the reciprocal of the marginal propensity to save (s) and the marginal propensity to import (m). Accordingly, the size of the multiplier varies inversely with the combined value of these two propensities; the greater their value, the smaller the multiplier, and vice versa.

But in addition to indicating the probable magnitude of a change in income, the multiplier analysis enables us to observe *how* an initial rise or fall in expenditures works its way through the economy. Thus guided, we can trace the actual process by which total income increases (or decreases), noting at the same time the changes induced in its individual components. These components—that is, the uses to which income can be put by recipients—consist of expenditures for domestically produced consumption goods (C), savings (S), and the purchase of imports (M). And since the sum of the changes in these three components must be equal to the total change in income itself, we can express any change in income in an open economy as follows

$$\triangle Y = \triangle C + \triangle S + \triangle M$$

where

$\triangle Y =$ total change in income
$\triangle C =$ total change in induced domestic expenditures for consumption
$\triangle S =$ total change in induced savings
$\triangle M =$ total change in induced imports

We may now proceed to explore the possible relation between income changes and balance-of-payments adjustment. Suppose that there is a sudden increase in country A's exports to country B, amounting to $1,000. If both countries had previously enjoyed balance-of-payments equilibrium vis-à-vis each other, then the rise in A's exports (provided it is sustained for some time) would cause a surplus in its own balance of payments and a deficit in the balance of payments of country B. How would B's deficit and A's surplus be eliminated or at least reduced?

Calling upon the multiplier, and assuming that in country A the marginal propensity to consume domestic goods is 3/5, the marginal propensity to save is 1/5, and the marginal propensity to import is also 1/5, we can conclude that the initial $1,000 rise in A's exports would produce a $2,500 total rise in its national income.

$$1,000 \cdot \frac{1}{\frac{1}{5} + \frac{1}{5}} = 1,000 \cdot \frac{1}{\frac{2}{5}} = 1,000 \cdot \frac{5}{2} = 2,500$$

We may also conclude, however, that the increase in income was partly spent on domestic consumption, partly saved, and partly spent on imports. Or, to put it differently, the total increase in income represents an increase in consumption expenditures, an increase in savings, and an increase in imports, all of which have been induced by the rise in income itself.

In order to find out just how much of the increase in income is accounted for by each of these components, we need only recall what the marginal propensities represent. In brief, these propensities indicate how each additional dollar of income is allocated to its three possible uses. Hence, we may compute the actual increases in C, S, and M by multiplying in turn the total increase in income by the respective marginal propensities. Using our present data, we arrive at the following.

$$\triangle C = \triangle Y \cdot c = 2,500 \cdot \tfrac{3}{5} = 1,500$$
$$\triangle S = \triangle Y \cdot s = 2,500 \cdot \tfrac{1}{5} = 500$$
$$\triangle M = \triangle Y \cdot m = 2,500 \cdot \tfrac{1}{5} = 500$$

We can now write

$$\triangle Y (2,500) = \triangle C (1,500) + \triangle S (500) + \triangle M (500)$$

Actually, only the last item ($\triangle M$) should concern us, for in it lies part of the answer to our question. Indeed, the very rise in A's exports had planted the seed of the income-adjustment process. For by causing a multiple expansion of A's income, the autonomous rise in exports was bound to induce a subsequent increase in A's imports. And the increase in imports served, in turn, to reduce the size of A's surplus and hence B's deficit. The skeptic may satisfy himself on this point by recalling that the initial rise in A's exports led to a $1,000 surplus in A's (equal to the deficit in B's) balance of payments. Yet as a result of the expansion of A's income, which in turn induced a $500 rise in its imports, the surplus (deficit) was reduced to $500.

But what about the remainder of the deficit, amounting to $500? Here we must turn to country B and briefly consider the likely consequences of the initial rise in imports on *its* national income. The autonomous rise in B's imports would in all probability cause a multiple contraction in its income. This contraction, in turn, would probably induce a subsequent decline in imports, some of which may come from country A. Depending on the value of its marginal propensity to import, the induced reduction in B's imports may or may not be large enough to eliminate the remaining deficit in the balance of payments. But to the extent that such a reduction takes place at all, supplementing the induced increase in A's imports, both A and B would be closer to the re-establishment of balance-of-payments equilibrium.

In reality, however, the income effect alone cannot be counted upon to bring complete relief in the event of balance-of-payments maladjustments. For one thing, the hoped-for income changes, following an increase in exports or in imports, may not automatically materialize. Thus, an autonomous rise in imports, which would normally be expected to cause income to fall, might be offset by an autonomous increase in domestic investment. Or, an autonomous increase in exports, if accompanied by a decline in domestic investment, might fail to result in an expansion of income. Moreover, even if they do occur, income changes may not generate sufficiently large changes in imports. (In technical language, we may say that the marginal propensities to import, in the surplus and/or deficit countries, are relatively small.) And finally, induced changes in imports may not necessarily be confined to the exports of the countries directly involved, but may be spread among other countries as well. If, in our example, part of the reduction in B's imports affects the exports of countries other than A, the deficit of B with A cannot be fully adjusted. And by the same token, if the increase in A's imports is accounted for by increased purchases from countries other than B, its surplus with the latter would persist.

In the final analysis, then, neither income changes nor price changes can be expected to correct single-handedly a balance-of-payments disequilibrium. For even in the absence of officially imposed obstacles, which may prevent the appropriate income or price changes from occurring at all, such changes may not be able to produce individually the kind of economic reactions upon which the adjustment process ultimately depends. Indeed, it is now generally recognized that the adjustment process under a system of fixed exchange rates must be explained in terms of a combination of *both* income and price changes. Moreover, it is hardly conceivable that changes in income would fail to produce some changes in general price levels, and vice versa. Thus, while under different circumstances one or the other of these changes may play a larger role in the adjustment process, the two kinds of changes are essentially interdependent. As such, they must be thought of as mutually reinforcing processes whose *combined* effect on exports and imports may result in the restoration of balance-of-payments equilibrium.

Adjustment Through Freely Fluctuating Exchange Rates

When foreign-exchange rates are regarded as fixed and unchangeable, the burden of balance-of-payments adjustments must necessarily fall on forces operating within the economy. Fixed exchange rates were the order of the day under the international gold standard; therefore we associate primarily with the gold standard the adjustment process based on changes in domestic price levels and/or changes in income. That standard, as we have seen, dominated the international economy for a period of about fifty years, beginning about 1870 and ending abruptly in 1914. Restored in 1925, the gold standard managed to survive for a few years until it finally collapsed in 1931, never again to return. With its collapse ended the system of balance-of-payments adjustment based solely on price-and-income changes.

It would be wrong to assume, however, that the disappearance of the gold standard was the only factor in the replacement of the price-and-income adjustment process with one working through exchange-rate variations. On the contrary, it would be more correct to argue that the growing dissatisfaction with, and the frequent violations of, the "rules of the game" necessitated by the gold standard rendered the price-and-income adjustment process increasingly ineffectual, and contributed in some measure to the eventual fall of the gold standard itself. Indeed, even while World War I was still going on, new ideas about international monetary relations began to circulate. In the years following the war, especially from 1918 to 1925 and to some extent from 1931 to the outbreak of World War II, these ideas translated themselves into a new kind of balance-of-payments adjustment process—a process based on freely fluctuating exchange rates.

The essential characteristics of an adjustment process working through freely fluctuating exchange rates—or, for that matter, any adjustment process based on exchange-rate variations—is that it places the burden of adjustment on external forces. In other words, a country's *domestic* prices and incomes do not change in response to balance-of-payments disturbances, but rather the rate of exchange between its currency and foreign currencies. To the extent that variations in the exchange rate affect the country's demand for, and supply of, foreign exchange, they contribute to the restoration of balance-of-payments equilibrium. One should not hasten to conclude, however, that changes in domestic prices and income must be completely ruled out as an equilibrating factor under these circumstances. In fact, price-and-income variations may exert a corrective influence even under a system of freely fluctuating or officially varied exchange rates. But inasmuch as most governments now regard the maintenance of domestic stability and high level of employment as a major goal of economic policy, one cannot expect that domestic prices and incomes will be allowed to rise or fall simply because there is a surplus or a deficit in the balance of payments. Hence, the main burden of adjustment in this case must fall on exchange-rate variations, with income-and-price changes playing only a secondary role.

To observe the working of a freely fluctuating exchange-rate process of adjustment, let us think of a balance-of-payments disequilibrium as a disequilibrium in the foreign-exchange market. Thus, instead of saying that a balance-of-payments disequilibrium reflects a change in the relationship between imports and exports (e.g., a sudden rise in imports or a sudden decline in exports), we may say that it represents a change in the relationship between the country's total demand for, and total supply of, foreign exchange at a given exchange rate. Thus conceived, disequilibrium assumes a more encompassing and a more realistic meaning, since it suggests that any number of different changes may cause a disturbance in a country's balance of payments. At the same time, it also suggests that the adjustment process need not concern one specific component in the balance of payments. Instead, it must re-establish a balance between the total demand and total supply of foreign exchange, arising out of the country's independently motivated debit and credit transactions.

To illustrate, consider a case in which the United States starts out from a position of balance-of-payments equilibrium vis-à-vis England. In Figure 10.1, the equilibrium reflects an equality between the demand for pounds $(D_\pounds)$ and the supply of pounds $(S_\pounds)$ at a given rate of exchange. More specifically, at the rate of £1 = $3, the quantity of pounds (OA) demanded by the United States to finance its normal transactions with England is equal to the quantity of pounds supplied in the foreign-exchange market. Now, suppose that due to a rise in the American demand for British goods or an increase in the exports of private capital to England, the demand for pounds increases. In Figure 10.1, such an increase is represented by a shift of the demand curve to the right, resulting in a gap between the quantity of pounds supplied and the quantity demanded at the existing rate of exchange. This gap (AA'), or, more specifically, the excess of demand over supply of pounds, can be conceived of as a deficit in the United States balance of payments—a deficit that, as long as it lasts, would have to be offset by compensatory credit transactions (e.g., sale of gold, borrowing, and so on).

But since the exchange rate can move freely, it would probably react to the shift in demand by rising above the £1 = $3 level. Indeed, in the absence of official intervention, the free-market price of the pound would continue to rise until it reached a level where the supply of and demand for pounds are again equal. Thus, moving along the new demand curve $(D'_\pounds)$ and the old supply curve $(S_\pounds)$, we observe that as the exchange rate rises, the gap is progressively reduced: Fewer pounds are being demanded and more pounds are being supplied than at the previous lower rates. When the exchange rate reaches the £1 = $4 level, the gap is

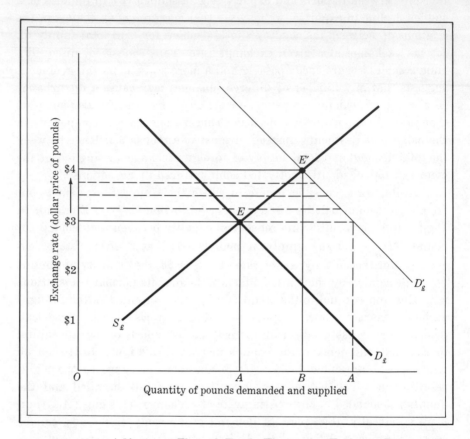

FIGURE *10.1*   Adjustment Through Freely Fluctuating Exchange Rates

completely eliminated—the new quantity of pounds demanded (*OB*) is exactly equal to the new quantity supplied. At this rate, then, an equilibrium in the balance of payments is re-established; the adjustment mechanism has accomplished its task.

It is not difficult to trace the same adjustment process in the event of a surplus in the United States balance of payments. Thus, should the American demand for pounds fall, the market price of the pound, in terms of dollars, would tend to decline until the excess of supply over demand is eliminated. In this case, however, the new equilibrium would involve not only a lower rate of exchange, but also smaller quantities of pounds demanded and supplied. To verify this, we may draw a demand curve on Figure 10.1 to the left of $D\pounds$ and trace the consequences until a new equilibrium position is reached.

Two powerful arguments are usually advanced in favor of this adjustment mechanism. First, since it is based entirely on the automatic reaction of free-market forces, the adjustment process is self-activating, necessitating no official action. Moreover, since under normal conditions any free market tends to establish a price at which supply and demand are equal, there is no reason why a freely operating foreign-exchange market cannot do the same with the demand and supply of foreign exchange. Second, to the extent that the adjustment can be automatically accomplished through variations in the exchange rate, domestic prices and incomes can remain undisturbed at their existing levels. To this we might add a practical consideration: Since exchange rates are in any case more responsive to changes in trade relations than are domestic prices and incomes, they are likely to react commensurately with balance-of-payments disturbances.

Against these virtues, we must consider three major disadvantages of a freely fluctuating exchange-rate system. First, there is the matter of uncertainty and risk. Frequent changes in exchange rates add the risk of losses due to exchange-rate variations to the normal risks of exporters and importers. And although exchange risks may be covered to some extent through forward-exchange transactions, this protection involves additional costs that reduce profit margins. The same holds true in the case of investors: If they do not cover their exchange risks, they stand to experience a loss; and if they do cover themselves, they must accept a lower return on their investment. Thus, because freely fluctuating exchange rates place additional burdens on those engaged in international trade, they are said to hinder international flows of goods and services as well as international movements of capital.

The second disadvantage of a freely fluctuating exchange-rate system lies in the possibility that instead of effecting a return to equilibrium, exchange-rate variations may further worsen an existing disequilibrium. The danger of such a development is especially great if market conditions are unstable to begin with. Under the circumstances, a change in the exchange rate may lead to speculative activities that would serve only to intensify the problem. To illustrate, suppose that due to a deficit in the United States balance of payments, the exchange rate between the pound and the dollar rises, say, from £1 = $3 to £1 = $3.50. If the rise in the dollar price of the pound leads to the expectation that it would continue to rise even further, the quantity of pounds demanded would be likely to increase rather than decrease, while the quantity of pounds supplied would tend to remain relatively the same. Under this set of "abnormal" conditions, the initial deficit may become larger before it is corrected. Similarly, should a fall in the exchange rate, from £1 = $3 to, say, £1 = $2.50 (due to a deficit in England's balance of payments) be regarded as the first of many subsequent reductions, the quantity of pounds supplied would probably increase while the quantity demanded would tend to remain the same. As a result, the excess of supply over demand would increase, making the adjustment all the more difficult to achieve.

Such perverse speculative behavior, intensified by unstable economic and/or political conditions, may undermine the working of a freely fluctuating exchange-rate system. This is borne out by historical experience. For example, during the early 1920's and to some extent during the 1930's, exchange-rate variations were often accompanied by speculative activities that spread from foreign-exchange markets to stock exchanges and commodity markets, and caused further destabilization of both international and domestic monetary relations. Moreover, anticipation of future exchange-rate movements often resulted in speculative flows of short-term capital that exerted their own pressure on the exchange-rate structures of countries with capital outflows. And as the pressure on exchange rates increased, so did speculative activities, thereby contributing in some cases (notably Germany in 1923) to a complete collapse of the monetary system.

It might be suggested, however, that the extent of speculative activities, caused by exchange-rate variations, is at least in part a function of the magnitude of the variations themselves. Thus, in cases where adjustment can be effectively brought about by relatively small changes in the exchange rate, one is unlikely to find excessive speculative activity. On the other hand, should large variations be necessary to correct a relatively small deficit (or a surplus), speculators will probably react in a manner that would hinder rather than help the adjustment process. The size of exchange-rate variations that are required to produce an adjustment depends, in any given case, on the elasticities of the demand and supply of foreign exchange. The more elastic the demand or supply schedule (or both), the smaller the necessary changes in the exchange rate. Conversely, the more inelastic (or less elastic) either one or both schedules are, the larger the exchange-rate variations would have to be. But since wide fluctuations in the exchange rate are likely to induce destabilizing speculative activities, the adjustment process may fail to accomplish its task in cases where either the demand or supply of foreign exchange is inelastic.

Herein lies the third major disadvantage of a freely fluctuating exchange-rate process of adjustment: Its effectiveness is generally limited to cases where foreign-exchange supply and/or demand are fairly elastic. For unless either of these schedules is sufficiently responsive to small changes in the exchange rate, the adjustment process may prove to be self-defeating—that is, instead of restoring equilibrium, it may unleash forces that aggravate the existing disequilibrium. Moreover, since supply and demand elasticities cannot be readily known in advance, one can never be certain that a particular change in the exchange rate would be sufficient to bring about the necessary adjustment, or at least to prevent undesirable speculation. In short, an adjustment through freely fluctuating exchange rates is at best a trial-and-error affair; given the right conditions, it may accomplish its task quickly and with a minimum of friction, but more often it may prove to be a long and drawn-out process.

Adjustment Through Flexible Exchange Rates: Devaluation

The collapse of the gold standard on the one hand, and the dissatisfaction with freely fluctuating exchange rates on the other, led many countries during the 1930's to seek new bases for international monetary relations. What finally emerged proved to be a middle-of-the-road solution; we referred to this earlier as a flexible exchange-rate system.

As we noted in Chapter 8, a flexible exchange-rate system features a combination of free-market forces and official participation in the foreign-exchange market—that is, exchange rates are determined by day-to-day supply and demand conditions, but the resulting fluctuations are kept within certain prescribed limits through official purchases and/or sales of foreign exchange in the open market. Thus, to the extent that they possess sufficient foreign-exchange reserves, the authorities can iron out market-price variations and keep the exchange rate at a fairly stable level. In so doing, the authorities actually perform an adjustment function. For inasmuch as exchange-rate fluctuations reflect a discrepancy between the demand and supply of foreign exchange, official open-market operations tend to eliminate the discrepancy by adding their share, either to the total demand or total supply of foreign exchange.

Yet the success of the authorities in maintaining a stable exchange rate through open-market operations depends not only on the size of their foreign-exchange holdings but also on the severity and duration of the balance-of-payments disturbance. And should fundamental changes in trade patterns persist for a considerable period of time, it may become necessary to adjust the exchange rate accordingly and to peg it at a higher or lower level. In this respect, the adjustment process under a flexible exchange-rate system resembles that associated with freely fluctuating exchange rates. For in both cases, the adjustment is carried out through exchange-rate variations instead of changes in domestic prices and income. But here, too, lies a major difference between the flexible-rate system (also known as *adjustable peg*) and the freely fluctuating rate system of adjustment: Under the latter, exchange rates are free to seek their own levels in response to balance-of-payments disturbances, whereas under the former, the exchange rate is varied from one level to another only by official decree. Moreover, once the rate is changed, the authorities are committed to support it at the new level.

Official variations of the exchange rate may move upward or downward, depending on the circumstances in each case. For example, the rate of exchange between the pound and the dollar may be officially raised (e.g., from £1 = $3 to £1 = $4) in the face of a surplus in Britain's balance of payments, or it may be lowered (e.g., from £1 = $3 to £1 = $2) in the face of a deficit. Or, using more technical terms, the pound may be *appreciated* or *devalued* in the event of a surplus or a deficit, respectively. But since it is unlikely that a country would deliberately appreciate its currency in order to eliminate a balance-of-payments surplus,[6] the discussion of the adjustment mechanism under a flexible

[6] Two recent exceptions might be mentioned. In 1961, both West Germany and The Netherlands revalued (appreciated) their currencies vis-à-vis the dollar in an effort to reduce persistent balance-of-payments surpluses and to slow down the steady accumulation of gold and foreign-exchange reserves.

exchange-rate system is usually couched in terms of devaluation and its supposed effect on a balance-of-payments deficit.

Briefly defined, devaluation, or depreciation of a currency, means the lowering of its value in terms of a foreign currency (or currencies). Thus, a devaluation of the pound vis-à-vis the dollar can be viewed as a decrease in the dollar price of the pound. At the same time, it can also be regarded as an increase in the pound price of the dollar. Here lies one of the basic features of devaluation: As the value of the home currency goes down in terms of the foreign currency, the value of the foreign currency, in terms of the home currency, must go up. For example, the depreciation of the pound, from £1 = $3 to £1 = $2, means an appreciation of the dollar, from $1 = £1/3 to $1 = £1/2. By the same token, a depreciation of the dollar from, say, $1 = £1/3 to $1 = £1/4, means an appreciation of the pound from £1 = $3 to £1 = $4.

How can depreciation help correct a balance-of-payments deficit? The answer becomes apparent if we consider the effects that depreciation is expected to have on the volume—and ultimately value—of a country's exports and imports.

Suppose that in view of a persistent deficit in its balance of payments, England depreciates the pound, lowering its dollar price from £1 = $3 to £1 = $2.[7] The immediate consequence of this move is a decrease in the dollar price of British exports and an increase in the pound price of British imports. For if we assume, for the moment, that commodity prices in England and the United States remain the same, fewer dollars would now be required to buy a given quantity of British goods, but more pounds would be needed to buy a given amount of American goods. To illustrate, consider a bottle of scotch whiskey that costs £4 in England, and a bottle of bourbon priced at $6 in the United States. Before the devaluation of the pound, an American consumer had to pay $12 for a bottle of scotch, whereas after the devaluation he could obtain the same bottle for only $8. Conversely, an Englishman who could previously import American bourbon for £2 would now have to pay £3. As a result of these price changes, American buyers might be expected to

[7] This is equal to a 33 per cent reduction in the dollar price of the pound. In 1949 Britain did, in fact, devalue the pound (by about 30 per cent), lowering its dollar price from $4.03 to $2.80.

demand larger quantities of scotch while Englishmen would presumably curtail their purchases of bourbon.

This illustration points to the supposed remedial effects of depreciation insofar as balance-of-payments ills are concerned. For as the price of its goods decreases, in terms of foreign currencies, the country that depreciates its currency may expect an increase in foreign demand for its exports. At the same time, its own residents will probably curtail consumption of those imported goods whose prices have risen in terms of the depreciated currency. Working simultaneously, these two tendencies (i.e., a rise in exports and a decline in imports) will supposedly reduce or eliminate the balance-of-payments deficit.

But inasmuch as the adjustment process just described rests on the response of consumers (in both countries) to price changes, the question of demand elasticities immediately arises. Thus, only if the American demand for British goods and/or the British demand for American goods are fairly elastic, would depreciation be expected to cause a sufficiently strong expansion of British exports and/or a significant reduction in British imports. Under such circumstances, the deficit in England's balance of payments might indeed be reduced or eliminated. If, on the other hand, one or both demand schedules are inelastic, depreciation may leave matters as they are or, worse still, cause them to deteriorate even further. For with an inelastic demand, the rise in the quantity of British goods that American consumers demand may not be large enough to compensate for the fall in their unit price; the result will be a smaller total amount of dollars spent on British exports than before. By the same token, a relatively small decline in the quantity of British imports, following the rise in their unit price, may actually result in a larger expenditure for them than before. In short, under fairly inelastic demand conditions, depreciation may widen rather than narrow the gap between the demand for, and supply of, foreign exchange, thereby worsening the deficit that it was supposed to eliminate.

To this we might add another by-product of depreciation that may hinder the adjustment process. It is generally agreed that if the country that depreciates its currency is already operating near or at full employment, depreciation is almost certain to produce domestic inflation. For to the extent that depreciation succeeds in stimulating its exports and/or curtailing imports, it increases the total demand for home-produced goods and services and thus exerts additional pressure on domestic resources. As a result of this pressure, prices and wages tend to rise, leading to increased production costs and causing further rises in prices. Costs may also rise if domestic production relies heavily on raw-material imports, whose prices, in terms of the depreciated currency, have risen. And as costs and prices rise, the remedial effects of the depreciation itself may be nullified, rendering the adjustment process ineffectual.

Finally, depreciation may prove fruitless if it inspires other countries to retaliate by devaluating their own currencies. The danger of such a possibility is particularly great when not one but several countries experience balance-of-payments difficulties, with each attempting to correct its own deficit through exchange-rate depreciation. And when depreciation is undertaken not only in order to correct a balance-of-payments deficit, but also to stimulate domestic employment through export expansion, the danger of retaliation is further increased. Under such circumstances, no country can hope to reach its goal. For the advantage that one country might gain by reducing the external value of its currency would probably be offset by the depreciation of other currencies. In the end, such competitive devaluation can only result in a further deterioration of balance-of-payments conditions, and may well lead to the imposition of direct controls over international trade.

Conclusions

What are we to conclude from our rather lengthy discussion of balance-of-payments adjustments? Perhaps the most significant conclusion is that none of the adjustment processes described in this chapter constitutes a foolproof measure of correction in the face of balance-of-payments maladjustments. Indeed, inasmuch as each of these processes depends on the appropriate reaction of free-market forces, which may or may not materialize, neither can always be counted upon to accomplish its task satisfactorily. Moreover, in each case, the successful operation of the adjustment process depends on the absence of official policies that either would prevent the necessary economic changes from taking place, or would nullify their intended effects. This condition can hardly be presumed to exist in today's world. To this we might add another disheartening note : Even proper market reactions may fail to correct a balance-of-payments disturbance if it is deeply rooted in basic structural changes that call for considerable economic readjustments within the countries involved.

A second important conclusion is that, in the absence of direct controls over international trade, a balance-of-payments adjustment must necessarily involve a choice between two distinct and essentially opposing alternatives : Should the adjustment burden be allowed to fall on internal variables (i.e., price-and-income changes), or should it be placed on external forces (i.e., exchange-rate variations) ? The implications of each of these alternatives make the choice between them all the more difficult. For in making such a choice, a country is actually choosing between the prices—domestic instability in one case and unstable exchange rates in the other—at which the balance-of-payments adjustment is to be purchased. And since, under certain circumstances, either one of these prices may be considered too high, the country may reject both alternatives in favor of still another : the imposition of direct controls over international payments. We will discuss this alternative and its implications in the next chapter.

11

Control Over International Payments

KEENLY AWARE OF THE WEAK-
nesses inherent in any free-market mechanism of adjustment, many
countries in the 1930's resorted to direct controls over foreign-exchange
transactions as a means of alleviating balance-of-payments difficulties.
In most cases, these were acts of desperation, prompted by severe current-account deficits and/or massive capital outflows that were accompanied by substantial losses of gold and foreign-exchange reserves. Indeed, when threatened with a sizable depletion of its reserves, a country
could hardly be expected to sit back and wait for free-market forces to
produce the necessary adjustments. In such a situation, they understandably chose to protect their precarious positions by means of direct controls and regulations rather than to rely on the slow and uncertain
response of market forces to exchange-rate variations or income-and-
price changes.

In a later chapter we shall describe in some detail the events that
contributed to international monetary disorder in the 1930's, and that
led to the widespread use of trade and payments restrictions. In this
chapter, however, we must examine the nature and implications of
exchange control with respect to balance-of-payments adjustments.

The Nature of Exchange Control

Briefly defined, a system of exchange control is a set of rules and regulations designed to ensure government supervision of foreign-exchange transactions. Although the extent of such supervision and the strictness of the regulations may vary from case to case, nearly all exchange-control systems share a basic feature: the establishment of a central authority through which foreign-exchange dealings must be processed. Thus, once exchange control is imposed, the citizens of a country can no longer freely buy and sell foreign currencies. Instead, anyone who wants a foreign currency must buy it, at the official rate, from the central authority or its authorized agents. Similarly, receipts from abroad, if they are denominated in foreign currencies, must be surrendered to the central authority and exchanged for the domestic currency at the official rate. In short, a rigid and all-encompassing exchange-control system assures the government of a virtual monopoly over foreign-exchange dealings; this monopoly enables it to regulate foreign-trade transactions as well.

Here lies the main attraction of exchange control from the standpoint of a country that has balance-of-payments difficulties. For by possessing a monopoly over foreign-exchange sales and purchases, the government can restrict imports simply by refusing to sell foreign exchange to importers. And should the difficulty stem, not from a current-account deficit but from excessive capital outflows, the government can check such outflows by refusing to allocate foreign exchange that is wanted for overseas investment. Moreover, exchange control enables the government to act as a *discriminating* monopoly, charging and offering different rates for a given foreign currency demanded for, or earned from, different transactions. In this manner, as we shall see shortly, the authorities can deliberately encourage some transactions while discouraging others. Finally, by controlling the effective demand for foreign exchange through rationing, the authorities can always equate it to the available supply, thus assuring the maintenance of a foreign-exchange rate at the officially chosen level.

But perhaps the greatest virtue of exchange control as a means of alleviating balance-of-payments difficulties is this: It gives the government a free hand to pursue its domestic economic policies without fear of balance of payments repercussions. In other words, exchange control serves as a safeguard against the possibility that monetary and/or fiscal policies at home would give rise to a balance-of-payments deficit, or would make it more difficult to achieve an adjustment of an existing one. Thus, whether it is committed to domestic price stability, the maintenance of full employment, or rapid economic growth, a country practicing exchange control need not sacrifice its domestic economic objective for the sake of maintaining balance-of-payments equilibrium. Nor need it court the danger of destabilizing speculative activities, capital outflows, or loss of reserves, by relying on exchange rate variations (either freely fluctuating or flexible) to take care of balance-of-payments disturbances. For by resorting to direct controls over international payments, it can pursue its domestic economic policies while enjoying the security of a rigidly fixed exchange rate and a tightly maintained balance in its international accounts.

There is no denying that exchange control provides an effective, though drastic, means of coping with immediate balance-of-payments difficulties. But neither can it be denied that the imposition of such control not only restricts the free flow of international trade, but may also give rise to practices that distort economically beneficial trade patterns. Two such practices—multiple exchange rates and bilateral payments arrangements—deserve special mention, and will be discussed in the next two sections.

Multiple Exchange Rates

We said earlier that under a regime of exchange control, the authorities may offer and/or charge different rates for a foreign currency, depending on the way in which it has been earned, or the use for which it is being demanded. This practice, which originated in Germany in the early 1930's and has since found its way to other countries (especially in Latin America), is made possible by the multiple exchange-rate system.

In its simplest form, a multiple exchange-rate system consists of only two rates, an official rate and a so-called "free" rate. The official rate is usually applied to foreign exchange demanded for approved transactions, such as the import of raw materials and other essential commodities. It is often also the rate at which the authorities purchase foreign-exchange receipts arising from exports that command a strong competitive position abroad. The free rate, which is usually lower (i.e., makes foreign exchange more costly), than the official rate, governs all other transactions—for example, travel, imports of luxuries and other nonessential materials, exports that must be subsidized, and so on.

To appreciate the working of a two-rate system, consider the following illustration. Suppose that, having established exchange control, the British authorities require exporters to surrender their dollar receipts at the official rate of, say, £1 = $3, and that importers of raw materials and foodstuffs can obtain dollars from the authorities at the same rate. Suppose, further, that at this rate not all the available dollars are demanded for the purpose of financing raw-material imports. In this case, the authorities can allow the remaining supply of dollars to be sold to anyone at whatever rate free-market forces establish, say £1 = $2. This means, in effect, that anyone who buys dollars other than for the purpose of importing raw materials must pay a higher price for them, namely, £1/2 instead of £1/3 per dollar. Consequently, imports that are deemed nonessential will tend to be discouraged

At the same time, the lower rate of £1 = $2 may encourage the exports of some commodities. Thus, the authorities may offer to some exporters the free rate instead of the official rate against their receipts of dollars, thereby enabling them to receive £1/2 instead of £1/3 for each dollar earned abroad. Consequently, these exporters could charge their foreign customers lower dollar prices in the hope of increasing their volume of sale. From the standpoint of the authorities, such an increase in sales represents a larger volume of exports that may help to correct a balance-of-payments deficit.

The opportunities for manipulating foreign trade through exchange control increase with the number of exchange rates the authorities specify. Indeed, an elaborate system of multiple exchange rates enables the authorities to discriminate not only between different commodities, but also between different countries. While the basic principle is the same as the one described above, the number of possibilities becomes quite large. Thus, some governments have adopted multiple exchange-rate systems featuring a multitude of official rates, treating differently almost every conceivable type of transaction. Other countries, notably the Soviet Union, have established different rates according to the source of imports and the destination of exports. Still others have combined multiple exchange rates with outright prohibitions on the use of foreign exchange for certain purposes. In almost all cases, multiple exchange-rate systems have been accompanied by rigid and all-emcompassing exchange controls; under them only the barest trace of a free market in foreign exchange could be said to operate.[1]

There is little doubt that a well managed system of multiple exchange rates can help ease a balance of payments deficit. For by assigning different rates to different import and export transactions, the authorities, in effect, either subsidize or penalize those engaged in them. And since a subsidy is supposed to encourage, and a penalty to discourage, a particular line of activity, the use of multiple exchange rates may achieve simultaneously an expansion of exports and a reduction of imports—the two major ingredients of balance-of-payments adjustment in the event of a deficit. As such, the effects of a multiple exchange-rate system can be likened to those of devaluation, except that under the former we have essentially a *partial* devaluation. In other words, only some exports and some imports are subject to exchange rates that reduce their prices in terms of the foreign currency, and raise their prices in terms of the domestic currency. Other exports and imports may be subject to overvalued exchange rates that induce neither substantial expansion nor significant contraction of sales.

In correcting a balance-of-payments deficit, the main advantage of multiple exchange rates over an across-the-board depreciation can be readily appreciated. One need only recall that the success of devaluation depends in large measure on the condition of demand elasticities. In the country that depreciates its currency, depreciation can increase the value of exports and decrease the value of imports only if the foreign demand for its exports and/or its own demand for imports are fairly elastic. Should these demand schedules be highly inelastic, depreciation would doubtless worsen rather than alleviate the deficit. But since in reality the elasticities of demand for different imports and exports are hardly ever

---

[1] Indeed, under the circumstances, the only existing free market may turn out to be an illegal one—i.e., a "black" market.

the same, a partial (or selective) devaluation may prove more fruitful than an across-the-board, uniform devaluation. To be more specific, the managers of a multiple exchange-rate system may exploit the differences in demand elasticities for different goods by setting their exchange rates accordingly. Thus, exports and imports for which the demand is estimated to be elastic would be assigned lower (devalued) exchange rates than commodities faced by a fairly inelastic demand. Through such manipulations—provided, of course, that they are based on correct estimates of demand elasticities—the authorities may be able to restore and preserve a balance between the value of exports and the value of imports.

While it may prove useful in correcting balance-of-payments deficits, a multiple exchange-rate system is a serious obstacle to the free flow of international trade. In the first place, the institution of such a system is bound to discourage some imports and exports, and hence serve to reduce the volume of internationally traded goods. Second, since a multiple exchange-rate system is basically a discriminatory device, it can lead to misallocation of economic resources both in the country concerned and elsewhere. For example, by assigning a devalued rate to exports that cannot normally compete in world markets, the authorities, in effect, subsidize and encourage the use of inefficient resources in the country's own export industries, and force unfair competition on more efficient foreign producers. At the same time, an undervalued rate tends to protect inefficient domestic producers of products that compete with imports. An overvalued rate, on the other hand, has the effect of a tax on exports and a subsidy for imports, and hence tends to discourage the use of efficient resources both in export industries and in industries competing with imports. Moreover, a multiple exchange-rate system that discriminates between different countries denies the consumer a free choice in obtaining imports from the cheapest possible source, and prevents the producer from selling his products where he can get the highest price. Under the circumstances, international trade is inevitably forced into uneconomic channels—channels that are dictated by balance-of-payments considerations rather than by comparative-cost differences. One such rechanneling of trade is known as *bilateralism*.

Bilateral Trade and Payments

In order to appreciate the nature of, and rationale behind, bilateral channeling of trade, we must first note briefly two basic features of a regime of exchange control. These are (1) generally overvalued exchange rates, and (2) currency inconvertibility.

By an overvalued exchange rate (or an overvalued currency) is meant an exchange rate at which the country's exports are overpriced in the world market, and its imports underpriced in the domestic market, under existing cost and price structures. As such, an overvalued currency tends to cause a decline in exports and an expansion in imports, either one or both of which are likely to produce a balance-of-payments deficit.[2] Under the circumstances, the deficit might conceivably be corrected by a downward adjustment of the exchange rate (devaluation of the currency) ; this would presumably stimulate exports and discourage imports. But if, instead of devaluating the currency, the authorities choose to counter the deficit by imposing exchange controls, the overvalued rate is merely frozen at its existing level, a level that prevents the country's exports from competing effectively in the world's free market. Hence, while the balance-of-payments deficit may be corrected through exchange restrictions, export opportunities are no greater than before; the country must, therefore, look for specific markets in which to sell its overpriced exports.

To this unhappy state of affairs, we must now add the second basic feature of exchange control: currency inconvertibility. Indeed, the very imposition of control over the sale and purchase of foreign exchange implies that the domestic currency is no longer freely convertible into foreign currencies. Since foreign-exchange dealings are regulated by, and carried out through, a central authority, one may convert his own currency into another only at the discretion of the authorities and with their permission. Similarly, one who possesses a foreign currency cannot sell it freely in the market or use it as he otherwise sees fit, but must surrender it to the authorities at the official rate. In a word, restrictions on the use of a currency for foreign-trade transactions actually mean

[2] You may recall (Chapter 9, footnote 3) that in such a case the deficit is said to be caused by exchange-rate disequilibrium.

that the currency is inconvertible. Since exchange controls are designed to do precisely that—to restrict the use of currencies—they must necessarily result in currency inconvertibility.

If, due to a widespread introduction of exchange controls, a great many currencies become inconvertible, the financing, and hence the ability to carry on free multilateral trade, becomes increasingly difficult. Thus, country A cannot pay for its imports from country B with the proceeds of its own exports to country C, if C's currency is not freely convertible. Nor can country B use A's currency to settle a deficit with country C, if A's currency is inconvertible. And neither of these currencies can be freely used to finance imports from, say, country D, if D's currency is also inconvertible. It is quite possible, of course, that one or all of these countries possess some foreign-exchange reserves denominated in E's currency, a currency that is not only fully convertible but is generally acceptable as a means of international payments (e.g., dollars). But rather than deplete such scarce reserves, each country would prefer to restrict its imports altogether or to buy them from a country whose currency—though generally inconvertible—can be earned through exports.

In such a set of circumstances lies the logic behind bilateral channeling of trade, a practice that first developed in the 1930's and that reached significant proportions during and immediately after World War II. The essential characteristic of bilateral trade is an arrangement between two countries whereby each agrees to accept the other's currency in payment for exports. But since one country's exports are the other's imports, the arrangement also implies the use of the currency, earned through exports, as a means of financing imports obtained from the trading partner. In other words, a bilateral trading arrangement typically concerns the settlement of financial claims, arising from imports and exports, in the trading partners' currencies; each is thereby enabled to conserve its reserves of gold and convertible foreign exchange. In actual practice, however, bilateral trade arrangements may take various forms; three are described in the following pages.

PRIVATE COMPENSATION SCHEMES

The most direct form of bilateral trade (and one of the earliest to develop) consists of barter exchanges between private firms in two countries. For example, subject to the approval of the authorities, an exporter in Germany might arrange with an exporter in Guatemala to exchange DM10 million worth of electrical equipment for DM10 million worth of bananas. Or, an exporter in Brazil might enter into a private arrangement with an Italian exporter to exchange a certain quantity of coffee for a quantity of Italian shoes of equal value.[3] Private compensation schemes like these have the advantage of eliminating the need for settlement of financial claims in foreign currencies. Goods are exchanged for goods; their value is determined either in one currency or another.

But private compensation schemes of this sort pose a problem for the firms involved: Each firm is forced to perform the function of both exporter and importer. Consequently, as time went on, more elaborate private compensation schemes developed, whereby *two* firms in each country would agree to settle claims and counterclaims arising from foreign-trade transaction Thus, a coffee exporter and a shoe importer in Brazil might enter into a barter arrangement with a coffee importer and a shoe exporter in Italy. Under such an arrangement, the Italian importer of coffee would compensate the Italian exporter of shoes, paying him in lire, while the Brazilian importer of coffee would pay his coffee-exporting countryman in cruzeiros—according to the agreed-upon value of the goods exchanged.

Participants in an elaborate private compensation agreement, however, must first find each other, and commodities to be exchanged must be approved by the authorities and be acceptable to consumers in each country. In view of the difficulties that a single firm might encounter in trying to fulfill all of these requirements, it was only natural that a new breed of entrepreneurs arose. Known as barter brokers, their specialty lay in finding prospective trading partners and bringing them together. Often, in fact, it was the broker who initiated such an arrangement, having discovered profitable trade opportunities based on barter exchange. Such broker-inspired barter arrangements, which had largely disappeared since the 1930's, seem to have made a recent comeback, though broker expertise in these matters is nowadays mostly confined to one or two countries.[4]

[3] Similar arrangements, as we shall see in Chapter 15, have at times been concluded between two governments and between a government in one country and private firms in another.

[4] For some interesting details on recent barter deals, see ''Barter is Respectable,'' *The Economist* (January 29, 1966), 428–429.

BILATERAL CLEARING AGREEMENTS

While private compensation schemes are necessarily limited to barter exchanges of specific commodities between specific firms, bilateral clearing agreements seek to provide a mechanism for settling financial claims arising from all imports and exports between the two countries concerned.[5] Such agreements are therefore made by the governments of the trading partners, and usually involve their central banks. To be more specific, each country sets up a special account in its central bank through which payments for imports and receipts from exports are cleared in its domestic currency.

To illustrate, suppose that France and Germany enter into a bilateral clearing arrangement, having determined in advance the exchange rate (between the mark and the franc) that would govern their bilateral trade. Under such an arrangement, a French importer buying DM1,000 worth of steel from Germany would pay the equivalent amount in francs to the Bank of France, where they would be credited to the German clearing account. French exporters who sell goods to Germany are paid, also in francs, out of this account; the sums paid are debited to the account. In Germany, a similar arrangement is at work. German importers pay marks to the Reichsbank, which then credits them to the French clearing account; German exporters are paid in marks from the same account.

If, given the predetermined exchange rate, the clearing account in each country shows a balance between credits and debits over a reasonable period of time, trade is said to be bilaterally balanced. In other words, all transactions between the two trading partners are financially cleared without any actual movement of funds across national boundaries. But since one country's exports to the other may at times exceed its imports from the other, bilateral clearing agreements usually contain provisions to handle the resulting discrepancies between payments and receipts. In most cases, the partners agree in advance on a certain amount, say $10 million, by which exports and imports would be allowed to deviate from each other; any discrepancies within this limit would be

[5] Unless the agreement is specifically limited to certain categories of exports and imports.

financed by an automatic line of credit extended by the export-surplus country.[6] In our example, such an arrangement—often called a "swing" credit agreement—would work something like this. Should German exports to France exceed its imports from that country, the Reichsbank would advance credit, in marks, to the French clearing account; this credit could then be used to pay German exporters. In France, meanwhile, the German clearing account would simply accumulate francs. Conversely, should French exports to Germany exceed German exports to France, the Bank of France would advance credit, in francs, to the German clearing account, while the French clearing account in the Reichsbank would accumulate marks

Please note, however, the possible consequences of such a "swing" arrangement for the domestic economies of the countries involved. In the export-surplus country, the central bank's advancement of credit to the clearing account, and the subsequent payment (in local currency) to exporters, would mean a net increase in the money supply; this may in turn generate inflationary pressures. Such pressures could be somewhat reduced if people were free to increase imports from other countries. But the existence of exchange control and the rationing of scarce foreign currencies militate against such possibilities. The central bank may, of course, reduce the threat of inflation by postponing payments to exporters until the clearing account shows more of a balance between in-payments and out-payments. But such a practice, whereby exporters receive no payment until imports from the bilateral partner have increased, would surely discourage them from increasing their shipments to the deficit country. As for the import-surplus (deficit) country, payments by importers, again in local currency, into the clearing account would exceed payments to exporters, thus draining money out of circulation. Unless this is offset by domestic credit expansion, the result would probably be deflationary pressures.

Nevertheless, a "swing" arrangement is superior to no arrangement at all. Since it sets a limit on the amount of credit that can be extended in inconvertible currencies, it removes the danger of excessive inflationary or deflationary pressures, as well as the possible accumulation by export-surplus countries of large unusable balances. Moreover, because

[6] Usually, the agreement also provides for the settlement, in gold or convertible currencies, of any discrepancy in excess of the prescribed limit.

any deficit in excess of the prescribed limit must be settled in gold or convertible currencies, an export-surplus country may be able to use at least part of its bilateral-export earnings to finance imports from other, and possibly cheaper, sources of supply. Under such circumstances, international trade may still be able to demonstrate some of its economic virtues.

PAYMENT AGREEMENTS

Unlike bilateral clearing agreements, which usually cover the settlement of claims arising from current trade transactions, payment agreements are wider in scope. Although the basic principles are the same in both cases (i.e., claims arising from credit transactions are used to settle claims arising from debit transactions) payment agreements can extend the clearing mechanism to past as well as to present transactions. As such, payment agreements may cover the entire range of a country's foreign-trade dealings, as reflected in all categories of its balance of payments.

As an illustration, consider a payment agreement concluded, let's say, between England and France. In addition to providing for the settlement of claims arising from exports and imports, the agreement may specify that a certain per cent of the proceeds earned by French exports should be used to repay a past loan advanced by British banks to French business concerns. Or, the agreement may provide for the gradual redemption, out of British export earnings, of long-term British government bonds held by French investors. Still another provision may cover the possibility of converting current claims into future ones—for example, Frenchmen may use the proceeds of French exports to England in order to buy British securities. Indeed the range of transactions that can be covered by a payment agreement is limitless, subject only to the prior consent of the countries involved. But in most cases, such agreements have been primarily designed to allow old debts to be repaid or frozen assets (e.g., blocked bank balances) to be gradually released.

In more recent times, however, a special kind of payment agreement has covered transactions resulting from the extension of foreign aid by one country to another. A concrete example: Almost all of the dollar loans or grants extended by the United States to other countries are specifically tied to purchases in this country. On the other hand, ship-ments of United States wheat to such countries as India and Egypt have mostly been paid for by local currencies (rupees and Egyptian pounds), which were then used to finance a variety of United States expenditures in these countries.

More will be said about the economic and political implications of bilateral trading agreements in Chapter 15. Here we might note in passing that although such arrangements may be rationalized on the basis of balance-of-payments difficulties and/or scarcity of convertible foreign exchange, their remedial effect on the balance of payments is generally at the cost of a loss in economic efficiency and a reduction in gains from trade. This is especially true if the parties to a bilateral agreement are of unequal strength, since the weaker partner will doubt-less be exploited by the stronger. And although both countries may regard bilateral trade as better than no trade at all, the supposed mutual advantages may be so unequally distributed as to become actual dis-advantages for the weaker partner. Such, as we shall see later, was often the case during the 1930's—the period that gave rise to bilateralism, and that perfected the use of it both as a balance-of-payments corrective measure and as a weapon of political and economic aggression.

The Implications of Exchange Control

Whatever else may be said about exchange control as a means of remedying balance-of-payments ills, one thing stands out clearly: It merely relieves the symptoms of the disease, it does not cure the disease itself. True, application of exchange control may well accomplish the immediate task of easing the pressure of a deficit, and of checking the losses of gold and foreign-exchange reserves. But a balance-of-payments deficit, as we have already learned, is merely a reflection of underlying economic changes. Unless its causes are properly attended to, the deficit will reappear as soon as exchange control is removed. Yet the treatment of fundamental economic changes is beyond the capabilities of a mere exchange-control system.

Indeed, when its overall accomplishments are measured against its cost, a regime of exchange control turns out to be a rather expensive medicine. At best, it is an effective stopgap measure that allows a country time to catch its breath and, if it wishes, to apply the necessary treatment to the underlying causes of a balance-of-payments disequilibrium. Whether the country chooses to make good use of the protection thus afforded is an entirely different matter; it depends not only on the nature of the necessary adjustments themselves, but also on the political feasibility of carrying them out. In any case, nearly every country, at one time or another, has found it more convenient to escape from balance-of-payments difficulties by prolonging the use of exchange control than by undertaking fundamental economic readjustment. In so doing, countries have had to pay a stiff price for what amounted to superficial relief: Not only has the basic cause of the disequilibrium remained untreated in most cases, but the widespread imposition of exchange control has tended to replace economically beneficial trade relations with uneconomic bilateral dealings, discriminatory practices, and inefficient use of economic resources.

12

The Need for International Liquidity.
Unilateral and Multilateral Sources

Looking back and reflecting on the last four chapters, we find ourselves up against a curious paradox. The smooth flow of free multilateral trade requires the existence of a well-functioning international-payments mechanism, under which national currencies can be freely converted into one another at fairly stable exchange rates. Such a freely operating international monetary system can thrive best only when nations are generally free from balance-of payments difficulties. Yet the very existence of a free-trade and payments network, which links different national economies closely to each other, is bound to give rise to balance-of-payments disturbances from time to time. And when such disturbances become sufficiently severe and/or widespread, they are apt to result in corrective measures that tend to restrict international payments, and thus reduce the scope for, and the benefits from, free multilateral trade.

How can this conflict between the desirability of free trade and payments, on the one hand, and the consequences of balance of-payments disturbances, on the other hand, be reconciled? Part of a possible solution must necessarily lie within the sphere of domestic economic conditions and economic policies. A fairly high level of prosperity and a reasonable degree of economic stability within each country can create an atmosphere conducive to free trade between them. Moreover, under generally prosperous and stable conditions, the correction of balance-of-payments disturbances may prove to be a relatively easy and painless task, involving a minimum of disruption in either domestic or international economic relations. In any event, a country whose domestic economy is in good health can afford to tolerate occasional ups and downs in its balance of payments, while still allowing its citizens freedom of action in matters pertaining to foreign trade.

In a more immediate sense, however, the solution to the conflict requires that individual countries possess adequate resources with which to finance temporary balance-of-payments deficits. For with such resources, the temptation to impose exchange control at the first sign of trade disturbances would be considerably reduced, and the free flow of trade would not have to be obstructed on the slightest pretext. This particular requirement, generally known as the need for *international liquidity*, has motivated much of the recent thinking concerning international trade in general and the position of two countries—the United States and England—in particular. But the origins of the so-called international-liquidity problem go back to the period following World War I; and its evolution during the past forty years or so has helped to shape the present international monetary system. Indeed, one can hardly appreciate the current preoccupation with trade problems and payments problems without examining the development of the institutional structure within which such problems exist. In tracing this development, one must answer the question: What *is* international liquidity and what are its sources?

The Nature of International Liquidity

International liquidity refers to the availability, in individual countries, of means of payments with which to finance a desired volume of foreign trade, especially the importation of goods and services. It makes little or no difference what forms these resources take, as long as they are fully acceptable to foreign payees. Indeed, it is this requirement (i.e., full acceptability) that lies at the heart of the liquidity problem. For if all means of payments were equally acceptable throughout the world, the problem of financing foreign trade, and particularly balance-of-payments deficits, could hardly exist.

We have noted earlier that a national currency constitutes a fully acceptable means of payment within the political boundaries of its issuing country. But whether country A's currency would be acceptable to country B would normally depend on the latter's need or desire to buy goods from A, or on its ability to use A's currency to pay for purchases from country C or D. This ability, in turn, would depend on the willingness of those countries to accept A's currency, as determined by *their* wish to buy imports from A, or *their* ability to use A's currency to finance purchases from other countries. Generalizing, we may say that the extent to which a currency is acceptable outside its own borders depends on the use to which other countries can put it. The more countries that can make use of it, the more widely acceptable the currency becomes. And by virtue of being accepted by *many* countries, that currency becomes more useful and hence more acceptable to each country individually.

Acceptability should not be confused with convertibility. True, in a period characterized by exchange controls and currency *in*convertibility, freely convertible currencies are likely to enjoy wide acceptability and hence be sought after as a form of foreign-exchange reserves. But convertibility per se is not the ultimate test of acceptability. Thus, although under the nineteenth century gold standard, and for a short while during the 1920's, nearly all currencies were freely convertible, only the pound sterling emerged as the most important and generally acceptable currency. This was due not so much to the free convertibility of the pound as to the dominant position of Britain in world trade and finance. To be more specific, it was the world-wide demand for British products, as well as the financial and banking facilities centered in London, that made the pound the world's most useful and hence most acceptable currency. As such, foreign-held sterling balances constituted a source of international liquidity, to be used in financing current foreign-trade transactions, or to be held as reserves against a rainy day.

Nevertheless, under the international gold standard, most countries' official reserves took the form of gold. Indeed, then as now, gold has enjoyed the unique position of being the world's most acceptable means of international payments. For since all governments have always been ready to purchase gold with their own national currencies (though not necessarily to sell it), gold has enabled its possessor to finance purchases from, or repay debts to, any country. Hence, the official gold holdings of any country can without hesitation be counted as part of the country's stock of international liquidity. And precisely because such holdings constitute the most valuable form of international reserves, nearly every country has always welcomed the accumulation of gold. By the same token, every country has usually regarded substantial reduction in its gold stock as a cause for concern, and an occasion for the adoption of some preventative measures.

In fact, fear of losing their entire gold reserves was the main reason why most countries went off the gold standard in 1914 and again in the early 1930's. And, as we shall see later, the abandonment of gold was usually accompanied by the imposition of controls over international trade and payments. At the same time, however, the depletion of many countries' gold reserves, following World War I, prompted a search for alternative sources of international liquidity. In the process, an institutional structure developed, known as the gold-exchange standard; its essential features constitute to this day the basis of international monetary relations.

From Gold to the Gold-Exchange Standard

Growing out of the economic and political upheavals of the post–World War I era, the gold-exchange standard was expected to perform two major functions: (1) to provide a basis for the determination and maintenance of stable exchange rates between national currencies, and (2) to furnish countries with acceptable means of international payments that, together with gold, could be used to finance current trade and also be held as reserves.

Judged by the first of these functions, the gold-exchange standard can be regarded as but a variation on the theme of its predecessor, the gold standard itself. For by adhering to a gold-exchange standard, a country committed itself to maintain, through open-market operations, a fixed exchange rate between its own currency and a particular foreign currency that *was* freely convertible into gold. Moreover, the country had to assure the free convertibility of its currency into the gold-based currency to which it was pegged. Hence, although the gold-exchange-standard country did not necessarily stand ready to buy and sell gold at an officially fixed price, its currency was nevertheless convertible into gold at a fixed rate. On that basis, exchange rates between currencies, all of which were pegged to a gold-based currency, could be established and maintained.

But in addition to linking their own currencies to one gold-based currency or another, countries that adopted a gold-exchange standard began to hold increasing portions of their reserves in the form of such currencies or claims thereon. Here, then, lies the second key aspect of the gold-exchange standard as it developed during the 1920's. In essence, it was a growing practice by many central banks to hold their monetary reserves in the form of bank balances or highly liquid assets denominated in gold-based currencies. And the two currencies in which most of these balances (and assets) came to be held were the pound sterling and (increasingly since the 1930's) the American dollar. As a consequence, the sterling and the dollar have assumed both the designation and the role of *reserve currencies*, or *key currencies;* their role, as we shall presently see, has continued to plague them, for better and for worse, until this very day.

From the standpoint of the international monetary system as a whole, many viewed the early development of the gold-exchange standard as just the medicine needed for a world whose total gold supply was believed inadequate to meet all the demands for it. Indeed, this diagnosis of the world's economic ills (i.e., the inadequacy of gold) led to the recommendation (by the Financial Committee of the Genoa Conference in 1922) that the monetary reserves of most nations should consist largely of gold-based currencies rather than of gold itself. In this way, so went the argument, the world's existing gold stock could be stretched to provide "backing" for the gold-standard currencies directly, and for the gold-exchange-standard currencies indirectly. More important still, the willingness to hold and to use reserves denominated in gold-based currencies was expected to reduce the danger of gold losses in countries with balance-of-payments deficits. For if, instead of insisting on settlement in gold, an export-surplus country were willing to accept and hold a gold-based currency, it could increase its own reserves without actually depleting the gold reserves of a deficit country. And with the danger of gold losses reduced (it was also believed), individual countries would have a less urgent need to impose trade and payments restrictions whenever a deficit appeared in their balances of payments.[1]

A moment's reflection should convince the reader that the gold-exchange standard of the 1920's was conceived of as a supplement to the gold standard rather than as a replacement for it. Indeed, gold continued to be regarded as the ultimate basis for domestic monetary systems as well as for stable international monetary relations. But if the available supply was to be conserved, additional resources had to be found to satisfy the needs of central-bank monetary reserves, on the one hand, and the need for international liquidity, on the other. Under the gold-exchange standard, these additional resources were to consist of foreign holdings of gold-based key currencies, holdings that could be converted into gold itself on demand.

While in theory the gold-exchange standard appeared to provide a reasonable solution to a pressing problem, in practice it soon revealed several basic weaknesses. Perhaps the most serious of these concerned the position of the key-currency countries themselves. Thus, proponents of the gold-exchange standard had obviously overlooked the fact that if key currencies are to be widely used as international reserves, foreign countries must be able to *accumulate* claims on such currencies. But accumulation by foreign countries of a particular currency can be accomplished only if the country that issues it is willing to run a deficit in its own balance of payments. Put differently, country A can acquire claims on country B's currency only by running an overall balance-of-payments surplus with the latter. This is the same as saying that country B is running an overall deficit with country A. In short, under the gold-exchange standard, any net addition to the total amount of foreign-held key currencies depends on the existence of deficits in the balances of payments of key-currency countries.

At the same time, the gold-exchange standard places key-currency countries in special jeopardy by exposing their own gold reserves to

[1] It was apparently not realized until much later that the fear of losing reserves, denominated in gold-based currencies, may also lead to the imposition of exchange controls.

sudden and severe drains. Since foreign holdings of a key currency must be convertible into gold on demand, there is always a danger that their owners will choose to exercise this option and convert them into gold or another key currency. Moreover, the slightest doubt about the ability of a key-currency country to meet its external obligations, or the slightest concern over its domestic economic conditions, may start a panic among foreign holders of its currency, and may well precipitate large conversions of their balances into gold. Under these circumstances, confidence in the currency may be further undermined, thus accelerating the rush of foreign creditors to cash in their claims for gold.

That this is not merely a hypothetical danger was forcefully demonstrated by Britain's experience in the late 1920's and early 1930's. During that period, British gold reserves came repeatedly under attack whenever private speculative activities or actions by foreign central banks resulted in pressure on the sterling in foreign-exchange markets. And as Britain's gold reserves declined, so did confidence in sterling, causing further conversions of sterling claims into gold. Indeed, a massive onslaught by foreign holders of sterling balances on her gold reserves finally forced Britain to suspend, in September, 1931, the free convertibility of the pound into gold. And since sterling had been until then the major gold-based key currency, the suspension of its gold convertibility shortly led to the collapse of the entire gold-exchange system and, with it, to "a sharp *reduction* in the aggregate of international currency reserves."[2]

The breakdown of the gold-exchange system marked the beginning of the end for the international gold standard as a world institution. To be sure, gold continued to be held and used as an international reserve by countries fortunate enough to possess it. And the pound sterling, though no longer convertible into gold, still retained its status as a widely acceptable currency until 1939, when its convertibility into other currencies was restricted by exchange controls imposed by the British authorities. Moreover, the United States dollar, which remained on the free gold standard until 1934, was beginning to gain international prominence during this period, and provided increasing international liquidity for foreign countries. By and large, however, the decade of the

[2] League of Nations, *International Currency Experience* (Geneva: 1944), p. 41. (Italics added.)

1930's witnessed a gradual disintegration of an international monetary system under which multilateral financial settlements of foreign-trade transactions could be freely and easily effected. In the place of such a system, the thirties saw the widespread use of exchange controls and other trade restrictions, recurring waves of currency depreciation, the development of bilateral trade and payments arrangements, and so forth—all of which reduced drastically the volume of world trade.

No doubt many of these developments were attributable to the failure of the gold-exchange standard to provide an effective international monetary mechanism at a time when rapidly changing economic conditions demanded it. And it was the lesson learned from this interwar experience that prompted later efforts to reconstruct the post–World War II world economy on a more solid footing by equipping it with, among other things, a better international monetary system than that of the 1920's.

Bretton Woods and the International Monetary Fund

The present international monetary order owes much of its strength, as well as some of its weaknesses, to an agreement that was reached by representatives of some forty-four nations at an international conference in Bretton Woods, New Hampshire, in 1944. That conference, which drew up and approved the Articles of Agreement of the International Monetary Fund and of the International Bank for Reconstruction and Development,[3] was preceded by a great many discussions among British and American officials. During these discussions, two major proposals competed for acceptance. For although the main objective of each was to create an institutional framework that would be conducive to the pursuit of free trade and payments, the proposals differed sharply in concept and detail. It was in large measure the task of the Bretton Woods conference to hammer out some compromise between them.

The British proposal, a brain child of Lord Keynes, sought the establishment of an International Clearing Union with powers to create an international currency unit—to be called "bancor"—that would

[3] Chapter 19 contains a discussion of the International Bank for Reconstruction and Development.

serve as an international means of payment. According to the proposal, the central bank of each country would be committed to accept, without limit, payment in bancors from foreign central banks in settlement of international financial claims. These payments would be made through a mere transfer of bancor demand deposits held at the clearing union. Moreover, countries with balance-of-payments deficits could obtain bancors by using automatic overdraft facilities with the clearing union. Keynes's proposal envisioned, in essence, the creation of an international central bank with power to create unlimited demand deposits that could be used to settle international financial claims.

The American proposal, associated with the name of Harry Dexter White, took a less visionary approach to future monetary relations. It also represented, however, a far-reaching innovation in international finance. Instead of a clearing union, the United States proposed the establishment of a fund into which each country would contribute a certain amount in its own currency, and from which it could borrow other countries' currencies whenever it needed them. In a word, the American proposal envisaged an international currency pool, consisting not of an unlimited amount of *international* currency units, but of specific amounts of *national* currencies.

The final compromise was the International Monetary Fund (IMF) which resembled the American proposal more than the British one. For the IMF is essentially a pool of currencies whose resources have come from the contributions of its member countries, based on their assigned *quotas*.[4] As set up originally, the total size of the Fund was the equivalent of $8.8 billion, of which the United States quota alone accounted for some $2.75 billion. In 1959, however, most of the members agreed to increase their contributions beyond the original quotas; as a result, the total resources of the Fund, as of 1965, stood at over $15 billion.[5]

The quota assigned to each member determines not only the size of its contribution to the Fund, but also the amount of the Fund's resources that it may borrow. The quotas themselves, however, consist of two

[4] These quotas were assigned on the basis of the relative importance of countries in terms of their foreign trade, national income, and similar considerations.

[5] In 1962, moreover, the IMF concluded an agreement with ten major industrial countries whereby they agreed to lend to the Fund, should the need arise, a total equivalent to $6 billion in their own currencies.

components: 25 per cent of the quota must be contributed in the form of gold and dollars,[6] and 75 per cent in the member's own currency. In determining the size of a member's drawing (borrowing) rights, both the total size of its quota and the Fund's holdings of its currency are taken into account. According to the general rule, the Fund's holdings of a country's currency cannot exceed, at any one time, 200 per cent of that country's quota. Although this rule can be waived at the discretion of the Fund, it means that the total borrowing power of a member country amounts to 125 per cent of its quota, since 75 per cent of the quota consists of the country's own currency.

This peculiar way of determining the extent of borrowing (drawing) rights will be better appreciated by understanding what is involved in a borrowing transaction. For example, when a country, say France, borrows from the IMF, it actually purchases the foreign currency it needs (e.g., pounds sterling), paying for it with its own currency (francs). Repayment of the "loan" involves the repurchase of the francs from the IMF by paying for them either in pounds or in gold. In other words, the IMF's lending activities, on which, incidentally, it levies interest and service charges, consist essentially of selling (and buying) different currencies needed by different countries. And, as can well be imagined, during the first years of its operation (it opened for business in 1947) the currency in greatest demand was the United States dollar. Since then, however, the demand for other major currencies has risen; from 1961 to 1965, for example, only 26 per cent of all drawings were of United States dollars.[7]

Judged by such activities, the IMF's main function has been to provide resources (in the form of needed currencies) that could be drawn upon by countries whose own reserves may at times be insufficient to finance balance-of-payments deficits. As such, the IMF must be regarded as a source of international liquidity. But in addition, the establishment of the IMF signified the acceptance by its members of certain principles and rules that would govern their conduct in inter-

---

[6] The proportion of gold to dollars was to be determined in each case. Moreover, this requirement was originally waived for countries whose own international reserves were very small.

[7] See L. Yeager, *International Monetary Relations* (New York: Harper & Row, 1966), p. 350.

national monetary affairs. Indeed, as claimed by its Articles of Agreement, some of the IMF's major objectives are: to promote international monetary cooperation; to facilitate the expansion and balanced growth of international trade; to promote exchange-rate stability and discourage competitive depreciation; to encourage the elimination of exchange controls and discriminatory exchange-rate practices; and, in general, to create an atmosphere of confidence and rapport among its members. In order to put teeth into these high-sounding goals, the Articles of Agreement endowed the new institution with certain powers and imposed on its members several obligations.

Thus, under the provisions of the IMF Agreement, each member was obliged to establish a par value of its currency either in terms of gold or in terms of the United States dollar, and to peg the exchange rates between its currency and foreign currencies within a range of 1 per cent above and below that par value. Moreover, the initial par value could be changed (i.e., devalued or revalued) only in order to correct, in the words of the agreement, a "fundamental disequilibrium" in the country's balance of payments.[8] In any event, such a change must be approved by the Fund—unless the change alters the exchange rate by no more than 10 per cent of the currency's initial par value. If a member violates this provision, by devaluating or revaluating its currency by more than 10 per cent without the Fund's permission, it runs the risk of being declared ineligible to draw on the Fund's resources, and may, moreover, be expelled from the institution.[9]

Similarly, members must refrain from imposing exchange restrictions on current-account transactions, and must avoid practices that discriminate against any currency. Interestingly enough, the imposition of exchange controls on capital-account transactions is *not* forbidden, and at times may actually be authorized by the fund. This provision undoubtedly reflects recognition of the fact that balance-of-payments difficulties may be rooted in excessive or destabilizing capital outflows. Currency discrimination may also be sanctioned by the IMF under

[8] The term "fundamental disequilibrium" was never clearly defined, but it has come to be interpreted as a prolonged or substantial balance-of-payments disequilibrium.

[9] The devaluation of the pound sterling in 1949 was, in a sense, a violation of this provision, since Britain merely informed the Fund of its intention instead of asking its permission.

certain conditions. To be specific, if the demand for a particular currency exceeds the Fund's supply, the currency may be officially designated a "scarce currency." As long as it is so designated, member countries are permitted to impose discriminatory exchange controls on the use of that currency.

The general prohibition of the use of exchange controls, moreover, was originally subject to a catchall exception, formally referred to as the "transitional period": the maintenance of exchange controls over current-account transactions was to be tolerated for a period of time following the establishment of the IMF. This time period had no specific termination date, but countries that maintained exchange restrictions on current transactions for more than five years after the beginning of the Fund's operation were obliged to discuss their expediency with the Fund each year. If the Fund finds no justification for the continuation of such restrictions, it may request their removal; a member who refuses to comply may be declared ineligible to use the Fund's resources. We might note, in passing, that although 1952 marked the fifth full year of the Fund's operations, many countries managed to retain exchange controls for many years beyond that date. Even today, some members of the IMF continue to exercise such restrictions on the use of foreign exchange.

No brief review of the IMF's operations during the first twenty years of its existence can hope to do it full justice. For while the Fund's supporters usually point to several of its important accomplishments, its critics have seriously questioned both its past performance and its ability to cope with the needs of an ever-expanding international economy. The existence of such divergent views obviously calls for a careful examination of the IMF's record. We do not have space for a thorough assessment, but a brief one will nevertheless be useful.

On the positive side, it can be said that the establishment of the IMF represented a new and bold approach to international monetary problems—an approach that emphasizes joint and cooperative efforts by many nations rather than efforts undertaken by each nation individually. This approach is surely a marked improvement over the attitudes and practices that dominated the international economy during the 1920's and 1930's. More important, from the standpoint of providing for adequate reserves to finance balance-of-payments deficits, the IMF constitutes a *multilateral* source of international liquidity, adding its resources to the reserves of individual countries. Indeed, a member of the IMF can count as reserves not only its own holdings of gold and convertible currencies, but also the amount of its drawing rights on the Fund's resources. And on several occasions, as we shall presently see, the Fund has made available additional financial resources—in excess of drawing rights—to countries whose currencies came under heavy speculative pressure, or whose balances of payments were threatened with a particularly critical development.

Also among its positive accomplishments is the technical advice and assistance that the IMF has rendered to underdeveloped countries. Although this function had not been envisaged in the Articles of Agreement, it has developed in the course of time and has grown in significance as more and more developing nations have become members of the IMF. By providing these nations with expert advice on how to formulate appropriate monetary and fiscal policies, the IMF has contributed a great deal toward their general economic development. And because the IMF is an important and respected international agency, its advice in such matters has in large measure been accepted by the underdeveloped countries. In addition, the IMF can rightly boast of a highly competent research staff whose publications and reports have furnished both governments and the general public with a great deal of useful economic and statistical information. And finally, like several other international institutions that came into being in the immediate post–World War II era, the IMF has provided a continuous forum for consultations and discussions among its member nations. As such, it has performed a service that had not previously existed in the area of international monetary affairs. In a sense, this service has been perhaps the greatest virtue of the IMF as a force for the maintenance of a smoothly functioning, frictionless international monetary system.

On the other hand, it cannot be denied that during its first ten years the IMF played a rather passive role in matters pertaining to international monetary policy, and failed to exercise the kind of leadership that had been envisaged for it at Bretton Woods. Nor was the Fund particularly active in its lending operations during its first ten years. In fact, after the first two years, at the end of which the total amount of net drawing (i.e., borrowing less repayment) came to about $750 million, the Fund assumed a rather conservative attitude toward lending. It took the position that drawing rights were not automatic and that each request for drawing (borrowing) had to be passed on by the IMF Executive Directors, who are empowered either to grant or to refuse such requests. Largely as a result, the net amount of drawing shrank from about $730 million in 1950 to $234.2 million in 1955.

Indeed, it was not until 1956 that lending activities picked up again. The occasion was the Suez Canal episode of 1956–1957, which led to a critical balance-of-payments situation in England and France, and brought heavy speculative pressures on their currencies—particularly the pound sterling. Coming to the rescue, the IMF made available to these two countries some $1.5 billion, mostly in the form of stand-by credits, which could be drawn upon when needed.[10] But in the three years following the Suez crisis, the Fund again became a *negative* lender—that is, each year total repayments exceeded total drawings; and by 1960, net drawings stood at $867 million. Since that time, however, the Fund engaged in large-scale lending operations on two occasions. In 1961 and again in 1964, it enabled Britain to draw substantial sums of foreign currencies, and arranged for additional stand-by credits. In both cases, these resources were urgently needed in order to defend the pound sterling from severe speculative pressures. In both instances, the IMF's assistance proved highly effective in combating the crisis.

Yet such recurrent speculative attacks on a currency, particularly a key currency such as the pound sterling or the dollar, have provided critics of the IMF with perhaps their strongest argument. They maintain that the establishment and subsequent development of the IMF have not removed the basic instability inherent in an international monetary system based on a gold-exchange standard. That instability, they claim, arises from the continued reliance, for needed international liquidity, on one or two key currencies—a reliance that places the burden of an entire international system on one or two countries. And while the critics do— as they must—concede that the IMF has been a useful additional source of international reserves, they rightly argue that its contributions are necessarily limited to the resources that it commands. Hence, should a

---

[10] A stand-by credit arrangement, first used by the Fund in 1952, guarantees that a member may draw from the Fund specified amounts of resources within a given period of time. It might be noted, incidentally, that in 1956–1957 not all the stand-by credits were actually drawn by England and France.

severe and widespread liquidity crisis occur, the Fund would be unable, given its present resources, to meet all the demands upon it. Under the circumstances, the international monetary system might come tumbling down as it did in the 1930's.

The seriousness of the charge, whose most vigorous exponent has been Professor Robert Triffin[11] of Yale, has given rise to considerable argument and debate. Much of the debate has centered on the question of whether the present system, including the IMF, can generate adequate reserves to provide a cushion against severe balance-of-payments difficulties, without at the same time imposing undue strain on the key currency countries; this strain, of course, opens the door to international monetary instability. To appreciate the significance of the question, and to test the validity of the charge that prompted it, we must briefly examine the impact of post–World War II international monetary developments on the balance-of-payments position of the United States.

Recent International Monetary Experience

Notwithstanding the advent of the IMF, the international reserves of most countries still take the form of official holdings of gold and foreign exchange, the latter consisting largely of dollars and pounds. As such, the existing international monetary system is properly called a gold-exchange standard, in which the major source of international liquidity consists of the world's holdings of these two key currencies. However, it must also be noted that from 1930 to 1959, when the pound sterling was inconvertible in varying degrees, the dollar was the one single currency acceptable to, and sought by, virtually all countries. And by 1960, foreign central banks accumulated a total of some $10.5 billion in dollar balances and dollar claims, holding them as reserves.

The ability of foreign countries to accumulate substantial dollar reserves, especially since 1950, was largely due to the massive economic and military aid that was extended by the United States government, and to substantial American private investment abroad. Up until 1950,

[11] Robert Triffin, *Gold and the Dollar Crisis* (New Haven: Yale University Press, 1960). In this book Triffin offers a diagnosis of, and a remedy for, what he considers to be the current international monetary ills.

however, all the dollars that foreign countries could possibly obtain were urgently needed to finance current-account deficits with the United States; most of them were, in fact, used for that purpose. Indeed, during the years immediately following World War II, the world at large, and Western Europe in particular, suffered from a severe "dollar shortage"; they needed more dollars to finance imports from the United States than they could earn by exporting to that country. But from 1950 on, and increasingly so with each passing year, some countries managed to run overall balance-of-payments surpluses with the United States. As a result, they were able to accumulate increasing amounts of dollar claims that they were content to hold as reserves.

However, the increased accumulation of dollar claims by foreign countries meant an almost continuous overall deficit in the United States balance of payments. Indeed, in nearly every year since 1950, total United States expenditures abroad exceeded its total receipts. And while these annual deficits, which were relatively small on the average, provided foreign countries with a source of additional reserves, their cumulative growth could not help but contain a potential threat to the United States own international financial position. By allowing other countries to accumulate dollar claims, the United States, in effect, exposed its own gold reserves to possible depletion in the event that foreign central banks wanted to convert their dollar holdings into gold. Although during most of the 1950's, such a danger seemed fairly remote, the climate of opinion changed rather abruptly in 1958. In that year, the overall deficit in the United States balance of payments suddenly reached $3.5 billion, and resulted in an unprecedented gold outflow of $2.3 billion.

Nor was this a passing phenomenon. In 1959, the annual deficit stood at $3.7 billion, and in 1960 it climbed further and reached about $3.9 billion. Since then, and partly as a result of several measures undertaken by the United States, the yearly deficits have been confined to the $1.5–$3 billion range. More alarming, however, was the fact that during 1958–1965, sizable amounts of foreign-held dollar claims were converted into gold, causing a substantial reduction in the United States gold stock. Although such conversions have been in part motivated by the desire of several foreign (mostly European) central banks to maintain a higher ratio between their gold and foreign-exchange holdings, they have also reflected the recurrent suspicion that sooner or later the United States may be forced to devalue the dollar by raising the dollar price of gold.[12] In any event, the main consequence of these conversions has been a decline in the United States gold stock, from a high of $24.6 billion in 1949 to about $13.8 billion at the end of 1965— a decline that was hardly viewed with equanimity either by the United States or by official holders of dollar claims abroad.

Whatever else may be said about the recent condition of the United States balance of payments and its gold losses, these phenomena must be viewed essentially as arising from the existing international monetary system. Indeed, critics who charge the IMF with failure to eliminate the inherent weaknesses of the gold-exchange standard, point to the recent experiences of the United States, and of Britain as well, as evidence in favor of their case. To them, the gold-exchange standard—even with the IMF as presently constituted—is at best a paradoxical, and at worst a self-defeating, kind of arrangement. While under the present system, they argue, any substantial increase in international liquidity requires continuously increasing deficits in the balances of payments of key-currency countries, such deficits breed lack of confidence in, and destabilizing speculative attacks against, the key currencies themselves. On the other hand, should the key-currency countries refuse to tolerate balance-of-payments deficits, and attempt to reduce or eliminate them, the chief source of international liquidity might well dry up. More significantly, since the world's gold production alone cannot meet even the present needs for international liquidity, it can hardly be expected to meet future needs. Under the circumstances, the reduction or elimination of balance-of-payments deficits by the present key-currency countries would surely jeopardize the continued growth of world trade.

These, then, are the main charges that have been leveled at the present international monetary system: (1) that the system is inherently fragile and is liable to collapse if severe pressure is brought to bear on the present key currencies, and (2) that the present sources of international liquidity cannot be relied upon to generate the adequate re-

---

[12] From the standpoint of foreign governments holding dollar claims, it is better to convert dollars into gold *before* the price of gold is raised. By so doing, they accumulate gold that, after devaluation, would be worth more in terms of dollars than it was before.

serves that will be needed as world trade continues to grow. Although different critics have pressed one charge more than the other, they generally agree that the present international monetary system could and should be improved. This sentiment, incidentally, is shared even by some who are basically satisfied with the IMF and its contributions. Hence, it is hardly surprising that a number of plans have appeared in recent years for the reform of the international monetary system. And it is only fitting that we conclude our long discussion of international monetary problems by briefly acquainting ourselves with the various solutions that have been proposed.

Proposals for International Monetary Reform

The plans for international monetary reform that have been advanced in recent years generally fall into one of two major categories. Some proposals are designed to strengthen the present system without changing its essential character. Others call for the replacement of the gold-exchange standard as it now exists with new international monetary structures, based on different sets of principles. Yet even within each group, significant variations can be found. Although a detailed account that would identify each and every proposal lies beyond the scope of this book, we may conveniently distinguish between six types of proposals on the basis of the solutions they embody.[13]

1. Cooperation and mutual assistance among central banks
2. Extension of the gold-exchange standard through the adoption of additional key currencies
3. Centralization of reserves and reserve creation
4. Increase in the price of gold
5. Return to a genuine gold standard
6. Introduction of freely flexible exchange rates

Of the six "solutions" listed above, the first two are the least drastic. The measures they suggest neither call for the elimination of the

[13] For a detailed account and critical analysis of most of the proposed schemes, see F. Machlup, "Plans for Reform of the International Monetary System," in *International Payments, Debts, and Gold* (New York: Charles Scribner's Sons, 1964), pp. 282–366. This section is based heavily, though not exclusively, on Machlup's work.

gold-exchange standard nor urge basic changes in its structure. They are merely intended to bolster the defense of the existing system by reducing its vulnerability to sudden and severe crises. Indeed, one of the measures suggested has already been put into practice in recent years; it takes the form of "swap" arrangements between central banks of different countries. Such arrangements, which were initiated by the United States in 1962, provide for the reciprocal exchange of lines of credit by central banks in their respective currencies. Thus, should one country's currency come under speculative pressure, its central bank could swap its own currency for foreign currencies with foreign central banks. The foreign currencies thus obtained could in turn be used to defend, through open-market operation, the exchange rate of the currency under pressure. Within an agreed period of time, the swap would be reversed: The foreign currencies previously obtained would be exchanged for the domestic currency.

But in addition to central-bank swap arrangements, which are designed to provide a besieged currency with immediate help and thus ward off its attackers, the gold-exchange standard might be strengthened if its base were broadened. In other words, the instability of the present system, which stems largely from the reliance on only two key currencies, might be somewhat reduced if several key currencies shared the burden of international liquidity. This, in fact, is the essential argument behind the second solution listed above—a solution that is sometimes called the multiple-key-currencies proposal.

There is something to be said for this proposal, especially since in recent years several European currencies (e.g., the German mark, the Dutch guilder, the French franc) have attained wide international acceptability. Indeed, the continued economic growth and expansion of trade of European countries, particularly the members of the European Economic Community, may enhance the status of their currencies and may lead to their wide use as a form of international reserves. Such a source of additional international liquidity could certainly lighten the load now carried by the dollar and sterling, thus reducing the instability inherent in a two-currency gold-exchange standard.

Whether a multiple-key-currencies system would actually develop within the framework of the present gold-exchange standard is anyone's guess. Moreover, even if such a system did develop, its effectiveness would depend upon a high degree of confidence in the monetary and

202 PART III : *Barriers to Free Trade*

fiscal policies of all key-currency countries. For should confidence frequently shift from one key currency to another, the danger of destabilizing speculative activities would be magnified many times. In any event,
even in the absence of speculative pressures, key-currency countries
would still be exposed to potential drains on their gold reserves, which
might in turn undermine confidence in one currency or another and
thereby spur speculators on.[14] Thus, from the standpoint of critics of the
gold-exchange standard, a multiple-key-currencies system is not any
more satisfactory than a two-key currencies system. To them, present-
day international monetary problems call for more drastic solutions. And
one of their proposed solutions calls for the centralization of reserves and
reserve creation (number three on our list).

The idea of centralized reserves—that is, the creation of a truly
international reserve unit, to be issued by an international agency—is
not new. As we have already seen, it was the central idea in Keynes'
proposal for an international clearing union. But although Keynes'
proposal was rejected in 1944, its basic idea has recently acquired a
number of champions, among whom Professor Triffin has been by far the
most vocal.

Like Keynes before him, Triffin envisages a system in which an
international agency—for example, an expanded IMF—could create demand deposits that would be used as international reserves by individual
countries. But unlike Keynes, Triffin carries the idea of reserve creation
one step further. His plan suggests that demand deposits by the re-
modeled IMF (designated as XIMF) may be created not only by the
requests of countries with balance-of-payments deficits, but by the XIMF
itself—whenever the latter felt it desirable to expand the volume of
international reserves. In effect, then, Triffin's proposal would transform
the existing IMF into a truly international central bank, having the
power to expand demand deposits through the granting of loans and
advances, as well as through open-market operations (e.g., by purchase of

---

[14] To lessen the danger of such speculative shifts, an interesting variation on
the multiple-key-currencies idea has been suggested. According to it, a composite
reserve unit (CRU) should be created, equal in value to a gold dollar but consisting
of fixed proportions of several major currencies (dollars, sterling, francs, and so on).
For details and elaboration, see E. M. Bernstein, ''A Practical Proposal for International Monetary Reserves,'' Model, Roland & Co., *Quarterly Review* (Fourth
Quarter, 1963).

securities in the money markets of its member countries). And since an expansion of XIMF demand deposits would mean an expansion of international reserves, the world could always be assured of an adequate supply of international liquidity that would grow with the growth in international trade.

In some of its technical and operational details, Triffin's plan resembles the one proposed by Keynes, although it contains certain operational safeguards—to placate the inevitable critics, one would assume. But the real significance of Triffin's proposal lies, not in its technical and operational aspects, but in its basic concept—namely, lessened reliance on increased gold production and balance of payments deficits of key currency countries as sources of international liquidity. As such, the proposal deserves hearty applause, even though its chances of being implemented (with or without modifications) in the foreseeable future are slight indeed. Moreover, it deserves credit for stimulating further thought concerning the present international monetary system, and for inspiring the formulation of other plans for its reform.[15]

Little need be said about the fourth and fifth solutions. For although some of their advocates are well-known economists, these measures are neither practical nor especially desirable. An increase in the price of gold, so it is suggested, would accomplish two things: (1) it would increase the monetary value of existing gold stocks and thereby increase the aggregate value of international reserves, and (2) it would create a faster rate of gold production that would result in a larger output of gold. True. But an increase in the price of gold would favor only a few countries: those that possess large gold reserves and those that produce most of the world's gold. At the same time, however, such an increase would hurt countries whose foreign reserves consist primarily of gold-pegged foreign currencies.[16] And as for stimulating a faster rate of gold production, a once-and-for-all price increase would not do. For since the cost of producing (i.e., digging) gold will doubtless continue to increase, its price would have to be repeatedly raised in order to induce

[15] At least eight other similar proposals have been suggested, following the appearance of Triffin's plan. For a convenient summary, see Machlup, *op. cit.*, p. 336.

[16] This is so because an increase in, say, the dollar price of gold means in effect a devaluation of the dollar; as a result, countries holding dollar claims could not help but suffer a loss in the value of their international reserves.

additional supplies. The result : a perpetual chain of gold price increases, favoring one or two gold-producing countries.

Nor can a return to a genuine gold standard be regarded as a reasonable solution to present international monetary problems. Indeed, such a solution seems a sheer anachronism in a world in which most governments are committed to the maintenance of domestic economic stability and high levels of employment through the use of fiscal and monetary policies. The flexibility in the conduct of monetary and fiscal policies, which such a commitment requires, is surely at odds with the so-called "rules of the game" that are implied in a genuine gold standard. More significantly, the advocates of a return to gold are yet to demon-state how their solution would create an adequate growth of inter-national liquidity to meet the needs of an expanding world trade. And until they have managed to do so, we must conclude that at present a gold standard per se would serve no useful purpose, either as an element of stability or as a source of international liquidity in the world economy.

The sixth and last solution differs fundamentally from all the preceding five. For by sacrificing exchange-rate fixity (i.e., official peg-ging of currencies) to freely flexible exchange rates, it seeks to remove altogether the necessity for official holding of reserves, and relies instead on the price mechanism in the foreign-exchange market to produce the supply of needed currencies at any given time. This is indeed a marked departure from the present system, under which countries are committed to maintain rather fixed exchange rates for national currencies. Yet precisely this commitment, say the advocates of freely flexible exchange rates, necessitates the possession of gold and foreign-exchange reserves with which to finance balance-of-payments deficits and fight off specula-tive pressures. Under a freely flexible exchange-rates system, so they argue, there could be no such thing as a discrepancy between foreign-exchange receipts and expenditures, since any foreign currency could always be obtained at a price—the price that equates its current supply and demand. Consequently, the basic problem of international liquidity (i.e., the availability of acceptable means of international payments) would vanish and the services of so-called key currencies would no longer be needed. Under the circumstances, the obligations currently imposed on key-currency countries, and the dangers to which such countries are exposed, would mostly disappear.

Please note, however, that a freely flexible exchange-rates system does not in itself constitute a guarantee against balance-of-payments disturbances. Nor are its advocates unaware of the several disadvantages inherent in freely fluctuating exchange rates. Hence, few of them envisage a world in which exchange rates are allowed to fluctuate without *any* limits, however wide these limits might actually be. Moreover, few would expect that an adoption of freely flexible exchange rates would result in a demotion of gold from its present position as a domestic and international monetary reserve. And finally, few would expect to see monetary authorities stand by passively in the event of severe balance-of-payments difficulties—even if exchange rates were allowed to fluctuate. In short, the only flexible exchange-rates system that could be seriously considered for adoption would have to be one in which flexibility would be managed rather than left to its own devices. And even with this qualification, there are few signs that the leading countries of the world are presently contemplating the abandonment of fixed exchange rates in favor of freely flexible ones.

To sum up, of all the solutions, only one appears to have been acted upon concretely: cooperation and mutual assistance among central banks. And while the notion of reinforcing the present gold-exchange standard with additional key currencies has gained considerable acceptance, it still remains largely a matter of deliberation rather than of execution. This is not to suggest, however, that the need for increased international liquidity and for stable international monetary relations must wait for action on one or several of the solutions. For there is still much that can be done—and some that has already been done—within the framework of existing international institutions. Indeed, the 1959 decision by the IMF members to increase their quotas and the 1962 agreement between the IMF and ten major countries (see footnote 5) exemplify the kinds of measures that may strengthen the present system. Along similar lines, the IMF might perhaps undertake some internal reforms that would make access to its resources more speedily and easily available. To augment these resources, as the need for them rises, member countries might agree to increase their quotas periodically.[17]

Yet whatever measures might be taken in the future, this much is obvious: If international trade is to pursue economically advantageous

[17] In 1965, the Fund agreed to raise members' quotas to a total of $21 billion; but drawing rights have remained carefully controlled.

paths, it must be furnished with a free and effective international monetary mechanism, capable of generating adequate supplies of international liquidity. For in the absence of such a mechanism, international monetary problems would surely prompt solutions that would obstruct trade and divert it from its natural course.

PART IV

BARRIERS TO FREE TRADE:
PRIVATE AND PUBLIC POLICIES

13

Monopolies and International Cartels

MARKET IMPERFECTIONS WERE
not taken into account in the theoretical model that we used to explain
international trade. Our explanation as to why and how mutually beneficial patterns of trade are established was based on the assumption of
pure competition and on the absence of any artificial barriers to the
flows of goods between nations.

In Part III, however, we discussed one type of trade barrier—exchange controls—that constitutes a departure from the free-market
conditions assumed earlier. Although exchange controls can justly be
regarded as impediments to trade, they are usually needed in extenuat-
ing circumstances; in any event, they are not incompatible with the basic
requisites of pure competition. In other words, freely competitive markets can conceivably exist even if exchange controls are practiced. But
the opposite is not true: Pure competition is *not* automatically assured
by the mere absence of foreign-exchange regulations.

Because pure competition is, in reality, the exception rather than the
rule, we must now relax our earlier assumption and admit into the
picture another set of barriers with which trade flows may have to
contend: the presence of monopolistic elements within national and
international markets.

Competition Versus Monopoly

By way of introduction, consider briefly the basic features that distinguish a purely competitive market (or industry) from a monopolistic one. Three fundamental characteristics of pure competition come immediately to mind: (1) a large number of sellers, (2) free entry and ease of exit, and (3) a homogeneous (standardized) product. Under such conditions, it is unlikely that any single producer could influence the market price by varying his output. Each firm, in fact, is faced with an infinitely elastic (horizontal) demand curve, indicating that it can sell all it wishes at the prevailing market price. Should the firm raise its price single-handedly, it would lose sales to its competitors. Nor would a price reduction bring any benefits, for the firm would needlessly suffer a reduction in profit.

Given a market price of, say, P_1 (in Figure 13.1), and wishing to maximize its profit, the typical firm would produce at a point where its marginal cost is equal to its marginal revenue. But since at this output (OQ_1), average cost is below the price, the firm will reap abnormal profits, which would presumably attract new firms into the industry. The entry of additional firms and the resultant expansion of the industry's total output would send the market price down to, say, P_2, causing our firm to readjust its own output and produce OQ_2 units. Here, however, average cost is above the price, and the firm incurs losses. Under the circumstances, the firm may be forced to leave the industry; or it may be able to weather the storm and hold out until other firms leave, thereby sending the market price up.

Neither P_1 nor P_2 can be regarded as long-run equilibrium positions for the firm or the industry. In one instance, firms will be attracted into the industry, and in another, some may find it impossible to continue in operation. Only when movements in and out of the industry come to a standstill is an equilibrium established. In Figure 13.1, this will occur when the market price settles at P. For here the price (which is also the marginal revenue) would be equal to both the marginal *and* average costs, and the firm would experience neither losses nor excessive profits. Here, too, the output (OQ) yields the lowest average cost, which, given the size of the firm, represents its most efficient level of production.

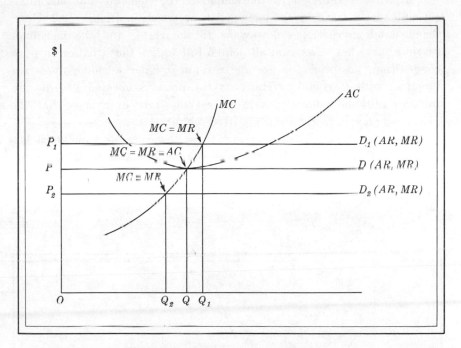

FIGURE *13.1* Profit Maximization (Pure Competition)

In contrast, a monopoly consists of a single producer, accounting for the entire output of a particular commodity. Moreover, the monopolist need not fear that other firms will enter the field; he is either protected by long-term patent rights or is sufficiently strong to nip would-be competitors in the bud. Thus, with the same impunity exhibited by Louis XIV, the monopolist may boast, "*L'industrie, c'est moi!*"

What does this mean? Since under a monopoly the industry and the firm are one and the same, the monopolist *can* influence the market price by varying the quantity he offers for sale. He may restrict output, thus driving prices up, or he may glut the market, bringing prices down. His action is limited, however, by the nature—or, more specifically, the elasticity—of consumer demand for his product. He cannot, for example, sell all he wishes at a given price. He must lower the price in order to induce consumers to buy more, and he must expect the quantity demanded to fall if his price goes up.

All this is reflected in the shape of the demand and marginal-revenue curves faced by the monopolist, as shown in Figure 13.2. Here, the demand curve slopes downward to the right, and the marginal-revenue curve lies below it at all points. For unlike the situation in pure competition, the price (or average revenue) under a monopoly is *not* identical with marginal revenue. As the price is lowered in order to induce additional sales, the marginal revenue falls even more than the price, and may, in fact, become negative.

When it comes to cost characteristics, however, the monopolist has average-cost and marginal-cost curves similar in shape to those of the purely competitive producer. The average-cost curve is U-shaped and is crossed, at its lowest point, by the marginal-cost curve. Moreover, the

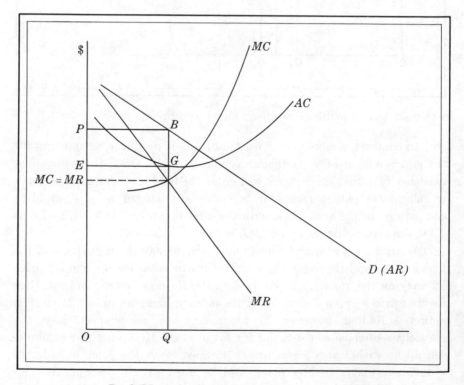

FIGURE *13.2* Profit Maximization (Monopoly)

same principle for profit maximization holds true in both cases. Thus, the monopolist described in Figure 13.2 will produce the output OQ, for here his marginal cost and marginal revenue are equal. The price at which he can sell this particular output is OP and his (maximum) profit is represented by the area $PEGB$. Having settled on the profit-maximizing output, the monopolist can sit back and enjoy the fruits of his labor. For since entry into the field is restricted, he is in little danger of having to readjust his output or change his price in the face of new competition. Even in the long run he can continue to make excessive profits.

Two major conclusions about monopoly[1] are usually drawn from the foregoing analysis. First, the price charged by the monopolist is always higher than his marginal cost. Thus, the principle of marginal cost pricing, so closely identified with efficient allocation of resources, is absent in a monopoly situation. Second, under monopoly, output is never produced at the lowest point on the average-cost curve (except, of course, by accident). Hence, it is claimed that given its resources, the monopolistic firm does not operate at the most efficient level of production possible.

Against these monopolistic ''vices,'' there is at least one virtue. Due to its large size, the firm in a monopoly (or oligopoly) may reap the benefits of economies of scale that are normally denied to firms operating in a purely competitive market. Indeed, the advantages of large-scale production constitute a valid justification for a market structure based on a few large firms, rather than on many small firms. This is especially true in those lines of production (e.g., automobiles, steel) in which increased productive efficiency is technologically tied to, and dependent on, increases in the size of output. And as efficiency rises, average costs fall, making reductions in price possible.

It does not necessarily follow, therefore, that because in the long run the purely competitive firm produces at the lowest point on its average-cost curve, the resulting cost figure will be actually lower than under monopoly. On the contrary, Figure 13.3 shows that a monopolistic firm may produce a given output at a *lower* average cost than the firm under pure competition—and this, despite the fact that the latter does, and the former does not, operate at the lowest point on their respective average-cost curves. The reason is fairly obvious. Because the monopoly enjoys

---

[1] Similar conclusions apply, in varying degrees, to other types of imperfectly competitive markets, e.g., oligopoly, monopolistic competition, and others.

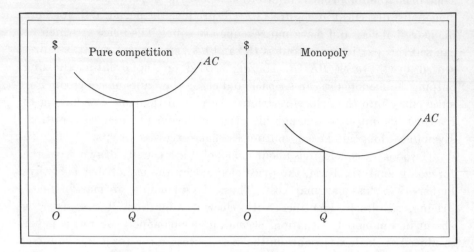

FIGURE *13.3*   Average Costs of Producing a Given Output (Pure Competition and Monopoly)

large-scale economies, its *entire* average-cost curve lies below that of the purely competitive firm; it can, therefore, produce any output at a lower cost.[2]

At the same time, the monopolist may not choose to share his cost savings with the consumer. He may charge a much higher price than is warranted by actual per-unit costs, or he may purposely hold back output, driving prices still higher. Moreover, taking advantage of variations in demand conditions, he may charge different prices in different markets, even though his per-unit costs are the same. Practices like these—cost-plus pricing, output restrictions, price discrimination, and so on—provide the critics of monopoly with their heaviest ammunition. Bearing these practices in mind, let us consider now the effects of monopolies and cartels on the volume and patterns of international trade.

---

[2] Another consideration is the availability of resources to finance research and development that may result in new and better products, and also greater efficiency and lower costs. Small firms do not normally possess such financial resources.

International Monopolies and Cartels: Nature and Extent

A desire to avoid competition, especially price wars, is often the major reason why national monopolies and trusts are formed. Indeed, many of the monopolies that have existed in the United States and elsewhere resulted from collusive agreements between firms in the same industry (or closely related industries) to pursue common price policies and to respect each other's share of the market. At times, such agreements were forced by a strong firm on its weaker competitors; but more often several large firms would voluntarily agree to a common mode of market behavior. Voluntary or not, collusive agreements have basically one main purpose: to eliminate the threat of competitive behavior within a particular industry, and to assure each participating firm a reasonable amount of profit.

Similar considerations underlie the formation of international monopolies, or *cartels*. Although they vary, international cartels may be generally defined as arrangements between producers in different countries to restrict competition in all or part of a particular industry. As in the case of domestic monopolies, international cartels may be voluntarily or involuntarily formed. They may involve a formal and explicit agreement or merely a gentlemen's agreement. Finally, they may cover either one or several aspects of international business relationships. For example, the famous international lamp cartel provided both for the division of markets and for price fixing in the home territories of its members. The international steel cartel, on the other hand, was mainly concerned with restrictions on output. Other cartels, such as the aluminum cartel, sought to limit productive capacity in various countries.

The list of companies that were at one time or another involved in cartel arrangements reads like the Who's Who in the Industrial World. It includes such famous names as Du Pont, Alcoa, General Electric, IBM, Standard Oil of New Jersey, DeBeers, I. G. Farben, Imperial Chemical Industries, and many others. The type of commodities that have been subject to cartel agreements range all the way from tin and zinc to motion-picture recording instruments and aspirin. They are far too many to enumerate; but they involve nearly all branches of manufacturing as well as many raw materials and foodstuffs.

Estimates vary, but they suggest that between one-third and one-half of total world trade was carried on under some kind of cartel arrangement during the interwar period.[3] This is hardly surprising. For, as later chapters will reveal, the 1920's and, more particularly, the 1930's were characterized by a general tendency to restrict international trade and payments. Partly in an effort to cure economic ills domestically and partly in retaliation against action by other countries, most governments adopted high tariffs and employed a variety of other trade controls. Aided by such restrictive policies, producers could more easily and effectively divide world markets and engage in price discrimination. Moreover, in an era when governments themselves tightly regulated the flow of trade, the atmosphere was ripe for private businessmen to do the same. Is it any wonder that cartels flourished during this period?

International cartels owe their origin to a variety of causes and circumstances. They should not be identified with any one period in history. Cartels exist today, and will undoubtedly continue to remain with us. To what extent they should be tolerated is a question that will be discussed in the last section of this chapter. For the moment, let us familiarize ourselves with some of the specific practices associated with international cartels.

International Cartels: Practices and Effects

It has been claimed that while domestic monopolies tend to distort comparative-cost advantages, international cartels often seek to prevent cost advantages from being realized at all.[4] Considering the seriousness of the charge, the "accused" deserve a fair hearing. The question to be decided is: How do cartel activities interfere with, and distort, mutually beneficial patterns of international trade?

In answering this question, it is best to examine the various methods that cartels use, and also some individual monopolistic practices that cartels and their methods make possible. These can be conveniently

[3] For actual estimates, see F. Machlup, "The Nature of the International Cartel Problem," in C. D. Edwards *et al.*, *A Cartel Policy for the United Nations* (New York: Columbia University Press, 1945), p. 11; and E. Mason, *Controlling World Trade* (New York: McGraw-Hill, 1946), p. 26n.

[4] See D. Snider, *Introduction to International Economics*, 3rd ed. (Homewood, Ill.: Richard D. Irwin, 1958), p. 458.

discussed under three headings: price policies, output restrictions, and allocation of markets.

Since the primary objectives of cartels are to avoid competition and to assure their members a reasonable degree of profit, they cannot tolerate price wars in particular and price fluctuations in general. To guard against them, cartels typically resort to price fixing, either imposing a uniform price throughout the area under control, or specifying different prices for different market territories. Such arrangements may well be preceded by severe price wars. But once cartelization has been achieved, price stability is the order of the day.

That price fixing is the antithesis of competition is obvious. It permits inefficient producers to remain in business, thereby causing a waste of economic resources. What is more important, prices set by cartels are higher than they would be under competition; they are seldom reduced and are usually increased even more whenever the opportunity presents itself. Thus, by setting and maintaining prices at a high level, cartels prevent consumers in one country from availing themselves of low-cost production in another. Worse still, by fixing prices in the home territories of their members, cartels enable a domestic monopolist to charge higher prices than he could if he had to face competition from foreign producers in his own home market.

Often used to illustrate this last point is the case of tungsten carbide, an industrial product of considerable importance. In the late 1920's, this product sold in the United States for $50 per pound. But under a 1927 agreement with the German firm of Krupp, General Electric was given control over the selling price in the United States—a privilege that Krupp promised to honor. Following this agreement, the price of tungsten in the United States rose meteorically, reaching a maximum of $453 per pound; during the 1930's, it ranged between that figure and a minimum price of $255. Only in 1942, as a result of an antitrust indictment, did the price fall—to a range of $27 to $45 per pound.[5] This admittedly is an extreme case. But many examples, though

[5] C. D. Edwards, *Economic and Political Aspects of International Cartels*, Subcommittee on War Mobilization of the Committee on Military Affairs, U.S. Senate (Washington: U.S. Government Printing Office, 1944), Monograph No. 1, pp. 12–13.

less dramatic, could be cited to illustrate the evils of price-fixing agreements by international cartels.

Not only do cartels fix prices, they often provide for, or encourage, price discrimination. As already mentioned, a monopolist may take advantage of local demand conditions by charging different prices in different markets. Instead of selling his entire output at the same price everywhere, he can charge a higher price where demand is inelastic and a lower price where it is fairly elastic. Behind this practice lies a simple fact: Since the cost of production is the same, regardless of where the output is sold, the monopolist stands to increase his total revenue—and hence his profit—by juggling his price according to different demand elasticities.

Thus, as Figure 13.4 shows, a monopolist may either charge a uniform price of, say, $10 in both markets, or he may discriminate by charging $15 in market A and only $9 in market B. If he pursues a uniform-price policy, his total revenue would amount to $300. (Multiply the quantity sold in each market by $10 and add the results.) But by charging $15 in market A (and selling 7 units) and $9 in market B

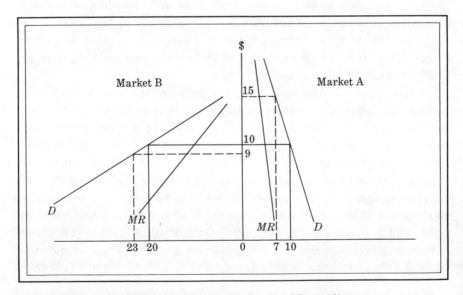

F I G U R E *13.4* Price Policies of a Discriminating Monopolist

(selling 23 units there), the monopolist could actually reap a total revenue of $312. Would he not be better off, then, in discriminating between these two markets?

The success of the monopolist in practicing price discrimination depends on the distance that separates markets from each other. The farther apart they are, the less chance that consumers in the expensive market would switch their purchases to the cheaper one. Geographic distance, however, is not the only factor involved. Equally if not more significant is the absence or presence of artificial barriers to the movement of goods and services between the two markets. Tariffs and other restrictive trade policies constitute such barriers, and thus enable a monopolist to charge higher prices in his home market than he might charge for the same products abroad. Cartel agreements serve a similar purpose. By protecting the domestic producer from encroachment by other cartel members, they strengthen his hand in discriminating between his home market and a foreign market. Such agreements, moreover, may enable a monopolist to divide his home market into segments according to prevailing conditions of demand.

When price discrimination involves both a domestic and a foreign market, it is commonly called *dumping*. The term, however, is misleading, for dumping refers specifically to selling a product abroad at a *lower* price than at home. Though often the case, it need not always be. In fact, in some cases producers may discriminate in the opposite way—they may sell abroad at a *higher* price than at home; and for lack of a better term, this is referred to as *reverse dumping*. In any event, the basic issue concerns, not problems of definition, but the economic effects of international price discrimination.

The main point is that price discrimination—especially when blessed by a cartel agreement—harms consumers in the country with the relatively inelastic demand. They must pay a higher price than would prevail in a competitive market, and are thus denied one of the basic benefits of international trade: availability of cheap sources of supply. But what about the effects of price discrimination on the "dumpee"— that is, the country where the particular good is sold at the lower price? The answer depends on the type of dumping—persistent, sporadic, or predatory—to which the country is being subjected.

When dumping is persistent—that is, occurring continuously over long periods of time—consumers have little to complain about. In fact, as long as the dumped goods are allowed to enter the country freely, consumers benefit from the steady stream of relatively low-priced imports. On the other hand, sporadic dumping (also called intermittent dumping), while beneficial to consumers in the short run, may have adverse long-run effects. For if, as a result of such dumping, local producers are forced out of business, consumers may suddenly find themselves at the mercy of a foreign supplier who, in the absence of local competition, may now raise his price.

Indeed, sporadic dumping is sometimes prompted by a producer's desire to gain a foothold and/or establish himself as a monopolist in a foreign market. If, in pursuit of this objective, he sells abroad at a loss (charges a price that is lower than his average cost) his action is called predatory dumping. As we shall see in the next chapter, many countries adopt defensive measures against this kind of dumping. And understandably so. For once it has accomplished its purpose (the elimination of local competition) predatory dumping comes to a stop. Thus, in the long run, neither consumers nor producers, in the country where such dumping occurs, benefit from it. And since predatory dumping is often made possible, if not actually provided for, by a cartel agreement, such agreements must take most of the blame for the consequences.

OUTPUT RESTRICTIONS

In actual practice, however, cartels shy away from stipulating exact prices. When they do so, it is mainly for the purpose of price discrimination between markets. For the most part, they strive to control prices in an indirect manner—through control over output and sales.

The underlying principle is the same as that which applies to the monopolist. He may drive prices up by curtailing the quantity offered for sale; and he can maintain the price at a high level (or raise it further) by refusing to increase output in the face of a rising demand for his product. In the case of cartels, the operation calls for setting quotas on the amount of output that each member may produce, sell, or export. The effectiveness of the system, however, depends on compliance by its participants. And to assure compliance, cartels have often prescribed penalties for violation of quota limits. Thus, under the first international steel cartel,[6] a fine was levied on producers who exceeded their allotted quotas, whereas those who produced below their full quotas were remunerated according to a previously agreed-upon formula.[7]

Output restrictions, as practiced by cartels, do more than just raise prices unnecessarily. These restrictions also produce severe shortages of goods and materials, both domestically and internationally. For since cartels typically impose quotas not only on domestic sales but on exports as well, a shortage created in one country cannot always be relieved by purchases from abroad. Moreover, limitations of output are sometimes accomplished by restricting productive capacity.[8] Thus, not only is current supply curtailed but future production is greatly jeopardized. Finally, output is often restricted through patent-licensing agreements or the outright buying up of patents. A company holding patent rights to a certain product or process will grant them to another firm only under certain conditions; these conditions often include restrictions on the amount to be produced or the uses to which it can be put. In some industries, in fact, control over patent rights assures virtual control over the entire output and sales. Similarly, the buying-up of patents prevents competitive products from seeing the light of day and from threatening existing firms in the industry.

So much for the evils of output restrictions. We turn now to consider the third major practice of cartels: allocation of markets.

ALLOCATION OF MARKETS

By stretching the point a bit, we may say that the allocation of markets by cartels rests on a do-unto-others-as-you-would-have-them-do-unto-you philosophy. For in allocating markets, cartel members agree to respect each other's sales territories and to refrain from encroaching on

---

[6] Formed in 1926, this important cartel included the iron and steel producers of Germany, Luxembourg, Belgium, the Saar, and France. It later broke down, but a second steel cartel was formed in 1933; it was joined by British producers in 1935, and by American producers in 1938. See George W. Stocking and Myron W. Watkins, *Cartels in Action* (New York: Twentieth Century Fund, 1946).

[7] For details, see *ibid.*, pp. 183–184.

[8] A case in point concerns a series of agreements between Alcoa, Dow Chemical, and I. G. Farben to limit the production of magnesium in the United States; this actually resulted in some plants closing down. See C. D. Edwards, *op. cit.*, p. 31.

them. This "courtesy," which is, of course, reciprocally extended, gives each member a free hand in a particular area (or areas), and enables him to maintain a monopoly position there.

Markets may be allocated either on a geographical basis or by type of product, or both. For example, under a 1933 agreement between Du Pont and Imperial Chemical Industries, which covered many different products, Du Pont obtained exclusive sales rights in the United States and Central America, while Imperial Chemical Industries was assured control over markets in the British Empire (except Canada). The agreement also provided for the formation of jointly owned subsidiaries to produce and import the products in question in the Canadian, Brazilian, and Argentinean markets.[9] Under a similar agreement, the Swedish Match Company agreed to stay out of the United States and appointed the Diamond Match Company, formerly its chief American competitor, its sole sales agent in this country. The latter, of course, promised not to encroach upon territories controlled by the former.

Whatever form they take, allocations of sales territories separate markets from each other and insulate producers in these markets from outside competition. If carried to an extreme, such practices may transform the international economy from a unified market area into isolated blocs between which there can be little or no exchange of goods and services. But even if practiced on a limited scale, market allocations obstruct trade flow, preventing it from following its natural course. As such, they strike at the very essence of international trade and undermine its basic purpose.

All in all, cartels stand guilty of the following crimes: raising prices unnecessarily; restricting supply; reducing the volume of international trade; subverting the patterns of trade; preventing the efficient allocation of the world's economic resources. Should the punishment fit the crimes? That is the next question.

Public Policies Toward Cartels: Facts and Issues

Strange as it may seem, some governments have actually encouraged and aided the formation of cartels, while others have openly tolerated

[9] *Ibid.*, p. 21.

their existence. Germany (especially in the interwar period) is usually singled out as the classic example of a cartel-loving nation; but other examples are not hard to find. Indeed, in most European countries, cartels have traditionally basked in the light of a favorable—or, at the least, of an indifferent—official attitude. And though the early years of post-World War II saw a slight change in European attitudes toward cartels, it was not long before a revival of cartel activities became evident. Similar trends have also been noted outside Western Europe; in Japan, where cartels played an important role before World War II, they have recently blossomed out again.

The United States, on the other hand, has long opposed monopolies and cartels, regarding them as injurious to the public interest. Beginning with the Sherman Antitrust Act of 1890, this attitude has been reflected in a series of laws that prohibit individual or collective business practices that would result in restraint of trade, whether domestic or foreign. The one notable exception to this attitude concerns the activities of American exporters. Under the Webb-Pomerance Export Trade Act of 1918, American firms were allowed to form associations (among themselves or with foreign firms) for the purpose of promoting exports of American products—provided that they did not thereby restrict domestic trade.[10] Enacted because of the operations of foreign cartels, this act was designed to bolster the position of American exporters in developing foreign markets. It did *not* intend to confer an official blessing on American participation in international cartels;[11] but inadvertently it enabled them to do precisely that.

Up until World War II, the United States stood virtually alone in championing the cause of anticartel policies. But although it practiced what it preached, its actions were necessarily confined to those in its own jurisdiction—namely, American firms suspected of violating antitrust laws. Only after World War II, from which it emerged as the world's leading power, was the United States able to spread its anticartel gospel more effectively, among both allies and former enemies. Thus, during the postwar occupation of Germany and Japan, the United States undertook

[10] See M. Fainsod *et al., Government and the American Economy* (New York: W. W. Norton, 1959), p. 449.

[11] At least, this was the interpretation of the Supreme Court in the case of *Alkali Export Association vs. the United States, ibid.,* p. 574.

to break up cartels in these two countries. But what is more important, it sought to obtain an *international* recognition of the evils of cartels and to secure international cooperation in controlling their activities.

This last objective found expression in the Havana Conference (1947–1948). The conference, sponsored by the United States and attended by fifty-seven nations, set out to draft a charter for an International Trade Organization (ITO). Article 46 of the Havana Charter specified several objectionable cartel practices, and charged member nations with prosecuting those who were guilty of them. Although the ITO, as we shall see later, never got off the ground, some of the provisions in its charter were subsequently incorporated into other international institutions. Among these was Article 46, which provided the inspiration for a United Nations resolution (adopted in 1951), requesting member nations to prevent restrictive business practices that might affect international trade. But this was as far as the resolution went; it left the actual matter of enforcement to the members themselves.

More recently, however, two breakthrough developments occurred with regard to cartel policies. Under the treaties establishing the European Coal and Steel Community (1951) and the European Economic Community (1957), cartels are subject not to national control, but to supranational control. In both cases, the authority to regulate cartels and to enforce anticartel laws is vested in centralized agencies[12] rather than in individual member governments. Moreover, restrictive business practices are explicitly declared incompatible with the aims and purposes of the organizations established under these treaties. The agencies are therefore given the power to formulate criteria with which to judge violations of anticartel rules.[13]

Do these and other developments spell doom for international cartels? Not necessarily. In fact, neither economists nor politicians are in clear-cut agreement concerning a proper policy toward cartels. At one

[12] The High Authority, in the case of the European Coal and Steel Community, and the Commission, in the case of the European Economic Community. With the merging of the ECSC, the EEC, and Euratom, such powers would no doubt be vested in one agency.

[13] For actual developments during the first few years of the EEC, see D. L. McLachlan and D. Swann, ''Competition Policy in the Common Market,'' *Economic Journal*, Vol. LXXIII (March, 1963).

extreme are those who urge complete abolition of cartels; at the other extreme are advocates of a laissez-faire attitude. Opponents of cartels rightly argue that practices such as price fixing, output restrictions, allocation of markets, and buying-up of patents undermine the basic purpose of international trade and conflict with the interests of consumers. The latter, they claim, would be better served by competitive market structures. Defenders of cartels, on the other hand, point to at least four of their virtues: economies of scale, exchange of technical information, price stabilization, and minimization of excess capacity. In any event, their trump card is the argument that the mere abolition of cartels would not necessarily assure pure competition.

It is not easy to balance the credit items against the debit items in the cartel ledger. What seems clear from such an attempt is the need for some middle-of-the-road solution. Since it is not cartels per se, but their restrictive practices that are considered undesirable, the objective of a cartel policy should be to regulate cartels, not eliminate them. Such a cartel policy, in other words, should permit the exploitation of economic advantages associated with large-scale business enterprises, while at the same time minimizing the economic dangers inherent in monopolies and cartels. Indeed, this kind of compromise solution can draw on a well-established precedent—the tolerance of privately owned, yet publicly regulated, "natural" monopolies (i.e., utilities) in the United States. And the more recent development of antitrust policies within the European Economy Community attests to a similar philosophy; such policies are not intent on destroying big business but rather on curbing their inherent economic powers.

In conclusion, one might note that to agree on a cartel policy is one thing, but to secure its implementation quite another. Unilateral action, especially if undertaken by a small and weak country, would have little or no success in restraining the activities of giant international cartels. The latter can be effectively controlled only through the joint effort of a large number of countries, all pursuing more or less similar policies. Yet the greater the number of countries involved in an attempt to formulate a multilateral approach to the regulation of cartels, the harder it is to reach unanimous agreement as to who should do what. In the absence of such an agreement, few tangible results can be expected. Indeed, with the exception of the programs contemplated by the European Economic Community, which is still to demonstrate its success, no *international* scheme to regulate cartels has ever been carried out, nor is one likely to be in the near future.

14

The Tariff Issue

NATIONAL MONOPOLIES AND international cartels are not the only forces that impede the flow of international trade and divert it from its natural course. The commercial policies of sovereign states are often just as obstructive and distortive as the policies of private business. In fact, governments probably influence trade more, if for no other reason than that governmental actions have a more comprehensive effect on economic activities.

Restrictive commercial policies, then, constitute still another set of barriers that interfere with freely established patterns of international specialization and exchange. Such policies can be distinguished on the basis of the tools used to implement them. In this chapter, we focus attention on one of these tools: the tariff.

The Meaning and Nature of Tariffs

Simply stated, a tariff is a tax—commonly referred to as *duty*—levied on imported goods when they cross the border of the importing country.[1] As such, the tariff is an indirect tax, similar in nature to a

[1] Although our concern here is with import duties, two other kinds of duty might be mentioned: (1) *export* duties, which are levied on goods leaving a country, and

sales or excise tax that is levied on domestically produced goods: Its imposition raises the prices of imported goods above their prices in the exporting countries, the actual rise being determined by conditions of supply and demand in the countries involved, and by the amount of the duties levied on the commodities in question.

As for the duties themselves, they are of two major types: *ad valorem* and *specific*. The ad valorem duty is stated as a percentage of the value of an imported good. Thus, a 10 per cent ad valorem duty, imposed on a commodity valued at $50, would amount to $5; if the commodity is valued at $100, the same duty requires a payment of $10. A specific duty, on the other hand, is a flat amount charged for each physical unit of a particular import—for example, 10¢ per pound of butter or $2 per ton of steel. To convert a specific duty into its ad valorem equivalent one need only know the price of the commodity in question. For example, if the price of butter is 50¢ per pound, a specific duty of 10¢ would be the same as a 20 per cent ad valorem duty. If the price of butter rises to, say, $1 per pound, the same specific duty would equal an ad valorem duty of only 10 per cent.[2]

To these two types of duties we might add a third, known as a *compound* duty. This represents a combination of the other two; when levied on a particular import, that article is subject to both specific and ad valorem charges. To illustrate, here are a few choice items, drawn from the United States tariff schedule.[3] The United States tariff on clocks ranges from 27½¢ to $2.25 per clock *plus* an ad valorem duty of 32½ per cent. On clay floors and/or wall tiles, the tariff varies from 5¢ to 10¢ per square foot *plus* 15 per cent to 35 per cent ad valorem charges. And knives (with folding blades) are subject to a 25–27 per cent ad valorem duty plus 17¢ for each knife!

All of a country's dutiable imports are listed, together with their respective duty rates, in its tariff schedule, while those goods that are exempt from the tariff are said to belong to the "free" list. It is not unusual, however, to encounter a particular commodity—at different

---

(2) *transit* duties, which are levied on goods passing through one country en route to another. Reference will be made to export duties in the next chapter.

[2] Thus, the burden of a specific duty varies inversely with changes in the price of imports, a fact whose practical implication will be seen in a later chapter.

[3] The following examples are from H. Piquet, *Aid, Trade, and the Tariff* (New York: Crowell, 1953), Chapter X.

times, of course—on both lists. Nor should we be surprised to learn that the tariff schedule itself may vary from time to time, and that it can take different forms. Thus, the simplest and least discriminatory tariff structure is represented by the so-called "single-column" schedule, under which *one* duty rate is applied to each dutiable import. The "multi-column" schedule, on the other hand, features different rates for the same commodity, thereby subjecting imports from some countries to lower or higher duties than those levied on similar imports from other countries. This is not to suggest, however, that the more columns in a tariff schedule, the higher the tariff wall around the country in question. All we can say is that a multi-column schedule discriminates between the various sources of imports, while a single-column schedule treats them all alike. The actual height of a country's tariff wall is quite another matter.

Although there is no completely satisfactory method by which to measure accurately the height of a tariff wall, the following distinction between two kinds of tariffs may provide some helpful clues. A tariff may be employed either as a protective device, designed to eliminate or reduce imports by raising their prices; or as a means of obtaining revenue for the government. Since duties can be levied only on goods that actually enter the country, a *revenue tariff* must consist of duty rates that are low enough to permit imports to come in. For if the duties are so high that they exclude imports completely or greatly reduce them, the tariff would not fulfill its purpose of raising revenue. But if protection of domestic industries is the primary reason for the tariff, duty rates will be high enough to deter foreign producers from underselling competitors in the importing country.

In practice, however, tariffs are often made to serve both objectives —to provide protection and to raise revenue. Hence, the fact that a certain country must rely on tariffs as a source of revenue may not necessarily be reflected in its tariff schedule. For if that country is also anxious to protect its industries, it may well surround itself with a high tariff wall. And, unless the duty rates are so high that they exclude imports altogether, the tariff will still yield some revenue. Conversely, one need not dismiss the protective qualities of a particular tariff schedule simply because its duty rates are relatively low. For even a low duty may prove quite effective, especially in cases where foreign producers possess only a slight cost advantage over domestic manufacturers.

Where does this leave us? Although we may conclude that, in

general, protective tariffs are likely to be higher than revenue tariffs, we are still faced with a basic problem: How do we measure the height of *any* tariff, so as to compare it with tariffs of other countries or with tariffs prevailing at different times in one country? Two possible methods of tariff measurement are frequently suggested, though each of them presents difficulties.

In one instance, the total amount of duties collected is divided by the total value of goods imported. The resulting ratio, expressed in percentage terms, can then be compared with similarly computed ratios for other countries or other time periods. Underlying this procedure is the assumption that the higher the ratio of duty receipts to total imports, the higher the particular tariff wall, and vice versa. Often, however, a low ratio may actually conceal a high tariff—especially if the duty rates are sufficiently high and encompassing to exclude most dutiable imports. In that case, the bulk of the country's imports would consist either of duty-free commodities or of goods that are subject to very low duties. As a result, total duty receipts would be small and might constitute an insignificant percentage of the total value of imports. Thus, unless we actually know what lies behind a particular ratio of duty collected to total imports, we may be greatly misled by it.

A preferable—or, if you wish, a less unsatisfactory—method of measuring tariff heights involves two steps. All duties are converted into ad valorem terms; then an average duty rate is computed. This average rate provides in turn the basis for comparing different tariffs; a low rate is associated with a low level of tariff protection and a high rate with a high tariff wall. In computing such averages, however, a number of vexing problems may be encountered. For one thing, a choice must be made between the use of a *weighted* or an *unweighted* average, each of which has merits and shortcomings. If a weighted average is decided upon, proper weights must be assigned to the various commodities according to their relative importance in the trade of each country under comparison. But apart from the statistical hurdles that must be overcome before a meaningful average-duty rate can be calculated, one must avoid a possible pitfall in interpreting the numerical results. For depending on supply and demand conditions in the countries being compared, a low average rate may prove more protective in one case than a high rate is in another. Consequently, even statistically reliable figures may yield misleading results as to the actual degree of protection afforded by different tariffs.

Nevertheless, the second method is generally regarded as superior to the first. For despite the complexities involved in computing and interpreting average-duty rates, such averages do provide a rough index by which to measure and compare different tariff levels. Measuring the tariff, however, is only one aspect of the problem. We must now probe into the various economic effects of protection.[4]

Economic Effects of the Tariff

The most direct manifestation of a tariff is an increase in the prices of imported goods. Yet whether the price of a commodity will rise by the full amount of the duty depends on its supply and demand in the importing and exporting countries. While under certain circumstances the entire burden of a duty may fall on the buyers of imports, it is more likely that it will be shared by both importers and exporters. That is to say, the price of a newly protected commodity will tend to rise in the importing country and fall in the exporting country; the result is a price differential that is equal to the value of the duty itself.

A simple graphical illustration can explain this phenomenon. Consider Figure 14.1, which depicts the supply and demand curves for a given commodity in two countries, one of which (A) imports, and the other (B) exports, the commodity in question. In the absence of tariff, and assuming no transportation cost, one price (P_e) would be established in both countries—the price at which the quantity (MP) imported by country A is equal to the quantity (EX) exported by country B. (This is but a reflection of a principle discussed earlier—namely, that under free trade, the equilibrium price of each traded commodity tends to be the same everywhere.) The imposition of a duty (TT') by country A would cause prices in both A and B to differ from each other. And although the establishment of a new equilibrium (i.e., an equality between A's imports and B's exports) requires that the price *differential* be equal to the full amount of the duty, the price in A rises, and the

---

[4] We are concerned therefore with tariffs imposed for protective rather than revenue purposes.

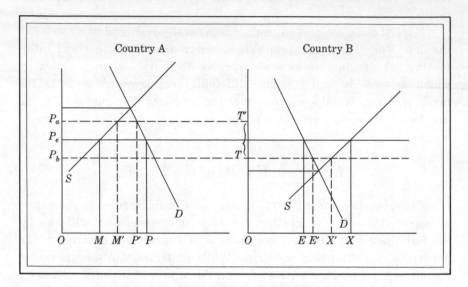

FIGURE *14.1* Effects of Tariff on Prices and Quantities

price in B falls, by less than the duty itself. Thus, in this instance, only part of the tariff burden was passed on to the importers in the form of a price increase ($= P_eP_a$) ; the other part was absorbed by the exporting country, where the price fell from P_c to P_b. Together, P_eP_a and P_eP_b are equal to TT'.

Under a different set of supply and demand conditions, however, the same duty would have produced price changes of different magnitude in each country. If, for example, B's supply curve had been less elastic, the fall in B's price would have been greater, and the rise in A's price smaller, than shown here. On the other hand, a more elastic supply curve in B would have resulted in a smaller fall in its price, and hence a larger increase in A's price. These contentions may easily be verified by drawing different supply and/or demand curves, and comparing the results with those obtained above. In the process, we may find another major "effect" of the tariff—its influence on the *volume* of traded goods.

Figure 14.1 shows this influence at work. As the price in A rises (from P_e to P_a), the quantity imported declines from MP to $M'P'$. And as the price in B falls (from P_e to P_b), the quantity exported is reduced from EX to $E'X'$. Similar results, though not of exactly the same magnitude, can normally be expected whenever tariffs are imposed. For by causing the prices of imported goods to rise, the tariff reduces the quantity demanded; and if, at the same time, exporting countries are experiencing a drop in *their* prices, they are apt to cut the supply of exports. Here lies an essential characteristic of the tariff: Its restrictive influence on the volume of trade is exerted *indirectly*. Unlike other trade controls (quotas, exchange regulations, and so forth), the tariff works through the market-price mechanism, relying on it to do its own "dirty work." In other words, changing prices bring about changes in the quantities of imports and exports; the tariff merely initiated the price changes themselves.

In addition to restricting the volume of international trade, tariffs can claim credit—or invite blame—for influencing various economic activities within the countries involved. Of particular interest, however, are the possible effects of a tariff on the very country that imposes it— that is, the country whose imports of a certain commodity (or commodities) are subject to duty. Some of these effects are more easily identified than others, and to appreciate their implications, we will resort once again to a graphical analysis.

In Figure 14.2, the domestic supply and demand curves of a particular commodity are S_d and D_d, respectively. To simplify the analysis and to dramatize the effects of the tariff, we may assume that the foreign supply curve of this commodity (S_f) is perfectly elastic (i.e., the commodity is produced abroad under constant-cost conditions). Under free trade, consumers in the importing country are faced with a combined supply curve (the line passing through S_d, G . . . S_f),[5] which, together with the demand curve, sets an equilibrium price of P_e. At that price, the total quantity demanded is ON; a small part of it (OA) is supplied by domestic producers and the rest (AN) is imported.

The imposition of a duty (equal to T) jolts the free-trade price

[5] Don't panic! This curve simply reflects the fact that foreign producers would not offer any quantities as long as prices are below P_e, while domestic producers would be willing to supply certain small amounts at such prices. Hence, the combined supply curve is derived by adding the portion (S_dG) of the domestic supply curve that lies below P_e to the foreign supply curve.

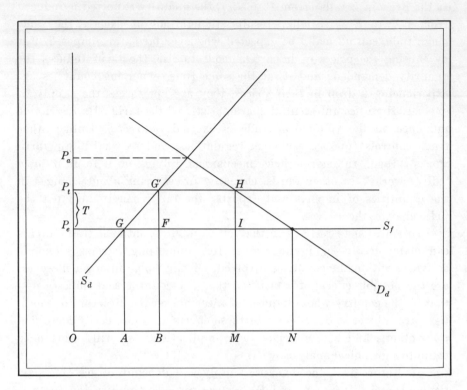

FIGURE *14.2*   Various Effects of the Tariff

from its equilibrium position. But since in this case the foreign supply curve is perfectly elastic, the export price of the commodity remains unchanged. Consequently, the entire burden of the tariff falls on the importing country, where the price rises by the full amount of the duty. (In Figure 14.2, the new domestic price is P_t, the vertical distance $P_e P_t$ being equal to T.) Confronted with a higher price, consumers react accordingly: They buy less than before, and the total quantity demanded is reduced from ON to OM. The horizontal difference between ON and OM (equal to MN) reflects the *consumption effect* of the tariff— that is, the tendency of a newly imposed tariff to reduce the total consumption of the good(s) subject to duty. By how much consumption is actually curtailed, depends on the elasticity of demand for the commodity in question. But as long as demand is not perfectly inelastic, the consumption effect will manifest itself to a greater or lesser degree.

But while a tariff curtails the consumption of a protected good, it usually results in an expansion of the domestic production of that good. This so-called *protective effect* of the tariff is confirmed by Figure 14.2, where, at the new price (P_t), domestic suppliers account for OB of the total quantity demanded, while imports only amount to BM. The expansion of domestic output from OA to OB can be directly attributed to the imposition of the tariff. For by raising the domestic price, the duty enables local producers to cover the high marginal costs that are associated with the additional output (AB). Indeed, were it not for the higher price, local producers would have little incentive to increase their output, and domestic production would have remained at OA. Thus, while benefiting the local industry, the protective effect of the tariff usually results in a double loss to the country as a whole: It enables high-cost domestic production to expand at the expense of lower-cost imports, thus harming the consumer; and it encourages misallocation of domestic resources, which are now drawn into less efficient use.

The magnitude of the protective effect depends not only on the amount of the duty, but also on the domestic conditions of supply of the protected commodity. In general, if the slope of the domestic supply curve is fairly flat, a given duty would result in a large expansion of domestic output; under a steeply sloped supply curve, the same duty would induce a smaller expansion. Of course, the duty may be so high that it excludes imports completely, in which case the domestic demand would be met entirely by domestic production. Thus, in Figure 14.2, a duty of P_tP_a would prove prohibitive; for in raising the price to P_a, the duty would enable local producers to supply the entire quantity demanded at that price. But as long as the duty is not prohibitive, some imports would continue to come in—and this, despite the protective effect.

This brings us to still another effect with which the tariff is usually credited—its *revenue effect*. Any tariff, even if its main purpose is protective, may provide some revenue for the government of the importing country. As long as it does not exclude all imports of the protected good, the tariff must result in a certain amount of duty receipts; the actual sum is determined by the value of the duty and the volume of incoming imports. As shown in Figure 14.2, the quantity of imports that comes in under tariff is BM $(= FI)$. And since each unit of these imports is subject to a duty of P_eP_t ($= FG'$), the revenue effect (i.e., the amount collected by the government) is represented by the rectangular area $FG'HI$.

Finally, as a result of the tariff, local producers are enjoying a higher income; their total receipts have risen from $OAGP_e$ to $OBG'P_t$. While part of this increase is attributable to the larger quantity now being supplied domestically, another part is made possible only by virtue of the tariff, and cannot be justified on economic grounds. In order to identify these parts, we may begin by comparing the actual consumer outlay on the quantity OB with what it would have been in the absence of the tariff. At the free-trade price (P_e), the quantity OB could have been obtained for a total outlay of $OBFP_e$, whereas at the higher price, occasioned by the tariff, the same quantity costs the consumer an amount equal to $OBG'P_t$. The difference between these two sums (the area $P_eFG'P_t$) represents an *increase* in consumer expenditures that is also an increase in the receipts of local producers.

To what do we owe this increase? A small part of it, measured by the triangular area GFG', can be attributed to the rising marginal costs incurred in the production of the additional domestic output (AB). But the rest, corresponding to the area $P_eGG'P_t$, is essentially a surplus: It is a payment, made to producers, in *excess* of what is necessary to induce them to supply the quantity OB; or, to put it differently, it is an addition to producers' *net* revenue. This additional revenue is possible only because the tariff has caused the domestic price to rise—and to remain—above the actual supply price of domestic producers (i.e., the price at which they would have been willing to offer the quantity[6] in question). As such, it represents a mere transfer of income from consumers to producers which, while benefiting the latter must be regarded as a loss to the former. The actual amount involved in this transfer reflects what is often termed the *transfer* or *redistributive effect* of the tariff.

But there is more to the redistributive effect than meets the eye in Figure 14.2. For apart from its direct impact on the producers and consumers of protected commodities, the tariff—like free trade—is likely to affect the distribution of income among factors of production. You

[6] Except for the last units offered.

will recall that as a result of the opening up of (free) trade, the demand for, and the price of, a country's abundant factor tend to rise; and for the opposite reason, the price of its scarce factor tends to fall. The imposition of a tariff produces exactly opposite results: It tends to raise the price of the scarce factor and to lower that of the abundant factor. Hence, while free trade is generally expected to redistribute income in favor of the country's abundant factor(s), the tariff favors the scarce factor(s). And, as we will see in the next section, much of the opposition to free trade comes from those domestic interests that stand to gain more from the redistributive effect of the tariff.

To sum up: The various effects of the tariff can be simply regarded as a series of economic changes. And although the effects of a particular tariff are seldom confined to the country that imposes it, they usually are manifested most forcefully there. From our standpoint, however, the lesson of the foregoing analysis concerns the more fundamental implications of the tariff insofar as international trade is concerned. For ultimately, it is not with the specific effects of the tariff that we must reckon, but with their influence on the course of, and gains from, trade. With this in mind, we may bring two major charges against the tariff. First, a tariff, especially a protective tariff, encourages the diversion of resources from more efficient to less efficient uses; in addition, it prevents the full exploitation of comparative-cost differences among nations. Put differently, tariffs lead to a *mis*allocation of the world's economic resources, and give rise to less profitable patterns of international specialization and exchange than those which would be established under free trade. Second, under a tariff, consumers find themselves losers on two counts—they are compelled to pay higher prices for, and curtail their consumption of, commodities subject to duty. Thus, the tariff not only restricts consumer choice, but also lowers real income.

The Case for Tariff Protection

Question: If free international trade brings about the most efficient allocation of the world's economic resources and hence the maximization of real income, why do nations deliberately set out to distort its patterns and reduce its volume?

Answer: That which is desirable from the viewpoint of the world may not necessarily be the most desirable from the viewpoint of a single nation. And what may be beneficial to a nation as a whole may be viewed as undesirable by a particular group or groups within it.

In this question and answer lies the essence of the discussion that follows. The case for protection, however well it may be disguised, nearly always reflects the interest of some group or groups in the economy. To such groups, little or no trade may be more desirable than free and unrestricted trade. And although at times it may be in the interest of the nation as a whole to restrict trade, these instances are few and must always be qualified. In short, what follows is a series of arguments in support of tariff protection. Each argument has come to be identified by a title that suggests its main thesis; in terms of this thesis the economic validity of the argument must be assessed.

Defense against pauper labor. As the title suggests, this argument concerns the interest of a particular group—wage earners—and purports to defend them against an alleged evil of free trade. It asserts that free trade would enable countries whose labor forces receive low wages to undersell producers in higher-wage countries, flooding their markets with cheaply produced, low-priced goods. In order to withstand such competition, local producers would be forced to lower wages to the level prevailing in foreign countries. The imposition of a tariff, it is declared, would avoid this sad necessity; for the tariff would shelter highly paid domestic workers from the competition of cheaply paid foreign labor, thus enabling them to enjoy their present high living standard.

Implicit in this contention are two basic assumptions: (1) that labor is the only factor of production, and (2) that the cost—and hence price—of the finished article is determined by wage rates. Since the logic of the argument rests on these assumptions, let us examine them more closely.

Is labor the sole factor of production? Definitely not. Everyone knows that all goods are produced by a *combination* of labor, capital, and other resources. What is more important, the proportion in which labor is combined with other factors varies from commodity to commodity, depending on its technological requirements. Hence, only in the production of labor-intensive goods may low-paid labor claim cost advantage over labor that receives high wages. For when it comes to capital- or land-intensive goods, the prices of these factors determine how cheaply (or expensively) they can be produced in one country as compared to another. And since international differences in factor prices reflect differences in their relative supply, countries endowed with relative abundance of labor may generally be expected to produce labor-intensive goods more cheaply than countries where labor is the scarce factor. This does *not* mean, however, that highly paid labor cannot successfully compete with low-paid labor in the production of other goods.

Yet even in the production of labor-intensive goods, a high wage nation can possess a cost advantage over a low-wage nation. For contrary to the second assumption, it is not only wage rates but also the level of productivity that determine per-unit costs of production. Indeed, where high money wages are justified by high labor productivity, per-unit costs may be lower than those resulting from low wage rates combined with an even lower productivity. To illustrate, suppose that hourly wage rates in the women's handbag industry are $1 in Italy and $3 in the United States, but that output per man-hour is one bag in the former and six bags in the latter. In this case, the labor cost per handbag is $1 in Italy but only 50¢ in the United States.

Such differences in productivity, combined with the fact that labor is not used in the same proportions in the manufacture of all goods, help explain why high-wage countries can—and do—compete effectively with low-wage countries in many lines of production. In so doing, they serve to reveal the basic fallacies in the ''pauper-labor'' argument, thereby rendering its conclusions invalid. For if the threat posed by low-paid labor is not as serious and encompassing as it is made to appear, a high-wage country need not surround itself with a protective tariff wall. And to the extent that such a need does exist, it can only mean that some commodities *can* be produced more efficiently abroad than at home. If so, why should consumers be denied the opportunity to obtain them from the lower-cost foreign source?

Keep money at home. Based on the fallacious notion that money is synonymous with wealth, this argument typifies one of the most popular misconceptions concerning the relation between international trade and economic well-being. Imports, it claims, result in payments to foreign countries and thereby reduce the domestic money supply of the importing country. Hence, if imports are restricted by a tariff, the outflow of money is checked and the domestic money supply can be maintained at a high level.

One may ask, "So what?" After all, money is simply a medium of exchange whose real value stems from the function it performs: to pay for goods and services. Consequently, the quantity of money per se does not determine a country's prosperity; it is the amount of goods and services that its money can buy. And since imports represent goods that either cannot be produced domestically or can be produced only at high cost, why should a nation have any qualms about exchanging its money for such goods?

But apart from erroneous views on the significance of money, the present argument fails to comprehend the practical connection between imports and exports. By implying that money that is paid for imports is forever lost, it overlooks the fact that one country's currency is of no use to foreign recipients unless they can spend it in that country. The payments that a country makes for imports must ultimately be used by other countries to pay for its exports. Or, to put it differently, if it wants to export its own products to other countries, a country must be willing to import from them. To imply otherwise is misleading and fallacious.

Protection of the home market. Equally fallacious is the claim that domestic producers, no matter how inefficient they may be, have more right to the home market than foreign producers—a "right" that must be protected by a tariff. This claim, however, is usually hidden behind a seemingly logical argument that is designed to prove that those seeking protection have the general interests of the economy at heart. Thus, it has often been argued that by stimulating production in the protected industries, the tariff will increase the incomes of owners of the resources involved. As a result, the market for products of other domestic industries would be enlarged, causing an expansion in their output as well. In other words, the benefits of the tariff are said to extend beyond the protected industries themselves, and permeate the economy as a whole.

Using this line of reasoning, one can justify protection for, say, manufacturing industries on the grounds that it helps create a larger market for domestic agricultural products; or one may clamor for a tariff on agricultural imports by suggesting that it would stimulate manufacturing activities. Better still, one can make a case for total tariff protection that would eliminate most, if not all, imports—that is, if one accepts the logic of the so called "home-market" argument!

But as it stands, the argument does not hold water. For if protection leads to a substantial reduction in a country's imports, it must also curtail foreign demand for its exports. Hence, while domestic production of import-competing goods may be expected to expand under the tariff umbrella, the production of export goods is likely to decline. And since these two tendencies may cancel each other, there is little reason to presume that the economy as a whole would experience a *net* expansion in its production activities. On the contrary, there is more reason to suspect that by causing resources to be shifted from the efficient export industries to the inefficient protected industries, the tariff will result in a reduction of total output—especially if domestic resources are already fully employed.[7]

But even if total production is maintained at its previous level, it is wrong to suggest that the economy as a whole gains from the tariff. In fact, benefits to producers of the protected goods may be more than offset by the losses of domestic industries that cater to foreign markets. As for the consumer, he is compelled to pay a higher price for whatever he buys, whether it is an imported article or one that is now produced domestically. In short, the tariff benefits only the protected industries. Any attempt to claim otherwise must be dismissed as invalid.

Equalization of production costs. Strictly speaking, the cost-equalization principle is not an argument *for* protection but a suggested guide *to* it. Proponents of this idea, which is sometimes called the "scientific tariff," argue that in order to eliminate "unfair" competition from abroad, the tariff should equalize average costs of production between domestic and foreign producers. Accordingly, they propose that duty rates be just high enough to bring the prices of imported articles into equality with the costs of producing similar goods at home. The result, they maintain, would be "fair" competition that would bestow on every producer—both foreign and domestic—the same opportunity to win or lose.

The attraction of this proposition lies mostly in its appeal to a sense of fair play; but some of it is due to its seemingly "scientific" over-

---

[7] As we shall see shortly, there is some justification for protection when resources are *not* fully employed.

tones—that is, the implication that duty rates should not be determined in a haphazard manner, but should be carefully and objectively calculated. But neither the appeal to fairness nor the claim of objectivity should fool anyone into believing that a cost-equalizing tariff is economically logical or practically feasible.

As for feasibility, two closely related problems are involved: Whose costs are to be equalized, and how are costs to be compared? Since even within a single industry costs differ from firm to firm, how can the many different types of producers in one country be compared, with respect to costs, to their many competitors abroad? Are we simply to average the costs of all domestic producers of a certain commodity, lumping together the efficient with the inefficient producers; or should we single out for comparison only some producers? And what about foreign costs of production? Should the price, say, of Danish butter be averaged with the price of butter produced in New Zealand, or should they be treated separately and be subject to different duty rates?

None of these questions can be answered with any degree of certainty. Nor, for that matter, should any of them be dignified with an honest answer. For if the cost-equalization principle is carried to its logical conclusion, it can mean only one thing: To be truly equalizing, the tariff must be so high that it enables the least efficient domestic producer to compete on an equal footing with the most efficient foreign producer. Since under such circumstances one can hardly expect competitive imports to come in, the entire idea is reduced to a mere protectionist gimmick, designed to shield domestic producers from *any* foreign competition and to favor them at the expense of consumers and of the country's more efficient export industries. Indeed, the true implication of the cost-equalization idea can best be appreciated if one recalls that, after all, cost *differences* between nations provide the basis for mutually beneficial trade. To eliminate such differences is not only to reduce the gains from trade but ultimately to destroy any basis for it.

Improving the terms of trade. The terms of trade to which we refer are the "commodity" or "net-barter" terms of trade—that is, the ratio between the prices a country receives for its exports and the prices it pays for its imports. This ratio, you will recall, improves whenever export prices rise relative to import prices, or whenever import prices fall relative to export prices. And since a tariff tends to force down the prices of protected commodities in the *exporting* countries (see Figure 14.1), it is sometimes advocated as a means by which a tariff-imposing country can obtain its imports at lower prices and thereby improve its terms of trade.

The fact that consumers are forced to pay higher prices for protected commodities does not destroy the analytical validity of the argument. For it is not changes in *domestic* prices that are measured by the terms of trade, but changes in the ratio at which traded goods exchange for each other internationally. Hence if the prices of its imports decline while the prices of its exports remain the same, a tariff-imposing country can now obtain more imports for a given quantity of its exports. And this, after all, is just another way of saying that its commodity terms of trade have improved.

Yet the extent to which the imposition of a tariff would lower the *export* price of a protected import, depends on the conditions affecting its foreign supply. If, as seen in Figure 14.2, the latter is infinitely elastic, no reduction in the foreign price can be expected. And even if the foreign supply is subject to increasing costs (i.e., the supply curve slopes upward), a tariff may fail to bring about a reduction in the foreign price of a particular import, especially if the country that imposes it represents only a small fraction of total world demand for the product in question.

Nor can the possibility of retaliation be ruled out. Indeed, the imposition of a tariff by one country is often an invitation to another to follow suit. Consequently, any initial improvement in the country's terms of trade may be nullified—or worse, turned into outright deterioration—once other nations counter with tariffs of their own. And since retaliation usually leads to counter-retaliation, no country can use tariffs to win a lasting victory in the battle to improve the terms of trade. On the contrary, all combatants will undoubtedly lose, especially the country that fired the first shot.

But even if retaliatory actions could be disregarded, the terms-of-trade argument would still provide a poor excuse for tariff protection. Improvement of its terms of trade is at best an ambiguous test of a country's gains from trade. And when such an improvement is brought about by the imposition of a tariff and the subsequent decline in imports, its dubious virtues are more than offset by the losses that result when domestic resources are diverted from efficient to inefficient use. In the final analysis, a policy designed to improve the terms of trade by restricting trade itself makes no more sense than "the operation was successful, but the patient died."

Bargaining and antidumping tariffs. Of the various "practical" arguments for protection, two deserve special mention. One rests on the proposition that a country that does not maintain a tariff, or whose tariff is very low, cannot coax other countries into reciprocal tariff reductions. By imposing a tariff, so the argument goes, the country arms itself with a bargaining weapon that can be used to obtain trade concessions, and thereby expand foreign markets for its exports. Proponents of the so-called bargaining tariff present it as a temporary device, which is to be discarded once it has served its purpose.

This reasonably valid argument is nevertheless open to serious question. For while a bargaining tariff may lead toward the eventual reduction of trade barriers, it involves the danger of creating vested interests that would effectively bloc its removal. In this case, the tariff would fail to accomplish its intended mission and, worse, would tend to perpetuate itself to the detriment of the country concerned. Moreover, when a bargaining tariff is imposed, not to effect future tariff reduction but to retaliate against protectionist policies of other countries, the case for it is further weakened. Since retaliation breeds counter-retaliation, the end result is likely to be an overall increase in protection and a consequent decline in the volume of international trade; neither can be justified on economic grounds.

Something is to be said, however, for a retaliatory tariff specifically designed to protect a country against predatory dumping by foreign producers. Dumping, you will recall, is a form of price discrimination that involves a domestic and a foreign market : It is the practice of selling a product abroad at a lower price than at home. When dumping is motivated by a desire to take advantage of a more elastic demand in the foreign market, it may continue indefinitely and would normally benefit the consumers in that market. But if the exporter undertakes such price cutting in order to drive foreign competitors out of business, it may prove quite harmful to the country where the dumping occurs. For once he has effectively eliminated local producers, the foreign producer may well establish himself as a monopolist, and charge consumers higher prices than ever before. Thus, any short-term benefits that consumers enjoyed during the dumping may be more than offset by the long-term adverse effects suffered by the economy as a whole when the dumping ends.

Although antidumping duties may be justified when the country has been a target for predatory dumping, use of the tariff to prevent such dumping entails several difficulties; moreover, it is subject to many abuses.[8] For one thing, it is not easy to determine whether predatory dumping does in fact take place, since it is only after imports have come in that price comparisons can be made and evaluated. Hence, by the time a duty is imposed, the dumping may have ceased and the damage already done. On the other hand, to impose an antidumping tariff *before* any dumping has occurred is tantamount to denying consumers the benefit of low-priced imports, and to encouraging inefficient domestic production. Indeed, there is always the danger that a supposed antidumping tariff would be pressured into adoption by domestic producers who cannot withstand foreign competition of any kind. In that case, the tariff could hardly be justified on so-called antidumping grounds.

Increasing employment or reducing unemployment. When faced with a severe depression, a country may resort to a tariff in an attempt to stimulate domestic production, incomes, and employment. Under such circumstances, reminiscent of the Great Depression of the 1930's, a tariff may help create additional employment or to prevent a further rise in unemployment. By restricting imports, the tariff induces domestic producers of the protected goods to expand their output, thereby creating new employment. Moreover, the initial spurt of activity in the protected industries may spread to other sectors of the economy via an increased demand for investment goods and the subsequent increase in consumption expenditures; in the process, incomes and employment may be further raised. Thus, the imposition of a tariff during a depression may help to cure existing economic ills and speed the country's recovery. That, at least, is the essence of the so-called "employment" argument for protection.

But the use of a tariff as a remedial measure has its price. This consists of several side effects that may slow the recovery process or,

[8] For a discussion of antidumping practices in the United States, see the interesting article by P. Ehrenhaft, "Protection Against International Price Discrimination: U.S. Countervailing and Anti Dumping Duties," *Columbia Law Review* (January, 1958), pp. 44–76.

worse, completely prevent it. First, imposition of the tariff, especially at a time when other countries are also suffering from economic slumps, is almost certain to lead to retaliatory action that would reduce the country's exports. As a result, any expansion of production and employment in the protected industries may be offset by a contraction of employment in the country's export industries, thereby leaving matters pretty much as they were. Second, even if other countries do not retaliate, the country that imposes the tariff may still experience a decline in exports, due to falling incomes abroad. For, as we saw earlier (Chapter 2), a reduction in one country's imports must be matched by a like reduction in its trading partners' exports. Falling exports, in turn, cause incomes to fall by a greater amount; and as their incomes fall, foreign countries will doubtless curtail their own imports, some of which constitute the exports of the country imposing the tariff. Third, to the extent that the tariff succeeds in stimulating domestic production and employment, it leads to a less efficient use of resources; for the expansionary effects of the tariff are most likely to be felt in inefficient industries. And since a tariff imposed during a depression may continue long after the need for it has passed, its short-term virtues may be quite costly when measured by long-term misallocation of resources.

The "employment" argument for protection is also open to the charge of aiding and abetting one of the worst kinds of beggar-thy-neighbor policies. To cure a depression by restricting imports is tantamount to "exporting" the depression to other countries; it makes them pay the "medical bill." Such a selfish policy creates ill feeling toward the country pursuing it, and may cause serious political repercussions in its foreign relations.

A much preferable way to stimulate a depressed economy is to apply liberal monetary and fiscal measures that encourage greater expenditures for investment and consumption. Easy credit policies, tax cuts, government expenditures for public projects, and so on—all these are recognized and tested methods of dealing with the problem of domestic unemployment. In their effect on the economy, such policies have the advantage of being far more direct and comprehensive than a tariff on selected commodities. Second, they can achieve their objective without causing injury to, and inviting retaliation from, other countries. Finally, they leave the flows of international trade unimpaired and do not result in a misallocation of economic resources.

Promotion and diversification of industry. Two separate arguments are involved here. Although each is invoked in response to a specific need, both share the distinction of providing the most valid—or least invalid— economic justifications for the use of tariff protection. Moreover, the two arguments are closely related. For each is a variation on a broad theme: that industrialization is the key to economic growth, stability, and fruitful participation in international trade; therefore, when free trade threatens to jeopardize a country's efforts to industrialize itself, temporary protection may be warranted.

1. Infant industries and growth

Of the two, the "infant-industry" argument is the more widely known and more frequently used. Associated originally with Alexander Hamilton and Friedrich List,[9] it correctly asserts that competition from older and well-established industries abroad may prevent the growth of potentially efficient home industries. A certain amount of protection is, therefore, necessary in order to shelter these new industries during their early stages of development, so that they can reach maturity and prove their worth.

So stated, the argument cannot be logically refuted. For regardless of how efficient a firm or an industry may turn out to be, at the beginning it is always characterized by high per-unit costs of production. Hence, a newly established industry cannot possibly withstand the competition of foreign producers who, by virtue of an earlier start, have already attained lower costs through economies of scale. Under a tariff umbrella, however, the new industry can expand its production, reach a more economical scale of operation, and be able to face foreign competitors on its own.

However, the validity of the infant-industry argument hangs on the observance of two important qualifications. First, the "infants" to be protected must be chosen on the basis of their suitability to the country's particular resources and their ability to stand on their own feet within a reasonable period of time. Second, the protection that is granted must be removed once the new industries are able to operate without it. Unfortunately, these qualifications are mostly honored in the breach. National pride, particularly in the case of newly independent nations, often

---

[9] Hamilton's ideas were expressed in his famous *Report on Manufactures*, submitted to Congress in 1791. List presented a much broader thesis, which appeared in his *The National System of Political Economy*, published in 1840.

influences economic policy more strongly than objective economic calculations. As a result, protection is given to industries whose prospects of ever surviving without it are slight. And even where the promotion of a new industry *is* justified on economic grounds, it is often difficult to remove the protection when it is no longer needed. Having become accustomed to the comforting shelter provided by the tariff, such an industry may effectively lobby for its continuation.

However, the practical misuse and abuse of the infant-industry principle does not invalidate its basic logic. For if the efficient allocation of resources within each country is to be fostered, then any industry whose growth would contribute to that end should be encouraged—with the aid of temporary protection, if necessary. Indeed, the only objection to a tariff in this case lies in the suggestion that the development of new industries might also be accomplished with government subsidies. The granting of subsidies, it is claimed, has the advantage of leaving market forces alone, and thereby enabling consumers to obtain commodities at competitive prices. At the same time, producers are compensated for losses resulting from prices that are below per-unit costs; prices are set below cost, of course—at least initially—in order to meet foreign competition. Another advantage of a subsidy over a tariff is this: it is easier to discontinue it when the need for it no longer exists. Finally, subsidies are said to represent a more equitable distribution of the burden involved in promoting new industries; for since they are usually granted out of general tax revenue, all taxpayers share in the country's development efforts.

But the ability to grant subsidies on a significant scale depends on a country's financial resources. While a country such as the United States may have little difficulty in appropriating large sums for the development of new industries, the same cannot be said of a poor, underdeveloped nation. The latter may have no choice but to use temporary tariff protection in order to stimulate economic growth.

2. *Diversification and stability*

Temporary protection is sometimes urged as the way in which a country might diversify its industries and thus achieve a more balanced and stable economic structure. This suggestion is not without merit if made in reference to highly specialized economies in which exports consist of only one or a few items, and which depend on a wide range of imports for their supply of goods and services. Such countries (most of the underdeveloped nations are among them) are particularly vulnerable to economic disruptions due to changing economic and/or political conditions abroad—for example, wars, depressions, technological changes, and so forth. Thus, the danger of economic instability, which in any case is inherent in a highly interdependent world economy, assumes added significance for these countries. And if diversification of domestic industries would help reduce or eliminate this danger, much can be said for it.

Though desirable in principle, however, the achievement of economic stability through diversification may prove more costly than it is worth. For in order to insulate itself effectively from economic fluctuations originating abroad, a highly specialized country may have to embark on a huge diversification program that would require, in effect, the reshuffling of its entire economic system. And if such reorganization could be accomplished only behind a highly protective tariff wall, it would probably result in a gross misallocation of the country's resources. Since inefficient use of resources tends to reduce real savings, it limits the society's efforts to accumulate capital—an important ingredient of economic growth. Thus, a slowing of economic growth may well be the price of economic stability.

This does not mean, however, that the problem of instability should be ignored, or that the use of tariffs to promote industrial diversification can never be sanctioned. What matters is the way in which a country goes about using tariff protection to solve the problem. A gradual approach, based on a careful selection of the industries to be developed, may be quite justified provided, of course, that protection is used with restraint. Indeed, such an approach is essentially the same as that advocated for infant industries. And understandably so. For in the final analysis, the promotion of new industries, especially in a young and developing nation, is no more or less than a way in which the nation tries to diversify its economic pursuits and widen its economic base. When justified on economic grounds (e.g., availability of the necessary resources) such efforts may yield both stability and growth.

National defense and national security. Unlike the preceding arguments, the appeal for a tariff as a means of safeguarding a nation's military and political interests cannot be judged solely in economic terms. For even though the "national-security" argument for protection involves economic considerations, it is based on the proposition, enunciated—of all people—by Adam Smith, that ''defense'' is of much more importance than ''opulence.'' In the face of such an admission, the economist's role in this case becomes that of a juror instead of a judge; it is not up to him to pass sentence on the validity of the objective, but to consider the evidence that is presented to support the use of a tariff to achieve it.

Briefly stated, the national-security argument maintains that too great a dependence on foreign suppliers may put a country in jeopardy in the event of a war or any other international crisis. This, it is claimed, is particularly true in the matter of strategically important goods. Hence, industries that are considered essential because of military and strategic reasons, but which cannot normally compete with foreign producers, should be kept alive by tariff protection. For although the industries in question may be economically inefficient, their continued existence would assure the nation of necessary supplies in time of emergency.

What constitutes an ''essential'' industry? If the term is broadly interpreted, practically any industry can somehow manage to fit the description, and clamor for protection in the name of national security.[10] It might, in fact, be claimed that to be perfectly secure, a nation must be completely self-sufficient—a claim that may have considerable appeal to national pride, but that is, in fact, economically illogical. But even if the term is narrowly defined to include only industries that bear most directly on the requirements of the military machine (e.g., munitions, aircraft, precision instruments, chemicals, steel), protection may not be the most economical—or fair—method of assuring military preparedness.

Indeed, if the survival of an inefficient industry is justified by national defense considerations, the government might just as well take it over and operate it. Or, if this raises objections, the industry might be granted subsidies, in a manner suggested earlier in connection with the development of infant industries. Either of these methods would be more desirable from the viewpoint of the economy in general and the consumer in particular. For in each case, the cost of national defense and security

[10] Examples of this in American industry are given in Chapter 17.

would be shared equitably, and the goods in question would be available at reasonable prices.

Summary and Conclusions

No summary can do justice to all of the foregoing. The best we can do is to recall that while free trade leads to the most efficient allocation of resources and results in a maximization of real income, protection encourages the *misallocation* of resources and tends to reduce real income.

Judged in these terms, most of the arguments for tariffs turn out to be economically indefensible; some, moreover, connote undesirable political repercussions. Even those arguments that have considerable merit derive their validity from special and highly qualified circumstances. In any event, the use of a tariff to achieve a particularly meritorious objective should always be avoided if a better alternative exists.

15

Quantitative Controls
and Discriminatory Practices

Odd as it may seem, tariffs are actually one of the lesser evils among protective devices. True, the tariff is one of the oldest and best-known instruments of commercial policy, and for many years was the most common form of trade restriction. But with the passage of time, it has been increasingly supplemented by other, more sophisticated trade controls. Compared to these controls, the restrictive impact of the tariff is mild. And although tariffs have never been completely abandoned, their significance has been gradually overshadowed by the development and use of other policy measures. The present chapter concerns these other measures.

Import Quotas

Like the tariff, a quota exerts a restrictive influence on the volume of imports. It does so, however, more directly: It sets a limit on the total physical quantity, or total value, of a particular import(s) that may enter the country during a given period of time. Often referred to as *quantitative restrictions,* quotas have a long history, dating back at least 300 years. But only since the 1930's have they come to be used extensively as a tool of commercial policy. Today there is hardly a country that does not use this tool to a greater or lesser extent.

In broad terms, we can distinguish between two kinds of quotas: "absolute" quotas and "tariff" quotas. The former set outright limits on the amounts of different commodities that can be imported (e.g., 1 million tons of steel or $5 million worth of tobacco per year). In its extreme form, an absolute quota may completely prohibit the importation of a particular product(s), in which case it can be termed an "embargo." Under a tariff quota, on the other hand, limits are imposed, not on the total quantity (or value) of an imported product, but on the amount that may come in free of duty, or at a specially reduced duty rate. Imports in excess of this amount are permitted, but are subject to the regular duty or even a higher duty. Thus, a tariff quota may actually be thought of as a device for trade liberalization, making possible at least some reduction in import restrictions. In recent years, however, such quotas have been employed sparingly; in the United States, for example, they apply to only a few items (e.g., petroleum and certain agricultural products).

Quotas, regardless of type, may also be classified according to the manner in which they are administered. Thus, a quota may be *global,* in which case the total allowable amount can be imported, regardless of source, until the quota is filled; or it may be *geographical.* In this case, the quota may be assigned entirely to one country, or be divided among several foreign sources of supply. Still another method of allocating quotas involves a system of *import licensing,* whereby the amount to be imported is allocated among individual importers and/or foreign exporters of the commodity in question.

Import quotas are at once a more effective and a potentially more discriminatory instrument of commercial policy than are tariffs. Indeed, one of the main reasons for the use of quotas, especially during periods of great emergency, is the certainty of their results. For unlike the tariff, whose success in limiting the quantity of various imports depends largely on supply and demand conditions in the countries involved, quotas can nearly always be relied upon to keep out undesired imports, or to reduce them to predetermined amounts.[1] Moreover, by their very nature, quotas

---

[1] Barring, of course, smuggling or other violations of the quota.

lend themselves to discrimination in the treatment of supplying countries as well as individual importers. As such, they pose much more of a threat to the cause of free multilateral trade than do tariffs.

While quantitative restrictions assure tighter control than a tariff over the volume and sources of imports, they involve a number of serious problems. To begin with, decisions must be made concerning the types of products whose imports should be curtailed by quotas, the sizes of these quotas, the manner in which they are to be allocated, and the portions that should be granted to different exporting countries and domestic importers. None of these decisions is easy to make, especially if quantitative restrictions are adopted, not by a desire to discriminate between various sources of supply, but by the need to limit imports in general. One might argue that in the latter case, global quotas provide the perfect answer. But such an arrangement creates the danger that importers, in their haste to get under the quota, would exhaust it within a relatively short time. As a result, the glut of imports during the early part of the quota period would soon give way to severe shortages. Moreover, global quotas tend to favor nearby sources of supply whose geographical proximity, and not necessarily their productive efficiency, enables them to fill the quota more rapidly than distant producers. Finally, it is not always possible to determine precisely how much of the quota has already been filled, and whether additional imports should be permitted to enter the country.

To avoid or at least minimize some of these hazards, quotas, whether global or geographical, are usually allocated by means of import licensing. Yet a system of import licensing poses problems of its own and is, moreover, open to bureaucratic abuses. Thus, if import licenses are issued on a first-come-first-served basis, the rush of applicants would once again result in the almost immediate exhaustion of the quota. On the other hand, any attempt to assign the quota according to past shares of the market would discriminate against newer importers and in favor of old, established interests. And if the same principle is used in allocating quotas among foreign exporters, it may favor traditional but perhaps inefficient suppliers at the expense of new and possibly more efficient suppliers. In short, no formula for assigning quotas is ever completely satisfactory on this score. For even when quotas are not intended to be discriminatory, their administration is likely to lead to some discrimination.[2]

The Effects of Quotas

It is best to discuss the major effects of quantitative restrictions by comparing them with those resulting from the tariff. And since both tariffs and quotas are designed to curtail imports, they can be compared mainly in terms of their effects on the quantities and prices of the goods whose importation is being restricted. We may begin by considering the quantitative effect.

As we saw earlier, a tariff is relied upon to restrict imports by raising their prices in the importing country. The rise in price, in turn, is expected to cut down the demand for imports, and at the same time to enable domestic producers to expand their output and capture a larger share of the market for the protected goods. Yet the extent to which the price rise would reduce the quantity of imports and/or increase domestic production depends on supply and demand conditions in the countries involved. Thus, fairly inelastic supply conditions at home, combined with a highly elastic foreign supply, would militate against a substantial expansion of domestic output. Moreover, if consumers insist on buying imported goods, and are willing to pay the higher prices resulting from the duties, imports would continue to come in. In any event, when a particular tariff leads to only small price increases, its effect in limiting the quantities of imports may be negligible.

Such considerations need not concern a country that employs quotas in order to restrict its imports. For under a quota system, neither supply and demand, nor even the price, play an active role in determining the actual amounts of incoming imports. These are set by administrative decree and are not dependent on prevailing market forces. To be sure,

---

[2] This is not to suggest, however, that discrimination must always be condemned. In an ingenious analysis, the Norwegian economist Ragnar Frisch has demonstrated that in certain instances of balance-of-payments disequilibrium, discriminatory import restrictions would actually result in more trade than if imports from all sources were cut back in the same proportions. See his "On the Need for Forecasting a Multilateral Balance of Payments," *American Economic Review* (September, 1947), pp. 535–551.

decisions as to what, how much, and from whom, may be imported are often guided by the nature of the domestic demand for particular imports, as well as by the conditions of their supply at home and abroad. But the decisions themselves are made not in the market place but in governmental quarters; hence their execution lies outside the influence of the price mechanism. For this very reason, the effects of quantitative restrictions on the volume of imports are much more predictable than the quantitative effects of the tariff. Indeed, quotas leave little room for guesswork concerning their effect on quantities that will be imported. Only the amounts specified by the quotas are permitted to enter; and once the quota limits are reached, further importation ceases.

When it comes to effects on prices, the positions are reversed. Since tariffs affect the prices of protected goods in a restrained way, any price changes that follow the imposition of a tariff are more easily predictable than those resulting from quotas. As we know, the prices of protected goods under a tariff tend to rise by less than the duties themselves, and the increase in price is unlikely to exceed the full amount of the duty.[3] In fact, there is little reason why prices should rise above the duty; for as long as the commodities in question can be imported—subject, of course, to duty payment—any rise in price would be checked by an increased supply of imports. In other words, the imposition of a tariff enables market adjustments to be made through changes in supply. And although the tariff causes prices to rise, the increases tend to be confined within a fairly narrow range.

Not so, however, with quantitative restrictions. If, at the prevailing market price, the quantity allowed under a quota is smaller than that which is actually demanded, prices of those commodities affected will rise. Moreover, any subsequent increase in demand will serve to push prices still higher. By the same token, a sudden decrease in demand will cause prices to fall sharply. In short, by rigidly fixing the supply of imports, quotas place the burden of market adjustments on changes in price rather than on changes in quantities. Consequently, they open the door to much wider price fluctuations than do tariffs.

But quotas do more than that. They enable domestic producers and/or importers to assume a strong monopoly position in the domestic

---

[3] Allowance should be made, however, for possible markups that may raise the price by more (but not much more) than the full amount of the duty.

market and reap unreasonably high profits—something that cannot easily be done under a tariff. Indeed, since under a tariff anyone willing to pay the duty is free to import unlimited amounts, no single producer (or importer) can charge a price that exceeds the world price plus the duty. Even a monopolist, protected by a tariff, must adjust his prices accordingly; for if he raises the price to a much higher level, he will only invite additional imports and lose some of his sales. But with a quota to protect him, the same monopolist enjoys a much freer hand. He can confront consumers in the home market with high prices without fear of losing ground to competing imports. As a result he stands to earn what is sometimes called "quota profits"— profits that are directly attributed to the more restrictive nature of quotas as compared to tariffs.

Similar profits may accrue to those importers who, by virtue of having obtained import licenses, constitute the only source of import supply in the domestic market. The smaller the quota and/or the fewer the importers among whom it is shared, the greater the potential profits for each importer. This is especially true if the goods subject to quota are not produced domestically, or if the demand for them is fairly inelastic. In this case, an import license is, in effect, a passport to abnormally high profits; and in some countries importers often resort to corruption and bribery of public officials in their efforts to obtain such licenses.

Much of the abuse associated with import licensing could be avoided if quota profits were limited or eliminated. This can be accomplished by setting up a price-control system, under which the government would closely regulate the prices of goods subject to quotas. Such a system would assure sellers of reasonable profits and protect consumers against monopolistic exploitation. Another possibility is for import licenses to be auctioned off to the highest bidders. In this way, the government itself would receive part (or possibly all) of the potential profits resulting from the quota and could use them in the public interest.[4] Unfortunately, neither of these suggestions has ever been put into practice in conjunction with the establishment of quota systems. And since the main opposition to their adoption usually comes from powerful vested interests, they will probably remain no more than textbook proposals.

In later chapters we shall return to quotas and describe their use in

---

[4] In this respect, proceeds from the auctioning of import licenses can be likened to the revenue effect of the tariff.

specific instances. For the moment, we may simply conclude that quantitative restrictions—no matter how administered—allow a country to manipulate its foreign trade much more directly than it can with tariffs. And although direct controls may be justified on occasion, one must not lose sight of their undesirable economic and political implications. Just how undesirable these can be will become increasingly evident in the discussion that follows.

Export Restrictions and Export Subsidies

Direct controls over trade are often used not only to restrict a country's imports, but also to regulate its exports. In this context, the "regulation of exports" assumes a rather broad meaning: It may involve policies designed either to restrict exports or to promote them, or both. And although these two objectives may appear at first glance to contradict each other, this need not be the case. Indeed, from the viewpoint of a particular country, the restriction of some kinds of exports (e.g., raw materials) may be deemed quite compatible with the promotion of others (e.g., manufactured goods). Similarly, the expansion of exports to certain countries may be regarded as desirable—and hence encouraged— while exports destined to other areas may be frowned upon and therefore restricted. But whatever form they take, and for whatever purpose they are undertaken, export regulations constitute a barrier to the flow of goods between nations, and distort the patterns of trade. In inquiring into the nature of such regulations, as well as the reasons behind them, we will begin with export restrictions.

A country wishing to restrict its exports may do so by instituting a system of export licensing, under which the types, amounts, and/or destination of potential exports are specified in advance and are tightly regulated. The government may, in fact, declare a complete embargo on certain exports, thus serving notice on domestic firms not to sell these items to foreign customers. Or, it may impose a geographical embargo, prohibiting the exportation of *any* goods to certain countries. (The United States embargo on exports to Red China and, more recently, to Cuba are cases in point.) Less stringently, exports may also be restricted by export taxes. Here, however, the primary objective is not to curtail exports per se, but to raise their prices and thereby improve the country's terms of trade.

Indeed, the restriction of exports—whether through licensing or taxation—may be undertaken for the sole purpose of improving the terms of trade. And to the extent that such a policy bears fruit, it closely resembles the establishment of output and export quotas, as practiced by private monopolies and cartels. In both cases, the immediate objective is to raise the prices of traded goods by deliberately limiting their supply. But whereas cartels seek high prices in order to assure high profit margins for their members, government action in this sphere is based on the familiar idea that as export prices rise, relative to import prices, the terms of trade become more favorable. This is not to suggest, however, that export restrictions, as practiced by governments, are any more desirable than those of cartels. For although a rise in the ratio of export to import prices does indicate an improvement in the net-barter terms of trade, such an "improvement" has little real value if it is brought about by a reduction in the volume of trade. Indeed, to improve the terms of trade by means of export restrictions makes no more economic sense than to improve them by restricting imports through tariffs. In any event, the success of such policies depends on supply and demand conditions as well as on the reaction of other governments—neither of which can be counted upon in advance.

There is something to be said, however, for policies designed to limit or prohibit the exportation of commodities that are needed at home. For example, nations have been known to impose export quotas (or complete embargoes) on shipments of various raw materials, foodstuffs, scrap metals, highly specialized machinery, and so on. But the reasons behind such restrictions are not always purely economic. For while the requirements of domestic consumption and production play an important role in shaping a country's export policies, they are often superseded by strategic and political considerations. In fact, many of the items whose exports are usually restricted consist of goods that bear directly or indirectly upon the nation's military needs. And even where such goods are plentiful, their exportation may be viewed as undesirable from the standpoint of national security, and is therefore limited.

Confronted with national defense requirements, Cold War politics, communist menace, and similar considerations that may prompt the restriction of exports, the free-trade economist must bite his tongue and admit that there is perhaps more to economic policies than economics alone. He may observe, however, that export restrictions, practiced by one country or a small group of countries, are in the end self-defeating. For if such policies succeed in cutting down the supply and/or raising the prices of the affected commodities, they are bound to encourage the development of substitutes or alternative sources of supply. This is likely, regardless of whether the commodities in question happen to be cotton textiles and cocoa beans or atomic bombs and guided missiles!

So much for export restrictions. When it comes to the promotion of exports, we have an altogether different set of considerations. Here the objective is not to curtail exports but to expand them. In pursuit of this objective, governments often resort to "export subsidies." The main purpose of export subsidies is to enable exporters to sell their products abroad at lower prices than actual cost or profit considerations would otherwise permit. Put differently, subsidies are intended to make it possible for high-cost domestic producers to compete on the world market with more efficient foreign producers. Such subsidies take many different forms. To illustrate the principles involved, we will examine four of the more common methods of subsidization.

In its simplest form, a subsidy consists of a direct payment by the government to the exporter, after the latter has completed his sale. The payment may be based on the number of units sold (e.g., so much per ton or per bushel), or it may be geared to the difference between the price received by the exporter and his actual per-unit costs. In any case, the payment is designed either to cover any possible losses suffered by the exporter or to assure him a higher profit than he could obtain without the subsidy. Similar results may be achieved in a more indirect way. The government itself may purchase the commodities in question from domestic producers at certain fixed prices, and in turn "dump" them in foreign markets at lower prices than those prevailing at home. This, as we shall see in Chapter 17, has long been the practice of the United States in connection with agricultural exports—a practice, incidentally, that grew out of the domestic farm-support program. But the same procedure may be adopted with respect to any commodity whose domestic production is being subsidized or whose exports are being encouraged.

Still another form of subsidization, involving foreign trade, is typified by the support that governments normally grant to their merchant marines. Some governments, in fact, go so far as to participate in the ownership of national shipping lines; thus they provide some of the original capital. But even where transportation industries are owned entirely by private interests, shipping operations are usually subsidized in one way or another. Thus, governments entrust to their merchant marines (as well as airlines and railroads) the carrying of mail, and pay them for their services. In addition, some governments (the United States among them) help to finance private shipbuilding, and may on occasion sell navy surplus material (including ships) to private concerns for very low prices.

Lastly, export subsidies may consist of tax concessions to exporters. In several countries exporters are either exempted from, or reimbursed for, payment of various business taxes.[5] As is well known, the existence of such taxes serves to raise the selling prices of the finished products. Hence, removal of these taxes enables exporters to reduce their prices and presumably to expand their sales abroad. But since these concessions are granted only in connection with the sale of exports, they discriminate against domestic consumers, who must pay a price that includes indirect business taxes; this price is therefore higher than the price that foreign buyers pay for the same commodity.

This is hardly surprising. For, as stated earlier, subsidies are specifically designed to promote the expansion of a country's exports by reducing the prices charged for them abroad. As such they tend to create a differential between the domestic and foreign prices of the subsidized commodities—a differential that, more often than not, favors foreign over domestic consumers. Thus, government grants of export subsidies impose a double burden on domestic consumers: Not only do they, as taxpayers, share in the direct cost of the subsidies, but they must pay higher prices (for the very commodities they help subsidize) than do consumers in foreign markets.

But that is not all. Inasmuch as export subsidies result in higher prices at home than abroad, they open the door to a possible influx of imports consisting of the very commodities whose exports are subsidized.

[5] For examples, see W. C. Gordon, *International Trade* (New York: Knopf, 1958), p. 223.

In order to guard against this possibility, the government may be obliged to impose tariffs or quantitative restrictions. In fact, one can hardly think of any attempt to promote exports through subsidies that did not also involve some measures to control imports. At times, governments may be driven to the use of export subsidies and import restrictions by severe balance-of-payments difficulties. This, for example, was the case during the 1930's when, in an effort to reduce trade deficits, country after country adopted measures to increase exports and limit imports. Although one cannot condone this kind of commercial policy, one can appreciate the context within which it was pursued. But when export subsidies are merely intended to enable high-cost domestic producers to compete with more efficient foreign producers, they deserve no sympathy. Under these circumstances, neither the subsidies nor the import restrictions to which they inevitably give rise serve a useful purpose—except, of course, to their recipients. On the contrary, they distort the patterns of international trade and encourage the misallocation of economic resources.

Bilateral Agreements and Preferential Arrangements

The 1930's saw not only the widespread use of import restrictions and export subsidies, but also the emergence of a trading system known as *bilateralism*. One aspect of bilateralism was encountered in Chapter 11. There we found that in the general atmosphere of exchange controls and currency inconvertibility, which characterized the interwar and early post-World War II periods, many nations resorted to bilateral-payment agreements as a means of settling their international transactions. These agreements, which provided for the balancing of trade between pairs of countries, enabled nations to finance significant amounts of their trade without the loss of scarce foreign exchange. But although the practice of bilateral balancing grew out of, and was designed to cope with, balance-of-payments difficulties, it soon acquired new purposes and new dimensions. It became, in fact, a versatile tool of commercial policy, which, when cleverly manipulated, permitted countries to exploit foreign-trade relations for selfish political and economic ends.

The best-known practitioner of bilateralism was Nazi Germany, whose commercial policies during most of the 1930's were geared primarily to the strengthening of the state's military and political powers. In pursuit of this objective, Germany entered into a series of bilateral trade agreements with many European and non-European countries. Since she was usually the stronger party to such agreements, she was able to extract from her trading partners many concessions that worked to her advantage. Specifically, Germany sought to make other countries dependent on her as a major market for their exports, hoping thereby to isolate them from the general network of world trade. Hence, she agreed to buy most of their exports, paying relatively high prices for them, but on the condition that the proceeds be used to purchase German made goods or be allowed to accumulate as bank balances in Germany. Moreover, she managed to assume the position of a large debtor vis-à-vis many of her weaker partners, and could thus threaten to default on her payments unless her conditions were met. These and other tactics[6] enabled Germany to use bilateral trade not only to her immediate economic advantage, but also as an effective instrument of power politics.

Even in its less obnoxious applications, bilateralism leaves much to be desired. To appreciate the extent to which bilateral agreements can subvert international trade and force it into uneconomic channels, one should recall some of their essential qualities. Thus, under a bilateral agreement, the volume (or total value) of the goods to be exchanged is largely influenced by the need or desire to *balance* the accounts between the two trading countries. And since it is easier to reach agreement on the figure to be balanced by reducing the imports of one country than by increasing the imports of the other, bilateral balancing tends to reduce the volume of trade. This idea was recently echoed by the astute and influential London *Economist*. "Bilateral trade," it stated, "inevitably pushes trade down to the lowest common denominator."[7] And although *The Economist* made the statement while commenting on a specific case (the trade of the Soviet Union with its East European satellites) the validity of its observation is supported by other cases.

To this we might add two other observations concerning the nature

[6] For a neat but detailed summary of Germany's foreign-trade policies during this period, see Albert O. Hirschman, *National Power and the Structure of Foreign Trade* (Berkeley: University of California Press, 1945), pp. 34–35.

[7] *The Economist* (October 9, 1965), p. 184.

of bilateralism. First, the parties to bilateral agreements usually agree to pay, for each other's exports, higher prices than either could obtain in the free world market. As a result, consumers in both countries are forced to buy their imports from a more expensive source than if they had a choice. Second, when trade is conducted on a bilateral basis, the choice of consumers is limited to the kinds of goods that the trading partners agree to exchange. These goods may either be inferior to similar goods produced elsewhere or altogether unsuitable to consumers' tastes and preferences. Under such circumstances, the actual exchange would surely fail to satisfy the needs and desires of consumers, and might prove of little benefit to the nation as a whole.

In sum, under a bilateral regime neither cost and price considerations nor consumers' preferences play a significant role in determining the volume and patterns of international trade. What and how much is to be imported *and* exported, and by whom—these questions are now left to administrative discretion rather than to free-market forces. Indeed, in name as well as character, bilateralism is the antithesis of multilateralism; whenever it predominates, it obstructs trade flows and diminishes the gains from trade. If proof is required, one need only look at the 1930's and some years of the 1940's. During both periods, world trade reached its lowest ebb, largely as a result of the general trend toward bilateralism.

Only slightly less obstructive are trade agreements whose aim is not to balance trade bilaterally but to extend special privileges to the exports of a particular country or countries. Known as "preferential arrangements," they usually provide for an exchange of tariff (or quota) concessions between the signatories—concessions that are denied to other trading partners. As such, preferential arrangements are essentially discriminatory; they are not intended to liberalize a country's trade but to direct its course in specific channels. And because they are motivated at times by political considerations, their economic virtues are open to question.

Among the best-known preferential agreements are those concluded between mother countries and their overseas colonial possessions or dependencies; one example is the Ottowa System of Imperial Preference. Signed in 1932 by the United Kingdom and various members of the British Commonwealth, this agreement provided for preferential tariff rates to be granted by Britain to a wide range of agricultural products exported by Commonwealth countries. The latter, in turn, agreed to extend preferential treatment to British exports of manufactured goods. Similar arrangements have existed between France and her colonial empire, as well as between various other pairs or groups of countries

Whether imposed by a colonial power on its dependencies, or voluntarily entered into, preferential agreements distort the patterns and composition of trade. They enable countries to discriminate between the sources of their imports and to select the commodities for preferential treatment. Consequently, the concessions exchanged under such agreements may have little or no effect in stimulating the total trade of the countries involved or the world as a whole. On the contrary, they are more apt to result in a mere *diversion* of trade—often from a more efficient to a less efficient source of supply—and possibly in an actual reduction of world trade.

State Trading

Although state trading is highly suggestive of a behavior that has come to be identified with totalitarian regimes (e.g., U.S.S.R., Red China), it is found in the so-called free or mixed enterprise economies as well. Briefly defined, the term means direct involvement of the government, or some of its agencies, in importing and exporting. It is a practice in which all countries have engaged at various times and in varying degrees.

For example, during World War II and in early postwar years, the British government concluded "bulk-purchase" (and sale) agreements with many foreign governments and with private companies abroad. These agreements, most of them lasting for several years, provided for an exchange of various goods in specified quantities and predetermined prices. (At one time, they covered a substantial portion of British imports in general, and imports of foodstuffs and raw materials in particular.) Other West European countries have employed similar devices in dealing with communist-bloc countries; and many of today's developing nations are using the same techniques in *their* trade. Even the United States, an avid champion of free enterprise, has not shied away from a certain amount of state trading. This is evidenced by the official importation of strategic raw materials for stockpiling purposes, the "offshore procurement" purchases of military goods and services, and the sale of surplus food by the Commodity Credit Corporation to countries overseas.[8]

Neither the mechanics of state trading nor the reasons for it need detain us. Let us merely note that while state trading is practiced in some countries to the complete exclusion of privately conducted commerce, in most countries the two exist side by side. As for the reasons that prompt direct government participation in foreign trade, these range over a wide field. On the economic side, we may list balance-of-payments difficulties, scarcity of foreign exchange, the need to coordinate foreign trade with national planning programs, and the desire to drive hard bargains with trading partners as the major causes that have given rise to state trading. But economic considerations do not alone guide a nation's commercial policies, and state trading is no exception. Indeed, even where it accounts for only a small part of a country's international economic transactions, state trading can be made to serve political and military interests as well as economic needs. Nor is it surprising that many countries, including the United States, have relied on state trading as an important instrument in conducting their foreign policies.

Our immediate concern, however, is with the *economic* effects of state trading. Accordingly, we may well ask: Is government involvement in importing and exporting activities an obstacle to the establishment of mutually advantageous patterns of international specialization and trade? Or, to put it differently, is trade that is carried on by governments any less beneficial, economically, than trade resulting from the interplay of free-market forces?

It is conceivable, of course, that government-conducted trade can be governed solely by cost and price considerations; and if this were the case, its economic effects would resemble those we associate with private commercial activities. That is to say, government purchases of imports and sales of exports could presumably follow the dictates of comparative advantage, the result being an efficient allocation of the country's (and

[8] One might also mention the Export-Import Bank, an institution formed with United States government funds; its purpose is to extend credit to foreign governments for purchases of American goods. (More about it in Chapter 19.)

world's) economic resources. Yet we must frankly admit that government participation in foreign trade is seldom motivated by the cost-price-profit calculations of private business. Thus, even if its ultimate objective is economic in nature, the government may go about achieving it in an uneconomic way. In any event, the very entry of the government into the international market—regardless of its underlying objective—often implies a desire to alter or regulate, rather than to accept, existing economic conditions.

To be sure, there are instances when state trading, though it interferes with the free-market mechanism, may turn out to the advantage of a country. This is the case when the government, by posing as a monopsony vis-à-vis individual foreign sellers, can obtain imports at lower prices than under freely competitive market conditions. Similarly, state trading may enable a country to assume a monopoly position and force higher prices on foreign buyers for its exports. Yet if state trading is carried on through bilateral agreements between governments—and this is very often the case—the gains to its practitioners are far from clear. For when two state-trading countries face each other across a bargaining table, they cannot bring the strength of a monopoly (or monopsony) position to bear upon the negotiations. Hence, neither can hope to gain a substantial advantage over the other.[9]

Indeed, one of the charges commonly leveled against state trading is that it leads to the worst possible kind of bilateralism—one from which the participants derive questionable benefits in the short run and no gains at all in the long run. This may or may not be true. For, given the particular objective that it had set out to achieve, a country may rightly feel that bilaterally conducted state trading has actually served its purpose well. Moreover, bilateral agreements, covering government-sponsored trade, may prove to be the speediest and surest way to cope with an emergency situation faced by one or two countries. But of one thing there can be little doubt: State trading, whether pursued bilaterally or unilaterally, is a departure from a freely operating competitive market system. And to the extent that it is motivated by noneconomic objectives, it may well be conducted without any regard to cost and price considerations. As such, state trading takes its place among other devices

[9] Unless, of course, one of the countries is in a much stronger position than the other.

that governments use to divert trade from its natural course and that cause a less than optimum allocation of economic resources.

"Invisible" Barriers to Trade

To complete the list of government-instituted trade restrictions, brief mention should be made of several types of import rules and regulations. These measures operate behind a facade of innocence; they may seem to have little to do with conscious efforts to restrict trade. But the fact that they are often well-disguised does not diminish their effectiveness as tools of commercial policy. To appreciate their insidious ways, consider a few representative samples.

One set of "invisible" trade barriers may be properly called "health and sanitary regulations," a term whose facetiousness is more than matched by its cynical application to foreign trade. For example, the United States prohibits (with few exceptions) the importation of fresh fruits and vegetables, and justifies its action by the need to protect home-grown products from agricultural diseases that might exist abroad. Similar prohibitions apply to imports of meat products and livestock, as well as to certain dairy products. Moreover, all imports of processed foods, drugs, and cosmetics are subject to rigorous requirements specified by the Food, Drug, and Cosmetic Act; failure to meet even the most minute requirement of this law disqualifies a product from entering the country.

No one can object to laws designed to safeguard a nation's health standards and to protect it from foreign born diseases. But one may well wonder whether oranges grown in Italy or Spain are necessarily more prone to nature's afflictions than Florida oranges; or whether cattle raised on the plains of Argentina are more apt to contract hoof-and-mouth disease than cattle raised in Texas or Oklahoma. For that matter, one might question the motives behind many sanitary regulations that the United States and other countries impose on their imports—especially requirements that make little sense medically, and whose main effect is to make it exceedingly difficult for foreign producers to comply with the law.

Indeed, it has often been claimed—and not without some justification—that the real purpose for various health regulations is to insulate unhealthy domestic producers from vigorous foreign competition, or else to discriminate between different sources of import supply. Although the issue is certainly open to debate, at least one poignant example might be cited in support of the above contention. In 1902, Germany reduced her tariff on cattle imports, but limited these concessions to cattle "reared at a spot at least 300 meters above sea level and having at least one month's grazing each year at a spot at least 800 meters above sea level." Perhaps there is something to be said for cattle whose lungs have been filled with pure mountain air. But it requires very little knowledge of European geography to realize that this particular provision was not so much a reflection of concern over the quality of imported cattle as of a desire to favor Swiss exporters over other cattle suppliers.[10]

Enough said about sanitary regulations. Another seemingly innocent device, often used to restrict imports, is the *mixing quota*. Many countries use mixing quotas to specify the proportions of locally produced (or grown) material that must be used in the manufacture of domestic finished products. For example, several countries require that domestically milled flour contain a certain amount of home-grown wheat, and/or that a specified minimum of domestic flour be used in baking all breads. Other countries provide for specific proportions in mixing such items as domestic and foreign tobacco leaf, natural and synthetic rubber, domestic beet sugar and imported cane sugar, coffee and chicory, raw wool and synthetic fibers. And so on. Similarly, the United States has decreed that at least half of foreign-aid goods shipped overseas must be carried in American vessels.

Ostensibly designed to assist some domestic producers by assuring them a part of the domestic market, mixing regulations actually constitute a serious barrier to trade and may lead to inefficient use of resources. For by specifying the proportions in which domestic and foreign materials must be combined in various manufacturing processes, such regulations effectively limit particular imports (usually raw materials and semifinished goods) to certain fixed amounts. In so doing, they

[10] One should not assume, however, that sanitary regulations are always so devious in nature. For example, the recent prohibition, placed by the United States, on imports of novelty ice balls from Hong Kong, *was* prompted by medical findings attesting to their harmful effects.

force domestic producers of *finished* goods to utilize materials that may be more costly than, and possibly inferior to, similar materials produced abroad. As a consequence, the unsuspecting consumer may have to accept goods that are higher-priced and of lower quality than is necessary.

Of the various "invisible" barriers which may confront imports, however, none are perhaps more frustrating than the legislative and bureaucratic complexities surrounding a country's customs administration. Not by accident has the term "invisible tariff" been coined to describe the vast array of customs regulations and procedures with which imports and importers must comply. Indeed, in some respects, the process of clearing goods through customs may prove just as burdensome, if not actually more so, than the tariff (i.e., duty payment) itself. And rather than fight their way through the customs machinery—thereby subjecting themselves to uncertainties, long delays, additional expenses, and possible court proceedings—importers may at times abandon some plans for purchases from abroad.

To be sure, some of the hazards encountered by importers at the customs gate can be attributed to "normal" bureaucratic inefficiencies. But one cannot—and should not—dismiss the possibility that a great deal of their difficulty stems from deliberate legislative efforts to discriminate against foreign-made goods. Indeed, customs legislation provides a perfect haven for a variety of rules and regulations designed to augment the protective effects of tariffs and quotas. This fact, whose significance is not lost on either lawmakers or domestic business interests, accounts for a great many administrative abuses that affect imports. Nor can any one country be singled out as a shining exception to the general rule. For while some nations may subject their imports to less rigorous entrance requirements than do others, no country has ever hesitated to use customs regulations as a restrictive device if it thought this necessary.

A more detailed account of restrictive customs regulations, as administered by the United States, will appear in Chapter 17. But one last point needs to be made here. The mere fact that imports must undergo a kind of administrative scrutiny from which domestically produced goods are exempted, impedes the international flow of goods and services. Put differently, the very existence of customs regulations— whether or not they are imposed for protective reasons—discriminates against foreign products and hence constitutes a barrier to trade. One can hardly expect this barrier to disappear as long as nations trade with each other. But one may hope for reforms designed to simplify and clarify customs procedures.

Summary

Tariffs, quotas, export restrictions, bilateral agreements, state trading, and various administrative regulations comprise a formidable arsenal of protectionist weapons. Some are old, some of more recent origin. But every one of them, singly or in company with others, has been used at one time or another in the battle against free trade. That battle—or, more precisely, the struggle between free trade and protection—has been raging off and on for the past two centuries. The next four chapters provide a historical account of this struggle.

PART V

FREE TRADE VERSUS PROTECTION
IN A CHANGING WORLD

16

From Mercantilism to Free
Trade and Back

PARALLELING THE RISE OF
strong, unified nation states in Europe, a series of economic ideas and
practices developed during the sixteenth and seventeenth centuries that
have since been labeled "mercantilism." These ideas and practices were
dominated by the proposition that wealth is a requisite for national
power, and that in order to assure the accumulation of wealth, the
nation's economic activities must be centrally controlled and regulated.
This central idea shaped governmental actions throughout most of the
period from 1500 to 1800; and although actual policies differed from
country to country, they were governed by a basically similar purpose:
to make the nation wealthy and powerful.

As an economic philosophy, mercantilism touched upon almost all
aspects of economic life. Of special interest to us, however, are the
mercantile ideas about foreign trade. For these not only constituted the
earliest body of thought dealing with the theory of international trade,
but also provided the basis for commercial policies, some of which have
persisted to this day.

Mercantilism in Theory and in Action

Viewed through mercantilist eyes, wealth consisted of precious metals; consequently, the more gold and silver a country acquired, the wealthier and more powerful it would be.[1] Accumulation of precious metals thus became a prime national objective, and in searching for ways and means of achieving it, the mercantilists were led to the conclusion that foreign trade was the chief source of wealth. Indeed, most mercantilistic policies were directly or indirectly influenced by the belief that a favorable balance of trade—excess of mechandise exports over imports—was the surest way to obtain large amounts of precious metals.

The concept of a favorable balance of trade was later elaborated and broadened into the idea of a favorable balance of payments, which took account of expenditures (and receipts) for freight, insurance services, tourism, and so forth, as well as for merchandise.[2] Yet the basic principle remained the same: An excess of receipts from abroad meant an inflow of gold and silver, while an excess of payments to other countries involved an outflow. Accordingly, every effort was made to maintain—and increase—the size of a favorable trade balance. Such efforts included not only direct regulations over trade, but also the encouragement of industry, agriculture, large merchant marines, and the acquisition of colonies.

A detailed account of mercantilism in action would require more space than we can give it here. But a few representative examples will indicate its general features. Thus, because a favorable trade balance required an excess of exports over imports, mercantilists advocated heavy import duties and generous export subsidies. While the exportation of manufactured goods was encouraged, however, that of raw materials was mostly prohibited. Conversely, although merchandise imports were subject to a host of restrictions, the importation of raw materials was generally favored. In this connection, we might note that the quest for colonial empires, so characteristic of the period, was at least

---

[1] This notion gave rise to the terms ''bullionism'' and ''bullionist,'' which are often used to describe early mercantilist ideas.

[2] See S. B. Clough and C. W. Cole, *Economic History of Europe* (Boston: D. C. Heath, 1941), pp. 199–200.

partly influenced by the fact that colonies provided sources of raw material supply and, at the same time, constituted overseas markets for exports of finished products. Indeed, the many wars fought to gain control over colonial possessions attest to their importance within the mercantile system.

Another aspect of mercantilist policy, identified especially with England, took the form of intricate shipping regulations. The so-called Navigation Acts, passed by Parliament in 1651 and 1660, assured British vessels an almost complete monopoly in carrying freight in and out of British ports. Although the basic motive was undoubtedly to limit expenditures for foreign shipping services, there was another important reason: encouragement of shipbuilding and naval improvements. In addition, mercantilism (particularly in France) involved deliberate efforts to foster industrial development. Subsidies, tax exemptions, and other privileges were granted to domestic producers in order to stimulate manufacturing activities. Even espionage was used to spirit trade secrets away from other countries, and turn them to one's own advantage.[3] At the same time, however, industries were subject to strict government supervision, and were closely regulated as to the types and quality of goods produced, the use of raw materials, wage payments, and so on.

In sum, mercantilism in action was basically an expression of a doctrine that stressed centralized control, rather than free-market play, as the way to achieve economic objectives. And given their particular objective (i.e., the accumulation of gold and silver) the mercantilists can hardly be blamed in retrospect for advocating and pursuing the kind of policies we have just described. Indeed, under the circumstances, theirs seemed a logical course of action. Hence, it was the objective itself, as well as the short-sighted concepts on which it was based, that had to stand trial if mercantilist policies were to be discredited. A kind of trial did in fact take place, and acting on behalf of the "prosecution," Adam Smith submitted his famous brief, appropriately entitled *An Inquiry into the Nature and Causes of the Wealth of Nations*. This exhaustive brief, as we shall see, had far-reaching consequences.

---

[3] One of the most dramatic coups was accomplished by Colbert, minister under Louis XIV. He arranged for smuggling a few glass workers out of Venice, and thus secured for France one of the most guarded manufacturing secrets of the time—the making of Venetian glass.

From Mercantilism to Free Trade: Britain
Takes a Lead

The intellectual attack on mercantilist thought and policies did not come about until the latter part of the eighteenth century—Smith's *The Wealth of Nations* appeared in 1776. But mercantilism as a system had begun to lose force even earlier. The development of industrial enterprise and the rise of a business class were perhaps the major factors that spelled doom for a system based on strict regulation and control of industry and commerce. For with the rise of the business class to prominence, new economic and political ideas were beginning to spring up. Specifically, a cry for laissez faire—nonintervention by the state in economic activities—was increasingly heard, especially in England. Accompanying it were demands for relaxation of controls over foreign trade.

The decline and fall of mercantilism, however, was a gradual process that (though it gathered momentum with the passage of time) was not completed until about the middle of the nineteenth century. To be sure, some changes in the direction of more liberal commercial policies had already appeared during the last two decades of the eighteenth century. In 1786, for example, England and France signed the Eden Treaty, whereby each country granted to the other important tariff concessions. But the French Revolution and the Napoleonic Wars put a stop to any further progress of this kind. If anything, the period saw widespread economic warfare, which included blockades, embargoes, and the use of other trade restrictions.

Britain emerged from the Napoleonic Wars as the most advanced industrial nation in the world. Her industries were in a good position to compete with foreign producers both at home and abroad. And this fact was no doubt greatly responsible for renewed efforts by British merchants to secure liberalization of trade policies. In 1820, commercial interests in London signed and circulated a petition urging the abolition of trade restrictions—a document that marked the beginning of the practical movement for free trade.[4]

[4] Clough and Cole, *op. cit.*, p. 473.

The initial results of this movement were: (1) reductions in some of the more restrictive tariff duties, (2) simplification of customs regulations, and (3) modification of the Navigation Acts. These and other reforms were largely the work of William Huskisson, who was the president of the Board of Trade from 1823 to 1827. Although a follower of Adam Smith's ideas, Huskisson did not seek absolute free trade but rather the freeing of trade from its most restrictive regulations. Moreover, in reducing trade barriers, he insisted on reciprocal concessions from other countries. In any event, despite his remarkable accomplishments, many protectionist devices still remained, hardly touched—devices that British agricultural interests demanded and received.

Huskisson's work was continued by Robert Peel, under whose leadership as Prime Minister (1841–1846) major tariff reforms were put into effect. His crowning achievement was the repeal of the famous Corn Laws. This set of laws, which provided for the most restrictive measures against agricultural imports, was regarded, together with the Navigation Acts, as the pillar of British protectionism. The landed aristocracy fiercely resisted any move to abolish these measures; and although they were somewhat modified in 1828, this did not lessen their general protective effect. The straw that finally broke the camel's back occurred in 1845–1846, in the form of a poor harvest and high food prices in Europe, and of a potato famine in Ireland. Food imports had to be permitted, and the Corn Laws were suspended temporarily. While they were still suspended, Peel convinced his government that they should not be re-established; in June, 1846, they were repealed. Abolition of the Navigation Acts followed three years later.

Thus, by 1850, Britain had adopted a free-trade policy, a policy to which she would stubbornly adhere throughout the remainder of the nineteenth century. It was not a policy born of pure idealism. Rather, it was based on the conviction that freer trade would enable Britain to find new markets for its exports, and that expanding trade would increase her economic power. The price to be paid—allowing foreign goods to come into the home market—was not considered excessive, especially since such imports would offer little competition to domestic producers. This assumption, incidentally, proved to be correct. For it was not until the latter years of the nineteenth century—and then only with respect to agricultural goods—that foreign suppliers were able to make much of a dent in the British home market.

Leaving Britain at midcentury, let us now cross the Channel and view events on the Continent.

Protection and Free Trade on the Continent

In contrast to England, most continental countries continued to pursue protectionist trade policies well into the 1850's, and some until the 1860's. France, the leading nation on the Continent, adopted extremely high tariffs in 1814 and 1816, and supplemented them in 1819 with her own version of a Corn Law. Anxious to develop the merchant marine, the state itself went into the maritime business in 1835; through the use of subsidies and grants, it tried to encourage private shipbuilding as well. At the same time, France was vigorously developing a preferential trading system with some of her colonies to the exclusion of other countries.

Similarly, Belgium, still enjoying protection under tariff laws enacted in 1821 and 1822, added another tariff in 1834 and passed its own Navigation Act in 1844. Austria maintained an exceedingly high tariff during this period, and so did the Italian states. Russia's tariff duties were perhaps the most prohibitive in all of Europe. In the second quarter of the nineteenth century some of her duties were slightly reduced, but only in order to discourage smuggling. Holland began to reduce its tariff duties as late as 1846, and did not repeal its navigation laws until 1851. Of all continental states, only Prussia had adopted reasonably low tariff rates early in the nineteenth century (1818). These rates were later incorporated into the common tariff of the Zollverein, the customs union formed in 1833 by Prussia and several other German states.[5] But although the Zollverein in a sense represented a move toward freer trade, its tariff on products from outside the union tended to increase from 1834 to 1848.

Thus, during the first half of the nineteenth century, free trade made little headway on the Continent. Proponents of protection were generally successful in establishing and maintaining high tariff walls around most European countries. These high tariffs were supplemented by other restrictive rules and regulations. Not until the mid-1850's did

[5] Customs unions are discussed in great detail in Chapter 20.

signs of change, hardly noticeable at first, begin to appear. But when the change finally came, it came boldly and swiftly.

The Short Reign of Free Trade

In 1860 England and France signed a commercial treaty, often referred to as the Cobden-Chevalier Treaty.[6] Under this treaty, England pledged to wipe out most of its tariff duties on imports of French manufactures and to lower the duty rates on French wines and brandies. In return, France promised to reduce all its tariff rates within five years to a level not exceeding 25 per cent ad valorem.

Helpful as it was to the development of a friendly relationship between England and France, the Anglo-French treaty had more significance as a stimulant to free trade on the Continent. Within a few years after 1860, France negotiated similar treaties with all European countries except Russia. And England, though she had already opened her home market to all nations, managed nevertheless to secure tariff concessions from Belgium, Italy, the Zollverein, Austria, Turkey, and other states. Moreover, practically all commercial treaties that were signed by European countries during this period included a most-favored-nation clause, whereby the signatories agreed to extend to each other, automatically, the lowest duty rates that might be granted to any third country in the future. Together, these treaties constituted a wide network, which covered the trade of most European countries. And although they were bilaterally negotiated and signed, the general result was a multilateral reduction of tariff rates throughout Europe.

It would be a mistake to conclude, however, that through this network of treaties all tariffs were abolished. Only England, Holland, Denmark, and Turkey adopted a virtual free-trade policy; other countries merely reduced their tariffs. Enough tariffs remained to preclude the kind of international division of labor that the classical economists had envisioned. And behind these tariffs—low as they may have been— there occurred on the Continent a process of industrialization that

---

[6] After the Englishman Richard Cobden and the Frenchman Michel Chevalier, who were instrumental, in a semiofficial way, in bringing the two countries together to negotiate and conclude the treaty.

eventually enabled some nations to stand up and challenge Britain's industrial superiority. Still, in comparison with the age of mercantilism, the period beginning in 1860 was one of liberal commercial policies and great economic freedom in Europe. But in the background were forces that soon burst into the open and ushered in a new era of economic nationalism.

Return to Protection: Neomercantilism

There can be little doubt that economic factors had a great deal to do with the wave of protectionism that arose on the Continent in the late 1870's and reached a world-wide climax some six decades later. The immediate causes of the return to protectionism were: (1) increasing competition from cheap overseas grain exports, (2) a series of depressions that began in 1873, and (3) an almost steady decline in price levels from 1873 to 1896. It is hardly surprising that these developments caused a clamor for relief, and that protection seemed the best way to secure it. But behind the immediate causes were deeper ones. By the end of the nineteenth century, some manufacturing industries on the Continent had achieved a fairly high level of maturity. And with their development came strong demands to preserve—through tariff protection—the home markets for locally produced goods. Moreover, the return to protection was at least partly motivated by rising public expenditures for armament, education, welfare, and so on. And since customs duties provided a large part of government revenue, it was only natural to increase them in an hour of financial need.

But there was more to the revival of economic nationalism than economic factors. The protectionism of the late nineteenth and early twentieth centuries was in large measure conditioned by ideas and events not unlike those that had inspired mercantilism three centuries earlier: It was essentially an expression of *political* nationalism. The surge of nationalism itself owed a great deal to the liberal doctrines and forces that dominated the nineteenth century. For these forces provided the inspiration for—and at times concrete aid to—the formation of several new nations and the consolidation of existing ones. Greece, Belgium, the Italian states, and Germany—all achieved national unification or attained independence between 1829 and 1871. With independence came a desire for political assertion, which soon spread throughout Europe. Thus, perhaps ironically, the very forces of liberalism that had contributed to the downfall of the old mercantilist system, also paved the way for a new brand of nationalism that brought with it something disturbingly familiar: neomercantilism.

Although the actual timing and intensity of the swing to protectionism differed from country to country, the first step took almost the same form everywhere—a series of tariff increases. Russia, which had not been enthusiastic about lowering tariff duties in the first place, was the first European country to raise them, she did so in 1877 and again in 1892. Austria raised its import duties in 1878, 1882, and 1887. Germany raised its tariff in 1879, 1885, and 1888. France increased its duties on agricultural products in 1881 and 1885, and in 1892 undertook further revisions of its tariff law. In Italy, the low tariff, adopted in 1860, was upped in 1878, 1887, and again in 1891. And Belgium raised its duties in 1887.

The storm of rising tariffs gave way to relative calm, which lasted from about 1891 to 1902. At the beginning of this period, Germany negotiated a series of treaties, reducing duty rates on agricultural imports. But in 1902 she reverted to agrarian protection and followed it with a general tariff increase in 1905. Austria and Spain countered by raising their tariffs in 1906; France did the same in 1910. In fact, throughout this entire period only England, Holland, Denmark, Finland, and Turkey—each for its own reasons—clung to their free-trade policies. Turkey had little industry to protect; while Holland, Denmark, and Finland had developed highly specialized export items with wide markets abroad. And England, though facing increasing foreign competition, still held a dominant position in the world economy, and could therefore resist the pressure of protectionist interests at home.

Imperialism

But even free-trading England participated, along with most European powers, in a wave of overseas territorial expansion that began around 1880 and continued in high gear almost to the outbreak of World War I. Commonly referred to as *imperialism*, the scramble for colonial acquisitions in the late nineteenth century has been likened to the colonial policies that characterized the age of mercantilism. It might even be argued that the new trend represented a reawakening of mercantilist attitudes toward colonies, attitudes that had lain dormant for a time, but had never really disappeared. This view is understandable, for there was indeed a basic similarity of motives in the old and the new colonialism.

Thus, on the economic side, the imperialist movement found justification in the need for export markets, on the one hand, and supplies of raw materials, on the other. Politically, the acquisition of overseas territories and the struggle for spheres of influence seemed the perfect medicine for pent-up nationalistic feelings, since it provided many opportunities to enhance the power and prestige of the state. One side effect was a naval rivalry between major European powers, very much reminiscent of the naval rivalries of the old days. But this time it was Germany, rather than France or Holland, whom England had to face on the high seas.

The new imperialism, however, was distinguished from the old in several major respects. As compared with the overseas expansion of the sixteenth and seventeenth centuries, the expansion in the nineteenth century was more rapid, and the penetration deeper and more effective. Between 1875 and 1914, one-half of the habitable surface of the earth, where some 500 million people lived, was opened up to European domination or influence. Second, the new expansion was accompanied by heavy exports of capital and capital goods that, while designed to return a handsome profit to the investing countries, aided the economic development of the colonies. And third, unlike the old colonial expansion, which concentrated on the Americas and India, the new movement turned primarily to Africa, the Middle and Far East, China, and the South Seas. Thus, with the exception of Abyssinia and Liberia, all of Africa had come under some kind of foreign rule by 1914. And in the Middle East, Far East, and South Seas, most areas were either seized by one European power or another, or came under its sphere of influence.

In Retrospect

Whatever else might be said about the new mercantilism, one thing stands out clearly. In the latter part of the nineteenth century, almost all aspects of international economic relations were subordinated to, or influenced by, political and diplomatic considerations. Protection—though often demanded by special interest groups that could profit by it—became an instrument of economic warfare and power politics. Similarly, the acquisition of colonies, the establishment of special trading ties, the attempts at greater national self-sufficiency, the building of strategic industries—all were carried on in the name of nationalism and were designed to further the political rather than the economic interests of the nation. Once committed to this battle, protectionism could not be easily withdrawn; in fact, it tended to grow stronger with each crisis, political or economic, that arose.

It is easy to imagine the effects of these protectionist policies. As we saw earlier, the raising of a tariff by one country usually invites retaliation by another; and during this period European countries fought several tariff wars. These wars brought no lasting victory to any of the combatants; they merely served to reduce trade between them. Besides breeding tariff wars, protection encouraged the formation of monopolies and cartels. Although their full effect was not felt until much later, they nevertheless contributed to the general trend of restrictive trade practices.

One might have expected trade to decline sharply in the face of these restrictions. But the volume of world trade continued to grow, though at a slower rate than before,[7] right up to the outbreak of World War I. Its continued growth can be partly explained by the fact that the period 1880–1913 was not characterized by a complete departure from free trade. Rather, it was a transitional phase, during which the free-trade system was eased out and a new protectionist period ushered in. Just as the latter part of the eighteenth century and the first half of the nineteenth century saw the transition from mercantilism to free trade, so the last decades of the nineteenth century and the opening decade of the twentieth century witnessed a movement from free trade to protectionism. Neither of these transitions was swift and clear-cut. It had taken the old mercantilism about one hundred years to bow out completely, and it took

[7] Between 1850 and 1880, the volume of international trade increased by 270 per cent. From 1880 to 1913 it grew by 170 per cent. See R. Nurkse, *Patterns of Trade and Development* (New York: Oxford University Press, 1961), p. 19.

the new protectionism some sixty years (to the mid-1930's) before it reached its peak.

Indeed, the story of European commercial policies in the nineteenth century is a story of overlapping phases, alternating between protection and free trade. It is a story whose denouement is not yet in sight; we shall therefore have more to say about it in subsequent chapters.

17

United States Commercial Policies

QUITE A DIFFERENT STORY CAN
be told about the foreign-trade policies of the United States. Unlike
Europe, this country did not even flirt with the free-trade doctrine
during the nineteenth century, let alone court it in earnest. On the
contrary. From 1789, the year Congress passed the first tariff act, until
the mid-1930's, American commercial policy was marked by a consistent
trend toward higher tariffs and increased protection. True, tariff rates
were reduced periodically, but rarely to their former levels. In any
event, tariff increases far outnumbered tariff reductions; as a result,
the modest duties (averaging about 5 per cent ad valorem) that were
enacted in 1789 reached an all-time high in 1931 (averaging 53 per
cent ad valorem).

But although the United States did not practice free trade, it did
not regard—or use—protectionism as an instrument of international
power politics. From the very outset, tariff legislation was shaped more
by economic than by political considerations; and inasmuch as politics
inevitably crept into the picture, it involved domestic rather than
international issues.[1] However, the reasons for imposing tariffs and the

[1] However, other instruments of commercial policy have been used on occasion
to further foreign policy objectives.

issues involved in tariff legislation have changed over the years. Practically every argument for protection has been advanced at one time or another; but often the real economic questions were lost in the heat of oratory and debate.

Tariff Issues and Tariff Laws: 1789–1930

The need for revenue was the main reason Congress passed the first tariff law and followed it up with several others. All in all, thirteen tariff bills were enacted between 1789 and 1812; but although revenue remained the overriding consideration, some duty rates actually reached protective levels. Protectionist sentiment, moreover, found explicit expression as early as 1791. In that year, Alexander Hamilton submitted to Congress his famous *Report on Manufactures,* urging a moderate amount of protection in order to encourage and promote the growth of domestic industries. Hamilton's reasoning—the now familiar "infant-industry" argument—furnished the advocates of protection, in the years before the Civil War, with a major intellectual weapon. But not until the close of the War of 1812 did protection as such become an element in American tariff legislation.

During the War of 1812 and the embargo that preceded it, American foreign trade virtually came to a standstill. The absence of competing imports stimulated domestic manufacturing activities, and a number of industries were established in this period. Trade was resumed when the war ended in 1814; a flood of imports followed, and seriously threatened the newly established industries. Particularly vulnerable to import competition were the textile firms of New England. Their plea for help—to be heard over and over again—led to the Tariff Act of 1816, which provided for higher duties on woolen and cotton imports. Other manufacturers soon joined the chorus, and in 1824 another tariff law imposed duties on iron, glassware, cutlery, and other manufactured imports.

Once started, the protectionist trend seemed to feed on itself. In 1828, Congress passed a tariff bill, often referred to as the Black Tariff or the Tariff of Abomination. This law, which contained duties averaging more than 45 per cent ad valorem, gave the country its highest tariff in the pre-Civil War period. It also strained, almost to the breaking point, the growing conflict between North and South. The South, whose plantation economy was geared to the export of agricultural products and the import of manufactured goods, favored low tariffs. Its representatives in Congress, who had earlier opposed the Tariff Act of 1824, were now doubly vehement in their opposition to further tariff increases. Indeed, the South so strongly resented the 1828 tariff that some states, notably South Carolina, pronounced it "null and void, nor binding . . .," while others threatened to secede from the Union.

Tempers subsided, however, with the passage of the tariff of 1833. This so-called Compromise Tariff provided for a gradual reduction in duty rates and a lengthening of the "free" list The reductions were to take place over a period ending in 1842. But in that year, a new administration came into office and replaced the previous law with a stiffer tariff bill; this remained in force until 1846.

In the 1840's and 1850's, fiscal considerations once again became a dominant factor in tariff legislation. Embarrassed by an excess of revenue over expenditures, the government resorted to tariff *reductions* as a means of balancing the budget. Thus, under the Walker Tariff (1846), duty rates were reduced to an average of 23 per cent ad valorem, though several luxury items continued to be taxed rather heavily. Further reductions took place in 1857, bringing the tariff wall to its lowest level since 1816. But four years later, just before the outbreak of the Civil War, the Tariff Act of 1861 went into effect, thus signaling a return to protectionism.

The Tariff Acts of 1861, 1862, and 1864, known as the Morrill Tariffs, had two purposes: to meet the government's need for increased revenue with which to finance the war effort, and to eliminate any competitive advantage that imports might have over the heavily taxed domestic products. Under these laws, particularly the Acts of 1862 and 1864, duties were raised to an average of 47 per cent ad valorem, and many articles were added to the list of dutiable imports. But although justified as emergency measures at the time, the Civil War tariffs remained in force long after the emergency had passed. For with the return to peace a clamor for protection arose that was to influence, in one way or another, the course of American tariff policies for many years to come.

The strength of protectionist pressures after the Civil War is demonstrated by the tariff legislation enacted between 1865 and 1930.

Following the war, the Republicans continued in office for nearly twenty years; twice during this period—in 1867 and in 1870—many duty rates were increased to levels even higher than wartime levels. Not until 1883 was a (slight) reduction of duties undertaken—and this only because of a growing popular resentment against the prevailing high tariffs. After four years of a Democratic administration (1884–1888), during which several attempts were made to lower duties, the Republicans (under Harrison) returned to office. Their campaign platform had included a pledge to protect American labor against low-paid foreign labor, and they proceeded to honor this pledge by enacting the McKinley Tariff of 1890. The new law raised duties to an average rate of 50 per cent ad valorem; and, for the first time, extended protection to some agricultural products. The Democrats were re-elected in 1892 and managed to lower some duties (the Wilson-Gorman Tariff of 1894). But the Republicans restored them three years later, by passing the prohibitive Dingley Tariff of 1897.

After the Civil War the infant-industry argument was no longer the main weapon in the protectionist arsenal. True, this argument, which had been invoked by the textile industry after the War of 1812, was used by the steel industry during the 1860's and by the chemical industry after World War I.[2] Yet by and large, the case for protective tariffs during the last decades of the nineteenth century rested on the proposition that American workers and businessmen must be defended against unfair competition from low-paid labor. This "pauper-labor" argument, which formed the basis for the McKinley and Dingley tariffs, was supplemented in the early years of the twentieth century by another appealing notion: the "scientific tariff."[3] This provided much of the rationale for the Payne-Aldrich Tariff of 1909.

With the Woodrow Wilson Administration came the first serious challenge to American protectionism since the Civil War. The Underwood Tariff, passed in 1913, provided for sharp reductions of duties on a substantial range of imports, and added many items—especially raw materials—to the "free" list. But this experience with freer trade was

[2] See Peter B. Kenen, *Giant Among Nations: Problems in United States Foreign Economic Policy* (Chicago: Rand McNally, 1963), p. 41.

[3] To refresh your memory on this and the "pauper-labor" argument, see Chapter 14.

short-lived. For within nine months after passage of the bill, World War I broke out; and although the Underwood Tariff remained on the books for eight years, it had little practical significance during most of this period.

The years following World War I witnessed the return of the Republicans to office, a revival of import competition, and renewed pressures for protection. This combination of circumstances produced two tariff bills in rapid succession. An Emergency Tariff Act, passed in 1921, gave increased protection to American farmers by adding many agricultural products to the list of dutiable imports. A year later, the Fordney-McCumber Tariff extended further protection to both agriculture and industry. Under this act, the President was empowered to raise or lower duty rates, by as much as 50 per cent, in accordance with the "cost-equalization" principle; one may easily guess whether most of the rate changes were upward or downward.

Although the Fordney-McCumber Act resulted in extremely high duty rates in comparison with previous legislation, the most restrictive tariff law in American history was yet to come. In January, 1929, Congress began hearings on what was intended to be a limited tariff revision, designed to bring relief to the farmers who had been in economic difficulty since the end of the war.[4] But in the wave of panic that followed the stock market collapse, the cry for protection became general. Pressured from all sides, Congress responded by passing the Smoot-Hawley Act of 1930. This law brought American protectionism to its historic peak!

The Smoot-Hawley Act increased the number of dutiable items to over 3,000, and raised the average import duty rate to 53 per cent ad valorem. At a time when not only the United States but also the rest of the world was experiencing economic difficulties, the enactment of the Smoot-Hawley Act was a selfish move that invited criticism and retaliatory actions. Following this country's example, other nations soon raised their tariffs, supplementing them with quantitative restrictions and exchange controls. In the face of rising trade barriers everywhere, both imports and exports declined sharply. By 1933, world trade had been reduced to one-third of its value in 1929. Parenthetically, we might note

[4] See Kenen, *op. cit.*, p. 40.

that the United States, whose action in 1930 had contributed a fair share to the general protectionist trend, suffered a greater decline in its exports than any other major trading country in the world.[5]

The Reciprocal-Trade-Agreements Program: 1934–1962

The year 1934 marked a turning point in American tariff history. A deepening depression, coupled with a sharply declining volume of exports, led Congress to pass (in June) the Trade Agreements Act. Hailed by many as a great victory over protectionism, this act effected a major change in the conduct of this country's commercial policies: It empowered the President to negotiate and conclude bilateral tariff treaties with foreign countries, without having to secure Senate ratification. It also authorized him to cut existing duty rates by as much as 50 per cent in exchange for equivalent concessions. In essence, the Trade Agreements Act transferred from the legislative to the executive branch the power to change tariff levels, thereby permitting tariff rates to be determined through international agreements rather than by congressional action.

Thus empowered, the government embarked on a vigorous program of tariff reduction. From 1934 to 1947, it concluded thirty-two reciprocal trade agreements, exchanging tariff concessions with some thirty different countries. All these agreements contained an unconditional most-favored-nation clause, whereby concessions, though bilaterally negotiated, were, in effect, made multilateral. And when, in 1947, the United States and twenty-two other nations signed the General Agreement on Tariffs and Trade (GATT), the most-favored-nation clause became one of its basic provisions. The advent of GATT, which will be more fully discussed in the next chapter, did not end the reciprocal-trade-agreement program. If anything, it created a framework within which such bilateral tariff negotiations could flourish. Indeed, since becoming a party to GATT, the United States has been able to pursue tariff bargaining on a wider

[5] According to a League of Nations study, the volume of American exports in 1932 was only 53 per cent of the 1929 level, while the exports of France, England, Italy, and Japan were down to 59 per cent, 63 per cent, 77 per cent, and 94 per cent respectively of their 1929 levels. See League of Nations, *World Economic Survey 1933–34* (Geneva: 1934).

scale, reaching an ever-increasing number of countries. By 1962, twenty-eight years after its inception, the reciprocal-trade agreements program could boast of a very impressive record: Over these years, trade agreements were concluded with some sixty countries;[6] and the average duty rate, on dutiable imports into the United States, has been brought down from a high of 53 per cent ad valorem in 1934 to approximately 11 per cent.[7]

It would be wrong to suppose, however, that the Trade Agreements Act signified a wholehearted conversion of Congress to the principles and ideas of free trade. That the act was passed at all is in large measure a tribute to the relentless efforts of Secretary of State Cordell Hull, the chief promoter of the reciprocal-trade-agreements program. But Hull's efforts alone would not have sufficed to sell Congress on the virtues of tariff reductions in the midst of a severe depression. What did the trick was the line of reasoning that both he and President Roosevelt adopted in presenting their case to Capitol Hill. Tariff concessions granted by the United States, they argued, would induce foreign countries to reciprocate by reducing *their* trade barriers; this in turn would create increased opportunities for expanding American exports. It was emphasis on the "export expansion" qualities of the trade-agreements program, accompanied by a solemn promise that no concessions injurious to domestic industry would be offered, that finally moved Congress to acquiesce.

Acquiesce it did, but with an important reservation: The Trade Agreements Act was to expire in three years. In 1937, therefore, the tireless Hull again went before Congress and managed to wring from it a three-year extension, to be followed by similar extensions in 1940 and 1943. But by the time World War II ended, the authority to cut duty rates, which had been granted in 1934, had been exhausted. Most of the duties that could be reduced without injuring American industry had already been reduced to the maximum allowed under the act. Consequently, a curiously obliging Congress passed the Trade Agreements Extension Act (1945), which empowered the President to cut in half the

[6] Not all of these agreements were signed within the framework of GATT. Six of them—with Argentina, El Salvador, Iceland, Paraguay, Switzerland, and Venezuela—were concluded on a bilateral basis, outside GATT.

[7] However, a substantial part of this reduction has been accounted for by a general rise in prices, resulting in a lowering of the ad valorem equivalent of *specific* duties.

tariffs that were in effect in 1945. However, this act, like the previous one, was to last for only three years. But because of its existence at the time, the President was able to commit the United States to participation in GATT—a move fraught with important consequences.

One of these consequences was felt less than a year after the signing of GATT. In 1948, when the Trade Agreements Act came up for renewal, Congress insisted on writing a "peril-point" clause into the act before passing it. Under this clause, the U.S. Tariff Commission was to decide to what level duties could be cut without injury to domestic producers. And although the President could actually cut tariffs below this level, he would have to inform Congress of his reasons for doing so in each case. As an added show of defiance, Congress extended the act for only one year.

In 1949, a less hostile Congress granted a two-year extension of the Trade Agreements Act and freed it from the peril-point provision. But in 1951 the same provision was reinstated and supplemented by an escape clause; this authorized the withdrawal of tariff concessions if domestic producers claimed injury as a result of increased foreign competition. An escape clause had been previously inserted into a trade agreement signed with Argentina in 1941, and another that was signed with Mexico in 1943. A similar provision had been incorporated—at the insistence of the United States—into GATT.[8] But this was the first time that an escape clause was actually written into the Trade Agreements Act itself. It has remained there ever since.

During President Eisenhower's tenure in the White House, the Trade Agreements Act came up for renewal four times—in 1953, 1954, 1955, and finally in 1958. On each occasion, but particularly the last two, the act was subjected to modifications and amendments that reflected growing congressional opposition to trade liberalization, and that rendered less and less effective the tariff bargaining authority of the administration. Thus, under the Trade Agreements Extension Act of 1955, the President was permitted to reduce tariffs by no more than 15 per cent of the levels in effect on January 1, 1955; such reductions were to be spread over a three-year period. He could, however, reduce duty rates that were higher than 50 per cent ad valorem to the 50 per cent

[8] This provision enables GATT members to withdraw previously granted concessions in the face of unforeseen circumstances.

level. And the Trade Agreements Extension Act of 1958 allowed him to cut tariffs by no more than 20 per cent of the 1958 levels, provided that the reductions were spread over a four-year period. More important, both the 1955 and 1958 acts allowed a wide interpretation of what constitutes an injury from import competition, thereby broadening the scope of the escape-clause and peril-point provisions.

To appreciate the implication of these and other provisions in the execution of the trade-agreements program, consider the following comments by Professor Don Humphrey.

> In negotiating, the American team is bound by the statutory lists of negotiable items prepared beforehand by the Trade Agreements Committee and by its instructions as to concessions. . . .

> These rules of procedures are so restrictive that negotiating teams cannot press their demands upon the other country first and then consider what can be offered in return. . . . The maximum concession permitted by law is known to all in advance, as is the escape clause policy. Regardless of possible gains, no branch of domestic industry may be exposed to serious injury, and if a mistake is made, the concessions [may] be withdrawn.[9]

Fortunately, the escape-clause provision allows both the Tariff Commission and the President some leeway Although any producer may petition the commission for relief against import competition, it is not obliged to go along with the request. And should the commission find that an injury has occurred, and recommend relief, the President may still refuse to grant it. In fact, out of ninety-six escape-clause cases, involving some seventy-six different products, that came before the Tariff Commission between 1947 and 1959, only thirty-two were recommended for relief. And of these, the President actually granted such relief to only twelve. Nevertheless, the constant possibility that concessions may be withdrawn has reduced American negotiating teams to a posi-

---

[9] Don Humphrey, *American Imports* (New York: The Twentieth Century Fund, 1955), p. 120.

tion of Indian givers, and has militated against a truly meaningful exchange of tariff concessions.

Nor were the escape-clause and peril-point provisions the only thorns in the side of the trade-agreements program. Since 1950, the White House has had to contend with restrictions, imposed on its trade liberalization efforts, in the name of national security and national defense. For example, a rider to the Defense Production Act of 1950 directed the President to restrict—of all things—cheese imports by placing them under quota, and to embargo imports of rice, butter, and other agricultural products. While pondering over the connection between Gouda cheese and national defense, we might also try our hand at determining the relationship to national security of clothespins, safety pins, dental burs, clinical thermometers, and wool textiles, to mention just a few. Perhaps a mysterious link does exist somewhere; if so, it is certainly hard to detect. In any event, the provisions of the Defense Production Act and the National Defense Amendment of 1955 have made it possible for these and other industries to apply for protection against competing imports, on the grounds that they are vital to national security. And some industries have actually managed to get away with it!

Lest anyone become concerned over national defense, it must be made quite clear that this is not at issue here. No one in his right mind would suggest that national security ought to be sacrificed on the altar of freer trade. It is an entirely different matter, however, when emotional appeals to national security are used by local producers as a device to obtain economic benefits at the expense of foreign manufactures. Such antics hurt local consumers on the one hand, and jeopardize tariff negotiations with foreign countries on the other. Indeed, the so-called national security restrictions, together with the escape-clause and peril-point provisions, have acted as powerful brakes on the progress of American commercial policy in general, and on its tariff-reduction program in particular. Because of them, the United States has found it increasingly difficult to strike hard bargains with its trading partners, in and out of GATT. And as the 1950's drew to a close, it became apparent that the reciprocal-trade-agreements program would have to undergo a major overhauling if it were to meet new challenges (e.g., the rise of the European Common Market) and serve our economic interests more effectively.

The Trade Expansion Act: 1962–?

The "tune-up" job was undertaken by the Kennedy Administration, which came into office in 1961. The result was a 1962 model of the Trade Agreements Act, officially entitled the Trade Expansion Act. Enacted for a five-year period, the new law does not do away with all the limitations of previous laws. It does represent, however, a serious attempt to come to terms with changing world realities. And as a tool of commercial policy, it contains several innovations—both conceptual and procedural—that may open the door to another era in American tariff history.

Under the Trade Expansion Act, the President is empowered to reduce duties on most manufactured products by as much as 50 per cent of the 1962 levels. He may completely eliminate duties on those products of the United States and the European Common Market that account for 80 per cent or more of world exports. More significantly, the act allows tariff reductions to be negotiated on broad commodity classifications rather than on a product-by-product basis, as was the case previously. Finally, the President may eliminate all duties on tropical products if the European Common Market agrees to do the same.

Another significant innovation is the disappearance of the peril-point provision. Thus, instead of advising the President by how much duties can be reduced without injuring domestic producers, the Tariff Commission henceforth merely reports on the probable impact of proposed tariff concessions. It will be up to the President to weigh the possible adverse effects against the possible benefits resulting from an exchange of tariff reductions—and then act accordingly.

Equally significant are the changes, two in particular, in the escape-clause provisions. First, the act makes it more difficult for local producers to claim injury due to import competition. Henceforth, a claimant will have to demonstrate that an increase in imports, directly connected with a tariff concession, was the major factor in causing (1) idling of productive facilities, (2) inability to operate at a level of reasonable profit, and (3) unemployment or underemployment. Unless the Tariff Commission is satisfied on these counts, it cannot declare that a serious injury has occurred. Second, the act empowers the President to extend trade-adjustment assistance to companies that are injured by rising imports. Such companies will be entitled to receive technical assistance, loans, and tax relief; and workers in these companies will be eligible for special unemployment compensation, aid in training for new skills, and cash allowances to move to other locations.

However, the new provisions do not completely replace the old escape clause. Injured firms may still prefer to ask for protection, and the President may still oblige them by withdrawing concessions previously granted. Yet the mere existence of an alternative—the opportunity for domestic producers to receive help in making new use of their resources—is likely to minimize recourse to protection. Thus, the Trade Expansion Act reflects a more wholesome attitude toward the essence of free international trade. Rather than encourage the protection of inefficient local producers and thereby deny consumers the gains that come from trade, it seeks to ease the adjustment process of dislocated resources while permitting the flows of trade to continue.

Along with its virtues, the Trade Expansion Act has its drawbacks. It contains a number of restrictions—some carried over from previous legislation, some newly adopted—that could set back any efforts toward greater liberalization of American trade policy. Among the restrictions from previous legislation are the national security provisions. These allow the President rather wide discretion in interpreting what constitutes a threat to national security. Moreover, the new act forbids the reduction of tariffs that had previously been imposed to protect injured domestic industries.[10] As for future action under the escape clause, the act permits Congress to override the President, should the latter disregard recommendations made by the Tariff Commission. Thus, if the Tariff Commission recommends a tariff increase but the President refuses to grant it, Congress may impose the recommended duty for a four-year period.

In addition, the Trade Expansion Act empowers the President to withhold concessions from, and/or raise tariffs against, foreign countries that restrict American exports (especially farm products) through quotas. But almost in the same breath, the act permits the imposition of

---

[10] In other words, no tariff concessions can be made in the case of products that the Tariff Commission had earlier recommended for relief action—regardless of whether or not such relief had actually been granted by the President.

quantitative restrictions on agricultural imports. Finally, the act continues the long-standing prohibition against granting most-favored-nation treatment to any communist country.

Shortly after the passage of the Trade Expansion Act, preparations got under way for a round of tariff negotiations between the United States and its GATT partners, especially the members of the European Common Market. From the very start, however, the so-called Kennedy Round was beset by complications of one sort or another; and it had taken some four years of hard bargaining before an exchange of tariff concessions was finally agreed upon, in May 1967. Although it is too early, at this time, to assess the full implications of these concessions, it cannot be doubted that the conclusion of the Kennedy Round represents several significant achievements. In the first place, it will result in tariff cuts averaging 35 per cent and covering some 60,000 internationally-traded products. Second, it provides for an antidumping agreement, designed to protect businessmen from unfair selling practices by foreign competitors. Third, it commits the developed nations (particularly the United States and the members of the European Common Market) to an international aid program which would provide the underdeveloped countries with substantial amounts of wheat and other food grains over the next several years. Finally—and perhaps most important—it signifies the ability and willingness of the major trading nations to overcome their individual differences and reach a meaningful compromise, in order to further the cause of trade liberalization.

"Buy American" Practices and Customs Administration

Apart from the tariff, the United States has used various methods to restrict or discourage imports. Some of these measures, though they give preference to domestic producers, do not actually prohibit the entry of imported articles. Others, however, constitute direct trade barriers designed to exclude certain products completely, and to limit to fixed amounts the importation of others.

Among the less restrictive measures, two deserve special mention: the "Buy American" Act and the "Ship in American Bottoms" regulations. A relic of the Great Depression, the "Buy American" Act (1933) directs the government to purchase goods and services from domestic suppliers if their prices are not "unreasonably higher" than those of foreign producers. The interpretation of what is "unreasonably higher" has been modified—originally a 25 per cent difference between domestic and foreign bids was considered reasonable, but in 1954 the margin was reduced to 6 per cent. However, there is little question that strong preference is always given to domestic producers in awarding public contracts. Thus, to all intents and purposes, the Buy American Act accords a certain degree of protection to domestic suppliers when dealing with the government—protection that in most cases has increased the cost of public projects, and has aroused ill will in foreign countries.

A similar law, enacted in 1934, accords preferential treatment to American shipping interests: American goods, purchased for foreign countries with funds lent or granted by any federal agency, must be transported in American vessels, whenever they are available. In practice, this provision is interpreted as permission to ships of foreign flags to share in carrying such goods, provided that at least 50 per cent of the cargo is reserved for American carriers. But even this slice—which guarantees American shippers carriage rights to half the materials sent abroad under the foreign-aid program—does not always seem to satisfy all concerned. Thus, in 1963, the maritime unions blew up a storm of complaint against the shipment of United States wheat to Russia in foreign vessels. In an attempt to placate the unions, President Kennedy issued an executive order requiring that half the sales of commercial wheat to Soviet bloc countries be carried in American ships.

Both the "Buy American" and "Ship in American Bottoms" legislations discriminate against foreign suppliers, and favor domestic suppliers. As such, they must be regarded as impediments to free trade. To these, one might add the vast array of import regulations and cumbersome customs procedures that, in their own way, impede the entry of imports into the United States.[11] According to the law, imported goods must be classified and valued for duty assessment; and in carrying out these tasks, customs officials are guided—or, more correctly, *mis*guided—by conflicting rules. Hence, not only does it often take a

[11] For a detailed account of customs regulations and procedures, see E. Pratt, *Modern International Commerce* (New York: Allyn and Bacon, 1956), Chapter 12.

long time before a final appraisal is made, but until recently an importer was liable to a heavy fine if his own declared valuation was lower than that eventually determined by the customs officials. To avoid delays, importers may clear their goods through customs by posting bond to cover whatever the final duty payment turns out to be. But since the actual amount of payment may not be known until after the goods are sold, the importer runs the risk of losing his anticipated profits, or, worse, actually incurring losses.

Other import regulations include the so-called "mark-of-origin" requirements, under which imported articles must be properly labeled to show the country of origin. This rule, from which domestically produced goods are naturally exempt, serves no purpose other than to increase the cost of goods manufactured abroad for export to the United States. That it has little more than nuisance value is demonstrated by the fact that under the Customs Simplification Act of 1953, certain imports were exempted from labeling requirements.[12] The same act also did away with some of the more complicated accounting and auditing procedures of the past, as well as with the heavy penalties for undervaluation of imports. A similar bill, the Customs Simplification Act of 1956, removed another administrative barrier by greatly simplifying the basis for import valuation by customs officials. But although the two acts represent a step in the right direction, much more can be done to improve our customs administration so as to remove from it the stigma of an "invisible tariff."

Protection of Agriculture: Import Quotas

If the "Buy American" practices and the customs administration constitute "invisible" obstacles to trade, the imposition of quotas is a direct barrier against imports, surpassing in restrictive effect the tariff itself. As noted in Chapter 15, quotas are of two basic types—absolute quotas and tariff quotas. And although the United States has used both types, we will center our attention on absolute quotas.

It may perhaps seem ironical that our use of quotas is rooted, not in

[12] More recently, suggestions have been made to exempt *all* imports from labeling requirements.

any weaknesses in the field of international trade, but in a perennial domestic problem : the economic plight of the American farmer. In fact, it was the Agricultural Adjustment Act of 1938 that initially empowered the administration to determine the quantities of certain goods that "may be permitted to enter the country *without interfering with the domestic production or marketing programs* of the Department of Agriculture."[13] Imports in excess of the amounts so determined were to be restricted by quotas or through import licensing.[14] Later, an amendment to the Defense Production Act of 1950 broadened these powers by directing the President to restrict imports which may unnecessarily burden *any* domestic farm support program.

The reasoning behind these provisions is easily understood. For under the present farm program agricultural prices are supported indirectly, as follows. The Commodity Credit Corporation (ccc) lends money to the farmer, who pledges his anticipated crop as collateral. If market prices are below support prices when he is ready to sell his crop, the farmer can turn it over to the ccc in repayment of his loan. Such crops are accepted, of course, on the basis of the official support price.

Unlimited entry of farm products from abroad would tend to depress domestic prices, thus widening the gap between the support and free-market prices. The ccc would then be faced with increased expenditures and an aggravated storage problem. Consequently, the United States restricts the importation of those products covered by the price-support program (e.g., wheat, rice, rye, cotton, tobacco, corn, peanuts), and, for good measure, a few others as well. At the same time, the ccc sells part of the ever-present surplus to other countries, at prices below the support level, and often below prevailing world prices.[15]

It is well known that this combination of quantitative restrictions and dumping has angered friendly nations—for example, Canada, Australia, and other grain producing countries—and has embarrassed the United States at gatt meetings. (The use of quotas, incidentally, is a flagrant violation of gatt rules, and the United States has had to obtain

[13] H. Piquet, *Aid, Trade, and the Tariff* (New York: Crowell, 1953), pp. 61–62. (Italics added.)

[14] *Ibid.*, p. 62.

[15] In addition, the government is authorized (under Public Law 480) to sell farm commodities abroad, for which payment may be made in foreign currencies.

a special waiver in order to pursue its policies that concern agricultural imports.) But apart from this, the policy of dumping farm products on the world market involves certain economic disadvantages for our own producers. Thus, producers of cotton textiles often claim that the sale of cotton abroad, below its domestic support price, has enabled foreign countries to produce cotton textiles more cheaply than domestic producers; as a result they can undersell domestic producers in the American home market.[16] Similar complaints have also been heard from other manufacturing circles.

As with national defense, the issue here does not lie in a choice between extremes that is, letting the farmers starve or restricting trade. Indeed, most industrial countries face vexing farm problems. But the solutions to these problems—mainly, the decrease in farm incomes relative to those of the nonfarm population—should be sought nowhere but at home. No country—least of all the United States—should rely on restrictive commercial policies to cure its domestic farm ills. For aside from inviting foreign retaliation, such a course of action is economically indefensible. Yet as these lines are written, most of the United States restrictions on agricultural imports are still in force. And they are not likely to disappear as long as powerful farm lobbies continue to apply strong political pressures on Congress and the administration.

[16] Kenen, *op. cit.*, p. 80.

18

From Bilateralism to Multilateralism

REVIVAL OF PROTECTIONISM was the dominant trend in Europe for thirty years or so before World War I. True, world trade continued to expand despite rising tariffs and other restrictions; but this expansion, as we have seen, lost much of its resiliency after 1880. And as one diplomatic crisis followed another, and as the threat of war kept increasing, the international structure that had supported the system of free multilateral trade for much of the nineteenth century began to give way under an increasing weight of political and economic nationalism.

The outbreak of war in 1914 dealt a crippling blow to the liberal doctrines and policies of the nineteenth century. During the war, trade relations were disrupted and trading activities came under strict regulations and controls. Moreover, many governments, belligerent as well as neutral, suspended the free operation of the gold standard—a move that opened the door to monetary chaos in several countries in the early postwar years. Finally, the four years of fighting resulted in an unprecedented destruction of productive facilities and a great drain on human resources. It was in such an atmosphere that a tired Europe emerged from the "war to end all wars," and began the task of rebuilding its political and economic life.

Yet within a few years, most of the war damage had been repaired; production activities outstripped their prewar levels, and international trade expanded vigorously. Indeed, so strong was the recovery and so buoyant the economic advance of the middle and late 1920's that between 1925 and 1928 the great majority of countries reinstated the gold standard as the basis of their monetary systems. And although, as we have seen earlier (Chapter 12), the gold standard of the late 1920's did not quite measure up to its prewar predecessor, it made possible the re-establishment of a fairly well functioning system of international payments, under which most currencies were freely convertible at stable rates of exchange.

Significant as it was, the restoration of the gold standard was merely one aspect of the post-World War I economic scene. It provided a basis for the return to stable international monetary relations and—so it was hoped—a mechanism of adjustment for balance-of-payments disturbances. But the disturbances that soon arose, as well as the burdens imposed by rapidly changing political and economic conditions, proved to be more than a match for the new international monetary system. The system could not by itself withstand the mounting pressures of the late 1920's and early 1930's. And in the absence of any other international arrangements, it finally collapsed, ushering in a period of protectionism the like of which the world had never seen.

The Interwar Period: Disintegration and Collapse

It was mainly a severe financial crisis in 1931 that led to the breakdown of the international monetary mechanism and set in motion a chain of events that culminated in the almost complete disintegration of the world trading system two years later. The crisis began with the failure of the Credit-Anstalt, Austria's largest and one of its most respectable banks. In the ensuing panic, banks in other countries (especially Germany) found themselves subject to huge withdrawals of foreign-held deposits, and several governments were soon forced to institute exchange controls in order to stem the outflow of gold and foreign-exchange reserves. England, too, came under heavy financial attack, as foreign claimants rushed to withdraw their sterling balances from British banks and convert them into gold and/or dollars. So strong was the pressure on the pound that in September, 1931, the Bank of England suspended the free conversion of sterling into gold, thereby terminating England's adherence to the free gold standard.

Britain's abandonment of the gold standard was a signal for other countries to follow suit. Within a short time, all but five nations—the United States, France, Switzerland, Belgium, and Holland[1]—had replaced the gold standard with various other kinds of monetary arrangements. For example, by tying the value of their currencies to the pound sterling, a large number of countries adopted a pegged currency system. These were countries (e.g., members of the Commonwealth, the Scandinavian and Baltic nations, and others) that had developed extensive trade relations with England and had previously kept large portions of their foreign reserves in the form of sterling assets. By continuing to do so now, these countries in effect constituted a currency bloc—which later became known as the Sterling Area and was joined by others—throughout which the stability of individual currencies was maintained; and maintained not in terms of gold parities, but in terms of the relation of each to the pound sterling.

Although the members of the Sterling Area cleared most of their international transactions through London, they permitted their currencies to remain, by and large, freely convertible—at least, up until World War II. The same was not true, however, of the other countries that had left the gold standard. Most of them, in fact, imposed exchange controls as well as specific restrictions on capital movements, thereby making their currencies inconvertible. Indeed, as we learned earlier, it was the widespread use of exchange controls and the resultant currency inconvertibility that prompted the trend toward bilateral balancing of trade. This, together with the fact that many currencies were allowed to depreciate, placed a considerable number of countries, including those still adhering to gold, in an untenable balance-of-payments position : Their exports began to decline and their imports to rise, as their currencies became overvalued in relation to currencies that had depreciated. And to prevent further balance-of-payments deterioration, imports had to be restricted and/or exports somehow stimulated; neither could be accomplished without increasing government control of trade.

[1] Of these five, the United States left the free gold standard in 1934 (though not for balance-of-payments reasons), and France abandoned gold and pegged its currency to the pound sterling in 1938.

Before long all countries were drawn into a protectionist race, and found themselves forced to adopt one restrictive measure or another. Most countries raised their tariffs and imposed quantitative restrictions in their efforts to curtail imports. Others resorted to devaluation and export subsidies; still others tightened their existing exchange controls and relied almost exclusively on bilateral balancing arrangements. And as country after country barricaded itself behind trade barriers, leaving only narrow passageways here and there, world trade plunged. By 1933, volume was down to two-thirds of the 1929 level. And although it began to climb again after that year, it did not regain its 1929 level until the last year or so before the outbreak of World War II.

It would be a mistake to conclude, however, that the decline of world commerce during the thirties can be explained entirely in *monetary* terms. To be sure, the financial crisis of 1931 and the subsequent collapse of the international monetary system played a leading role in effecting the disintegration of trade relations and the imposition of restrictive measures. Yet the severity of the collapse and the intensity of the reaction to it must be attributed to other forces as well. In looking back on the interwar period as a whole, one sees several such forces.

One of these was undoubtedly the downward trend of American business activities, which began in 1929 and reached a low in 1932. As production, employment, and incomes fell, so did the volume of American imports; as a result there was a decline in the exports and incomes of foreign countries. Accompanying the decline in United States imports was a sharp reduction in American foreign lending and investment, and a cutback in payments for service items. All told, the three years from 1929 to 1932 saw a drop of approximately $5 billion in the level of United States expenditures abroad, a drop that could not fail to depress the production, employment, incomes, and trade of many other countries. And as if to add insult to injury, Congress passed, in June of 1930, the notorious Smoot-Hawley Act, raising United States tariffs to the highest level in history.

There can be little doubt that the combination of falling incomes and rising tariffs in the United States set the stage for many of the developments described earlier in this section. For by touching off a general economic decline abroad, the reduction in American imports and foreign investment led many countries to adopt various restrictive measures even before 1931. Thus, some countries—especially the exporters of primary products—found it necessary to depreciate their currencies as early as 1929 and 1930. Others, while adhering to the idea of fixed exchange rates, resorted to tight domestic monetary and credit policies in order to counteract balance-of-payments difficulties. Still others responded to the contraction of exports and incomes by raising tariffs and/or instituting quantitative restrictions and exchange controls.

Each country, in fact, sought to insulate itself from economic difficulties originating abroad by pursuing its own brand of trade and payments policies. And in the absence of any cooperative plans, each country acted independently, with little regard to the possible adverse effects of its own policies on other nations. Thus, when the financial crisis came in 1931, it fell on a world already weakened by a major depression, and greatly unbalanced by a variety of restrictions imposed upon it in the name of economic nationalism.

Indeed, the failure of the early post-World War I years to produce a working international arrangement that would facilitate economic adjustments and coordinate national policies must be regarded as yet another factor that contributed to the economic collapse of the thirties. Had such an arrangement existed, it is quite possible that some of the difficulties, both individual and collective, could have been alleviated and their consequences avoided. As it was, the vacuum created by the lack of international cooperation was filled by increasing economic nationalism which, by taking the form of selfish beggar-thy-neighbor commercial policies, only added fuel to the spreading fire.

That no international plan existed was in itself a symptom of a rising nationalism that originated in the prewar period. Reinforced by the war, nationalistic feelings manifested themselves in several ways, not the least of which was a desire for great independence of action in political and economic matters. Weary of wars, yet feeling uncertain about the future, most countries were reluctant to delegate substantial powers to any internationally instituted body. Nowhere was this tendency more forcefully demonstrated than in the structure and operations of the League of Nations. This organization, to which were pinned ardent hopes for a lasting peace and international stability, was limited from its very beginning by nationalistically inspired provisions that had been inserted into its Covenant. And as the League's effectiveness grew progressively weaker, the forces of nationalism grew stronger, thus precluding any meaningful international agreements.

Efforts to reach international agreement on economic matters were, on the whole, no more successful than those that were later aimed at securing collective action against military and political aggression. In fact, of the four international conferences that were called in the twenties to deal with monetary and commercial problems, only one—a diplomatic conference that met in Geneva in 1923—managed to produce concrete results: It drafted a convention for the simplification of customs procedures, which was accepted by most nations [2] The other conferences—in Brussels (1920), in Genoa (1922), and in Geneva (1927)—either did not produce any meaningful suggestions, or recommended measures that were never acted upon. A fifth conference, the World Monetary and Economic Conference, which convened in London in 1933, soon reached a deadlock on the question of currency stability. While wrestling with this and other problems, the conference was jolted by an unexpected shock: the devaluation of the American dollar. Shortly thereafter it, too, adjourned without accomplishing anything.

The London Conference was the last of its kind prior to World War II. Its failure to reach agreement on either monetary or commercial problems, at the time when collective action was desperately needed, shattered the hope for any solution in the immediate future, and intensified the protectionist trend after 1933. What is more important, this failure demonstrated how strongly the forces of economic nationalism had become entrenched. For in the final analysis, it was not the devaluation of the dollar that undermined the conference, but a basic disagreement among several major powers concerning the appropriate measures to be recommended for action. It was this kind of paralyzing disagreement that had characterized most of the other attempts at joint action undertaken during the interwar years.

Reviewing the experience of the interwar era, we may therefore conclude that the economic (*and* political) disintegration in the thirties was largely an inevitable consequence of the failure in the twenties to create a climate more conducive to international cooperation. To this must be added, of course, several burdens on the international economy

[2] See M. Heilperin, *The Trade of Nations* (New York: Knopf, 1947), p. 150.

throughout the period: structural changes that altered the patterns of production and trade, and caused severe maladjustments in many countries; problems involved in settling war debts and reparation payments after World War I; agricultural overproduction that depressed world prices of raw materials and foodstuffs, and forced some countries to impose trade restrictions in the late 1920's; and finally, the general decline of economic activities that was sparked by the American depression and spread rapidly from country to country. These were heavy burdens indeed for a weak economic structure. But given a genuine willingness to cooperate, reasonable solutions to some of the problems might have been found, and the international economy could have been given a breathing spell in which to try and adjust itself. Such cooperation, however, was lacking; without it, there was little to stop the economic nationalism and growing militancy of Germany and Italy that led to another global conflict in 1939.

Post-World War II : Recovery and Reconstruction

The Second World War lasted longer, and involved more nations and a larger total effort, than World War I. It was truly a global war, from which only a few countries managed to escape without injury. When it was over in 1945, it had done far greater damage and caused more economic disruption than the earlier conflict. Fortunately, the lessons taught by the interwar years were not entirely lost on those who gathered to reconstruct the world. Determined to prevent the repetition of past mistakes, they sought ways and means to effect the transition from war to peace without the added burdens that characterized the post-World War I period. Hence, while the war itself was still in progress, the Allies were giving serious consideration to the economic problems that would undoubtedly follow it, and to the appropriate measures with which to cope with them.

Out of these wartime deliberations grew various proposals, some of which became blueprints for action. We have already called attention (Chapter 12) to the Bretton Woods Conference that met in 1944 to plan the international monetary future of the world. That conference drew up and approved the Bretton Woods Agreement, which provided, among other things, for the establishment of the International Monetary Fund (IMF) and the International Bank for Reconstruction and Development (IBRD). But in addition to preparing a joint defense against possible monetary disorder, several Allied governments, led by the United States and Britain, sought to secure international cooperation on a wide range of matters relating to trade policies. In particular, they directed their efforts to an all-out attack on protectionism, seeking to obtain a *multi-lateral* commitment to the reduction of trade barriers and the elimination of discriminatory trade practices.

While these efforts (to be discussed in some detail in the next two sections) were in progress, more pressing problems presented themselves, the most urgent of which concerned the economic future of Western Europe. Ravaged by war, Europe's economy was incapable of meeting the demands made upon it when peace returned. With production facilities mostly destroyed, and with surviving factories slowed down for lack of raw materials and skilled labor, demand for goods and services far exceeded supply. Severe shortages led to inflationary pressures, and these were further aggravated by the lack of sufficient foreign exchange to finance imports and relieve local scarcities. And since the major source of imports in the immediate postwar years was the United States, it was the lack of dollar reserves that particularly threatened to undermine Europe's chances of economic recovery. Put in balance-of-payments terms, Europe's needs for imports from the United States far surpassed her ability to produce the exports with which to pay for them. The result was a serious balance-of-payments deficit that could not be financed without substantial aid from the outside.

The deficit, which in 1946 and 1947 alone amounted to some $13 billion, was financed partly with funds provided by the United Nations Relief and Recovery Administration (UNRRA), and partly by loans advanced by the IBRD, the IMF, and the United States Export-Import Bank. In addition, the United States and Canada granted $5 billion to England, under the terms of the Anglo-American Financial Agreement of 1946. But it soon became quite clear that if the cause of the deficit was to be removed, Europe's productive capacity would have to be thoroughly rebuilt and her mounting inflation somehow be brought under control. It also became clear, however, that neither task could be accomplished without massive and prolonged aid from the United States; moreover, unless such aid was forthcoming, Europe might soon be headed for economic and political collapse.

America's response to this challenge was first expressed by Secretary of State George Marshall, in his commencement address at Harvard, on June 5, 1947. Calling upon European nations to get together and agree on a common plan for action, he pledged America's help in formulating and financing a comprehensive program for the economic reconstruction of Europe. In less than a year, the European Recovery Program (ERP)— or the Marshall Plan, as it came to be called—began to take shape. In Europe sixteen countries formed the Organization for European Economic Cooperation (OEEC)[3] and outlined a four-year (1948–1951) recovery plan. In the United States, Congress in 1948 passed the Economic Cooperation Act, setting up the Economic Cooperation Administration (ECA) and authorizing funds for its operation. Charged with America's part in the execution of the Marshall Plan, the ECA soon established administrative and technical missions in all of the OEEC countries. These missions, working in close cooperation with the OEEC, were to help determine the needs of the various countries and supervise the distribution of aid directed to them. At the same time, they were to assist in drawing up long-range recovery plans in the light of the conditions that prevailed in each country. For their part, the members of the OEEC promised to make every effort to increase productive efficiency and output, to work for domestic monetary stability, and to promote cooperation in intra-European trade.

Judged by its results, the Marshall Plan turned out to be an unqualified success. Although its accomplishments cannot be measured solely in economic terms, there is little question that the massive aid extended under its auspices was the single most important factor in the rapid economic progress of the OEEC countries from 1948 to the early 1950's. During that period the index of industrial production climbed back to its 1938 level, and then proceeded to climb at an annual rate of

---

[3] The OEEC grew out of the Committee for European Economic Cooperation (CEEC), which was formed about a month after Marshall's speech. At the insistence of the United States, the CEEC was made into a permanent organization—the OEEC. The sixteen countries involved were Austria, Belgium, Denmark, France, Greece, Iceland, Ireland, Italy, Luxembourg, Holland, Norway, Portugal, Sweden, Switzerland, Turkey, and the United Kingdom. West Germany became a member of OEEC upon becoming independent of Allied occupation control.

approximately 10 per cent. Inflationary pressures, which had charac-terized the immediate postwar years, yielded to relative price stability. And the combined balance-of-payments deficit of the OEEC countries, which had exceeded $7 billion in 1947, was reduced to a little over $2 billion in 1950. Indeed, by 1951 Europe had reached a stage from which it could hope to advance largely on its own power. And although United States economic aid continued beyond that year, it became less and less crucial as time went on.

The year 1951 also marked a new development in the administration of American foreign aid. In that year Congress passed the Mutual Security Act, placing the various assistance programs—economic as well as military—under the supervision of a Director for Mutual Secu-rity. The ECA, which until then had administered over $10 billion in Marshall Plan aid, ceased to exist as a separate agency and its functions were taken over by a new organization, the Mutual Security Agency. With this reorganization, the Marshall Plan as such came officially to an end.

The Marshall Plan left an important legacy: the OEEC. This organi-zation, which had originally devoted itself to the immediate problems of Europe's postwar economic recovery, soon turned to broader and more general tasks. Having established itself as a permanent, smoothly func-tioning institution,[4] it undertook to build a Europe based on close intergovernmental cooperation in economic and political matters. Of particular interest to us, however, are the accomplishments of OEEC in liberalizing intra-European trade and payments. In order to appreciate the extent of these accomplishments, one needs to be reminded that international trade in the early postwar period was largely dominated by the very restrictive policies that had characterized the 1930's. Thus, most countries still relied on exchange controls and quantitative restrictions to regulate their imports. Moreover, intra-European trade was conducted almost entirely on the basis of bilateral clearing arrangements, of which over 200 were in force in the early 1950's.[5] Finally, many of the high

---

[4] In 1961, the OEEC was transformed into the Organization for Economic Cooperation and Development (OECD); it includes, in addition to the OEEC countries, the United States, Japan, and Canada. More will be said about it in Chapter 19.

[5] Of these, ninety-two agreements covered intra-OEEC trade. The remaining agreements governed trade between OEEC countries and other European nations, as

314 PART V : *Free Trade vs. Protection*

tariffs that had been adopted during the 1930's were still in effect at the end of World War II.

Anxious to create an atmosphere more conducive to freer trade within Europe, the OEEC sought first of all to minimize the need for bilateral balancing arrangements. Its efforts resulted in an agreement to establish a European Payments Union (EPU), which began operations in July, 1950, and continued until 1958. The EPU could best be described as a multilateral clearing system; each of its members could settle its accounts with all its trading partners simultaneously. Thus, instead of running a deficit or a surplus with each other separately, EPU members ran credit and debit balances with the union itself; these balances were settled monthly according to an agreed-upon formula.[6] In this way, any EPU member could use surpluses earned by trading with some countries to cancel deficits arising from trade with others—and this, despite the fact that the currencies of the countries involved may not have been freely convertible into one another.

Indeed, during a period when currency *in*convertibility was the general rule, the EPU offered a sensible avenue of escape from the clutches of bilateralism. For by providing a *multilateral* clearing mechanism, it permitted the participating countries greater freedom in choosing between their various sources of imports, thereby reducing their dependence on bilateral channeling of trade. By the same token, it eliminated the need of any EPU member to discriminate against the exports of another member on balance-of-payments grounds, since a deficit with one member could easily be offset by a surplus with another. That the EPU performed its task well cannot be doubted for a moment. In fact, no greater tribute could have been paid to it than the unanimous decision of its members each year, from 1952 to 1957, to renew its existence for another twelve months. Only in 1958, following the establishment of free convertibility of eleven European currencies, were the EPU facilities considered no longer essential to the smooth functioning of an intra-

---

well as between OEEC members and non-European areas. For a complete listing of postwar bilateral agreements, see M. Trued and R. Mikesell, *Postwar Bilateral Payments Agreements* (Princeton: International Finance Section, Department of Economics and Sociology, Princeton University, 1955).

[6] For a more detailed account of EPU operations, see W. M. Scammell, *International Monetary Policy* (London: Macmillan, 1961), Chapter 10.

European payments system. In December of that year, the EPU was replaced by the European Monetary Agreement (EMA)—an arrangement that, in the words of one observer, was intended to "play [only] a limited role in a free-currency Europe, *lubricating* and *servicing* the new payments mechanism, rather than operating it.'"[7]

The replacement of the EPU by the EMA was largely a tribute to the OEEC, whose earlier efforts had made possible a return to currency convertibility and freely operating foreign-exchange markets in Western Europe. Yet while working to restore Europe's *monetary* health, the OEEC did not ignore other obstacles to the flows of intra-European trade. Soon after its inception, the organization enacted a Code of Liberalization, setting up a schedule for the removal of quantitative restrictions by its members. In accordance with this code, quotas—but not tariffs—were progressively eliminated on private trade between the OEEC countries; and by the mid-1950's, some 80 per cent of intra-OEEC imports had been "liberalized" in this manner. Encouraged by the success of the quota-liberalization program, several OEEC members began exploring the possibility of joint action with respect to tariff reductions as well. And although few could have suspected it at the time, these explorations led to the most ambitious ventures in close economic cooperation ever witnessed in the course of modern European history: the establishment of the European Economic Community (1957) and the European Free Trade Association (1960).

In the final analysis, it is neither the EPU nor the Code of Liberalization, but rather the development of economic regionalism in Europe, that must be regarded as the most significant and lasting achievement of the OEEC. For although the establishment of the EPU and the institution of a quota-liberalization program were remarkable accomplishments in themselves, they were essentially the manifestations of a new European spirit—a spirit born of the Marshall Plan, but kept alive and nurtured by the OEEC itself. This spirit—based on the concept of close intergovernmental cooperation and mutual confidence—facilitated Europe's rapid economic recovery after World War II. And it was the same spirit, as we shall see in Chapter 21, that helped reconstruct Western Europe, transforming it from an area dominated by selfish economic nationalism and bilateralism into a well-integrated community of nations, linked together in an expanding network of free multilateral trade.

[7] *Ibid.,* p. 314. (Italics added.)

A Charter for World Trade: The Proposed International Trade Organization (ITO)

Postwar efforts to replace bilateralism with multilateralism were not confined to Europe. As mentioned earlier, some of these efforts originated in wartime discussions among the Allies and were aimed at securing an *international* adherence to the principles of free trade and nondiscrimination. One such effort deserves special mention; for although it fell short of expectations, it paved the way for a new and unique experience in international commercial policies. To this effort, initiated by the United States immediately after the war, we now turn our attention.

In a document entitled "Proposals for Expansion of World Trade and Employment," issued by the State Department in November, 1945, the United States presented a series of guidelines for action in such matters as tariffs, quantitative restrictions, discriminatory trade policies, monopoly and cartel practices, and the maintenance of full employment. The same document also urged the creation of an International Trade Organization (ITO) whose members would be committed to the reduction of trade barriers and to the promotion of mutually advantageous international economic relations. The proposed organization, it went on to suggest, would be governed by a charter, to be drafted by a special International Conference on Trade and Employment. And it concluded by calling for an early meeting of such a conference, under United Nations auspices.

Preliminary discussions of these "Proposals" took place, in late 1945 and early 1946, between the United States and Britain, and between the United States and several other governments. Following an agreement in principle on the major points contained in the "Proposals," an international conference was convened to consider them more fully. The conference started in London in the latter part of 1946, changed its location to Geneva the next year, and moved on to Havana in the winter of 1947–1948. There a charter for an International Trade Organization was finally agreed upon and was signed by some fifty-four countries in March, 1948.

The Havana Charter was signed but never ratified. Its sweeping and revolutionary provisions on the one hand, and the many qualifications and exceptions on the other, apparently proved too much for most parliaments to swallow. If the United States Congress had ratified the agreement, however, a sufficient number of other countries would quite possibly have followed suit; and since only twenty ratifications were needed to bring the charter into force, the ITO might still have been created. But in 1948, less than a year after it had been confronted with America's commitment (via the Trade Agreements Act) to GATT, Congress was hardly in a mood to approve participation in another far-reaching scheme for trade liberalization. And aided by a storm of protests and denunciations, directed at the proposed ITO from various domestic interest groups, it refused to ratify the charter. Its action ended all hope for ratification by any other signatories of the charter.

But although the ITO failed to materialize, the efforts that had gone into shaping it were not entirely lost. Indeed, even as the charter was being drafted, it inspired some twenty-three nations, meeting in Geneva in the summer of 1947, to start negotiations for multilateral tariff reductions. These negotiations resulted in a General Agreement on Tariffs and Trade (GATT), an international agreement that has remained in force to this day. Moreover, the original parties to GATT borrowed several provisions from the proposed ITO Charter, using them as the framework within which to conduct their negotiations; and these provisions were later embodied in GATT's own code of commercial relations. Thus, through the development and accomplishments of GATT, the spirit of ITO managed to survive despite the parliamentary defeat suffered by the Havana Charter.

The General Agreement on Tariffs and Trade (GATT)

Like ITO, GATT owed its origin to American initiative. For it was largely at the suggestion of the United States that, having adjourned from London to Geneva, the participants in the preparatory committee of the ITO Charter set out to test some of the new ideas it contained. More specifically, while awaiting completion of the final draft of the charter, the assembled nations embarked upon a series of trade negotiations; in the course of these negotiations each country simultaneously exchanged tariff concessions with several other countries. Though bilaterally negotiated, the concessions were extended to all participants via a general most-favored-nation clause. Moreover, the concessions were formalized by the signing of the General Agreement on Tariffs and Trade—a document that included, not only a list of the tariff reductions themselves, but also the set of rules and principles under which the negotiations had been carried out.

GATT—or, more specifically, those of its provisions pertaining to the conduct of commercial policy—had been intended to serve as a temporary arrangement, pending the signing and ratification of the ITO Charter. Consequently, no plans for an elaborate organizational structure were made for it at the 1947 Geneva conference. The agreement did provide, however, for annual meetings of the signatories as well as for a small secretariat to handle administrative matters that might arise between the annual sessions. But no other organizational fixtures had been added until 1954, when a permanent Council of Representatives was created.

Indeed, as originally conceived, GATT's main function was merely to establish a framework for multilateral trade negotiations—a function that was expected to be assumed later by ITO. But as it turned out, ITO died at birth while GATT survived and grew to maturity. Although its purpose has remained essentially the same—that is, to help reduce trade barriers and promote the expansion of multilateral trade—it has acquired additional duties with the passage of time. More important, GATT has come to be regarded as a permanent institution; together with such bodies as the IMF, the IBRD, and UNESCO, it is one of the specialized agencies of the United Nations.

Permanency, however, has not changed the basic character of GATT. It is still essentially a contractual agreement, consisting of two parts. One of these may properly be termed a ''book of records,'' for in it are listed all the trade concessions (tariff reductions and quota liberalizations) made by GATT's members. The other part constitutes a code of commercial policy, made up of rules, regulations, privileges, and obligations that govern the conduct of, and the relations between, the contracting parties.

This code reflects two major principles that had been embodied earlier in the ITO Charter: (1) a multilateral and nondiscriminatory approach to international trade, and (2) condemnation of quantitative trade restrictions. To implement the first of these principles, the code contains a most-favored-nation clause, through which concessions made by any member are automatically extended to all others; in the same vein, it prohibits any preferential trade arrangement designed to favor one nation over another.[8] As for quantitative restrictions, the code forbids them in principle but allows for exceptions in certain circumstances—in the case of countries suffering from balance-of-payments difficulties, and in the case of developing nations that impose quotas to protect infant industries. Another exception permits the use of quantitative controls to restrict imports of agricultural products, provided that domestic production of such products is controlled in a similar manner. Finally, the code features an escape clause that allows member nations to raise tariffs or impose quotas if any of their domestic industries are injured by increased import competition.

Today GATT can justly claim credit for several accomplishments, not the least of which is the marked increase in its membership. Numbering twenty-three signatories in 1947, it now comprises some seventy-two nations that together account for over 80 per cent of total world trade. Second, in less than twenty years of existence, GATT has sponsored several rounds of multilateral trade negotiations—held in Annecy, France (1949); Torquay, England (1950–1951); and Geneva (1956 and 1960–1962); these have resulted in substantial reductions of tariffs and other trade barriers. More recently it served as the stage for the Kennedy Round of trade negotiations.

Equally significant are GATT's contributions to the peaceful settlement of commercial disputes. By providing a forum for consultation and discussion, GATT encourages its members to air any grievances and, if necessary, to submit them to arbitration or adjudication. As a result, very few conflicts—whether arising from a member's failure to honor obligations or from an outright violation of GATT's provisions—have remained unresolved. And in cases where persuasion or arbitration has failed, GATT authorizes retaliation against the offending nation, allowing the other countries involved to place restrictions on its exports.[9]

In addition to its general concern with the reduction of trade

---

[8] An exception to this rule allows for preferential arrangements that take the form of customs unions or free-trade areas. These will be discussed in Chapter 20.

[9] For example, a 1963 ruling by a GATT's panel of arbitrators allowed the United States to raise tariffs on $26 million worth of selected imports from EEC countries in retaliation for their restrictions on United States exports of frozen chickens.

barriers and the settlement of commercial disputes, GATT has increasingly turned its attention to the specific problems of the underdeveloped nations. These problems, as well as some of the suggested solutions, will be discussed in the next chapter. We might note here, however, that in 1963, while preparing for the forthcoming Kennedy Round, a GATT ministerial meeting adopted a new and important principle: It relieved the developing nations within GATT from the necessity to reciprocate fully for the concessions granted by the economically advanced countries in the course of the Kennedy Round of tariff negotiations.[10] In other words, the developing nations would be entitled to receive the full benefit of any tariff reductions, to be negotiated by GATT's industrial nations, without having to offer substantial concessions in return.

It is too early to assess the practical significance of this principle. For one thing, only nineteen of the fifty-three nations that participated in the Kennedy Round have been designated as Less Developed Countries (which is the official UN term for the underdeveloped nations). More-over, the developing nations in general have taken a rather skeptical view of GATT's contributions to their cause. Nevertheless, the fact that the nonreciprocity principle was unanimously adopted at the 1963 ministerial meeting signifies a formal recognition of the plight of the economically less developed countries, and suggests the possibility of additional joint efforts on their behalf in the future.

GATT : *Past and Future*

As early as 1953, several of GATT's members proposed that the agreement be better defined and more solidly based. The matter was discussed further in the following year, and in 1955 an agreement was reached to create an Organization for Trade Cooperation (OTC). It must be emphasized that the proposed organization was not conceived of as a replacement for GATT. On the contrary, it was designed to assure GATT's continuity by providing it with an administrative arm and permanent organizational machinery. To state it succinctly, the OTC was expected to

[10] See R. Stern, ''Policies for Trade and Development,'' *International Conciliation No. 548* (New York: Carnegie Endowment for International Peace, May, 1964), p. 43.

help implement GATT's purposes and provisions rather than to formulate new provisions and policies of its own.

Before it could become effective, the OTC agreement required ratification by countries that together represented at least 85 per cent of the total trade of GATT's membership. As can well be imagined, the fulfillment of this requirement depended to a large extent on positive action by the United States. But when the OTC agreement came before Congress, it received similar treatment to that accorded the ITO. If anything, congressional opposition to international commercial commitments had stiffened between 1948 and 1955. And although a bill to approve the OTC passed through the House Ways and Means Committee, it never reached the floor of either the House or the Senate.

Despite the failure of OTC to receive congressional approval, GATT has continued to exist and, as stated earlier, has achieved the status of a permanent international institution. Its future course will depend, of course, on the attitudes of its members and on their willingness to cooperate in matters relating to international trade in general and to the problems of the developing nations in particular. Although the future role of GATT is unknown, its accomplishments have already earned for it a place of honor in the history of international commercial policies. For ever since its inception, and despite occasional setbacks, GATT has been the major force in guiding the world economy on an expanding path of multilateral trade.

19

The Developing Nations and World Trade

Sɪɢɴɪғɪᴄᴀɴᴛ ᴀs ɪᴛs ᴀᴄᴄᴏᴍ-plishments have been, ɢᴀᴛᴛ has invited frequent scorn and criticism from a large group of countries—the so-called underdeveloped nations. They have claimed that ɢᴀᴛᴛ's contributions to the liberalization of trade policies have done very little to enhance their economic well-being and their prospects for rapid economic growth. More specifically, they have charged that, both as an institution and as a code of commercial policy, ɢᴀᴛᴛ has been primarily geared to the accommodation of the advanced countries and has failed to consider the special problems faced by the developing nations in today's international economic setting. Largely because of this failure, their argument continues, they have actually been hindered in the pursuit of their main goal, which is to advance economically and to achieve equality with the developed nations.

In recent years, these charges have been heard with increasing sympathy within ɢᴀᴛᴛ's councils, and some steps have already been taken to exempt ɢᴀᴛᴛ's economically less developed members from some of the requirements of ɢᴀᴛᴛ's commercial code. One such step, to which we referred in Chapter 18, was the decision to exempt developing nations from the reciprocity principle during the Kennedy Round of tariff negotiations, without denying them the benefit of tariff concessions reciprocally exchanged by the advanced countries. Another step was to convene the United Nations Conference on Trade and Development, which met in Geneva in 1964, and in which all GATT members took part. Out of this conference came several proposals for changes in the commercial policies of the advanced nations, changes geared to the special needs of the developing countries.

But although it is highly desirable to have measures that are designed to bring about readjustments in commercial policies, so that the needs of developing nations may be met, such measures cannot in themselves be regarded as a final solution. For the plight of today's developing nations stems from a variety of circumstances, only one of which involves the problems relating to the commercial policies of the advanced nations. Indeed, a comprehensive solution to the problem of economic underdevelopment would call for a simultaneous attack on several fronts, covering almost every aspect of the developing nations' economic structures and their trade relations with the advanced countries. In order to appreciate the need for such a comprehensive approach, let us consider briefly the nature of economic underdevelopment and the problems that it involves.

The Nature of Economic Underdevelopment

Some terms are more easily coined than defined and among these one must surely include "underdeveloped areas." In fact, the widely used distinction between economically "developed" (or advanced) and "underdeveloped" (or backward) nations is essentially nothing more than a convenient way of pointing to the sharp contrasts in economic welfare and living standards that exist in the world today. Such a distinction, however, does not in itself provide an accurate or meaningful definition of economic underdevelopment. Nor does it throw much light on the reasons behind it.

Yet while the terminological division of the world into developed and underdeveloped areas begs the question of what *is* economic backwardness, it implies the possibility of quantitatively assessing and comparing the relative economic status of nations. One quantitative measure is an international comparison of per capita incomes. Thus if we accept the proposition that the level of a country's per capita income reflects the stage of its economic development, we may get some impression of the meaning of economic underdevelopment by comparing existing levels of per capita national incomes in the world.

A comparison of per capita national incomes reveals the startling fact that nearly half (approximately 49 per cent) of the world's population lives in countries whose annual per capita incomes fall within a $40–$100 range—as compared with a per capita income of over $2,500 per year in the United States, and of between $700 and $1,500 in most West European countries! Between these extremes are some 16 per cent of the world's inhabitants, with annual per capita incomes ranging from $100 to $300; and another 18 per cent, with per capita incomes between $300 and $700. All told, roughly two-thirds of the world's population live in countries whose per capita national incomes are below $300 per year, while less than 15 per cent enjoy per capita incomes of $700 and above.[1] Here, in a nutshell, lies the meaning of today's economic underdevelopment: It is the existence of a huge gap, insofar as per capita incomes and economic well-being is concerned, between a few countries and the rest of the world (virtually all of Africa and Asia, and most of Latin America). But here, too, lies the problem of economic *development*—namely, the desire and need of the underdeveloped countries to close this gap as rapidly as possible by accelerating the rate of their economic growth.

Stating the problem is one thing, solving it is quite another. Chapter 1 told us that economic growth—and especially a rapid rate of growth—rests in large measure on rapid accumulation of capital, technological progress, expansion of markets, and efficient organization of productive activities. In the absence of these conditions, economic growth—though, strictly speaking, still possible—can proceed only very slowly. But a country that, besides lacking adequate capital resources and technological knowledge, is also afflicted with (1) rapidly growing population in relation to resources, (2) primitive methods of production, (3) lack of skilled labor, (4) extremely low levels of nutrition, (5) social and

[1] These figures are based on 1957 estimates of per capita national incomes. For a more detailed breakdown, see E. Hagen, "Some Facts About Income Levels and Economic Growth," *Review of Economics and Statistics,* Vol. XLII (February, 1960).

cultural superstitions and taboos, (6) inability to generate savings because of low levels of income, (7) absence of efficient monetary institutions, (8) lack of adequate transportation and communications facilities, and (9) a generally unskilled and often corrupt civil service— such a country may find it extremely difficult even to get started in the direction of sustained economic growth, let alone experience a rapid rise in per capita national income. And since most of today's underdeveloped countries can be generally characterized by these conditions, is it any wonder that their intense desire for rapid economic growth is out-matched by formidable obstacles to its attainment?

Of particular interest to us, however, are the problems that confront the underdeveloped countries in the field of foreign trade. For these problems—and the circumstances from which they arise—bear directly on the role that international trade has played (and can play) in promoting, or possibly hindering, the economic growth of these countries. At the same time, the existence of such problems helps to explain both the attitude of the underdeveloped countries toward the commercial policies of the advanced countries, and their reluctance to lower their own trade barriers. Indeed, the prospects for a truly free, multilateral network of world trade rest largely on a solution to the external problems that plague the underdeveloped countries. Let us take a look at these problems.

The Underdeveloped Countries and Foreign Trade

What are the problems that the underdeveloped nations face as members of the twentieth-century international economy? Two such problems are usually singled out: (1) The export earnings of under-developed countries are unstable and subject to severe fluctuations, and (2) the prospects for expanding their exports and export earnings are rather dim.[2]

These two problems are closely interrelated, for they spring from the same basic source—the heavy concentration of exports, and hence export

[2] In addition, it is often claimed that the underdeveloped countries have suffered a long-run deterioration in their commodity terms of trade (i.e., a decline in the ratio of their export to import prices). This claim, however, is open to serious question both on statistical and analytical grounds, and hence will not be dealt with here.

earnings, in a few primary products. The extent of such concentration is strikingly illustrated by the fact that in many underdeveloped countries over 50 per cent of total export earnings are derived from *one* exportable product; in some cases, two or three products account for over 80 per cent of the country's export earnings. For example, 95 per cent of Colombia's export earnings are from coffee, petroleum, and bananas; 88 per cent of Ceylon's are from tea, rubber, and coconut products; 74 per cent of Burma's, from rice; 72 per cent of Egypt's, from cotton; and 62 per cent of Ghana's, from cacao.[3] Because the bulk of most under-developed countries' exports is so heavily concentrated in one or two primary products, their *total* export earnings are extremely vulnerable to fluctuations. For even the slightest change in the condition of world demand for primary products may result in a significant rise or fall in the export income of primary-producing countries.

Instability of export earnings leads to two additional problems that must be met if the underdeveloped countries are to enjoy the benefits of international specialization and trade. There is the immediate problem of recurring balance-of-payments deficits whenever export earnings unex-pectedly fall below the intended level of import expenditures. Unless deficits can be readily financed, imports must be reduced, thereby jeopardizing development projects that are dependent on certain import requirements. However, since most underdeveloped countries can hardly boast of large holdings of gold and foreign-exchange reserves, they must look elsewhere for sources of international liquidity with which to counter their balance-of-payments deficits. One such source, we already know, is the IMF. But although in recent times the IMF has been rather sympathetic toward balance-of-payments problems of underdeveloped countries (especially problems that arise from instability of export earnings), its resources have not been extended automatically upon request. Nor would an automatic extension of short-term credit by the IMF necessarily solve the problem. For as long as instability prevails in export earnings, the underdeveloped countries would be in almost con-stant need of credit to finance balance-of-payments deficits. Under the circumstances, automatic granting of credit by the IMF might well exhaust its resources.

[3] See J. Bhagwati, *The Economics of Underdeveloped Countries* (New York: McGraw-Hill, 1966), p. 59.

Indeed, if balance-of-payments difficulties that arise from instability of export earnings are to be alleviated, the instability itself must somehow be reduced. And this raises another major problem: how to stabilize the world markets for primary products, the very markets on which the underdeveloped countries are presently dependent for their export earnings?

Over the years, various stabilization schemes have been proposed; and some of these have been put into effect: international commodity agreements, which have sought mainly to stabilize the *prices* of particular primary products (e.g., wheat, tea, coffee, tin, and so on) by regulating their supply on the world market. In general commodity agreements have set limits on the quantities of certain primary products that may be exported and/or imported by countries participating in the agreements.[4] In some cases, moreover, international commodity agreements have provided for a range of prices at which specified quantities of given commodities would be purchased by the importing countries, regardless of prevailing free-market prices. Still other schemes have been based on the notion of a "buffer stock," whereby an international agency (or a group of countries acting together) would stand ready to buy a commodity in the open market when its supply was excessive and prices were low; and sell it, out of storage, when supply was low and prices high.

Yet because international commodity agreements have been basically price-stabilization schemes, they have not completely satisfied the real need of the underdeveloped countries—a need for stability of *total* export earnings rather than of individual export prices.[5] Moreover, the operation of such agreements often adversely affects consumers by compelling them to pay higher prices than under free-market conditions. And finally, by fixing and stabilizing prices at fairly high levels, price-stabilization schemes interfere with allocation of resources based on the free-market price mechanism, and may actually encourage inefficient patterns of production and trade. Thus, neither the need of the under-developed countries for stable export earnings nor the cause of economic

[4] Governments, not individuals, enter into international commodity agreements. Accordingly, limitations on exports and/or imports are effected through the use of export restrictions and import quotas, respectively.

[5] Stability of prices does not necessarily assure stability of earnings; for while the price may be kept stable, the quantities demanded or supplied may fluctuate, thus affecting total revenue.

efficiency has been served well by existing international commodity agreements. And until more effective means of coping with the problem of stabilizing primary-product markets can be devised and implemented, underdeveloped countries will be continuously plagued by fluctuations in export earnings and consequent balance-of-payments difficulties.

But in addition to vulnerability in their current export earnings, and its implications for their short-run balance-of-payments position, the underdeveloped countries *as a group* face a serious long-term problem. Their ability to finance an increasing volume of imports—especially imports of essential capital goods—depends to a large extent on the future *expansion* of their exports and export earnings. Such an expansion, however, requires steady and significant growth in the demand for primary products by the economically advanced countries. But during the past forty years or so, the demand for primary products has grown very slowly, and at present there are no indications that its future rate of growth will be accelerated. Moreover, many of the advanced countries, including the United States, at present restrict the imports of agricultural and other primary products by quotas and by tariffs. And such restrictions constitute another obstacle to the expansion of primary-product exports by the underdeveloped countries.

This is not to suggest, however, that the prospects for export expansion are equally gloomy for all the underdeveloped countries. For depending on the particular primary products they export, and the special relations they may enjoy with one advanced country or another, some underdeveloped nations fare better than others. Furthermore, some underdeveloped countries have slowly begun to shift their resources to the production of light manufactures, in an attempt to diversify their exports and to reduce their dependence on imports. But here again the prospects for significant export expansion seem uncertain, in view of the widespread use by the advanced countries of quotas and tariffs aimed against imports of so-called "cheap labor" products from the underdeveloped nations. Finally, as newcomers to the field, exporters of manufactures in the underdeveloped countries must face stiff competition in the world markets from well-established producers in the advanced countries.

All in all, heavy concentration in the production and export of a few primary products has placed the underdeveloped countries in an unenviable and paradoxical position as members of the world trading community. To attain more rapid growth, they must take full advantage of the benefits of international specialization and trade. Yet the very products in which they have to specialize cannot always be relied upon to yield stable, expanding export earnings with which to finance an adequate volume of imports. Hence, their ability to engage in mutually advantageous trade relations with the advanced countries is severely limited. Nor can they fully avail themselves of the contributions of international specialization and trade to a better utilization of resources and greater economic efficiency, both of which are indispensable to economic growth. In short, while international trade is of crucial importance to the underdeveloped countries, they are at present denied some of its most important benefits—a predicament that seriously impedes their growth.

Indeed, unless the underdeveloped countries can extricate themselves—or be extricated—from this and related predicaments, their prospects for more fruitful trade relations, as well as for a more rapid rate of growth, remain dim. However, a "pulling out"—or better, a "pulling up"—process requires technical knowledge and a rapid accumulation of capital. But given their extremely low levels of domestic savings, along with a paucity of technical and administrative skills, the underdeveloped countries are hardly in a position to meet these requirements entirely on their own. Hence, in their efforts to overcome obstacles to growth, they must rely on considerable financial and technical assistance from the economically advanced nations. While this idea (i.e., the need to provide capital and technical resources to underdeveloped countries) is not new, it raises a number of important questions, which we will discuss now.

Aid for Development: Some Basic Questions

In their present predicament, the underdeveloped countries cannot finance their development without assistance from abroad. Nor can there be doubt that the extension of capital and technical resources by the economically advanced nations would help to accelerate economic development in these countries and enhance their prospects for self-sustaining growth. But questions arise as to how much aid is needed, and how it might be transmitted. Some of these questions are: How much capital is required to enable the underdeveloped countries to attain a reasonable annual rate of growth over the next few years? Through what institutions and under what terms should funds be transmitted? What criteria should be used to determine the needs of various underdeveloped countries? How much reliance should be placed on private, as opposed to public, capital? And so on.

Admittedly, none of these questions can be answered readily; and even painstaking investigations usually yield widely different conclusions. For example, some estimates of the total amount of foreign assistance that the underdeveloped countries need over the next decade or two have placed it at approximately $5 billion per year;[6] other estimates are double this figure. Nor can one be certain of what exactly is meant by the "needs" of the underdeveloped countries. For if we mean—as we usually do—the amount of assistance that would enable these countries to attain a certain annual *rate* of growth, then the question arises as to what this rate ought to be—2, 3, perhaps 5 per cent—and whether it should be applied equally to each and every one of the underdeveloped countries. By the same token, it is difficult if not impossible to predict whether a given amount of aid would actually enable a particular country to attain its projected growth rate within a "reasonable" (another ambiguous concept) period of time.

Another vexing question concerns the form that financial assistance should take—whether outright grants or loans—and the terms and conditions under which it should be extended. This question is indicative of the character and composition of international capital flows in the last few decades. More specifically, it reflects the fact that *private* foreign investment, which during the nineteenth century had provided the then developing nations with most of their capital needs, has been largely replaced by *public* capital transfers as a source of development funds. Indeed, it is not surprising that private foreign investment, whose chief motivating force is the expectation of profit, has shied away from today's underdeveloped countries, where profitable investment opportunities are

---

[6] See, for example, P. N. Rosenstein-Rodan, ''International Aid for Underdeveloped Countries,'' *Review of Economics and Statistics*, Vol. XLIII (May, 1961).

very limited, and where political instability and the danger of expropriation add to the already high risk of overseas business ventures. Moreover, it is doubtful that private capital flows, even if they were somehow to increase significantly, would be used to finance basic needs, such as roads, hydroelectric projects, hospitals, training centers, irrigation networks, and so forth. Nor is it likely that private foreign capital— with the exception of short- and intermediate-term bank credit—would be available to finance the so-called "general purpose" import requirements and needs of the underdeveloped countries. In the final analysis, officially sponsored financial assistance must continue to carry, at least for the foreseeable future, the main burden of aid to the underdeveloped countries.

Given this premise, the question of loans vs. grants, as well as the terms and conditions attached to the granting of aid, assumes great practical significance. For since the profit motive, characteristic of private foreign investment, is not the determining factor in public capital transfers, other considerations must take its place. More important, because the bulk of public aid to underdeveloped countries is extended *unilaterally* by developed countries, aid programs are necessarily influenced by political, as well as economic, considerations. And depending on the criteria and objectives that may govern such considerations, the question would yield different answers according to the circumstances in each case.

Yet even *multilaterally* extended public aid—that is, assistance offered by, or channeled through, international and interregional agencies—poses problems regarding the types of aid, its purpose, its terms and conditions, and so on. And although multilateral aid may be less susceptible to direct political considerations than aid extended by individual countries, it is similarly influenced by a variety of conditions and circumstances that are bound to change as time goes by. Indeed, neither national nor international public-aid institutions can escape the need to constantly reassess the character of the aid they extend, in accordance with the questions that have been raised here. To appreciate the various ways in which these questions have been acted upon, we devote the next two sections to a brief examination of the major public sources of development aid in existence today.

Unilateral Sources of Aid

During the past twenty years, the United States has been by far the largest unilateral source of public aid to both developed and under-developed countries. Its total aid throughout this period (1947–1966) amounted to some $100 billion. In its early days, however, some 85 per cent of the total aid was directed toward Western Europe and Japan, and immediately after the Korean War, much of it consisted of military assistance. But beginning in the mid-1950's, both the composition and direction of United States foreign-aid programs have undergone signifi-cant changes. Thus, during the ten years from 1955 to 1965, some $20 billion in aid was allocated for economic assistance, and practically all of it went to the underdeveloped countries of Latin America, Asia, and Africa.[7] Moreover, in 1961 the administration of foreign economic aid, for which several agencies had been previously responsible, was entrusted to a new agency, the Agency for International Development (AID). Through this agency has flowed the largest portion of America's foreign economic aid in recent years.

THE AGENCY FOR INTERNATIONAL DEVELOPMENT (AID)

Established by the Foreign Assistance Act of 1961, AID was charged with carrying out economic aid programs of its own, and with co-ordinating various other aspects of United States foreign assistance activities. Thus, its operations have included a rather wide range of different though interrelated functions. But insofar as economic assis-tance programs are directly concerned, AID operations can be classified under three major headings: (1) programs designed for long-term economic development, (2) programs intended to meet immediate and present needs, but aiming at economic development in the long run, and (3) limited aid programs involving rather restricted objectives.[8] These,

[7] See AID, *Foreign Aid in Perspective* (Washington: U.S. Government Printing Office, 1964), pp. 2–3.

[8] See AID, *Principles of Foreign Economic Assistance* (Washington: U.S. Gov-ernment Printing Office, 1963), pp. 5–7.

in turn, reflect the types of *financial* assistance provided by AID to developing and underdeveloped nations.

Broadly speaking, AID's contributions to economic development consist of four types of financial aid.

1. Long-term development loans, with maturities of up to forty years and interest rates from 3/4 to 5¾ per cent. These loans, most of which are repayable in dollars, are intended primarily to help finance basic capital projects (e.g., transport and communication systems, water resources, and so on). But they may also be used to finance "general purpose" imports if they are related to development efforts, or to overall development programs (as opposed to specific projects).

2. Local-currency loans, extended either to American investors or to local private firms for the purpose of encouraging private investments. These loans are made out of the accumulated proceeds from the sale of surplus agricultural products by the United States government, under Public Law 480 (see footnote 15, Chapter 17), and are repayable in local currencies.

3. Technical cooperation and development grants. These are used primarily to hire experts and technicians to help train administrative and technical personnel in the underdeveloped countries. Such grants may also be used to pay for goods and equipment needed in technical training (e.g., textbooks, demonstration apparatus, and so on), as well as for training of personnel from underdeveloped countries in American colleges and universities.

4. Supporting assistance funds (in the form of either loans or grants), which are used primarily in conjunction with military assistance programs, and are designed to provide aid for an emergency situation (e.g., refugee relief projects, internal security requirements, severe balance-of-payments difficulties, and so on).

It is interesting to note, in this connection, that while the bulk of United States economic aid during the 1950's was extended on a grant basis, AID policies have resulted in increased emphasis on aid through loans. According to recent estimates, some two-thirds of AID economic assistance in the last three years has taken the form of loans, repayable in dollars. Moreover, over 80 per cent of the funds disbursed by AID during this period has been tied to purchases of United States goods and services. It should also be noted that AID is entirely dependent for its financial resources on annual congressional appropriations. As a result, it has had to contend with whatever conditions, qualifications, and/or limitations Congress has chosen to insert into its foreign-aid appropriation bills in the past few years. More important, in submitting its financial requests to Congress, AID can never be certain that the full amount requested will be appropriated. (In fiscal year 1964, for example, AID requested some $2.9 billion in new appropriations for economic assistance, but Congress slashed this amount by over one billion dollars, appropriating only $1.8 billion.) But despite congressional vicissitudes, AID has been able during its first five years to expand its operations considerably. As of 1966, it has conducted assistance programs in over seventy countries, and from 1962 to 1965 it has extended economic assistance (including loans and grants) totaling some $10 billion.[9] Largely through its efforts, some developing nations are approaching the stage where they can begin to rely for their capital needs on sources whose terms are more exacting than AID's. One such source, the Export-Import Bank of Washington, will be described next.

THE EXPORT-IMPORT BANK (EXIMBANK)

Chronologically, the Export-Import Bank is the United States government's oldest foreign lending agency. It was established in 1934 as a District of Columbia banking corporation, and was reincorporated in 1945 as an independent government agency.[10] Its major purpose is to aid American exports by extending credit to foreign purchasers of American goods, and by providing credit and guarantees against credit risks (and, more recently, against political risks) to American exporters. The Eximbank, whose capital stock of $1 billion was subscribed to by the U.S. Treasury, may borrow up to $6 billion from the same source. All its loans are repayable in dollars and carry interest charges, averaging in recent years about 5½ per cent. Its short-term loans involve maturities of up to 180 days, while medium-term credits range in maturity from six months to seven years.

[9] Calculated from statistical data in AID, *Proposed Economic Assistance Programs FY 1967* (Washington: U.S. Government Printing Office, 1966).

[10] For additional information and a brief critical appraisal of the Eximbank, see R. Mikesell, *Public International Lending for Development* (New York: Random House, 1966), pp. 81–89.

In terms of this information, the Eximbank can hardly be described as a source of foreign assistance to developing nations. But while most of its operations are indeed related to the financing of United States exports, the Eximbank also extends long-term development loans ranging in maturity from eight to twenty years. And since a significant portion of such loans have been granted to developing and under-developed countries (especially in Latin America), the Eximbank has come to be regarded as an important source of development finance.[11] Indeed, many of its long-term loans have been used to finance basic industrial and public utilities projects in underdeveloped countries, projects which depended on imports of heavy machinery and equipment from the United States. The Eximbank has also made a number of long-term loans to underdeveloped countries with balance-of-payments diffi-culties, so as to enable them to maintain their levels of imports from the United States. And finally, on a number of occasions, the Eximbank extended general lines of credit to developing nations, to be used in the financing of future projects.

Unlike AID, however, the Eximbank has provided very little technical assistance to developing nations, either in connection with projects it has helped to finance, or for economic development in general. But this is not surprising. For since the Eximbank is, strictly speaking, a banking institution, it is not equipped to deal with the variety of technical and administrative problems that are involved in development plans. More-over, its basic interest has always been to promote United States exports, not to plan development projects in underdeveloped areas. Hence its contribution to economic development has been largely confined to aiding underdeveloped countries in financing necessary imports from the United States. But despite the limited nature of its contribution, the Eximbank has emerged as one of the most important sources of develop-ment finance in recent years. And it is to be expected that its role in extending financial resources to developing nations will increase as they begin to rely more and more on conventional sources of foreign capital.

11 Thus, in 1965 the Eximbank's long-term loans totaled $771.5 million, of which $457 million went to non-European countries. Of this, the share of Latin American countries was $258 million. Source: statistical data in *Proposed Economic Assistance Programs FY 1967, op. cit.*

THE OECD COUNTRIES

In addition to the United States, some thirteen other countries have developed their own foreign-aid programs in recent years. (Most of these countries had been themselves recipients of United States aid during the early post-World War II period.) Between 1956 and 1959, eleven of these countries extended a total of $5.3 billion in financial assistance to under-developed countries, of which some $1.3 billion took the form of loans; the rest were grants.[12] But although each country has channeled its development assistance through its own agencies and institutions, since 1961 all have conducted their foreign-aid operations within the general framework of an important international organization—the Organization for Economic Cooperation and Development (OECD).

As we noted in Chapter 18, the OECD is a successor to the OEEC. It was set up under an agreement signed in Paris in December, 1960, and came into being in September, 1961. The new organization, including the OEEC members plus Canada, Japan, and the United States, committed it-self to several goals and principles pertaining to the expansion of multi-lateral trade, to rising standards of living, and to continued economic growth of its member countries. But one of its most significant objectives was to "contribute to sound economic expansion" in countries undergo-ing the process of economic development. In line with this objective and as early as January, 1960, several members of OECD had created a specialized body, the Development Assistance Committee (DAC), for the purpose of "providing a central point where suppliers of assistance to less developed countries might consult together on various problems connected with the channeling of development aid, as well as the effectiveness of their efforts."[13]

The DAC possesses no lending funds of its own. It is merely a framework for consultations and discussions. And while its members

[12] Computed from data in OEEC, *The Flow of Financial Resources to Countries in Course of Economic Development 1956–59* (Paris, 1961).

[13] OECD, *Development Assistance Efforts and Policies, 1965 Review* (Paris, 1965), p. 9. The original members of the DAC were Belgium, Canada, France, Ger-many, Italy, Japan, The Netherlands, Norway, Portugal, the United Kingdom, the United States, and the Commission of the European Economic Community. In 1961, Denmark also became a member and, in 1965, Austria and Sweden.

from time to time adopt resolutions and recommendations pertaining to development assistance efforts, the DAC has no power to enforce these resolutions. Nevertheless, it has proved to be a major force behind development assistance activities of OECD countries other than the United States. Indeed, since 1961, the DAC countries—excluding the United States—have disbursed an average of some $2 billion per year in official aid to underdeveloped countries. However, the composition of official aid has varied from one DAC country to another. In some cases (notably France and Belgium), over 70 per cent of the official aid has taken the form of grants and grant-like contributions (i.e., repayments in local currencies or over very long periods of time). In other cases (U.S., Germany, Italy, and Japan), official assistance has consisted largely of loans. Such loans, too, have varied—with respect to maturities and interest rates—among the donor countries.[14] In addition to extending financial aid on an individual basis, the OECD countries have been the major contributors to a number of multilateral aid agencies (to be discussed in the next section). Through these contributions they have also made resources available with which to finance the development efforts of underdeveloped countries. Moreover, various OECD countries have participated in aid consortia and consultative groups, whose purpose is to secure and coordinate the flow of financial and technical assistance from several developed countries to specific underdeveloped nations. The first consortium, the Indian Consortium, was organized in 1958 at the initiative of the World Bank to help finance India's second Five Year Plan. Another consortium, the Pakistan Consortium, was organized in 1960 for a similar purpose. At present, there are several consortia and consultative groups that have been sponsored by DAC countries, and in which many OECD countries are full-fledged participants. Other consortia, sponsored by the World Bank or the Inter-American Development Bank, also rely on help from OECD members.

Finally, since 1958 the European Economic Community (EEC), whose six members are also members of the OECD, has channeled economic assistance to underdeveloped countries through two of its own institutions: the European Development Fund and the European Investment Bank. This assistance has been extended independently of the individual aid programs of the six EEC countries, although they have supplied the

[14] For details, see the statistical appendices in OECD, *op. cit.*

financial resources which made the assistance possible. More about this in Chapter 21.

Multilateral Sources of Aid

All of the financial resources that flow from developed to under-developed countries must ultimately originate in the developed countries. But some of the aid can be—and has been—channeled through international rather than national institutions. Indeed, since the end of World War II, four major international institutions have been created for the purpose of disbursing development assistance: the International Bank for Reconstruction and Development (IBRD), the International Finance Corporation (IFC), the International Development Association (IDA), and the Inter-American Development Bank (IDB). These, then, are the present multilateral sources of development aid, sources that in recent years have come to play an increasing role in promoting economic development. Each of them, therefore, deserves a brief mention.[15]

THE INTERNATIONAL BANK FOR RECONSTRUCTION AND DEVELOPMENT (IBRD)

Created at the Bretton Woods Conference, the IBRD, usually called the World Bank, began operations in 1946 and granted its first loan in 1947. Thus, the World Bank is, with the exception of its twin, the IMF, the oldest *international* financial institution of the post–World War II era. Moreover, its continuous record of operation in the field of development assistance exceeds that of almost any other aid-giving organization, national or international. Interestingly enough, the World Bank was originally designed to help in the financing of postwar economic reconstruction rather than to help extend aid to developing nations. In fact, the bulk of its loans before 1950 were earmarked for reconstruction projects in European countries. But since then, the World Bank's loans have been largely for economic development, and most of the recipients have been non-European countries.

[15] Mention should also be made of the most recently established multilateral source of development aid—the Asian Development Bank. Set up in late November, 1966, and capitalized at $1 billion, the ADB, with headquarters in Tokyo, is intended to serve the development finance needs of Southeast Asia.

The World Bank's authorized capital had been originally set at $10 billion, to be subscribed by its member countries. Each member paid in 20 per cent of its subscription (2 per cent in gold or dollars and 18 per cent in its own currency), the remaining 80 per cent being subject to call if needed to meet the bank's obligations. In 1959, the authorized capital was increased to $21 billion; and as of June, 1964, subscriptions amounted to $21.2 billion, of which the United States share is $6.35 billion.[16] Its capital stock, however, represents only a small source of its loanable funds. The bulk of its lending resources are derived from borrowing in the world's capital markets by issuing its own bonds. These bonds, it might be noted, are guaranteed by the governments in whose national currencies a particular issue of bonds is denominated.

Yet the very fact that the World Bank raises most of its lending funds in private money markets, and must pay for them according to prevailing interest rates, is a drawback insofar as the underdeveloped countries (the major borrowers of these funds) are concerned. For since the World Bank must eventually redeem its outstanding obligations, its loan portfolio must be geared to conventional banking principles, which in turn impose certain limitations on the types of loans it can grant. Thus, any World Bank loan is repayable in the currency in which it was made, or in the currency used by the bank to acquire the loan funds. Moreover, all loans carry a rate of interest that is largely determined by the prevailing rates in the capital markets where the bank sells its own bonds. In addition, there is a service charge (called a "commitment charge") of 3/8 per cent on undisbursed balances of authorized loans. Finally, the bulk of the bank's loans are made for specific projects and are normally tied to the direct foreign-exchange costs of the imports required by such projects.

On the other hand, World Bank loans are *not* tied to purchases in any particular country, and borrowers are free to spend loan proceeds wherever they think fit. Moreover, while most of its loans are made to governments, the bank may also lend to private investors in member countries—though all such loans require a guarantee by the government in each case. Also, the bank has made loans to development banks in underdeveloped countries, for the purpose of supplying them with funds to lend to private enterprises.

As of January, 1966, the World Bank's membership totaled 103

16 Mikesell, *op. cit.*, p. 216.

countries (the same as IMF's). Its total cumulative loan commitments amounted to about $9 billion, of which some $7 billion have been disbursed. And with the exception of $497 million classified as "reconstruction loans," the entire sum has been advanced for development financing. In addition, the World Bank has provided a variety of services to its less developed member countries, including advice on the preparation of projects, review of broad development plans, and suggestions concerning overall financial and economic policies. And, as noted earlier, the World Bank has been instrumental in organizing a number of consortia and consultative groups for the purpose of coordinating aid activities of various developed countries together with its own financial assistance to particular underdeveloped countries.

But despite its significant accomplishments, the World Bank's lending activities could not possibly meet the *variety* of financial needs of the developing and underdeveloped nations. Fully aware of this, the bank itself initiated action that led to the creation of two affiliated agencies whose range and type of activities could supplement its own operations. These agencies are the International Finance Corporation (IFC) and the International Development Association (IDA). Together with the IBRD itself, they constitute the World Bank Group.

THE INTERNATIONAL FINANCE CORPORATION (IFC)

The IFC was created in 1956 with a membership of some thirty countries and a total authorized capital of $100 million. By 1966 its membership had grown to eighty-two countries, all of whom, of course, are also members of the World Bank. Although the IFC is a separate entity, it is authorized to use the personnel, facilities, and services of the World Bank. The closeness of the affiliation is underscored by the fact that the two institutions (and the same is true of the IDA) have the same president and the same board of directors.

The main purpose of the IFC is to promote and encourage the growth of private enterprise in underdeveloped countries. Its loans are made exclusively to private firms, and do not require government guarantee. The loans are mainly long-term, and, with few exceptions, are repayable in dollars. Interest rates on IFC loans have varied from 5 to 8 per cent;

but unlike the World Bank, the IFC does not have the same interest rates for all borrowers at any one time. Moreover, from 1961 on, the IFC has been permitted to invest in equity capital (i.e., purchase of securities) of private enterprises, and to underwrite new issues of capital shares. Since then, a substantial portion of IFC investment has taken the form of equities.[17] This kind of investment (equity shares) is usually sold by the IFC in the open market, once the enterprise in question has proven sufficiently developed to attract additional private investors.

The IFC does not engage in business activities of its own. Along with other private investors, it merely invests in promising enterprises, and leaves the actual management and operation of the enterprises to their local promoters or private foreign investors. Thus, although its own limited capital resources have not permitted the IFC to make a significant financial contribution to economic development in general, it has often served as a catalyst in stimulating the flow of private investment into projects in underdeveloped countries. Indeed, by encouraging other private investors to participate in its investments, the IFC "has operated so that for every IFC dollar invested, some three or four more dollars from private channels have flowed into its projects. And in [some] special cases, a relatively small IFC participation has induced a very large investment of private capital."[18]

THE INTERNATIONAL DEVELOPMENT ASSOCIATION (IDA)

The creation of IDA in 1960 reflected a recognition of the need for a source of development finance that would not be bound by the rigid requirements of conventional loans. Thus, although it is an affiliate of the World Bank and is administered by its staff, the IDA extends financial assistance that is markedly different from that disbursed either by the IBRD or the IFC.

Indeed, as financial institutions go, the IDA is unique in development finance. For although it is a lending, rather than a grant-giving, institu-

---

[17] As of June, 1964, total loans and equities held by the IFC were $59.9 million, of which $17.8 million constituted equity investments. *Ibid.*, p. 218.

[18] IBRD, *The World Bank, IFC, and IDA. Policies and Operations* (Washington, D.C.: April, 1962), p. 102.

tion, most of its loans are made for a period of fifty years, and (apart from an annual ¾ per cent service charge) carry no interest rate! To be sure, IDA's loans must be made for specific projects, and these are expected to meet the same technical and economic standards of the IBRD itself. But the IDA can make, and has indeed made, loans for projects that would not ordinarily be eligible for IBRD assistance (e.g., housing projects, health and sanitation).

Terms are lenient because, unlike the World Bank, the IDA does not borrow its loanable funds in private money markets. Its financial resources are derived entirely from the contributions of its member governments (which numbered some ninety-six at the beginning of 1966); these take the form of capital subscriptions.[19] As of June, 1964, total subscriptions amounted to $987 million, of which $754 million were in convertible currencies. An additional $750 million in convertible currencies (including $312 million to be provided by the United States) is expected to become available during the fiscal years 1966–1968.[20] Against its existing resources, the IDA (as of June, 1966) has committed a cumulative total of some $1,300 million in loans.[21]

The ability of IDA to expand its operations in response to the increasing need for them depends on the willingness of its members to augment its resources through additional contributions. But inasmuch as the bulk of these contributions would have to come from the advanced nations, it would ultimately be up to them to decide whether IDA could keep expanding. One cause for concern in this connection is the possibility—in fact, the probability—that the advanced nations would prefer to continue channeling most of their aid efforts through their own national institutions rather than through an agency such as IDA. Indeed, given the fact that political, as well as economic, considerations play a significant role in determining the foreign-aid policies of individual advanced countries, it is understandable that these countries should feel reluctant to transfer large sums of money to an international agency

---

[19] In 1964 the IDA also received some $50 million as a grant from the World Bank; this represented a portion of the bank's net annual income. It is therefore expected that a portion of the bank's net annual income will regularly be made available to IDA. See Mikesell, *op. cit.*, p. 69.

[20] *Ibid.*, pp. 219–220.

[21] See IBRD, *Facts about the World Bank and the International Development Association* (Washington, D.C.: 1966). (Mimeographed.)

about whose day-to-day operations they have little or no say. As long as this is the case, the future of IDA—and any other international agency whose resources are derived from voluntary contributions by the advanced countries—remains unpredictable.

THE INTER-AMERICAN DEVELOPMENT BANK (IDB)

The IDB, which was established in December, 1959, and began operations in 1960, is an *interregional* rather than an international institution. It was born of long and relentless effort by Latin American countries to secure a regional development bank that would be geared to their special problems and needs. Thus, although in terms of its resources and volume of lending, the IDB is second only to the World Bank as a multilateral source of development aid, its membership is restricted to members of the Organization of American States (OAS), and its assistance is limited to Latin American countries. Currently, the IDB's membership totals twenty countries including the United States.

The IDB has conducted three kinds of operations, corresponding to three types of resources at its disposal.[22]

1. Ordinary Capital Resources. These are derived from members' subscriptions. As of October, 1964, the total Authorized Ordinary Capital was $2.15 billion, of which $1.8 billion was actually subscribed to, and some $500 million actually paid in. (The paid-in portion consisted of 50 per cent in dollars and the remainder in members' own currencies.)

2. Fund for Special Operations. This was originally set at $219 million, of which the share of the United States was $150 million. In line with a decision made in 1965, the resources of this fund are to be increased to $900 million during 1965–1967; the major contributor, of course, is the United States.

3. Social Progress Trust Fund. This fund, whose resources totaled $525 million in 1964, was set up by the United States in 1961 as part of its Alliance for Progress program. The United States has been the sole contributor to this fund, which is administered by the IDB under a trust agreement with the United States. However, the Social Progress Trust

[22] All data pertaining to the IDB's resources and operations are based on information in Mikesell, *op. cit.*, pp. 71–81, 220–222.

Fund is soon scheduled to be abolished and its functions merged with the Fund for Special Operations.

Out of its Ordinary Capital Resources, most of which incidentally must be raised in private money markets, the IDB makes long-term loans for specific projects. These loans are repayable in the currency loaned (mostly dollars) and carry, on the average, a 6 per cent rate of interest. Loan maturities range from eight to twenty years, and loan proceeds may be spent anywhere in the world. While most loans are made to governments, they may also be made to private firms, with or without government guarantee. As of December, 1964, the IDB has authorized loans totaling $554 million out of its Ordinary Capital Resources.

Loans from the Fund for Special Operations can be granted either for directly productive, or for social overhead projects. These loans involve maturities of from seven to twenty-five years and carry interest rates varying from 2 to 4 per cent. Such loans, moreover, may be repayable in the borrower's currency rather than in the currency loaned. (By December, 1964, approximately $117 million in loans had been authorized.) Finally, loans from the Social Progress Trust Fund are made primarily for social overhead projects. They are repayable in the borrower's currency, carry interest rates of from 2 to 3 per cent, and range in maturity from thirteen to thirty years. Proceeds from these loans must be spent in the United States, but under special circumstances may be spent in other member countries of the IDB. Some $450 million in loans had been made from the Social Progress Trust Fund as of December, 1964.

All told, the IDB has authorized loans totaling about $1.2 billion during the first five years of its operation. In addition, the IDB has encouraged the formulation of development plans by members, and has provided technical assistance related to these plans. It has also initiated the formation of aid consortia and consultative groups relating to several Latin American countries. And it has actively promoted the cause of regional economic integration in Central and South America. Indeed, the IDB has in large measure fulfilled the hopes—if not the precise expectations—of its early proponents. Although it is not the only source of development aid for Latin American countries, it has certainly shown a keener interest in the region's problems and aspirations than any of the other three multilateral-aid institutions.

Conclusions: Aid, Trade, and Development

This impressive line-up of national and international public-aid agencies should not be taken as an index of the magnitude of aid that has actually been extended. When all is said and done, the total volume of foreign economic assistance that the developed countries have provided during the last five years, both directly and through multilateral agencies, has remained at a fairly constant annual level of about $6 billion.[23] This figure, it might be noted, represents less than 1/5 of one per cent of the combined gross national product of the DAC countries in 1965, and about 8/10 of one per cent of the gross national product of the United States in the same year. And even when private capital flows to the underdeveloped areas are added, the relative magnitude of development aid in the twentieth century is pitifully low compared to the (private) foreign investment of Britain alone in the latter part of the nineteenth century.[24] Nor has the absolute magnitude of public foreign aid even begun to approach the level of financial assistance that could be fruitfully used by the underdeveloped countries as a group. And although some underdeveloped countries have been making steady economic progress, the overall economic gap between the underdeveloped and developed countries is far from being narrowed—a clear indication that more financial *and* technical aid is needed.

Yet increased aid is not the only answer to the dilemma faced by today's underdeveloped countries. For as noted earlier in this chapter, one of the grave obstacles to the economic growth of these countries is the peculiar position they presently occupy within the network of world trade. Indeed, unless their current export earnings can be stabilized, and their prospects for expanding export earnings somehow brightened, the underdeveloped countries will have to continue to use restrictive trade measures to protect their balance-of-payments positions, and conserve their scant foreign-exchange reserves. In so doing, they would deny themselves the full benefits of international trade, and add to the

[23] See *Proposed Economic Assistance Programs FY 1967, op. cit.,* p. 12.

[24] At their peak, British capital outflows averaged some 6–7 per cent of the British gross national product. See D. Snider, *Introduction to International Economics* (Homewood, Ill.: Richard D. Irwin, 1958), p. 551.

pressures already placed on their economic resources by rapidly growing populations and by increasing demands for goods and services.

Whether the underdeveloped countries will be able to overcome their present foreign-trade problems depends largely on the kind of commercial policies pursued by the advanced nations. By reducing their tariffs and liberalizing or eliminating their import quotas, the advanced nations would greatly contribute to the expansion of the underdeveloped countries' exports. At the same time, renewed efforts ought to be made to find effective means of stabilizing the world markets for primary products. Surely the GATT has an opportunity, as well as a responsibility, to play a leading role in tackling these problems. By so doing, it would not only promote the cause of economic growth in the underdeveloped countries, but would also enhance the prospects for the emergence of a truly free multilateral network of trade, from which all countries could derive the benefits of international specialization.

PART VI

THE REGIONAL APPROACH
TO FREE TRADE

20

Regional Economic Integration: Methods and Issues

THUS FAR WE HAVE DEPICTED the struggle between protection and free trade in universal terms. That is to say, we have presented a picture of the international economy as a whole, moving from one phase of commercial policy to another. And in describing recent efforts to remove trade barriers, we have concentrated on those whose main goal is the establishment of a *universal* system of free trade, in which multilateral trading relations could flourish on a world-wide basis.

Yet one of the most striking features of the post-World War II period has been the emphasis on a *regional* approach to trade liberalization and economic cooperation. The formation of the OEEC as well as the establishment of the European Coal and Steel Community (ECSC), the European Economic Community (EEC), the European Free Trade Association (EFTA), and, more recently, the Latin American Free Trade Association (LAFTA) and the Central American Common Market (CACM) —all these are manifestations of this trend. And, as we will see in Chapter 22, projects for regional economic cooperation are currently under consideration in other parts of the world as well.

It would be incorrect to assume, however, that the apparent popularity of regional economic blocs is due entirely to economic considerations. In fact, much of the enthusiasm about current economic integration efforts arises from political and strategic factors. Still, it is *economic* reasoning that provides the core of the argument for the regional removal of trade barriers. This argument, in turn, stems from the realization that universal free trade, though it may be economically desirable, is an ideal that cannot be fully attained in the foreseeable future.

That universal free trade is an ideal cannot be doubted. But whether the formation of closely integrated regional economic units represents progress toward its attainment is a question that has been the subject of many debates. Indeed, the fear has often been expressed that the division of the world into economic blocs would constitute a step away from freer multilateral trade, rather than a step toward it. While the question has no simple and clear-cut answers, it nevertheless suggests several issues that must be considered if a meaningful evaluation of any integration project is to be attempted. One of these issues concerns the very meaning of the term "integration," or, more precisely, the forms that regional integration can and/or should take.

Methods and Forms of Regional Integration

Regional integration is accomplished through the removal, by two or several countries mutually, of barriers to the flow of economic activities across their national frontiers—barriers such as tariffs, quotas, exchange controls, and immigration restrictions. But which of these barriers are to be removed, and to what extent, are matters left to the discretion of the participating countries. Their decision will determine in each case how closely their economies are brought together, and hence what form the particular integration project takes.

Generally speaking, four types (representing varying degrees) of regional economic arrangements can be distinguished: free-trade area, customs union, common market, and economic union. The least demanding of these is the free-trade area, an arrangement that removes barriers that inhibit trade between the participating countries, but retains for them independence in dealing with nonparticipating nations. Thus, while committing themselves to free trade vis-à-vis each other, the individual members of a free-trade area may pursue either liberal or restrictive commercial policies when it comes to their trade with non-members. In any event, the formation of a free-trade area requires little cooperation in matters that do not relate directly to the reduction of barriers on intra-area trade.

A somewhat greater degree of economic (and political) cooperation is exemplified by a customs union. In this case, the participating nations agree not only to eliminate restrictions on their mutual trade, but to pursue a common commercial policy vis-à-vis the rest of the world. Hence, the formation of a customs union involves the establishment of a single external tariff, to be levied on goods entering the union area, and second, the creation of a central agency to collect and distribute duty receipts. Moreover, the members of a customs union must agree to act as one unit in negotiating tariff and trade agreements with nonmember nations. Finally, the creation of a customs union implies at least some degree of coordination in its members' national economic policies.

If, in addition to the removal of trade barriers, the members of a customs union provide for the free flows of factors of production, the resulting arrangement is referred to as a common market. Indeed, as the term suggests, a common market constitutes a unified market area throughout which goods and services, as well as labor and capital, can move freely across national borders. As such, the common market represents a more closely knit integration scheme than the customs union, and consequently entails a higher level of cooperation.

The ultimate in regional economic integration, however, is represented by the economic union, or economic community. For although its members may still constitute separate political entities, an economic union implies an almost complete unification of economic institutions throughout the union area. Thus, it usually involves the setting up of *supra*national agencies whose decisions are binding on the union members, and whose powers may supersede, in part or in whole, those of national decision-making authorities. But even where institutional unification is less than complete, the satisfactory operation of an economic union demands close coordination and harmonization of its members' domestic economic and social policies.

The need for such coordination is easy to appreciate if we remember that removal of trade barriers by previously protected national economies increases their interdependence, and makes each of them more susceptible to cyclical economic fluctuations originating abroad. This is particularly true in the case of closely integrated regional blocs whose members open their respective economies to increased flows of intragroup trade and, in addition, permit the free movement of labor and capital between them. Under these circumstances, interdependence is likely to increase the danger of economic fluctuations, transmitted from one union member to another, and thereby undermine the successful operation of the union as a whole. Hence, the higher the degree of integration, the greater the need for the coordination of national policies designed to combat recession, prevent excessive inflation, and facilitate balance-of-payments adjustments. In carrying out such policies jointly, the members of a common market or an economic union may well find it necessary to create central institutions that are endowed with some supranational powers.

The Customs Union Issue

Of all forms of economic integration, the customs union has attracted the greatest attention in theoretical literature. This is not surprising, for the attraction can be easily explained on analytical and historical grounds.

Unlike a free-trade area, a customs union represents a *unified* tariff area instead of several independent tariff areas. Hence, it offers a more convenient model than the free-trade area for analyzing the beneficial as well as harmful effects of economic regionalism. Moreover, if regional free trade is to be judged primarily in terms of its effects on the movement of goods and services, rather than on factors of production, there is little need to concentrate on higher forms of integration—common markets or economic unions. In any event, both imply the prior existence of a customs union.

Highly relevant, too, is the fact that the customs union constitutes the earliest and most common type of economic regionalism in modern times. At least twenty customs unions have actually been formed during the past 150 years[1]—a record unmatched by any of the regional arrange-

[1] For a complete list, see United Nations, Dept. of Economic Affairs, *Customs Unions* (Lake Success, N.Y.: 1947), p. 1.

ments that were described in the preceding section. This predominance alone helps to explain why most of the inquiries into the nature and problems of regional economic integration have centered on the customs union issue.

EARLY VIEWS

Early discussions generally favored customs unions. "As a rule," wrote Professor J. Viner in 1931, "customs unions probably constitute a step toward freer trade "[2] Another leading economist went a step further, stating that "from an economic standpoint, based on free trade reasoning, customs unions are to be wholeheartedly welcomed."[3] These endorsements, however, were more a product of the times than of a careful and detailed analysis. During the 1930's, a period of extreme protectionism, customs unions were considered within the context of a broader question—how best to liberalize trade; and the merits of customs unions were judged largely on the basis of comparisons with other means of protection. Judgment in their favor was based on a choice, not between free world trade and customs unions, but between the latter and preferential reductions of duties. Such comparisons persisted, in fact, into the early 1940's. Regimes of preferential duties were regarded as "decidedly undesirable, both from a selfish economic point of view of the countries concerned and because they contain a serious threat of discrimination."[4] In contrast, the economic justification for the formation of customs unions was considered to be "identical with the old classical arguments for free trade."[5]

Here lies a curious paradox. It is true, on the one hand, that the replacement of separate national economies by a regional free-market area entails advantages that differ in degree only from those associated with universal free trade (e.g., opportunities for specialization, mass production, and so on). On the other hand, by eliminating tariffs

---

[2] J. Viner, "The Most-Favored-Nation Clause," in *International Economics* (Glencoe, Ill.: The Free Press, 1951), p. 102.

[3] G. Haberler, *The Theory of International Trade: With Its Application to Commercial Policy* (London: Hodge, 1950), p. 390.

[4] G. Haberler, "The Political Economy of Regional or Continental Blocs," in S. E. Harris (ed.), *Postwar Economic Problems* (New York: McGraw-Hill, 1943), p. 344.

[5] *Ibid.*, p. 330.

(and other restrictions) on their mutual trade while surrounding themselves by a common tariff wall, the members of a customs union practice the *highest* form of discrimination against the rest of the world. Thus, by definition, customs unions contain a much greater threat of discrimination than selective preferential arrangements; on this score, one might well question the logic of endorsing them while rejecting selective preferential arrangements.

How, then, can the case for or against customs unions be established? Actually, neither the virtues nor the drawbacks of economic regionalism are readily ascertainable or predictable. It cannot be argued conclusively that all customs unions will prove beneficial and that therefore regional integration is always desirable. But neither should possible adverse effects, due to discrimination, serve to condemn them completely. The results of regional tariff removals will vary from case to case; only through a careful analysis of each existing or proposed project can its probable consequences be assessed. Such an analysis, however, requires a set of valid criteria that can be applied generally. It is the task of theory to furnish these criteria.

TRADE CREATION AND TRADE DIVERSION

Within the familiar framework of static analysis,[6] integration is judged by its effects on resource allocation. More specifically, the question is whether the regional removal of trade barriers—accompanied by the erection of a common external tariff wall—would lead to a more—or less—efficient use of resources in the participating nations.[7]

Improvement in efficiency can be realized whenever a union effects the replacement of high-cost industries, operating behind tariff protection, with lower-cost sources of supply. For in this case, resources that were previously employed in protected industries can be channeled into more efficient lines of production; and consumers stand to gain from lower-priced goods. Not so, however, if the union merely enables high-cost industries in some member states to capture markets that were

[6] You may recall that the major assumptions of static analysis are: (1) a given supply function of productive factors, (2) a given state of technology, and (3) a given market structure.

[7] An equally important question—i.e., the effects of regional integration on efficiency of resources throughout the world—will be discussed later in the chapter.

formerly supplied by lower-cost producers outside the area. Inefficient production has been encouraged, not displaced, in this instance.

A seemingly clear-cut criterion suggests itself: A union may result either in *trade creation*, brought about by the substitution of low-cost imports for a previously protected high-cost domestic supply; or in *trade diversion*, representing a shift from a lower-cost outside source of imports to a higher-cost source within the union itself. Newly created trade leads to economic gains while diverted trade represents a loss. Depending on which of these outcomes predominates, the union is judged as desirable or not.

With this criterion in mind, consider a case involving three countries (A, B, and C), two of which (A and B) have decided to form a customs union. Suppose that before the formation of the union, country A levied an ad valorem tariff of 100 per cent on imports of steel from all sources. Suppose further that steel is produced in the three countries, its cost per ton being $200 in A, $120 in B, and $110 in C. The tariff imposed by A enables its inefficient domestic steel industry to supply consumers at a lower price than they would have to pay for imported steel from either C or B. For with the tariff, the price in A of B-steel would be $240 per ton, and of C-steel, $220 (as compared with a price of $200 for domestically produced steel). Once the union is formed and steel imports from B are tariff free, the price of B-steel will drop from $240 to $120 per ton, and A's consumers will shift their purchases from A's domestic producers to B's producers. The union has thus led to the creation of new international trade, and this clearly represents an improvement of economic efficiency.

The same union, however, may also cause undesirable consequences. Consider the following possibility. Before the union was formed, A may have levied a tariff of 50 per cent on imports of bicycles. The cost of producing a bicycle is $20 in B and $16 in C. (Assume that A produces none.) With the tariff, the price in A of a B-bicycle was $30, and a C-bicycle, $24; A's consumers imported bicycles from C. Once the tariff on B-bicycles is removed, their price in A drops to $20, and imports from B now replace C-bicycles (the import of which is still subject to tariff). Trade in bicycles has merely been diverted—from a lower-cost to a higher-cost source—and economic efficiency has suffered a loss.

To be sure, any union almost certainly involves elements of both trade diversion and trade creation. Therefore, the losses due to the former must be balanced against the gains due to the latter before the net outcome can be evaluated. It would be wrong, however, to judge a union simply by measuring the total value of newly created trade and the total value of diverted trade. For if the crucial test of economic efficiency lies in changes of per-unit costs, the total figures may not reveal them. Hence, one must also consider the extent to which costs have been raised on each unit of the diverted trade, and the extent to which they have been lowered on each unit of the newly created trade. In our example, the rise in cost on each unit of the diverted bicycle trade amounts to 25 per cent, but the cost saved on each unit of the newly created steel trade is 40 per cent. On balance, therefore, the union could still result in cost savings (i.e., greater efficiency), even though the value of trade diversion may exceed the value of trade creation.

Accordingly, the criterion suggested above must now be modified as follows: To evaluate the union's effects on efficiency, it is necessary to multiply the differences between production costs at the various sources of supply by the quantities of the goods traded; and then compare the resulting cost changes associated with trade creation and trade diversion.

Using the above cost figures, consider country A and assume that 1 million tons of steel, previously supplied domestically, are now imported from B, while 10 million bicycles formerly imported from C are now supplied by B. The cost differential between A-steel and B-steel is $80 per ton, and that between C-bicycles and B-bicycles is $4. Total cost savings on steel production are $80 million, whereas the total increase in the cost of bicycles is $40 million. Thus the union has effected a net saving in cost of $40 million, despite the fact that the total value of trade creation— $120 million—is smaller than the total value of trade diversion—$200 million.

CONSUMPTION EFFECTS AND WELFARE

Thus far it has been assumed that shifts from one source of supply to another involve no quantitative changes in the patterns of consumption. That is to say, the same quantity of a particular commodity is demanded before and after the formation of the union—the only difference being the source from which it is obtained. Hence, a union has been judged solely on the basis of *productive efficiency* (i.e., movements of costs).

The case for integration may be strengthened if another factor is brought into the picture: the effects of a union on consumption. It is possible—in fact, highly probable—that a reduction in the price of imported goods, following the removal of tariffs, will induce consumers to demand greater quantities than before. And this rise in consumption implies, *ceteris paribus*, an increase in economic welfare.

Consider, once again, the above example. At the price of $24 per unit, A's consumers imported 10 million bicycles from country C. Following the formation of a union with B, the price falls to $20, and unless the demand for bicycles is perfectly inelastic, A's consumers will now purchase *more* than 10 million bicycles. How much more will depend on actual demand conditions. Yet any increase in quantity purchased signifies a rise in welfare for which the union must be given credit.

To be sure, the final outcome will depend on how much of this additional demand can be supplied by country B, and at what price. The gain would be reduced if B's producers are unable to supply all of the additional quantity demanded, or can do so only at increasing cost (leading to a higher price). Worse still, if a comparison between C and B reveals that the former could have met all of the extra demands without increasing costs, whereas the latter cannot, the union has compounded the injury. Such possibilities, however, do not alter the main point of the argument—that regional integration must be judged by its effects on *consumption* as well as on production. Nor can it be denied that an importing member of a customs union may experience a gain in welfare even if trade diversion has occurred.

DYNAMIC ASPECTS OF INTEGRATION

The criteria provided by static analysis are necessarily confined to the short-run consequences of tariff removal. Integration, however, is expected to exert a far greater influence through its impact on economic growth. It is *dynamic* forces, unleashed by integration, that may contribute to an increase in productivity and thereby accelerate the rate of economic growth. Hence, no evaluation of integration can be complete without consideration of its dynamic aspects.

A qualification is in order. Dynamic processes do not permit accurate predictions, much less exact measurements. For such processes simultaneously affect and are affected by each other. But if the exact interactions that lead to growth cannot be measured, one can nevertheless identify the so-called dynamic effects of integration and assess their role in promoting productivity.

ECONOMIES OF SCALE   An increase in productivity implies a reduction in per-unit cost; and a well-known economic principle suggests that a close functional relationship exists between costs of production and the size of output: Costs fall (i.e., productivity rises) as production expands. Thus the term "economies of scale" refers to cost savings due to the greater efficiency of large-scale operation. Cost savings, however, may be realized either from expansion of the individual firm's output, or from expansion of the industry and/or other industries. Accordingly, a distinction is usually made between "internal" and "external" economies, indicating the source from which the gain to efficiency arose.

Internal economies. A firm's output is likely to depend on the size of the market for its product. The output that a small market can absorb may be smaller than the output that would enable the firm (or firms in an industry) to expand its scale of operation and realize cost savings. An industry where internal economies can be realized requires a market large enough to justify the production of the so-called optimum output—the level of production at which costs are minimized.[8] There would be no incentive to expand production if the optimum output of a single firm producing, say, automobiles was considered to be 500,000 cars per year, while the entire national market was capable of absorbing only 200,000 cars. But the creation of a larger market, *through regional integration,* may open the door to a full exploitation of large-scale internal economies.

It is by no means certain, however, that the relation between size and productivity applies to all lines of production. Nor can it be assumed that the mere creation of a regional market would automatically lead to increased productivity, even where such relationships do exist. It is quite possible that some industries in member nations had already achieved the optimum scale of production before integration took place. In other cases,

---

[8] Under pure competition, of course, there will be a tendency to produce at the optimum level; but pure competition is the exception, not the rule, in real life.

there may be neither the incentive nor the ability to expand operations and lower costs, despite enlargement of the market. The extent of the benefits of large-scale production depends, therefore, not so much on the act of integration itself as on circumstances in the member countries. And the essential question, with respect to any integration scheme, is: Do existing conditions offer opportunities for reaping the advantages of large-scale economies, once the market is enlarged?

External economies. Technological improvements, leading to cost reduction, are often transmitted from one firm or industry to another. When, due to interaction with other firms in the same industry (or in other industries), an individual firm experiences a rise in its own productivity, the source of gain is appropriately termed "external economies." An expansion of steel output may thus lead to a reduction in the cost of producing automobiles. Or a technical innovation in one firm producing steel may increase productivity throughout the steel industry. But the important question, once again, is whether integration stimulates external economies.

Enlargement of the market may indeed enable some industries to expand production and thereby lower costs. And the closer the interaction between industries, the greater the chances for these cost savings to be shared. Moreover, once trade barriers are removed, industries in different countries may come into closer contact with each other, and technological knowledge in one country may be transmitted to, and thus shared with another. Last but not least, industries that could not previously be supported may make their appearance, and favorably affect the operation of existing industries.

CHANGES OF MARKET STRUCTURE   Where the incentive to innovate and/or expand operations is lacking, integration in itself cannot be expected to increase productivity. And the presence or absence of such incentives depends largely on the nature of the market within which producers operate. Where, for one reason or another, the market is noncompetitive, the firm has little motive to expand; for it can enjoy high profit margins even if its costs are higher than they might otherwise be. Moreover, expansion may involve encroachment on the market share of a fellow firm, which might therefore retaliate and disturb the status quo throughout the industry.

Not so, however, if the market is highly competitive—that is, if there are producers who are able and willing to encroach on their competitors' share of it. Under these circumstances, the widening of the market may well result in exploitation of large-scale economies. Hence, if economies of scale are to be realized, the market must be competitive or such that integration will render it more competitive.

Here lies one of the major potential contributions of integration : increasing competitiveness in the market. A previously protected domestic market, characterized by producers with a live-and-let-live attitude, will become more competitive when exposed to producers in other member countries. Increased competition will put at least some pressure on existing producers to make innovations and lower their costs. At the same time, the disappearance of inefficient producers will enable those who remain to capture larger shares of the market and expand their operation.

Another obstacle to mass production and competition lies in consumer preference for differentiated products. Within a small market, such preferences enable inefficient producers to remain in operation. Yet the replacement of small national markets by a large free-market area can make possible large-scale production of different brand-name goods. More important, the interaction between consumers of different countries may bring about fundamental changes in consumption patterns, leading to a greater demand for mass-produced goods, and creating new opportunities for efficient production.

MISCELLANEOUS DYNAMIC EFFECTS   Other by-products of integration deserve at least some mention, although the extent of their influence is difficult to foresee.

Of major significance is the possibility that investment activities will be increased throughout a union area. This would be due in part to enlargement of the market and subsequent opportunities for large-scale production. Investment may also be stimulated, however, because removal of trade restrictions would do away with uncertainties that investors in member countries faced before. And where investment was previously limited because of a lack of funds, it may now be made possible, due to rising levels of incomes that would encourage a greater volume of savings.

Important benefits may accrue to member countries if provisions for the free movement of labor and/or capital are specifically included in an integration plan. Although such provisions are not a part of customs-union or free-trade-area arrangements, it is reasonable to expect that the removal of trade restrictions—and especially payment restrictions—between member countries would make intra-area flows of capital possible. Funds may thus find their way to capital-poor regions that offer profitable investment opportunities. Movements of labor, on the other hand, are much less likely to occur in the absence of specific provisions.

The justification for free movement of factors of production roots, of course, on a familiar theoretical principle. This principle states that the total output of a community can increase, even with the same supply of resources, if factors move from areas where their marginal productivity is low to areas where it is high. However, once marginal productivities have been equalized in different areas, no further gain from factor movements is possible. While this is, strictly speaking, a static principle, it has dynamic implications. For a rise in output, following factor movements, implies a rise in income, which in turn may stimulate additional investment leading to a further rise in output and income. And so on. Thus the original movement of factors may give rise to a chain reaction that would continue long after marginal productivities have been equalized and the factor movement itself has come to an end.[9]

THE IMPACT OF INTEGRATION
ON NONPARTICIPANTS

Theory, as well as common sense, suggests that formation of a union will affect both participating and nonparticipating nations. This would not be the case only if the countries that formed the union had not previously traded with any outside country. In reality this is unlikely; and since a customs union represents the highest form of trade discrimination, it is bound to cause changes in pre-existing trade patterns. Therefore, while a union may, on the whole, prove beneficial to the participants, its effect on nonmembers will depend on the extent and nature of these changes.

[9] This is not to suggest, however, that the process of expansion cannot eventually come to an end, or be reversed.

The confirmed free trader would not endorse a union unless it implied a gain for its members *and* the world at large. But how can the overall outcome be predicted? Once again, static analysis suggests an answer: If a union leads to trade creation, the member countries benefit while outside countries are not harmed. Consequently, trade creation implies a *net* gain for the world as a whole. Should trade diversion predominate, both the union members and outside countries that have lost their export markets would suffer. Thus, depending on which outcome predominates, the union can be endorsed or condemned.

Yet this suggestion is open to question. In the first place, we now know that even where trade diversion occurs, a union may prove beneficial to one or more of its members; but outside countries may still be hurt through loss of their export outlets. Second, once a union is formed, exports from member countries that were previously destined for non-union customers may now be rerouted to union partners. In such cases, outside countries may be injured regardless of whether the union has resulted in overall trade creation or trade diversion!

Generally speaking, how much a union may benefit or injure third countries depends primarily on the extent of their economic relations with the union members, both prior to and after the formation of the union. This, in turn, is affected by (1) how high individual tariffs were prior to the union, (2) the level of the common external tariff, and (3) the commodity composition of trade among the union members (before integration), and between individual union members and outside countries.

A good case can be made, however, if the external impact of regional integration is judged in terms of its long-run effects on the union members themselves. For as dynamic processes begin to take hold, any short-run harmful effects of trade diversion may be more than offset by long-run benefits. Thus, a faster rate of economic growth within the union may stimulate a larger volume of imports from, and exports to, third countries. Second, technological improvements that lead to cost reductions in industries of union members may benefit industries elsewhere. Finally, the emergence of efficient industries within the union may increase competitiveness—and through it productive efficiency—in the world at large. Yet the realization of these and other potential benefits will depend on the extent of interaction between the union on the one hand, and third countries on the other.

Conclusions

Does the formation of regional economic blocs (such as customs unions) constitute a step toward, or away from, free trade? Or, to put it differently, do customs unions lead to an increase or a decrease in world economic efficiency? The foregoing discussion suggests that this question is more easily asked than answered. In short, it is impossible to pass judgment on integration in general. For depending on the circumstances in each case, as well as the policies adopted by the participants, unions may or may not lead to greater economic efficiency. In any event, the final outcome of a particular union cannot be predetermined.

Yet the *likelihood* of one outcome or another can be inferred to some extent from the characteristics of the economies involved. Hence, let us rephrase the above question. Instead of asking, Will integration lead to freer trade?, let us ask, Under what circumstances is it likely to do so? This makes it possible to conclude by suggesting that the case for a particular integration plan rests on the presence of certain features. These may be summarized as follows.

The formation of a customs union is more likely to have beneficial effects on world economic efficiency (1) the more competitive the structure of the participating economies, (2) the larger the size of the union, (3) the greater the proportions of world production, consumption, and trade that the union members command, (4) the higher the level of preunion tariffs in the individual union members, (5) the greater the degree of preunion economic relations between the participating countries, (6) the greater the difference in per-unit costs of the commodities actually produced in the participating countries prior to the union, (7) the greater the scope for economies of scale among union members, (8) the lower the level of the common external tariff maintained by the union, and (9) the more elastic the demand and supply conditions in the participating countries.

With these observations serving as a background, we will proceed to discuss present and potential schemes for regional economic integration.

21

European Economic Integration

U NLIKE ALL OTHER REGIONAL
economic blocs currently in operation, the European Economic Community (EEC) has been regarded by many as but the first step in the development and eventual establishment of a close *political* union in Western Europe. This view is understandable. For the movement toward European economic integration was born of political, as well as economic, expediency. Indeed, its chief proponents have never concealed their hope that an economically unified Europe would eliminate the age-old political conflicts that have repeatedly torn European countries apart. At the same time, they argue, economic integration would help to create an all-around stronger Europe that could hold her own in a world dominated by two giants—the United States and the Soviet Union. In the light of these sentiments, it is hardly surprising that the development of the EEC during the past ten years has been analyzed and interpreted in both economic and political terms.

Yet as it now stands, the EEC, commonly referred to as the European Common Market, is still largely an economic institution. As such, it merely represents a stage in a process of European economic cooperation that began shortly after the end of World War II and that featured other, though less comprehensive, regional economic schemes. Even today the EEC does not constitute the only economic grouping in Western Europe; for soon after its inception, another bloc—the European Free Trade Association (EFTA)—was formed. Hence, a meaningful appraisal of the present state of European economic integration cannot be confined to the EEC alone. Nor can we appreciate the EEC's own development without first taking a look at the events that preceded its formation.

Forerunners of the EEC

We have already called attention (Chapter 18) to the significance of the Marshall Plan and the OEEC in promoting inter-European cooperation in matters pertaining to commercial policy. We have also noted the contributions of the European Payments Union (EPU) to the re-establishment of a freely functioning inter-European monetary mechanism. But in addition to these early examples of European economic cooperation, two other developments more directly influenced the course of economic integration in Europe. These developments—the formation of the Benelux and the establishment of the European Coal and Steel Community (ECSC) were the true forerunners of the EEC.

The formation of the Benelux—the customs union consisting of Belgium, Luxembourg, and The Netherlands—had actually been agreed upon as early as 1944. During their wartime sojourn in London, the governments-in-exile of these three countries embarked upon a series of negotiations, the first round of which resulted in the signing (October, 1943) of a monetary agreement betwen the Belgian and Dutch governments. Although the agreement was essentially a bilateral payments agreement, some of its provisions reflected the two governments' desire to cooperate in other economic and financial matters as well. Moreover, the agreement did not preclude adherence to it of other countries, provided, of course, that both the Belgian and the Dutch governments agreed. Finally, and most significantly, the signatories bound themselves to enter any wider multilateral monetary arrangements only jointly, and by the joint decision of the two countries.

This agreement was followed, in September, 1944, by the signing of a convention to establish a customs union between Belgium, Luxembourg, and The Netherlands. The convention stated, however, that the ultimate intention of its signatories was to form a full economic union, and it provided for setting up several joint administrative institutions to facilitate the attainment of this goal. Those who signed the convention had hoped that its provisions would become operative as soon as possible after the liberation of the three countries from German occupation. But as it turned out, the convention was ratified by the legislatures of the countries concerned only during the latter part of 1947; and not until January 1, 1948, did its provisions go into force.

The next several years saw only slow progress toward the transformation of the Benelux into an economic union. There was, to be sure, a great deal of ministerial activity during that period, and a number of steps were taken to unify, or at least harmonize, the fiscal, monetary, and social policies of the member countries. But balance-of-payments considerations, on the one hand, and domestic economic problems, on the other, made it difficult for the Benelux countries to abolish all controls and regulations over economic activities, and to throw open their respective economies to their partners. In fact, it was not until 1954 that an important step toward economic union was taken. In June of that year, an agreement was reached to allow freedom of capital movements between the three countries. And it took almost two more years for the partners to approve a draft treaty dealing with free movement of workers between them. But by that time, another treaty had been in preparation; when it was finally signed, on March 25, 1957, the three Benelux countries, together with France, Italy, and West Germany, found themselves partners in the EEC.

In fact, the same six countries had already joined forces in an earlier cooperative venture. In April, 1951, they had signed a treaty establishing the European Coal and Steel Community (ECSC). This treaty provided for the formation of a common market between the signatories, covering their trade in coal, iron, and steel. As such, the establishment of the ECSC typified the *sectoral* (or functional) approach to economic integration—that is, the abolition of barriers to the movement of only certain commodities between the member countries. But as set up in the treaty, the ECSC was intended to be much more than a sectoral integration scheme. It was to constitute, in effect, the first supranational organization in Western Europe—an organization whose decision-making authority concerning the production of, and trade in, coal, iron, and steel was to transcend that of its member countries, and whose decisions were to be binding on them.

The significance of the ECSC as a force working toward the eventual economic unification of its members can be gauged from the agencies and institutions that were set up by its treaty. These included a High Authority (the executive body), a Common Assembly (the parliamentary body), a Court of Justice, and a Council of Ministers. The first three of these bodies were designed to serve as representative of the ECSC as a whole, functioning in complete independence from the six governments involved. The fourth—the Council of Ministers was to act as a bridge between the ECSC and its member countries; it was to coordinate and harmonize the work of the High Authority with the general economic policies of the individual member governments. Moreover, in order to assure the High Authority of financial independence, the treaty endowed it with the power to levy and collect an excise tax on coal and steel production within the ECSC, and to negotiate loans with foreign governments. Finally, the treaty provided that the High Authority would be responsible, not to individual member governments, but to the Common Assembly. Only the latter would have the power to review and pass on the actions of the High Authority; and should it disapprove of them, it could, by a vote of censure, force the resignation of the High Authority in a body.

Signed in April, 1951, the treaty was ratified by the parliaments of the six countries in June of the following year; shortly thereafter the institutions of the ECSC were set up in the city of Luxembourg. The actual establishment of the common market, however, proceeded in three stages: The common market for coal, iron ore, and scrap entered into force in February, 1953; it was followed in May, 1953, and in August, 1954, by the introduction of common markets for steel and special steels respectively. Thus, from August, 1954 on, these products could be traded among the ECSC members free of tariffs, quotas, and other restrictions, while their importation from outside sources was subject to a uniform tariff. But not until 1957 was another major objective of the treaty attained—the free movement of labor between the six countries. Only since September of that year have skilled colliery and steel workers been able to take jobs anywhere within the ECSC.

The ECSC has compiled an impressive record of accomplishments. It stimulated a substantial increase of trade in coal and steel among its six members, as well as between them and outside countries; it has contributed to a spectacular expansion of steel production within the Community and to a significant improvement in the living standards of coal and steel workers; its concern with general economic development led to the formulation of various plans for efficient use of resources and for the development of new sources of energy; and, most important, it helped to create the kind of atmosphere in which further progress toward economic integration could be made. Indeed, there can be little doubt that the very existence of the ECSC constituted the main springboard for subsequent action by its members. And, in fact, three years after the establishment of ECSC, they embarked upon a series of negotiations that led to the signing of the so-called Rome treaties, and the creation of the European Economic Community and the European Atomic Community.

The Rome Treaties and the Structure of EEC

The first step in the negotiation for the formation of EEC was taken in June, 1955. During a conference in Messina, the foreign ministers of the six ECSC countries set up a committee to study and recommend ways and means of creating a customs union and a common market between them, and of pooling their resources for the development of atomic power in Europe. A little less than two years later, the committee's recommendations having been submitted, two treaties were drafted. These provided for the creation of two institutions: a European Economic Community (EEC) and a European Atomic Community (Euratom). On March 25, 1957, these treaties were signed in Rome by the representatives of the six countries.

Of the two Rome treaties, the one establishing the EEC was by far the more significant. It gave the initial shape to the most ambitious economic project thus far undertaken by European countries in modern times. Yet it was only natural that the treaty establishing the EEC would borrow some of the institutional framework for the new organization from the treaty that had previously established the ECSC. Thus, as in the case of the ECSC, the EEC was to have a Council of Ministers, a Common Assembly, and a Court of Justice. In addition, however, the EEC was to include a Commission, an Economic and Social Committee, a Monetary Committee, a European Investment Bank, and a European Social Fund. Quite significantly, the Rome treaty provided that the Common Assembly would be the same for the ECSC, the EEC, and Euratom, and that the Court of Justice would serve both the ECSC and the EEC.

There were, however, some basic institutional differences between the two communities. Thus, the ECSC treaty had vested the main powers and responsibilities in the High Authority. But in the EEC, the Council of Ministers was responsible for insuring the achievement of treaty objectives, and was given the real decision-making power. Moreover, while the members of the High Authority were to exercise their functions in complete independence, the EEC Council of Ministers could not be quite as free to act. For in the first place, the council was to consist of ministers representing their governments, not the EEC at large. Second, most of the council's decisions required a weighted majority vote, with France, Germany, and Italy having more votes than the smaller Benelux countries. In effect, then, the Rome treaty allowed individual governments to exert much greater influence on EEC affairs than they could under the ECSC.[1] But at the same time, the treaty assigned to the commission (the administrative arm of the EEC) a much wider range of duties and responsibilities than had been entrusted to the High Authority.

This is hardly surprising, for the Rome treaty concerned itself with almost every conceivable aspect of economic policy that might be involved in the creation and effective operation of a true common market. Hence, the drafters of the treaty included in it many more provisions than had been specified in the ECSC treaty. But because agreement could not always be reached on every single point at the time of actual drafting, many of the provisions were merely statements of general principles. In these cases, the treaty left it up to the commission and the council to formulate and enforce the exact rules and regulations in specific instances.

---

[1] Moreover, on many matters the decisions of the EEC Council required unanimous agreement. Thus, even the small countries could influence various decisions by threatening to vote negatively on a particular issue.

The tremendous scope of the treaty is reflected in its major provisions. These may be summarized as follows:

1. The gradual abolition of tariffs and other barriers to trade among the members, and the adoption of a uniform tariff on imports from the rest of the world.
2. The elimination of restrictions on the movement of labor, capital, and business enterprises within the EEC.
3. The prohibition of cartel and other restrictive business practices.
4. The formulation of a common agricultural policy.
5. The formulation of a common transport policy.
6. The harmonization and coordination of fiscal, monetary, and social policies of the member states.
7. The formulation and pursuit of joint commercial policies vis-à-vis nonmember countries.

In addition, the treaty provided for an association of the EEC with the dependent overseas territories of some of its member states.[2] The purpose of the association was, in the words of the treaty, "to promote the economic and social development of the [overseas] territories and to establish close economic relations between them and the Community as a whole."[3] To demonstrate its good intentions in a more specific way, the treaty provided that "goods originating in the [overseas] territories shall, on importation into member states, benefit from total abolition of customs duties."[4] Moreover, the signatories agreed to establish a Development Fund for the purpose of extending financial help to the overseas territories. The Fund, to be administered by the commission, was to receive specific contributions from all member states (totaling some $580 million over a five-year period), and to disburse these funds to the various member states on behalf of their territories.

All in all, the Rome treaty embodied a far-reaching and comprehensive plan of regional economic integration among politically sovereign nations. And for this very reason, there were many who, in March, 1957, expressed strong doubts that the treaty would even be ratified, let alone implemented. However, subsequent events proved the skeptics wrong.

2 The member states involved were France, Belgium, The Netherlands, and Italy.
3 Article 131, the EEC treaty.
4 Article 133, the EEC treaty

Although today, ten years after it was signed, the Rome treaty is still not completely fulfilled, the development of the EEC during this period has been quite spectacular—as the next few pages will reveal.

EEC: *Past Accomplishments and Future Prospects*

With the exchange of parliamentary ratifications on January 1, 1958, the Rome treaties went into force; and exactly one year later to the day, the first mutual tariff reduction among the six participants took place. According to the treaty timetable, the elimination of tariffs on intra-EEC trade was to proceed in three stages, each covering a period of four years. The treaty also specified the actual amount of each tariff reduction to be made during each stage. Thus, by the end of the first stage (1958–1962), tariffs were to be reduced by at least 25 per cent from their 1957 levels; and by the end of the second stage they were to be 50 per cent lower than in 1957. Any remaining tariffs were to be completely removed by 1970.

Yet by January, 1962, the duties on intra-EEC trade in industrial products had actually been reduced by 40 per cent, and those on agricultural products by an average of 30 per cent.[5] In May, 1962, moreover, the EEC decided to speed up the timetable; and as of July 1, 1963, cumulative tariff reductions on industrial products amounted to 60 per cent. At the same time, rapid progress was being made to align the individual members' tariffs on imports from nonmember countries. Thus, in July, 1963—two and one-half years ahead of schedule—the second stage in the formation of a common external tariff was reached, bringing the six separate tariffs still closer to the agreed-upon EEC common external tariff. Encouraged by these achievements, the commission set January, 1967, as the target date for the elimination of all internal tariffs and for the complete formation of a common external tariff. Since that time, however, the commission has lowered its sights and revised its estimates, setting July 1, 1968, as the new target date.

While the common external tariff was being formed, the EEC offered to reduce many of its eventually-established duty rates by as much as 20 per cent. This offer formed the basis for several rounds of negotiations

[5] European Economic Community, *The First Stage of the Common Market* (Brussels: 1962), p. 17.

within the framework of GATT, during 1960–1962. And these negotiations resulted in an exchange of substantial tariff concessions, affecting a sizable amount of the trade between EEC and other members of GATT. More recently, the EEC has been involved in the so-called Kennedy Round of negotiations, which began in 1964 and was concluded in 1967.

As it moved rapidly toward the establishment of internal free trade and a common external tariff, the EEC scored several important achievements in other areas. Thus, its members have made steady, though at times painfully slow, progress toward the harmonization of their divergent agricultural policies and toward the creation of central market organizations for various agricultural products. Along similar lines, important steps have been taken to formulate a common transport policy and to coordinate the fiscal, monetary, and social policies of the six member states. Moreover, the commission has already laid down several rules and regulations concerning cartel activities, and its rulings in several cases have been upheld by the Court of Justice. Finally, the commission has been instrumental in urging the creation of an atmosphere conducive to the movement of workers within the EEC. And although there are still obstacles to free-labor mobility, substantial movements of workers have indeed occurred.

Another important development concerns the association of EEC with the overseas territories of some of its members. As provided in the Rome treaty, that association was to expire five years after the EEC went into force. Yet when the date of expiration drew near, the overseas territories, most of whom had in the meantime attained political independence, expressed a desire to continue the association. Accordingly, on July 20, 1963, a new Convention of Association was signed. It provided for the association of eighteen African states and Madagascar with EEC, along the same general lines provided for in the Rome treaty. It also provided for the extension, by EEC, of some $800 million in aid to the associated countries, over a five-year period. The convention, which was ratified in 1964, is to run until 1969, when it may be renegotiated. More recently (July, 1966), Nigeria—a member of the British Commonwealth —also signed an association agreement with the EEC, providing for a wide range of reciprocal trade concessions.

Nor have these been the only countries to become associated members of the EEC. In fact, as early as 1959 two European countries—Greece and Turkey—applied for association. And in 1961 and 1962, following the start of negotiations for Britain's entry into the EEC, the latter received membership applications from about a half-dozen other European nations. More will be said about this development in the next section. For the moment, we might note that thus far the only European countries formally associated with the EEC are Greece and Turkey.

Perhaps the most significant achievement of the EEC is reflected in its decision to merge the executive branches of the three European communities—EEC, Euratom, and ECSC—into one body, and to create a single council of ministers to determine policies for the three communities. This decision, which was formalized by a treaty signed on April 8, 1965, clearly demonstrates how far the six nations have traveled toward economic and political unification. For the merger of the High Authority, the EEC Commission, and the Euratom Commission is generally regarded as a prologue to the fusion of the three communities themselves. And, in the words of the EEC Commission's former president, Walter Hallstein, "the economic integration of the three Communities is an important part of the *political* integration of Europe."[6]

On July 1, 1967, the merger went into effect, resulting in the creation of a single commission which will henceforth serve as the administrative arm of the three European communities. The commission, moreover, was charged with the task of drafting a new treaty providing for the merger of the three communities themselves. But even when such a treaty is drafted and the hoped-for merger of the three communities is executed, the six countries will still have to overcome many obstacles before they can hope to achieve complete economic (not to mention political) unification. One obstacle may well lie in the kind of relationships to be developed between the EEC and other West European countries. And to appreciate the possible impact of such relationships on the future course of Europe's economic integration, we must briefly examine the development of another European economic bloc, the European Free Trade Association.

The European Free Trade Association (EFTA)

Although the European Free Trade Association (EFTA) was officially established with the signing of the Stockholm Convention, on November 20, 1959, its origins go back to July, 1956. At that time, some nine

[6] *Bulletin from the European Community* (May, 1965), p. 3. (Italics added)

months before the Rome treaties were signed, the Council of the OEEC established a Special Working Party, and instructed it to "study the possible forms and methods of association between the proposed customs union [of the six ECSC countries] and other members [of OEEC] not taking part therein."[7] As a possible method of association, the Working Party was to consider the creation of a free-trade area that would include the customs union of the "Six" and the other OEEC countries.

In January, 1957, the Working Party published its report. Its conclusions were clear and precise. It found that it was "technically possible to conceive a system which takes account of the characteristics of a free-trade area and which would insure the satisfactory operation of the latter."[8] These conclusions were reinforced a month later by a White Paper issued by the British government. While lending moral support to the negotiations being carried on by the six ECSC countries, the White Paper stated that "Her Majesty's government believes that it is fully practicable for the United Kingdom and many other OEEC countries to enter a Free Trade Area."[9]

But that was as far as Britain went during the winter of 1957. Nor had she accepted an earlier invitation, extended by the six ECSC countries, to join them in the negotiations for, and formation of, the EEC. Indeed, not until the EEC became a living reality did Britain finally act more concretely with respect to Europe's economic integration. In 1959, Britain—together with Austria, Denmark, Norway, Portugal, Sweden, and Switzerland—formed the European Free Trade Association, a free-trade area covering trade in manufactured products among the participants.[10]

The EFTA agreement, which was concluded in Stockholm in November, 1959, went into effect on May 3, 1960. Two months later its members undertook their first mutual tariff reduction; this amounted to 20 per cent. By December, 1962, tariffs on industrial products within the EFTA had been reduced to 50 per cent of their 1960 level; and at the end of 1966 they were completely eliminated. However, since the EFTA is a free-

---

[7] OEEC, *Report on the Possibility of Creating a Free Trade Area in Europe* (Paris: 1957), p. 7.

[8] *Ibid.*, p. 27.

[9] *A European Free Trade Area*, Comnd. 72 (February, 1957), p. 4.

[10] In June, 1961, Finland joined the EFTA as an Associated Member.

trade area, and not a customs union, it has no common external tariff. Hence, each member has remained free to fix the level of its tariff on imports from nonmember countries. Moreover, because the agreement covers only trade in manufactured goods, trade barriers that are applicable to agricultural products and fisheries still remain within the EFTA. Finally, although the EFTA can boast of a permanent headquarters in Geneva and several joint administrative and consultative agencies, it does not approach the degree of institutional unification that has developed within the EEC. And if the events of the past few years are indicative, it is quite possible that instead of developing closer economic unification among its present members, some may depart and join the EEC.

Indeed, the possibility of EFTA's diffusion was forcefully demonstrated less than two years after its inception. In August, 1961, two of its members, Britain and Denmark, made formal applications for negotiations with the EEC, with the aim of joining it.[11] In October of that year, separate preliminary negotiations began between them and the EEC. Within two months after the start of the negotiations, the EEC received similar applications for negotiations from Austria, Sweden, and Switzerland. In May, 1962, Norway also applied for membership in the EEC, and a month later Portugal did the same. Thus, in one year's time, every member of the EFTA turned its eyes toward the EEC. And although the breakdown of negotiations between Britain and the EEC, in January, 1963, brought these overtures to a halt, and seemed to revitalize the EFTA itself, the last two years have again witnessed a trend toward closer association of individual EFTA countries with the EEC.

The story of Britain's negotiations with the EEC is long and involved. Suffice to say that after sixteen months of hard bargaining and extended discussions, many complex problems seemed to be on the verge of solution, and the prospect of Britain's admission into the EEC appeared reasonably good. But then came two hectic weeks, beginning with General de Gaulle's famous press conference on January 14, 1963, and ending with a last-ditch effort by France's five EEC partners to overcome

[11] These applications were based on the provisions of the EEC treaty itself. Article 237 states that ''any European State may ask to join the Community.'' The same article also states, however, that the decision to admit new members requires a unanimous vote of the Council of Ministers.

French objections and keep the negotiations going. The effort failed, and on January 29, 1963, the EEC announced its inability to continue the negotiations; and they were broken off.

Some three and one-half years later, Britain decided to try her luck again. On May 2, 1967, Prime Minister Harold Wilson announced his government's decision to apply anew for membership in EEC; and on May 11, a formal application was submitted to the EEC Council of Ministers. Barely five days later, in the course of another famous press conference, General de Gaulle declared that, while he would not prejudge any forthcoming negotiations, he believed that "the obstacles to be overcome [in connection with Britain's application] are formidable." Thus, at the time of this writing, it is not quite clear what course of action France would choose to follow if and when negotiations between Britain and the EEC do resume. Nor is it clear what position the other members of EEC might take should France again attempt to block Britain's bid for entry.

What is clear, however, is that the collapse of the negotiations in 1963 threatened to undermine the very unity of the EEC itself, by causing an open rift between its members. And the possibility that the new approach by Britain (or any other European country) might again produce a serious split within the EEC, must be considered as a potential obstacle which the six EEC members would have to overcome before achieving economic and political unification. Moreover, even if one or several EFTA countries were unanimously endorsed by the EEC nations, their admission as full (or associate) members might actually slow down, rather than accelerate, progress toward complete economic union. For, strange as it may seem, the addition of new members might at first lessen the sense of cohesion that, despite several setbacks, has developed among the six original members of the EEC over the years. Without such cohesion, little progress can be made either in economic or political spheres. Thus, in the final analysis, an expanded EEC would probably require more time to be transformed into a complete economic union than today's EEC. And as for the EFTA, its prospects for further unification are even less predictable than those of the EEC.

An Integrated Europe—Myth or Reality?

As one observer put it, Western Europe now stands at sixes and sevens. On the one hand, there is the closely integrated EEC; on the other, the rather loosely integrated EFTA. Apart from these, various other organizations exist in Europe—some essentially economic in nature, others political—to which the members of both EEC and EFTA belong, along with non-European countries. And at times it seems as though this multiplicity of overlapping alliances hurts rather than helps the chance for political unity in Western Europe.

However, it cannot be denied that the EEC and the EFTA have created a tremendous expansion of free trade among European countries, and have contributed to a remarkable economic growth in Western Europe as a whole. Out of this economic progress has grown a strong sense of political—or, if you will, emotional—solidarity that had not existed in Europe before. And it is this "European" spirit that may one day transform the myth of an economically *and* politically integrated Europe into a living reality.

22

Regional Integration: A Possible
Tool for Economic Growth

VARIOUS SCHEMES FOR RE-
gional economic integration have been discussed in recent years by non-
European countries, and some proposed projects have already reached
varying stages of implementation. But although these schemes differ
as to the number and size of the countries involved, and as to the degree
of integration each entails, they share a common characteristic: All the
non-European regional economic groupings—whether they are in actual
operation or are still on the drawing board—involve countries that, with
one or two exceptions,[1] can be designated as underdeveloped (or developing) nations. In all these cases, therefore, regional integration is
regarded not only as a means of expanding intraregional trade, but also
(and this is far more important) as a possible contributor to economic
growth.

Indeed, regional economic integration has much to recommend it as
a growth-promoting force insofar as today's developing nations are
concerned. For one thing, the creation of large regional markets could

---

[1] One of these exceptions is the Free Trade Agreement, concluded between
Australia and New Zealand in 1965, which provides for the elimination of duties on
some 60 per cent of their mutual trade over an eight-year period. See IMF, *Seventeenth Annual Report* (Washington, D.C.: 1966), p. 10.

help to overcome one of the major obstacles to growth that under-developed countries face—the small size of their individual national markets. An expanded market area would, in turn, open up greater opportunities for specialization and large-scale methods of production in these countries, thus contributing to increases in productivity. At the same time, the enlargement of their markets can be expected to create additional opportunities for profitable investment, and may well stimulate a larger flow of private capital to the developing nations. Moreover, the formation of regional groups by underdeveloped countries could enable their members to pool their own resources for the purpose of financing basic development projects. In fact, joint development of regional projects—such as transportation and communication networks, sources of electric power, harbor facilities, and so forth—has two distinct advantages. First, the cost of these projects can be shared by several countries, none of which could afford to finance them alone; and second, the development and use of regional projects would eliminate the wastefulness that duplication of such projects involves; within each country these projects could not attain an optimum scale of operation. And finally, regional integration can permit underdeveloped countries to plan their industrial development so as to complement each other's activities, thereby making efficient use of the special endowments and skills available in each country.

Despite the apparent virtues of regional integration, it is far too early to predict how much of a contribution any of the existing (or potential) regional groups of underdeveloped countries can make to the economic growth of each of its members. All we can attempt here is to briefly describe these projects. Two regional groups—the Latin American Free Trade Association and the Central American Common Market—deserve special mention.

The Latin American Free Trade Association (LAFTA)

Efforts to form regional economic groups in Latin America have their beginnings in the early 1940's. In 1941, for example, a commercial treaty was signed by Argentina and Brazil, providing, among other things, for the progressive establishment of a free-trade system between

them and for the development of complementary industries.[2] Similar
bilateral treaties were concluded between Argentina and two other
countries—Chile and Paraguay—in 1943.[3] But it was not until the mid-
1950's that several Latin American nations, under the active leadership
of the United Nations Economic Commission for Latin America (ECLA),
began a long series of discussions aimed at the establishment of some
regional trade and payments arrangement. After four years of discussions and negotiations, a treaty was finally drafted providing for the
creation of a free-trade area. This treaty, which instituted the Latin
American Free Trade Association (LAFTA), was signed in Montevideo on
February 18, 1960, and became effective in July, 1961. Its original
signatories were Argentina, Brazil, Chile, Mexico, Paraguay, Peru, and
Uruguay. By November, 1961, two more countries, Colombia and Ecua-
dor, had joined LAFTA; and in December, 1965, Venezuela was accepted
as the tenth member of the group.[4]

The Montevideo treaty envisioned the creation of a free-trade area,
to be achieved through negotiated tariff reductions over a twelve-year
period from the date the treaty went into effect. It also sought to promote
the development of industrial complementarity, by urging its signatories
to negotiate agreements for the establishment of regionally integrated
industries. Third, although the treaty did not spell it out, it strongly and
hopefully hinted that the formation of LAFTA might lay the foundation
for a common market consisting of all the Latin-American republics.[5]

Interestingly, the treaty stipulates two distinct methods whereby
tariffs are to be gradually eliminated. First, each member country must
negotiate an annual "national schedule," designating the tariff cuts that
it would grant to other members. The weighted average of the duties on

---

[2] See J. Viner, *The Customs Union Issue* (New York: Carnegie Endowment for
International Peace, 1950), pp. 71–72. Under an agreement for complementary industries, one country trades off its right to produce a certain product in return for
an agreement to supply another product to the other country.

[3] *Ibid.*, p. 168.

[4] At this time, Bolivia is the only country that had been involved in the negotiations for LAFTA, but that has not as yet joined.

[5] This sentiment recently received a more concrete form. A declaration, issued
by the Presidents' Summit Conference at Punta del Este, Uruguay (April, 1967),
called for the creation of a Latin American common market, to be completed by
1985. It remains to be seen, however, whether this proposal will actually be carried out.

items in the national schedule must be reduced each year by at least 8 per cent of the weighted average of duties applicable to imports from non-members. What the treaty says, in effect, is that in any one year during the transitional period, the *difference* between the average duty rates applicable to intra-LAFTA imports and those applicable to imports from other countries, must be equal to 8 per cent multiplied by the number of years the treaty has been in force. Second, the treaty requires that all signatories agree to a "common schedule," listing the products entering intra-area trade, on which they collectively agree to eliminate duties. Once a product is placed in the common schedule it cannot be removed, and any tariff cuts are irrevocable.[6] The treaty also sets up a timetable for the gradual expansion of the common schedule. Thus, the common schedule must consist of products that, in terms of aggregate value, represent at least 25 per cent of total intra-LAFTA trade by the end of the first three years (following 1961), 50 per cent by the end of six years, 75 per cent by the end of nine years, and substantially all intra-area trade at the end of the twelfth year.

Together, the national schedule and the common schedule constitute the avenue along which the elimination of trade barriers and the establishment of the free-trade area are to proceed. How successful has been the journey toward this goal?

During its first few years, riding on a high wave of initial enthusiasm, LAFTA's accomplishments appeared to be quite impressive. At the first annual conference (1961), tariff concessions were granted on some 3,300 items, and during the second annual conference (1962), an additional 4,500 items received tariff cuts.[7] Moreover, the total value of intra-LAFTA trade, which had averaged some $725 million annually in 1958–1960, rose to $775 million in 1962 and to $950 million in 1963.[8] But in 1963, LAFTA began to face its first serious difficulties, due in large part to the reluctance of several member countries to grant substantial tariff

[6] However, placing a product in the common schedule does not necessarily mean an immediate change in the duty rate applied to it. It simply means that by the time the free-trade area is fully established, all duties on it would be abolished.

[7] See Chase Manhattan Bank, *Latin American Business Highlights* (First Quarter, 1966), p. 9.

[8] See M. Wionczek, "Latin American Free Trade Association," *International Conciliation No. 551* (New York: Carnegie Endowment for International Peace, January, 1965), p. 30.

concessions. Thus, only 650 items received tariff concessions at the third annual conference (1963), and a mere 300 items at the fourth conference (1964). At the same time, the treaty's escape-clause provisions were being increasingly used; under these provisions, previously granted concessions on national-schedule items may be withdrawn by countries suffering from balance-of-payments difficulties, or other short-term economic difficulties. And as for industrial complementarity, only a handful of agreements have been negotiated and approved by LAFTA's members since the treaty went into effect. Consequently, duplicate manufacturing facilities are still being constructed throughout the region, thus making it all the more difficult to achieve regional industrial integration as time goes on.

On the other hand, LAFTA can point to a number of achievements that reflect gradual acceptance by its members of a *regional* viewpoint. For example, several permanent administrative bodies and commissions have been created within LAFTA, charged with the task of planning regional programs. Another significant development was the signing of an agreement, in September, 1965, by the central banks of the LAFTA countries, establishing a multilateral-payments clearing system between them. Under this agreement, balances between the individual central banks are to be settled on a bimonthly basis and cleared through the Central Reserve Bank of Peru, which was designated as the agent for the group.[9] This agreement is expected, of course, to facilitate both trade and payment flows within the region, and represents an important step toward closer regional cooperation. Finally, during the fifth annual tariff-negotiating conference (1965), the number of items on which tariff concessions were granted rose to about 800, more than double the number of the previous year; and the member countries approved a decision to restrict the use of the treaty's escape-clause provisions in the future.

But despite these and other accomplishments, LAFTA's progress toward economic integration has been slow, and the rate of increase of intra-LAFTA trade, since 1963, rather moderate. This can be explained, in part, by the geographical obstacles that have traditionally impeded the flow of intraregional trade in South America, and also by the fact that many of the import requirements of the LAFTA countries cannot yet be supplied by producers within the region. Yet perhaps the major obstacle to a more rapid *regional* economic development lies in the basic atti-

9 See IMF, *op. cit.*, p. 9.

tudes—shared by both Latin American businesses and governments—toward free trade in general and LAFTA in particular. Indeed, some of LAFTA's own member countries still view the organization with considerable suspicion and skepticism, regarding it as a mechanism that enables competing products from other member countries to penetrate their own markets and undermine their own industrialization efforts. As long as this attitude prevails, LAFTA's progress in carrying out the objectives, and fulfilling the hopes, of the Montevideo treaty will necessarily be slow.

The Central American Common Market (CACM)

In comparison with LAFTA, the five-nation Central American Common Market (CACM) has been more successful in opening up its members' national markets to each other's products, and has shown much more vigor in pushing ahead with its regional integration plans. Indeed, although both LAFTA and the CACM are the same age, the progress of each stands in sharp contrast.

The CACM is a product of efforts that began in the early 1950's and that gathered momentum in 1958 and 1959. During these two years, five Central American countries—Costa Rica, El Salvador, Guatemala, Honduras, and Nicaragua—signed three separate agreements, all pertaining to the establishment of close mutual economic ties. The first two of these agreements—the Multilateral Treaty on Free Trade and Central American Integration, and the Agreement on the Regime for Central American Integration Industries—were signed in June, 1958. The former provided for the establishment of a customs union among the five countries; the latter was designed to promote within the area the expansion of existing industries and the development of new ones. In September, 1959, the same countries signed the Central American Agreement of Equalization of Import Duties and Charges, which constituted the first step toward setting up a uniform external tariff for all of them. These three agreements were incorporated, in 1960, into the General Treaty on Central American Economic Integration, which by 1962 had been signed and ratified by all five nations.[10]

[10] Costa Rica was the last to sign and ratify the General Treaty; it did so in 1962.

The General Treaty provided for the establishment of a common market within five years after going into effect, and for the creation of common administrative and policy-making institutions. Moreover, the signing of the treaty was accompanied by the signing of a separate convention for the creation of still another regional institution: the Central American Bank for Economic Integration (CABEI). This bank, which was designed to foster closer economic integration within the CACM by promoting and financing a well-balanced economic development for its members, was established in May, 1961. The CABEI has proved to be highly dedicated to its mission. As of the beginning of 1965, it had granted credits totaling over $26 million.

Within five years after the General Treaty had been signed, its provisions concerning trade liberalization had been nearly fulfilled. Thus, by 1965, some 95 per cent of the internal customs duties on products originating within the CACM had been eliminated, and the formation of a common external tariff had been almost completed.[11] During this period (1961–1965), intra-CACM trade rose at an average rate of over 30 per cent per year, and total CACM trade also registered significant increases. At the same time, rapid progress was made along several other lines. The CABEI has recently begun to settle the local accounts of the central banks of the five nations in the area's new accounting currency—the Centro-american peso—which is at par with the United States dollar.[12] Moreover, in 1965 a common customs code went into effect for all five CACM countries. And in the same year, a Central American Integration Fund was established to finance infrastructure projects (e.g., transportation and communications systems) for the entire region.[13]

There can be little doubt that the geographical proximity of the CACM countries—and the fact that, despite some differences, all five are roughly at the same stage of economic development—has contributed to the remarkable accomplishments of the CACM. Another contributing factor has been the general absence of deeply entrenched industrial interests in these countries, which might possibly have strongly opposed the removal of trade restrictions on intra-area trade in manufactures.

[11] See Chase Manhattan Bank, *Latin American Business Highlights* (Second Quarter, 1965), p. 4.

[12] *Ibid.*, p. 5.

[13] See IMF, *op. cit.*, p. 9.

Yet precisely because the principal economic activity of the CACM countries consists of the production and export of agricultural products—mainly coffee, bananas, and cotton—future progress toward economic integration largely depends on the ability of the CACM countries to reach agreement on such matters as the kind of industries to be developed and the location of regionally integrated manufacturing facilities. How successfully the CACM countries can tackle these problems ultimately depends on how much they have learned from their past experience with regional integration, and on the continuation of the cooperative spirit that has made that experience possible.

Other Integration Schemes[14]

In contrast to LAFTA and the CACM, most other non-European regional economic schemes involve countries that have only recently gained political independence, and that had belonged until then to one of two colonial empires. This is particularly true of the newly independent African nations. All of them, with the exception of the former Belgian Congo, are either former French or former British colonies; and most of them, moreover, have continued to maintain close ties with their respective mother countries. More significant still is the fact that, within each of these groups of former colonies, various economic ties exist—for example, similar monetary systems and common monetary arrangements, a large measure of free trading, and so on. These ties have linked their members together for many years. It is not surprising, therefore, that out of these circumstances several economic groupings have recently emerged in Africa.

In 1961, twelve former French colonies, known as the Brazzaville Group,[15] met at Dakar and formed *l'Organisation Afro-Malgache de Coopération Economique* (OAMCE). Although the main objective of this organization was to foster economic cooperation among its members, it

[14] This section draws heavily on the material presented in Chapter 7 of S. Dell, *Trade Blocs and Common Markets* (New York: Knopf, 1963).

[15] The members of the Brazzaville Group are Cameroon, Central African Republic, Chad, Congo (French), Dahomey, Gabon, Ivory Coast, Madagascar, Mauritania, Niger, Senegal, and Upper Volta.

did not constitute a formal integration project. But even before the existence of the OAMCE, its members had already formed two closely integrated economic groups. In June, 1959, seven countries, formerly of the French West African Federation (Dahomey, Ivory Coast, Mali, Mauritania, Niger, Senegal, Upper Volta), concluded an agreement for the immediate establishment of a customs union. And in December of the same year, Chad, Gabon, the Central African Republic, and the former French Congo established the Equatorial Customs Union.

However, while the customs union of the countries of the former French West African Federation soon ran into serious difficulties that impeded its progress, the Equatorial Customs Union has scored several successes in its few years of operation. In 1961, barely two years after its establishment, its member countries agreed to include the newly independent nation of Cameroon as an associate member. At the same time they began preparations for setting up a common external tariff and for the harmonization of their individual tax systems. And in December, 1964, they signed an agreement to replace their customs union with a Central African Economic and Customs Union. Although the new agreement, which became effective in January, 1966, retains the basic features of the Equatorial Customs Union, it provides for further measures of unification, including provisions for the free movement of labor within the union area.[16]

Other measures to further the cause of regional economic integration among African states, especially the former British colonies, have not been particularly successful. To be sure, there presently exists a so-called East African Common Market, consisting of Kenya, Tanzania, and Uganda. But its recent actions can only be interpreted as a step away from, rather than a step toward, closer economic unification. Nor has much been accomplished in this respect by other African groups that involve both former French and former British colonies. One such grouping, the so-called Monrovia Group (consisting of the Brazzaville Group and Liberia, Libya, Nigeria, Sierra Leone, Somalia, Togo, Tunisia, Ethiopia) proposed, in 1961, a program for the establishment of a common market and an economic development bank. About the same time, the Casablanca Group (Egypt, Ghana, Guinea, Mali, Morocco) called for a similar program for its members. As of this moment, these

[16] IMF, *op. cit.*, p. 10.

projects have not advanced beyond the planning stage, and it is highly doubtful that they will take concrete form in the near future.

We might briefly mention regional integration activities among the nations of Southeast Asia. At present there is not a single customs or economic union comprised of Asian countries. Moreover, the few proposals made thus far for closer economic ties do not seem to contemplate the establishment of economic unions in the formal sense of the term. Thus, the Association of Southeast Asia (ASA), which was established in 1961 by Malaya, the Philippines, and Thailand, claimed rather limited objectives: promotion of trade relations, exchange of technical information, the establishment of joint air and shipping lines, and joint efforts to stabilize the world prices of its countries' primary products. A more ambitious plan—the creation of a Greater Malaysia—envisions a merger of Malaya, Singapore, and British Borneo. But the political obstacles to such a venture are as great as the doubts concerning its economic virtues. In any event, little progress has been made in carrying out this particular project. Nor has another proposal, aiming at the creation of a Pacific Free Trade Area,[17] advanced beyond the stage of consideration and discussion.

Much the same can be said about the current state of economic regionalism in two other underdeveloped areas of the world—the Middle East and the West Indies. Although in both areas, plans for economic (and even political) unification have been frequently suggested, none has taken concrete and permanent form. Thus, the political union that had been formed between Egypt and Syria in the latter part of the 1950's (i.e., the United Arab Republic) proved to be short-lived; it was dissolved in 1961. And in the West Indies, a federation of the eleven Caribbean islands,[18] which had been created in 1958 by the British government, lost three of its members (Jamaica, Trinidad, and Tobago) when they attained their independence. As of this moment, the Arab countries of the Middle East are still discussing the possibility of a Middle Eastern economic union—excluding, of course, Israel. And in the West Indies, two members of the Caribbean federation—Antigua and

[17] To include Hong Kong, Japan, Australia, and New Zealand, as well as the members of the ASA.

[18] The federation originally consisted of Antigua, Barbados, Dominica, Grenada, Jamaica, Montserrat, St. Kitts, St. Lucia, St. Vincent, Trinidad, Tobago.

Barbados—have apparently decided to look elsewhere for regional economic association. Together with the newly independent British Guiana, they recently signed an agreement establishing a mutual free-trade area.[19]

Conclusions: Cooperation or Rivalry?

The emergence of regional economic groups, composed of underdeveloped countries, reflects more than a desire to reap the advantages of larger markets and joint development of basic projects. It also represents an attempt by some underdeveloped nations to secure for themselves a more solid position in dealing with the developed countries. Indeed, in the eyes of some observers, this consideration has been the decisive factor in the formation of many regional economic groupings. And this very consideration, according to the same observers, would continue to govern any future trend toward economic regionalism in the developing nations. This view is not wholly without logic or justification. Given their present foreign-trade problems (see Chapter 19), the underdeveloped countries may well look upon regional unification as a way to improve their external bargaining position, and as a weapon with which to apply pressure on the advanced countries. And there can be little doubt that the formation of the European Economic Community (EEC) in 1957 has only intensified this feeling, and hastened the conclusion of several regional economic agreements among underdeveloped nations.

Yet one can hardly welcome the possibility—let alone the probability —that the formation of regional blocs by underdeveloped countries has been, and will be, mainly influenced by noneconomic considerations. For if the true economic benefits of regional integration are forced to play second fiddle to political and strategic considerations, then a continued trend toward economic regionalism would constitute a disruptive rather than a unifying force in international trade relations. One can envision, for example, a situation in which new regional blocs would be formed, not in order to further the cause of free trade and rapid economic growth, but to offset the political or military advantages enjoyed by existing blocs. Under such circumstances, one would not expect the various regional

[19] IMF, *op. cit.*, p. 10.

blocs to pursue the kind of commercial policies under which international trade could expand and economic growth could be accelerated.

The possibility that this might actually come about raises serious questions that concern developed and underdeveloped countries alike. Underdeveloped countries must avoid what is obviously a great temptation—to form regional blocs for the purpose of political bargaining, regardless of whether such arrangements would yield substantial economic benefits. And the developed nations must do everything in their power to help the underdeveloped countries to resist this temptation. For only if it is based primarily on proper economic reasoning can the regional approach to free trade prove effective in bringing about a multilateral system of free trade, under which both developed and developing nations would experience rapid economic growth and continuously rising standards of living.

SELECTED
BIBLIOGRAPHY

Selected Bibliography

This bibliography is designed to provide a comprehensive, though by no means an exhaustive, guide to the literature of international economics. Some of the most important contributions to this literature are products of the 1930's and 1940's. Here, however, greater emphasis is placed on more recent contributions—those of the last fifteen years or so.

I. General Treatises, Texts, Monographs, and Essays

Angell, James W. *The Theory of International Prices: History, Criticism, and Restatement.* Cambridge, Mass.: Harvard University Press, 1926.

Baldwin, Robert E., *et al. Trade, Growth, and the Balance of Payments.* Chicago: Rand McNally, 1965.

Caves, Richard E. *Trade and Economic Structure.* Cambridge, Mass.: Harvard University Press, 1960.

Condliff, John B. *The Commerce of Nations.* New York: W. W. Norton, 1950.

Corden, W. M. *Recent Developments in the Theory of International Trade* (Special Papers in International Economics No. 7). Princeton: International Finance Section, Princeton University, 1965.

Ellsworth, Paul T. *The International Economy.* 3rd ed. New York: Macmillan, 1964.

Enke, Stephen, and Virgil Salera. *International Economics.* 3rd ed. Englewood Cliffs, N.J.: Prentice-Hall, 1957.

Gordon, Wendell C. *International Trade: Goods, People, and Ideas.* New York: Knopf, 1958.

Graham, Frank D. *The Theory of International Values.* Princeton: Princeton University Press, 1948.

Haberler, Gottfried. *A Survey of International Trade Theory* (Special Papers in International Economics No. 1). Princeton: International Finance Section, Princeton University, 1955, 2nd ed., 1961.

――――. *The Theory of International Trade: With Its Applications to Commercial Policy.* London: William Hodge, 1950.

Harris, Seymour E. *International and Interregional Economics.* New York: McGraw-Hill, 1957.

Harrod, Roy. *International Economics.* Chicago: University of Chicago Press, 1958.

Heilperin, Michael A. *The Trade of Nations.* New York: Knopf, 1947.

Hirschman, Albert O. *The Strategy of Economic Development.* New Haven: Yale University Press, 1958.

Johnson, Harry G. "Effects on Changes in Comparative Costs as Influenced by Technical Change," in R. Harrod and D. C. Hague (eds.), *International Trade Theory in a Developing World.* London: Macmillan, 1963.

――――. *International Trade and Economic Growth.* Cambridge, Mass.: Harvard University Press, 1958.

Kindleberger, Charles P. *Foreign Trade and the National Economy.* New Haven: Yale University Press, 1962.

――――. *International Economics.* 3rd ed. Homewood, Ill.: Richard D. Irwin, 1963.

Marsh, Donald B. *World Trade and Investment: The Economics of Interdependence.* New York: Harcourt, Brace, 1951.

Meade, James E. *Theory of International Economic Policy.* Vol. I: *The Balance of Payments.* New York: Oxford University Press, 1951.

――――. *Theory of International Economic Policy,* Vol. II: *Trade and Welfare.* New York: Oxford University Press, 1955.

Meier, Gerald M. *International Trade and Development.* New York: Harper & Row, 1963.

Metzler, Lloyd. "The Theory of International Trade," in H. S. Ellis (ed.), *A Survey of Contemporary Economics.* Philadelphia: Blakiston, 1949.

Myrdal, Gunnar. *An International Economy.* New York: Harper & Row, 1956.

Nurkse, Ragnar. *Patterns of Trade and Development.* New York: Oxford University Press, 1961.

Ohlin, Bertil. *Interregional and International Trade.* Cambridge, Mass.: Harvard University Press, 1933.

Schelling, Thomas. *International Economics.* Boston: Allyn & Bacon, 1958.

Snider, Delbert A. *Introduction to International Economics.* 4th ed. Homewood, Ill.: Richard D. Irwin, 1967.

Tarshis, Lorie. *Introduction to International Trade and Finance.* New York: John Wiley, 1955.

Taussig, Frank W. *International Trade.* New York: Macmillan, 1927.

Vanek, Jaroslav. *International Trade: Theory and Economic Policy.* Homewood, Ill.: Richard D. Irwin, 1962.

Viner, Jacob. *International Economics: Studies.* Glencoe, Ill.: The Free Press, 1951.

———. *International Trade and Economic Development*. Oxford: The Clarendon Press, 1953

———. *Studies in the Theory of International Trade*. New York: Harper & Row, 1937.

Young, John P. *The International Economy*. 4th ed. New York: Ronald Press, 1963.

In addition, there are several volumes of readings containing broad selections of previously published articles.

Allen, William R, and Clark L. Allen (eds.). *Foreign Trade and Finance*. New York: Macmillan, 1959.

American Economic Association. *Readings in the Theory of International Trade*. Homewood, Ill.: Richard D. Irwin, 1949.

Balassa, Bela (ed.). *Changing Patterns in Foreign Trade and Payments*. New York: W. W. Norton, 1964.

Clement, M. O., R. L. Pfister and K. J. Rothwell (eds.). *Theoretical Issues in International Economics*. Boston: Houghton Mifflin, 1967.

Jensen, Finn B., and Ingo Water (eds.). *Readings in International Economic Relations*. New York: Ronald Press, 1966.

Taussig, Frank W. (ed.). *Selected Readings in International Trade and Tariff Problems*. Boston: Ginn, 1921.

II. The Pure Theory of International Trade

BOOKS

Kemp, Murray C. *The Pure Theory of International Trade*. Englewood Cliffs, N.J.: Prentice-Hall, 1964.

Linnemann, H. *An Econometric Study of International Trade Flows*. Amsterdam: North-Holland, 1966.

Meade, James E. *A Geometry of International Trade*. London: George Allen & Unwin, 1952.

Mookerjee, S. *Factor Endowments and International Trade: A Study and Appraisal of the Heckscher-Ohlin Theory*. Bombay: Asia Publishing House, 1958.

Mosak, Jacob L. *General Equilibrium Theory in International Trade*. Bloomington, Ind.: Principia Press, 1944.

Wu, C. Y. *An Outline of International Price Theories*. London: Routledge, 1939.

Yntema, Theodore O. *A Mathematical Reformulation of the General Theory of International Trade*. Chicago: University of Chicago Press, 1932.

ARTICLES

Amano, A. "Determinants of Comparative Costs: A Theoretical Approach," *Oxford Economic Papers* (November, 1964).

Baldwin, R. E. "Equilibrium in International Trade: A Diagrammatic Analysis," *Quarterly Journal of Economics* (November, 1948).

———. "The New Welfare Economics and Gains in International Trade," *Quarterly Journal of Economics* (February, 1952).

———. "The Role of Capital-Goods Trade in the Theory of International Trade," *American Economic Review* (September, 1966).

Bardham, P. K. "Equilibrium Growth in the International Economy," *Quarterly Journal of Economics* (August, 1965).

Bhgwati, J. "Growth, Terms of Trade and Comparative Advantage," *Economia Internazionale* (August, 1959).

———. "International Trade and Economic Expansion," *American Economic Review* (December, 1958).

———. "The Pure Theory of International Trade: A Survey," *Economic Journal* (March, 1964).

Black, J. "Economic Expansion and International Trade: A Marshallian Approach," *Review of Economic Studies* (1955–1956).

Chipman, J. S. "A Survey of the Theory of International Trade: Part I: The Classical Theory," *Econometrica* (July, 1965); Part II: The Neo Classical Theory, *ibid.* (October, 1965); Part III: The Modern Theory, *ibid.* (January, 1966).

Clemhout, S. "Efficiency, the Heckscher-Ohlin Theorem and Patterns of International Trade as Exemplified by the Leontief Paradox," *Economia Internazionale* (February, 1964).

Corden, W. M. "Economic Expansion and International Trade: A Geometrical Approach," *Oxford Economic Papers* (June, 1956).

Daniere, A. "American Trade Structure and Comparative Cost Theory," *Economia Internazionale* (August, 1956).

Elliott, G. A. "The Theory of International Values," *Journal of Political Economy* (February, 1950).

Ellsworth, P. T. "A Comparison of International Trade Theories," *American Economic Review* (June, 1940).

———. "The Structure of American Foreign Trade: A New View Examined," *Review of Economics and Statistics* (August, 1954).

Graham, F. D. "The Theory of International Values Reexamined," *Quarterly Journal of Economics* (November, 1923).

Haberler, G. "Real Cost, Money Cost, and Comparative Advantage," *International Social Science Bulletin* (Spring, 1951).

———. "Some Problems in the Pure Theory of International Trade," *Economic Journal* (June, 1950).

————. "The Relevance of the Classical Theory under Modern Conditions," *American Economic Association Papers and Proceedings* (May, 1954).

————. "The Theory of Comparative Costs Once More," *Quarterly Journal of Economics* (February, 1929).

Harrod, R. "Factor-Price Relations under Free Trade," *Economic Journal* (June, 1950).

Heckscher, E. "The Effect of Foreign Trade on the Distribution of Income," *Ekonomisk Tidskrift* (1919). (Reprinted in American Economic Association, *Readings in the Theory of International Trade*. Homewood, Ill.: Richard D. Irwin, 1949.)

Isard, W. and M. Peck. "Location Theory and International and Interregional Trade Theory," *Quarterly Journal of Economics* (February, 1954).

Johnson, H. G. "Factor Endowments, International Trade, and Factor Prices," *Manchester School* (September, 1957).

Keesing, D. B. "Labor Skills and Comparative Advantage," *American Economic Association Papers and Proceedings* (May, 1966).

————. "Labor Skills and International Trade: Evaluating Many Trade Flows with a Single Measuring Device," *Review of Economics and Statistics* (August, 1965).

Kemp, M. C. "Gains from International Trade and Investment," *American Economic Review* (September, 1966).

————. "The Gains from International Trade," *Economic Journal* (December, 1962).

————. "The Relation between Changes in International Demand and the Terms of Trade," *Econometrica* (January, 1956).

Kenen, P. B. "Distribution, Demand, and Equilibrium in International Trade," *Kyklos*, 1959 (4).

Kreinin, M. "Comparative Labor Effectiveness and the Leontief Scarce-Factor Paradox," *American Economic Review* (March, 1965).

Lancaster, K. "The Heckscher-Ohlin Trade Model: A Geometric Treatment," *Economica* (February, 1957).

Laursen, S. "Production Functions and the Theory of International Trade," *American Economic Review* (September, 1952).

Leontief, W. "An International Comparison of Factor Costs and Factor Use," *American Economic Review* (June, 1964).

————. "Domestic Production and Foreign Trade: The American Capital Position Reexamined," *Proceedings of the American Philosophical Society* (September, 1953). (Reprinted in *Economia Internazionale*, February, 1954.)

————. "Factor Proportions and the Structure of American Trade: Further Theoretical and Empirical Analysis," *Review of Economics and Statistics* (November, 1956).

————. "The Use of Indifference Curves in the Analysis of Foreign Trade," *Quarterly Journal of Economics* (May, 1933).

Lerner, A. P. "Factor Prices and International Trade," *Economica* (February, 1952).

————. "The Symmetry between Import and Export Taxes," *Economica* (August, 1936).

Lovasy, G. "International Trade under Imperfect Competition," *Quarterly Journal of Economics* (August, 1941).

MacDougall, G. D. A. "British and American Exports: A Study Suggested by the Theory of Comparative Costs," Part I, *Economic Journal* (December, 1951) ; Part II, *ibid.* (September, 1952).

Mason, E. "The Doctrine of Comparative Cost," *Quarterly Journal of Economics* (November, 1926).

Matthews, R. C. O. "Reciprocal Demand and Increasing Returns," *Review of Economic Studies* (February, 1950).

Meade, J. E. "The Equalization of Factor Prices: The Two-Country Two-Factor Three-Product Case," *Metroeconomica* (December, 1950).

Meier, G. M. "The Theory of Comparative Costs Reconsidered," *Oxford Economic Papers* (June, 1949).

Metzler, L. A. "Graham's Theory of International Values," *American Economic Review* (June, 1950).

Michaely, M. "Factor Proportions in International Trade: Current State of the Theory," *Kyklos,* 1964 (4).

Mishan, E. J. "International Factor Price Determination with Neutral Technical Progress," *Economica* (August, 1966).

Mundell, R. "International Trade and Factor Mobility," *American Economic Review* (June, 1957).

————. "The Pure Theory of International Trade," *American Economic Review* (March, 1960).

Myint, H. "The Classical Theory of International Trade and the Underdeveloped Countries," *Economic Journal* (June, 1958).

————. "The Gains from International Trade and the Backward Countries," *Review of Economic Studies* (June, 1955).

Pearce, I. F. and S. F. James. "The Factor-Price Equalization Myth," *Review of Economic Studies* (1951–1952).

Posner, M. V. "International Trade and Technical Change," *Oxford Economic Papers* (October, 1961).

Samuelson, P. A. "A Comment on Factor Price Equalization," *Review of Economic Studies* (1951–1952).

————. "International Factor-Price Equalization Once Again," *Economic Journal* (June, 1949).

————. "International Trade and the Equalization of Factor Prices," *Economic Journal* (June, 1948).

————. "The Gains from International Trade," *Canadian Journal of Economics and Political Science* (May, 1939).

————. "Theoretical Notes on Trade Problems," *Review of Economics and Statistics* (May, 1964).

————. "Welfare Economics and International Trade," *American Economic Review* (June, 1938).

Stolper, W. and P. A. Samuelson. "Protection and Real Wages," *Review of Economic Studies* (November, 1941).

Tinbergen, J. "The Equalization of Factor Prices Between Free-Trade Areas," *Metroeconomica* (April, 1949).

Vanek, J. "An Afterthought on the 'Real Cost-Opportunity Cost' Dispute and Some Aspects of General Equilibrium under Conditions of Variable Factor Supplies," *Review of Economic Studies* (June, 1959).

————. "An Alternative Proof of the Factor Price Equalization Theorem," *Quarterly Journal of Economics* (November, 1960).

———— "Unilateral Trade Liberalization and Global World Income," *Quarterly Journal of Economics* (February, 1964).

Williams, J. H. "The Theory of International Trade Reconsidered," *Economic Journal* (June, 1929).

III.   Foreign Exchange, the Balance of Payments, and International Monetary Relations

BOOKS AND SHORT MONOGRAPHS

Aliber, Robert Z. *The Future of the Dollar as an International Currency.* New York: Praeger, 1966.

Anfricht, Hans. *The International Monetary Fund.* New York: Praeger, 1964.

Aubrey, Henry G. *The Dollar in World Affairs.* New York: Praeger, 1964.

Bloomfield, Arthur. *Capital Imports and the American Balance of Payments, 1934–1939: A Study in Abnormal International Capital Transfers.* Chicago: University of Chicago Press, 1950

————. *Monetary Policy Under the International Gold Standard, 1880–1914.* New York: Federal Reserve Bank of New York, 1959.

————. *Short-Term Capital Movements Under the Pre-1914 Gold Standard.* Princeton: International Finance Section, Princeton University, 1963.

Brown, Weir M. *The External Liquidity of an Advanced Country.* Princeton: International Finance Section, Princeton University, 1964.

Crump, Norman. *The ABC of the Foreign Exchange.* 12th ed. London: Macmillan, 1955.

Einzig, Paul. *A Dynamic Theory of Forward Exchange.* New York: St Martin's Press, 1961.

————. *The Euro-Dollar System.* New York: St Martin's Press, 1964.

Factors Affecting the U.S. Balance of Payments. Joint Economic Committee, U.S. Congress, Washington, D.C.: Government Printing Office, 1962.

Gardner, Richard. *Sterling-Dollar Diplomacy.* New York: Oxford University Press, 1956.

Gilbert, Milton. *Problems of the International Monetary System.* Princeton: International Finance Section, Princeton University, 1966.

Haberler, Gottfried. *Money in the International Economy: A Study in Balance of Payments Adjustments, International Liquidity, and Exchange Rates.* Cambridge, Mass.: Harvard University Press, 1965.

Halm, George N. *The "Band" Proposal: The Limits of Permissible Exchange Rate Variations.* Princeton: International Finance Section, Princeton University, 1965.

Hansen, Alvin. *The Dollar and the International Monetary System.* New York: McGraw-Hill, 1965.

Harris, Seymour E. (ed.). *The Dollar in Crisis.* New York: Harcourt, Brace & World, 1961.

Hinshaw, Randall. *Toward European Convertibility.* Princeton: International Finance Section, Princeton University, 1958.

Holmes, Alan R. *The New York Foreign Exchange Market.* New York: Federal Reserve Bank of New York, 1959.

Iverson, Carl. *Some Aspects of the Theory of International Capital Movements.* Copenhagen: Levin & Munksgaard, 1936.

Johnson, Harry G. *Money, Trade and Economic Growth.* London: George Allen & Unwin, 1962.

Kenen, Peter B. *Reserve-Asset Preferences of Central Banks and Stability of the Gold-Exchange Standard.* Princeton: International Finance Section, Princeton University, 1963.

Kindleberger, Charles P. *Balance-of-Payments Deficits and the International Market for Liquidity.* Princeton: International Finance Section, Princeton University, 1965.

――――. *Europe and the Dollar.* Cambridge, Mass.: MIT Press, 1966.

――――. *International Short-Term Capital Movements.* New York: A. M. Kelley, 1965.

Lary, Hal B. *Problems of the United States as World Trader and Banker.* Princeton: Princeton University Press, 1962.

Lederer, Walther. *The Balance on Foreign Transactions: Problems of Definition and Measurement.* Princeton: International Finance Section, Princeton University, 1963.

Lutz, Friedrich. *The Problem of International Liquidity and the Multiple-Currency Standard.* Princeton: International Finance Section, Princeton University, 1963.

MacDougall, Donald. *The Dollar Problem: A Reappraisal.* Princeton: International Finance Section, Princeton University, 1960.

――――. *The World Dollar Problem.* London: Macmillan, 1957.

Machlup, Fritz. *International Payments, Debts, and Gold.* New York: Charles Scribner's Sons, 1964.

――――. *International Trade and the National Income Multiplier.* Philadelphia: Blakiston, 1943.

McKinnon, Ronald and Wallace Oates. *The Implications of International Economic Integration for Monetary, Fiscal, and Exchange Rate Policy.* Princeton: International Finance Section, Princeton University, 1966.

Nurkse, Ragnar. *International Currency Experience.* Geneva: League of Nations, 1944.

Robinson, Joan. *The Foreign Exchanges: Essays on the Theory of Employment.* Oxford: Blackwell, 1947.

Rolf, S. E. *Gold and World Power.* New York: Harper & Row, 1966.

Roosa, Robert V. *Monetary Reform and the World Economy.* New York: Harper & Row, 1965.

Salant, Walter, et al. *The U.S. Balance of Payments in 1968.* Washington, D.C.: Brookings Institute, 1963.

Scammell, W. M. *International Monetary Policy.* 2nd ed. London: Macmillan, 1961.

Schlesinger, Eugene. *Multiple Exchange Rates and Economic Development.* Princeton: International Finance Section, Princeton University, 1952.

Scitovsky, Tibor. *Requirements of an International Reserve System.* Princeton: International Finance Section, Princeton University, 1965.

Shannon, Ian. *International Liquidity: A Study in the Economic Functions of Gold.* Chicago: Henry Regnery, 1966.

Snider, Delbert. *International Monetary Relations.* New York: Random House, 1966.

Sohmen, Egon. *Flexible Exchange Rates: Theory and Controversy.* Chicago: University of Chicago Press, 1961.

——. *International Monetary Problems and the Foreign Exchanges.* Princeton: International Finance Section, Princeton University, 1963.

——. *The Theory of Forward Exchange.* Princeton: International Finance Section, Princeton University, 1966.

Southard, Frank. *Foreign Exchange Practice and Policy.* New York: McGraw-Hill, 1940.

Stein, Jerome. *The Nature and Efficiency of the Foreign Exchange Market.* Princeton: International Finance Section, Princeton University, 1962.

Triffin, Robert. *Gold and the Dollar Crisis.* New Haven: Yale University Press, 1960.

——. *The Balance of Payments and Foreign Investment Position of the United States.* Princeton: International Finance Section, Princeton University, 1966.

——. *The Evolution of the International Monetary System: History, Reappraisal, and Future Prospectives.* Princeton: International Finance Section, Princeton University, 1964.

——. *The World Money Maze—National Currencies in International Payments.* New Haven: Yale University Press, 1966.

Yeager, Leland. *International Monetary Relations: Theory, History, and Policy.* New York: Harper & Row, 1966.

A R T I C L E S

Alejandro, C. F. D. "A Note on the Impact of Devaluation and the Redistributive Effect," *Journal of Political Economy* (December, 1963).

Alexander, S. "Devaluation versus Import Restriction as an Instrument for Improving Foreign Trade Balance," *IMF Staff Papers* (April, 1951).

———. "Effects of Devaluation: A Simplified Synthesis of Elasticities and Absorption Approaches," *American Economic Review* (March, 1959).

———. "Effects of a Devaluation on a Trade Balance," *IMF Staff Papers* (April, 1952).

Aliber, R. Z. "The U.S. Role as a Reserve Currency Country," *Quarterly Journal of Economics* (August, 1964).

Allen, W. R. "The International Monetary Fund," *Oxford Economic Papers* (June, 1961).

Altman, O. L. "The Management of International Liquidity," *IMF Staff Papers* (July, 1964).

Black, J. "A Proposal for the Reform of Exchange Rates," *Economic Journal* (June, 1966).

———. "A Savings and Investment Approach to Devaluation," *Economic Journal* (June, 1959).

Bloomfield, A. "Foreign Exchange Rate Theory and Policy," in S. Harris (ed.), *The New Economics: Keynes' Influence on Theory and Public Policy.* New York: Knopf, 1948.

Bronfenbrenner, M. "The Keynesian Equation and the Balance of Payments," *Review of Economic Studies* (June, 1940).

Brown, A. J. "Trade Balances and Exchange Stability," *Oxford Economic Papers* (April, 1942).

Caves, R. E. "International Liquidity: Toward a Home Repair Manual," *Review of Economics and Statistics* (May, 1964).

Cheng, H. S. "A Collection of Elasticities and Propensities in International Trade," *IMF Staff Papers* (April, 1959).

DeVries, M. "Multiple Exchange Rates: Expectations and Experiences," *IMF Staff Papers* (July, 1965).

Elliott, G. "Transfer of Means-of-Payments and the Terms of International Trade," *Canadian Journal of Economics and Political Science* (November, 1936).

Ellis, H. "Exchange Control and Discrimination," *American Economic Review* (December, 1947).

Ellsworth, P. T. "Exchange Rates and Exchange Stability," *Review of Economics and Statistics* (February, 1950).

Fleming, J. M. "On Making the Best of Balance of Payments Restrictions on Imports," *Economic Journal* (March, 1951).

Frank, H. J. "Problems of the Dollar and the Pound," *Quarterly Review of Economics and Business* (Summer, 1965).

Friedman, M. "The Case for Flexible Exchange Rates," in *Essays in Positive Economics*. Chicago: University of Chicago Press, 1953.

Frisch, R. "On the Need for Forecasting a Multilateral Balance of Payments," *American Economic Review* (September, 1947).

Gray, H. P. "Imperfect Markets and the Effectiveness of Devaluation," *Kyklos*, 1965 (3).

Haberler, G. "The Choice of Exchange Rates after the War," *American Economic Review* (June, 1945).

————. "The Market for Foreign Exchange and the Stability of the Balance of Payments: A Theoretical Analysis," *Kyklos*, 1949 (3).

Harberger, A. C. "Currency Depreciation, Income, and the Balance of Trade," *Journal of Political Economy* (December, 1957).

Heller, H. R. "Optimal International Reserves," *Economic Journal* (June, 1966).

Hemming, M. F. W. and W. M. Corden. "Import Restriction as an Instrument of Balance-of-Payments Policy," *Economic Journal* (September, 1958).

Hicks, J. R. "The Long Run Dollar Problem: An Inaugural Lecture," *Oxford Economic Papers* (June, 1953).

Holzman, F. and A. Zellner. "The Foreign Trade and Balanced Budget Multiplier," *American Economic Review* (March, 1958).

Johnson, H. G. "The Transfer Problem and Exchange Stability," *Journal of Political Economy* (June, 1956).

Kemp, M. C. "The Rate of Exchange, the Terms of Trade and the Balance of Payments in Fully Employed Economies," *International Economic Review* (September, 1962).

Kenen, P. B. and E. B. Yudin. "The Demand for International Reserves," *Review of Economics and Statistics* (August, 1965).

Keynes, J. M. "The German Transfer Problem," *Economic Journal* (March, 1929).

Klopstock, F. H. "The International Money Market: Structure, Scope, and Instruments," *Journal of Finance* (May, 1965).

Laursen, S. and L. Metzler. "Flexible Exchange Rates and the Theory of Employment," *Review of Economics and Statistics* (November, 1950).

Machlup, F. "The Cloakroom Rule of International Reserves," *Quarterly Journal of Economics* (August, 1965).

(Most of Professor Machlup's many articles on problems of foreign exchange and balance of payments are in his *International Payments, Debts, and Gold*, *op. cit.*)

Metzler, L. "The Transfer Problem Reconsidered," *Journal of Political Economy* (June, 1942).

Michaely, M. "Multilateral Balancing in International Trade," *American Economic Review* (September, 1962).

Mikesell, R. "The Role of International Monetary Agreements," *Journal of Political Economy* (December, 1947).

Mundell, R. A. "A Theory of Optimum Currency Areas," *American Economic Review* (September, 1961).

————. "The Appropriate Use of Monetary and Fiscal Policy for Internal and External Stability," *IMF Staff Papers* (March, 1962).

————. "The Monetary Dynamics of International Adjustment under Fixed and Flexible Exchange Rates," *Quarterly Journal of Economics* (May, 1960).

Nurkse, R. "Domestic and International Equilibrium," in S. Harris (ed.), *The New Economics: Keynes' Influence on Theory and Public Policy.* New York: Knopf, 1948.

Ohlin, B. "The Reparation Problem: A Discussion," *Economic Journal* (June, 1929).

Orcutt, G. H. "Exchange Rate Adjustment and Relative Size of the Depreciating Bloc," *Review of Economics and Statistics* (February, 1955). .

————. "Measurement of Price Elasticities in International Trade," *Review of Economics and Statistics* (May, 1950).

Spraos, J. "Stability in a Closed Economy and in the Foreign Exchange Market, and the Redistributive Effect of Price Changes," *Review of Economic Studies* (June, 1957).

Stein, J. "International Short-Term Capital Movements," *American Economic Review* (March, 1965).

Stolper, W. "The Multiplier, Flexible Exchange Rates and International Equilibrium," *Quarterly Journal of Economics* (November, 1950).

Tinbergen, J. "The Relation between Internal Inflation and the Balance of Payments," *Banco Nazionale del Lavaro Quarterly Review* (October–December, 1952).

Tsiang, S. C. "The Role of Money in Trade-Balance Stability," *American Economic Review* (December, 1961).

Wexler, I. "EEC and International Liquidity: New Help for Dollars and Sterling," *Challenge* (1962).

IV.   Issues in Commercial Policy and Foreign Aid

BOOKS AND PAMPHLETS

Beveridge, William. *Tariffs: The Case Examined.* London: Longmans, Green, 1932.

Curzon, Gerald. *Multilateral Commercial Diplomacy.* London: Michael Joseph, 1965.

Diebold, William. *The End of ITO.* Princeton: International Finance Section, Princeton University, 1952.

Ellis, Howard S. *Bilateralism and the Future of International Trade.* Princeton: International Finance Section, Princeton University, 1945.

Galbraith, Virginia L. *World Trade in Transition*. Washington, D.C.: Public Affairs Press, 1965.

George, Henry. *Protection or Free Trade*. New York: Robert Schalkenbach Foundation, 1949.

Goldwin, Robert (ed.). *Why Foreign Aid?* Chicago: Rand McNally, 1963.

Hinshaw, Randall. *The European Community and American Trade: A Study in Atlantic Economics and Policy*. New York: Praeger, 1965.

Humphrey, Don D. *American Imports*. New York: The Twentieth Century Fund, 1955.

————. *The United States and the Common Market*. New York: Praeger, 1962.

Isaalu, Asher. *International Trade: Tariffs and Commercial Policies*. Homewood, Ill.: Richard D. Irwin, 1948.

Johnson, Harry G. *The World Economy at the Crossroads: A Survey of Current Problems of Money, Trade, and Economic Development*. New York: Oxford University Press, 1966.

Kenen, Peter B. *Giant Among Nations: Problems in United States Foreign Economic Policy*. Chicago: Rand McNally, 1963.

Manoilesco, Mihail. *The Theory of Protection and International Trade*. London: P. S. King, 1931.

Mason, Edward S. *Controlling World Trade*. New York: McGraw-Hill, 1946.

Nove, Alec and Desmond Donelly. *Trade with Communist Countries*. London: Hutchinson, 1960.

Nurkse, Ragnar. *Problems of Capital Formation in Underdeveloped Countries*. Oxford: Blackwell, 1953.

Piquet, Howard S. *Aid, Trade, and the Tariff*. New York: Crowell, 1953.

Robinson, Richard. *International Business Policy*. New York: Holt, Rinehart and Winston, 1964.

Stern, Robert M. "Policies for Trade and Development," *International Conciliation No. 548*. New York: Carnegie Endowment for International Peace, May, 1964.

Swerling, Boris C. *Current Issues in International Commodity Policy*. Princeton: International Finance Section, Princeton University, 1962.

Taussig, Frank. *Some Aspects of the Tariff Question*. 3rd ed. Cambridge, Mass.: Harvard University Press, 1931.

Tinbergen, Jan. *International Economic Integration*. Rev. ed. Amsterdam: Elsevier, 1965.

————. *Shaping the World Economy*. New York: The Twentieth Century Fund, 1962.

Towle, L. W. *International Trade and Commercial Policy*. 2nd ed. New York: Harper & Row, 1956.

Vernon, Raymond. *America's Foreign Trade Policy and the GATT*. Princeton: International Finance Section, Princeton University, 1954.

————. *Trade Policy in Crisis*. Princeton: International Finance Section, Princeton University, 1958.

Viner, Jacob. *Trade Relations Between Free-Market and Controlled Economies.* Geneva : League of Nations, 1943.

Weaver, J. H. *The International Development Association: A New Approach to Foreign Aid.* New York : Praeger, 1965.

ARTICLES

Balassa, B. "Tariff Reductions and Trade in Manufactures among the Industrial Countries," *American Economic Review* (June, 1966).

Baldwin, R. "The Effects of Tariffs on International and Domestic Prices," *Quarterly Journal of Economics* (February, 1960).

Black, J. "Arguments for Tariffs," *Oxford Economic Papers* (June, 1959).

Chenery, H. B. "Comparative Advantage and Development Policy," *American Economic Review* (March, 1961).

———— and A. M. Strout. "Foreign Assistance and Economic Development," *American Economic Review* (September, 1966).

Cohen, B. I. "Measuring the Short-Run Impact of a Country's Import Restrictions on Its Exports," *Quarterly Journal of Economics* (August, 1966).

Corden, W. M. "Tariffs, Subsidies and the Terms of Trade," *Economica* (August, 1957).

————. "The Effective Protective Rate, the Uniform Tariff Equivalent, and the Average Tariff," *Economic Record* (June, 1966).

Dagnino-Pastore, J. M. "Balanced Growth: An Interpretation," *Oxford Economic Papers* (July, 1963).

Flanders, J. M. "Measuring Protectionism and Predicting Trade Diversion," *Journal of Political Economy* (April, 1965).

————. "Prebisch on Protectionism: An Evaluation," *Economic Journal* (June, 1964).

Fleming, M. "The Optimal Tariff from an International Standpoint," *Review of Economics and Statistics* (February, 1946).

deGraff, J. "On Optimum Tariff Structures," *Review of Economic Studies,* 1949/50 (1).

Graham, F. D. "Some Aspects of Protection Further Considered," *Quarterly Journal of Economics* (February, 1923).

Haberler, G. "Integration and the Growth of the World Economy in Historical Perspective," *American Economic Review* (March, 1964).

Hagen, E. E. "An Economic Justification of Protectionism," *Quarterly Journal of Economics* (November, 1958).

Hilgerdt, F. "The Case for Multilateral Trade," *American Economic Review* (March, 1943).

Horwell, D. J. "Optimum Tariffs and Tariff Policy," *Review of Economic Studies* (April, 1966).

Johnson, H. G. "A Model of Protection and Exchange Rate," *Review of Economic Studies* (April, 1966).

——— . "An Economic Theory of Protectionism, Tariff Bargaining, and the Formation of Customs Unions," *Journal of Political Economy* (June, 1965).

———. "The Cost of Protection and the Scientific Tariff," *Journal of Political Economy* (August, 1960).

———. "The Costs of Protection and Self Sufficiency," *Quarterly Journal of Economics* (August, 1965).

Kahn, R. F. "Tariffs and the Terms of Trade," *Review of Economic Studies,* 1947/48 (1).

Kaldor, N. "A Note on Tariffs and the Terms of Trade," *Economica* (November, 1940).

Kelly, W. B. "The Expanded Trade Agreements Escape Clause, 1955–61," *Journal of Political Economy* (February, 1962).

Koo, A. Y. C. "Duty and Non-Duty Imports and Income Distribution," *American Economic Review* (March, 1953).

Little, I. M. D. "Welfare and Tariffs," *Review of Economic Studies,* 1949/1950 (2).

Meade, J. E. "International Commodity Agreements," *Lloyds Bank Review* (July, 1964).

Metzler, L. "Tariffs, International Demand and Domestic Prices," *Journal of Political Economy* (August, 1949).

———. "Tariffs, the Terms of Trade, and the Distribution of National Income," *Journal of Political Economy* (February, 1949).

Myint, H. "Protection and Economic Development," in R. Harrod and D. C. Hague (eds.). *International Trade Theory in a Developing World.* London: Macmillan, 1963.

Nurkse, R. "Some International Aspects of the Problem of Economic Development," *American Economic Association, Papers and Proceedings* (May, 1952).

Prebisch, R. "Commercial Policy in Underdeveloped Countries," *American Economic Association, Papers and Proceedings* (May, 1959).

Pryor, F. "Economic Growth and the Terms of Trade," *Economic Journal* (March, 1966).

Ranis, G. "Trade, Aid, and What?" *Kyklos,* 1964 (2).

Rosenstein–Rodan, P. N. "International Aid for Underdeveloped Countries," *Review of Economics and Statistics* (May, 1961).

Scitovsky, T. "A Reconsideration of the Theory of Tariffs," *Review of Economic Studies* (1942) (2).

Singer, H. W. "The Distribution of Gains between Investing and Borrowing Countries," *American Economic Association, Papers and Proceedings* (May, 1950).

Soligo, R. and R. M. Stern. "Tariff Protection, Import Substitution, and Investment Efficiency," *Pakistan Development Review* (Summer, 1965).

Stern, R. M. "International Compensation for Fluctuations in Commodity Trade," *Quarterly Journal of Economics* (May, 1963).

———. "The U.S. Tariff and the Efficiency of the U.S. Economy," *American Economic Association, Papers and Proceedings* (May, 1964).

Ward, B. "Foreign Aid: Strategy or Stopgap?" *Foreign Affairs* (October, 1962).

Yang, S. C. "Foreign Trade Problems in Economic Development," *Scottish Journal of Political Economy* (June, 1964).

Yeager, L. B. "The Size of Gain from an Optimum Tariff," *Southern Economic Journal* (October, 1964).

V.   Regional Economic Integration

A.   General Works

BOOKS

Balassa, Bela. *The Theory of Economic Integration.* Homewood, Ill.: Richard D. Irwin, 1961.

Dell, Sidney. *Trade Blocs and Common Markets.* New York: Knopf, 1963.

Lambrinidis, J. S. *The Structure, Function, and the Law of a Free Trade Area.* New York: Praeger, 1966.

Meade, James E. *Problems of Economic Union.* Chicago: University of Chicago Press, 1953.

———. *The Theory of Customs Unions.* Amsterdam: North-Holland, 1955.

Sannwald, Rudolph, and Jacques Stohler. *Economic Integration.* Princeton: Princeton University Press, 1959.

Shoup, Carl S. *Fiscal Harmonization in Common Markets.* 2 vols. New York: Columbia University Press, 1966.

United Nations, Department of Economic Affairs. *Customs Unions.* Lake Success, N.Y.: 1947.

Vanek, Jaroslav. *General Equilibrium of International Discrimination: The Case of Customs Unions.* Cambridge, Mass.: Harvard University Press, 1965.

Viner, Jacob. *The Customs Union Issue.* New York: Carnegie Endowment for International Peace, 1950.

ARTICLES

Allen, R. L. "Integration in Less Developed Areas," *Kyklos,* 1961 (3).

Balassa, B. "Toward a Theory of Economic Integration," *Kyklos,* 1961 (1).

deBeers, J. S. "Tariff Aspects of a Federal Union," *Quarterly Journal of Economics* (November, 1941).

Bhembri, R. S. "Customs Unions and Underdeveloped Countries," *Economia Internazionale* (March, 1962).

Bye, M. "Customs Unions and National Interests," *Economie Appliquée*. 1950. (Reprinted in *International Economic Papers No. 3*. New York: Macmillan, 1953.)

Gehrels, F. "Customs Unions from a Single Country Viewpoint," *Review of Economic Studies*, 1956–1957 (1).

Haberler, G. "The Political Economy of Regional or Continental Blocs," in S. E. Harris (ed.), *Postwar Economic Problems*. New York: McGraw-Hill, 1943.

Kreinin, M. "On the Dynamic Effects of a Customs Union," *Journal of Political Economy* (August, 1964).

———. "On the Trade Diversion Effect of Trade Preference Areas," *Journal of Political Economy* (August, 1959).

Lipsey, R. G. "The Theory of Customs Unions: A General Survey," *Economic Journal* (September, 1960).

———. "The Theory of Customs Unions: Trade Diversion and Welfare," *Economica* (February, 1957).

Makower, H. and G. Morton. "A Contribution Toward a Theory of Customs Unions," *Economic Journal* (March, 1953).

Meade, J. E. "The Removal of Trade Barriers: The Regional vs. the Universal Approach," *Economica* (May, 1951).

Meyer, F. V. "Complementarity and the Lowering of Tariffs," *American Economic Review* (June, 1956).

Rom, M. "Customs Unions and Third Countries in GATT," *Kyklos*, 1964 (2).

Scitovsky, T. "International Trade and Economic Integration as a Means of Overcoming the Disadvantages of a Small Nation," in E. A. G. Robinson (ed.), *Economic Consequences of the Size of Nations*. London: Macmillan, 1960.

Spraos, J. "The Condition for a Trade-Creating Customs Union," *Economic Journal* (March, 1964).

Werstate, C. "The Economic and Political Implications of a Customs Union," *Quarterly Journal of Economics* (May, 1948).

Wexler, I. "Trade Creation and Trade Diversion: A Geometrical Note," *Southern Economic Journal* (April, 1960).

B. *European Economic Integration*

BOOKS AND PAMPHLETS

Beloff, Max. *The United States and the Unity of Europe*. Washington, D.C.: Brookings Institute, 1963.

Benoit, Emile. *Europe at Sixes and Sevens.* New York: Columbia University Press, 1961.

Camps, Miriam. *European Unification in the Sixties.* New York: McGraw-Hill, 1966.

————. *The European Common Market and American Policy.* Princeton: Center of International Studies, Princeton University, 1956.

Diebold, William. *Trade and Payments in Western Europe.* New York: Harper & Row, 1952.

————. *The Schuman Plan.* New York: Praeger, 1959.

Frank, Isaiah. *The European Common Market: An Analysis of Commercial Policy.* New York: Praeger, 1961.

Haines, G. C. (ed.). *European Integration.* Baltimore: The Johns Hopkins Press, 1957.

Hallstein, Walter. *United Europe: Challenge and Opportunity.* Cambridge, Mass.: Harvard University Press, 1962.

Krause, Lawrence B. (ed.). *The Common Market: Progress and Controversy.* Englewood Cliffs, N.J.: Prentice-Hall, 1964.

Lamfalussy, Alexander. *The United Kingdom and the Six.* Homewood, Ill.: Richard D. Irwin, 1963.

Lindberg, Leon. *The Political Dynamics of European Integration.* Stanford: Stanford University Press, 1963.

Meade, James E. *Negotiations for Benelux: An Annotated Chronicle, 1943–1956.* Princeton: International Finance Section, Princeton University, 1957.

————, H. H. Liesner, and S. J. Wells. *Case Studies in European Economic Union.* London: Oxford University Press, 1962.

Meyer, F. V. *The European Free Trade Association.* New York: Praeger, 1960.

Pinder, John. *Britain and the Common Market.* London: The Cresset Press, 1961.

Scitovsky, Tibor. *Economic Theory and Western European Integration.* Stanford: Stanford University Press, 1958.

ARTICLES

Aron, R. "Problems of European Integration," *Lloyds Bank Review* (April, 1953).

Beckerman, W. "Distance and the Patterns of Intra-European Trade," *Review of Economics and Statistics* (February, 1956).

————. "Projecting Europe's Growth," *Economic Journal* (December, 1962).

Gehrels, F. "Monetary Systems for the Common Market," *Journal of Finance* (May, 1959).

———— and B. Johnston. "The Economic Gains of European Integration," *Journal of Political Economy* (August, 1955).

Gordon, L. "Economic Regionalism Reconsidered," *World Politics* (January, 1961).

———. "Myth and Reality in European Integration," *Yale Review* (September, 1955).

Haberler, G. "Economic Aspects of a European Union," *World Politics* (July, 1949).

Hald, M. W. "Social Charges in the EEC Countries: Some Economic Aspects," *Economia Internazionale* (November, 1959).

Kreinin, M. "European Integration and American Trade," *American Economic Review* (September, 1959).

———. "The 'Outer Seven' and European Integration," *American Economic Review* (June, 1960).

Letiche, J. M. "European Integration: An American View," *Lloyds Bank Review* (January, 1965).

Liesner, H. H. "The European Common Market and British Industry," *Economic Journal* (June, 1958).

Meade, J. E. "The Balance-of-Payments Problems of a European Free Trade Area," *Economic Journal* (September, 1957).

Stikker, D. "The Functional Approach to European Integration," *Foreign Affairs* (April, 1951).

Swann, D. and D. L. McLachlan. "Programming and Competition in the European Communities," *Economic Journal* (March, 1964).

Verdoorn, P. J. "A Customs Union for Western Europe," *World Politics* (July, 1954).

C. Economic Integration in Non-European Areas

BOOKS AND PAMPHLETS

Dell, Sidney. *A Latin American Common Market?* London: Oxford University Press, 1966.

Hirschman, Albert O. (ed.). *Latin American Issues: Essays and Comments.* New York: The Twentieth Century Fund, 1961.

United Nations, Economic Commission for Latin America. *The Latin American Common Market.* Santiago, Chile: 1959.

———. *The Latin American Movement Toward Multilateral Economic Cooperation.* Santiago, Chile: 1961.

Urquidi, Victor L. *Free Trade and Economic Integration in Latin America.* Berkeley: University of California Press, 1962.

Wionczek, Miguel S. "Latin American Free Trade Association," *International Conciliation No. 551.* New York: Carnegie Endowment for International Peace, January, 1965.

———. (ed.). *Latin American Economic Integration: Experiences and Prospects.* New York: Praeger, 1966.

ARTICLES

Alexander, R. J. "Trade Policies in Latin America," *Current History* (August, 1962).

Amin, R. K. "A Suggestion for a Closer Economic Integration between India and the Adjacent Territories," *Indian Economic Journal* (July, 1954).

Cochrane, J. K. "Central American Economic Integration: The Integrated Industries Scheme," *Inter-American Economic Affairs* (Autumn, 1965).

Gigax, W. R. "The Central American Common Market," *Inter-American Affairs* (Autumn, 1962).

Huelin, D. "Economic Integration in Latin America: Progress and Problems," *International Affairs* (July, 1964).

Keesing, F. A. G., and P. J. Brand. "Possible Role of a Clearing House in the Latin American Regional Market," *IMF Staff Papers* (November, 1963).

Mills, J. C. "Development Policy and Regional Trading Arrangements: The Case of Latin America," *Economic Development and Cultural Changes* (October, 1964).

Naleszkiewicz, W. "The Central American Common Market and the European Economic Community," *Caribbean Studies* (January, 1964).

Pryor, F. "Communism's Common Market," *Michigan Business Review* (July, 1962).

———. "Forms of Economic Cooperation in the Communist Bloc," *Soviet Studies* (October, 1959).

Stanley, C. E. "Central American Economic Integration," *Southern Economic Journal* (October, 1962).

Stewart, I. G. "Customs Unions in East and Central Africa," *Scottish Journal of Political Economy* (February, 1962).

Triffin, R. "International Monetary Arrangements, Capital Markets, and Economic Integration in Latin America," *Journal of Common Market Studies* (October, 1965).

United Nations, Economic Commission for Latin America, "Central American Economic Integration Programme: Evaluation and Prospects," *Economic Bulletin for Latin America*. Santiago, Chile: October, 1959.

Wilcox, C. "Regional Cooperation in Southeast Asia," *Malayan Economic Review* (October, 1964).

Wionczek, M. "The Montevideo Treaty and Latin American Economic Integration," *Banca Nazionale del Lavaro Quarterly Review* (June, 1961).

INDEXES

Name Index

Subject Index

419